A California Woman's Story

A California Woman's Story

Joan Irvine Smith

Essay by Jean Stern

Foreword by Maria Shriver

Preface by Donald Bren

Prologue by James Irvine Swinden

The Irvine Museum

© 2006 The Irvine Museum
18881 Von Karman Avenue
Irvine, California 92612
www.irvinemuseum.org

ISBN 0-9714092-7-7
Library of Congress Control Number: 2006927919

Art direction by Joan Irvine Smith
Printed in California by Typecraft Wood *&* Jones

P. 1: William Wendt, *Along the River Bed* (detail),
Private Collection, Courtesy of The Irvine Museum
P. 2: Photo of Joan Irvine Smith, 1993 by Lori Brysten

Table of Contents

Granville Redmond, *Poppies and Lupine*, The James Irvine Swinden Family Collection

Joan Irvine Smith is an original – a determined, formidable and inspiring woman who has made an extraordinary contribution to California.

Not long after my husband was elected Governor of California, I set out to create a special exhibit at the California State History Museum that would recognize and pay tribute to the achievements of many of the remarkable women of our Great State.

Of course, Joan Irvine Smith is one such woman – she is a protector of the environment, she is an avid art collector of California history, she is a tireless philanthropist and an accomplished equestrian. On one occasion, she told me the Irvine Museum would soon be publishing a book to document her accomplishments and she was busy gathering information and photographs to write her text. I encouraged her to do so and suggested the title, *A California Woman's Story*. She replied, "That's a great idea and that will be the title of my book!"

I am delighted to see the publication of *A California Woman's Story* and I send my friend Joan all my best wishes on the success of her book.

Maria Shriver

William Wendt, *A Clear Day*, 1903, The Irvine Museum

A View of the City of Irvine, 1995, photo by Jean Stern

THE IRVINE COMPANY

Donald Bren
Chairman of the Board

October 19, 2005

Ms. Joan Irvine Smith
P.O. Box 1453
San Juan Capistrano, CA 92693

Dear Joan:

I've only had a few moments to scan your monumental book, but I wanted to thank you for your generous references to me – most particularly your reflections on my efforts to permanently protect significant parks and open space on The Irvine Ranch. Over time, it has become one of my highest passions and priorities, and I am so pleased that you have recognized it in your book.

I also appreciate your kind words about my determination to keep the Irvine Ranch intact, respect the Master Plan, and follow the tradition of stewardship so firmly established by your family.

The Summer 2004 issue of *Orange County Coastkeeper* magazine contains a thoughtful and detailed article on our special efforts to manage and control runoff from the new hotel and improved golf courses at Pelican Hill on the Newport Coast. As we get closer to installation of the system, I would be pleased to arrange a briefing and site visit with me to learn more about it. We really are quite proud of what we are doing there with respect to water quality and runoff.

It was good to see you again Saturday at the very successful UCI Medal Dinner.

Best regards,

Donald

Guy Rose, *Point Lobos*, The James Irvine Swinden Family Collection

Introduction

JEAN STERN

The Irvine Museum opened to the public on January 15, 1993. At that time, it was a small startup museum with no history, experience or exhibition record. During the first five years, we astounded the museum world by producing seven traveling exhibitions and seven fully illustrated companion books, a feat unmatched by any other institution. As of this writing, that number has risen to thirteen, in only twelve years.

How does one explain this meteoric growth? In great part, it is due to the devotion of my dauntless staff, Merika Gopaul, Christine DeWitt, Judy Thompson and Don Bridges. Moreover, none of this would have occurred without the leadership and inspiration of James Irvine Swinden, the Vice President and Administrator of the museum. Most of all, the remarkable progress of The Irvine Museum is due to the singular vision and dedication of Joan Irvine Smith, its Founder and President.

Individuals of great vision are society's treasures. Joan Irvine Smith has inspired our small museum to reach out and realize unprecedented accomplishments. Imagine: a small startup museum in Irvine, staffed, incredibly, by only five people, sending exhibitions throughout California, across the country to cities such as Chicago and New York, and finally, organizing an international exhibition to Paris, Krakow and Madrid, all within the first ten years of its existence!

To proclaim and document her myriad accomplishments, The Irvine Museum decided to honor Joan Irvine Smith with a book that recounts her extraordinary life and portrays the history of our young museum. We call this book *A California Woman's Story*—not because her significance is limited to the Golden State, but because she, like the museum she founded, is the product of the social, intellectual and natural environment of California, a setting that promotes individuality, creativity and imagination.

I invite you to read the story of Joan Irvine Smith.

Frederick Shafer, *Mount Shasta*, c. 1885, Private Collection, Courtesy of The Irvine Museum

FRONT ROW FROM LEFT: Joan Irvine Smith, former California Secretary of State March Fong Eu, California First Lady Maria Shriver and, AT UPPER RIGHT: Governor Arnold Schwarzenegger

A Remarkable Woman

JAMES IRVINE SWINDEN

On a balmy spring evening in May 2004, at the California State History Museum in Sacramento, Joan Irvine Smith was honored by Maria Shriver, First Lady of California, as one of California's Remarkable Women. It was a fitting tribute for her to be included with the late architect Julia Morgan, who designed Hearst Castle, the former California First Lady Gayle Wilson and the former California Secretary of State March Fong Eu, to name a few, as one of the remarkable women who have contributed so much to the state of California. It was an exceptional event that I was doubly honored to attend, as Joan Irvine Smith is my mother.

As I stood in front of her display case in the museum, I realized that this brief tribute to such a multi-faceted woman touched on only a few of the fascinating events and accomplishments comprising her life. This book, *A California Woman's Story*, reveals her story in an engaging first-hand narrative. It is a tale of vision, perseverance, tragedy and determination. Tracing her life as a young girl riding across the vast expanse of the Irvine Ranch to becoming one of the leading environmental activists in the United States today, the volume sheds new light on this truly remarkable woman.

Born into one of the leading pioneer families of California, my mother had all the benefits of privilege, and yet at the same time suffered tragedy with the loss of her father at an early age. She inherited her deep love of animals and nature from her grandfather James Harvey Irvine, as she spent countless hours accompanying him as he inspected the Irvine Ranch. As a young girl, she became an accomplished equestrian. Her love of horses, which continues to this day, led to the establishment of three world-class horse facilities: The Oaks in Virginia and The Oaks and The Oaks Indian Hill Ranch in California. For the past three years, she has received the U.S. Equestrian Federation–Performance Horse Registry Silver Stirrup Leading Hunter and Jumper Breeder Awards, in keeping with her longtime dream of developing an American sport horse that is capable of competing with European horses.

She was also instrumental in bringing a campus of the University of California to Irvine. Her deep appreciation of the land that she had inherited from her grandfather led her to be the driving force in The Irvine Company, engaging William Pereira to develop a master plan for the ranch. Owing to her tenacity and energy in pursuing these and other causes, she became the first woman to receive the Orange County Press Club's "Man of the Year" award, in January 1961. Her achievements ultimately led to the development of the city of Irvine, which then embraced her vision of a planned community that encompassed both "economic growth and environmental preservation." In 1991, she was awarded the highest honor offered by the university when she received the UCI Medal in recognition of her vision and continued support of that institution. These successes were only accomplished through great determination, effort, perseverance and sacrifice, as she spent more than three decades in litigation fighting to achieve these ends.

One of my mother's early achievements came as a result of spending six years lobbying in Washington, D.C., which included testifying before the House Ways and Means Committee and the Senate Committee on Finance in support of the Tax Reform Act of 1969. This law, which she championed aggressively, required all charitable foundations to increase their charitable grants to be at least five percent of their asset value each year (in some cases, the total for grants had previously been less than one percent). The significance of her efforts in lobbying for this legislation can be demonstrated by the $26.3 billion that foundations contributed to charitable causes in 2003 alone.

She and her mother, Athalie Richardson Irvine Clarke, established the Joan Irvine Smith & Athalie R. Clarke Foundation in 1991, which over the years has supported numerous environmental, medical, historical and artistic endeavors. Most notably, it supports the National Water Research Institute, which they helped to establish through their vision and inspiration. Its mission is to "create new sources of water through research and technology and to protect the fresh water and marine environment." In 1993, the Association of California Water Agencies presented my mother with the President's Recognition Award for her inspiration and her contribution to the development of the National Water Research Institute.

My mother's profound love of art, which she inherited from her own mother—an accomplished artist in her own right—led to the formation of three fine collections of Oriental art, English sporting paintings and California Impressionist paintings, the latter of which is acknowledged to be the most important in the nation. Ultimately, my mother's and my grandmother's love of art led to the establishment of The Irvine Museum in 1992. Through its exhibitions and publications, The Irvine Museum has become a leader in the field of regional American art. Its important American paintings are exhibited not only for their beauty and merit, but also to inspire a greater environmental awareness and a renewed interest in the preservation and stewardship of this country's natural resources.

It was for these and a great many other services to the state of California that Governor Gray Davis proclaimed March 20, 2002, as "Joan Irvine Smith Day." The city of San Juan Capistrano followed suit on April 5, 2002, with a similar proclamation.

My mother's wide-ranging contributions to the people of the state of California have also included being a cofounder of the Children's Hospital of Orange County and leading the effort to save Crystal Cove State Park. In 2004, the Youth Employment Service of the Newport Harbor Area also honored her for her outstanding community work.

A California Woman's Story is indeed the unique story of a remarkable woman, but then again, I might be slightly biased.

FROM LEFT: Morton Irvine Smith, California First Lady Sharon Davis, Joan Irvine Smith, Governor Gray Davis, Russell S. Penniman, James Irvine Swinden, and Jean Stern

John Cosby, *Morning, Crystal Cove*, Courtesy of Gray and Sharon Davis Collection

William Wendt, *Sycamores*, Private Collection, Courtesy of The Irvine Museum

A California Woman's Story

JOAN IRVINE SMITH

Athalie Richardson Irvine holding
infant Athalie Anita, photograph,
The Irvine Family Archives

I was born in Los Angeles on May 29, 1933, and named Athalie Anita Irvine. I lived there with my mother's parents, Dr. and Mrs. George H. Richardson, as my mother, Athalie Richardson Irvine, and my father, James Irvine, Jr., lived in Banning, because my father had tuberculosis. He was vice president of The Irvine Company and owner of *Cinelandia*, a Spanish-language Hollywood news magazine. My mother was a commercial artist who excelled at fashion design, and the many covers she produced for the magazine clearly showed her great ability.

After my father died in 1935, my mother and I lived with her parents. I was devoted to my grandmother and grandfather Richardson, who continued to take care of me. I will always remember my grandmother reading to me and telling me stories about when she was a young girl. She loved flowers and had a garden behind the house, where I played. My grandfather, who was a very strict disciplinarian, would put me on his lap and spend hours teaching me to play solitaire. When we took Sunday drives, I sat beside him in the back seat, always on my best behavior.

Another of my vivid childhood memories is driving with my mother and grandmother Richardson to San Juan Capistrano to visit the mission, where I loved to feed the great flock of white pigeons that fluttered about the fountain in the courtyard and along the garden paths and then landed on my shoulders. Occasionally, one of the birds would fly high above my head into the sky, and my mother would tell me that that was where my father had gone. Even to the present day, when I walk through the mission grounds, my impressions reach me at a deep and personal level, far beyond that of just a beautiful and historic monument.

Dr. George H. Richardson and Cora
Margaret Mather Richardson, c. 1899,
photograph, The Irvine Family Archives

Father Hutchison at Mission San Juan
Capistrano, postcard, c. 1930

Paul de Longpré, *Papa Gontier Roses*,
The Irvine Museum

Paul de Longpré, *French Bridal Roses*, Private
Collection, Courtesy of The Irvine Museum

James Harvey Irvine Jr. (Jase) c.1926, photograph,
The Irvine Family Archives

Athalie Richardson, c 1926, photograph, The Irvine Family Archives

My mother immediately became immersed in the details of my father's estate. She also became managing director and publisher of *Cinelandia* and spent a great deal of time running the magazine, which was published for circulation in Spain, Cuba, Mexico and the Latin American market. My father strongly believed in the potential for future social and commercial relations with Mexico and other Latin American countries, and I think that by focusing on the movie industry, he showed great foresight in identifying an effective vehicle for improving international relations. Just as managing the magazine had been wonderful therapy for my father during his long illness, it was equally beneficial for my mother, I am sure, as it enabled her not only to carry on my father's work, but to bury her grief in that work as well.

Every week, my mother and grandmother, and my nurse Dear Dear and I would go to Forest Lawn to put flowers next to the urn that held my father's ashes. I always loved feeding the beautiful white swans that glided across a large pond just inside the gate. Sometimes my mother and my grandparents and I would drive out to Eagle Rock, where my mother had property she had inherited from my father. There was a pony ring there, and I would be allowed to ride one of the very quiet ponies around and around the small dusty ring. This was something I truly looked forward to, and I would always cry when I had to get off my pony. I inherited my love of horses from my grandmother Richardson, who as a young girl sold all of her mother's beautiful cut crystal perfume bottles to buy a buckskin horse while her parents were away. From my grandfather James Irvine II, I inherited my love of dogs and nature. My great affection for horses and dogs and other animals has taught me patience and perseverance over the years, helping me to overcome many of the obstacles life has put before me.

Athalie Richardson Irvine on her wedding day, photograph,
The Irvine Family Archives

Paul Grimm, *Eucalyptus and Clouds*, Private Collection, Courtesy of The Irvine Museum

Athalie Anita with her nurse Dear Dear, 1933, photograph,
The Irvine Family Archives

Athalie Anita takes first horseback ride on the Irvine Ranch
with Sheriff Bill Reed, 1934, photograph, The Irvine Family Archives

Hernando Villa, *The Helene J,* The Irvine Museum

Martin E. Hall, *The Prospector*, 1851, Courtesy of A.R. Phillips, Jr.

John Stobart, *The Vicar of Brey in Yerba Buena Cove, San Francisco*, 1849, © John Stobart, Courtesy of Maritime Heritage Prints

James Irvine I(1827-1886); photograph, The Irvine Family Archives

Nettie Rice Irvine, photograph, The Irvine Family Archives

My great-grandfather James Irvine I was born in Belfast, Ireland, in 1827 and was of Scotch-Irish Presbyterian descent. In 1846, when he was nineteen, he and his younger brother William immigrated to the United States.

For two years, my great-grandfather worked in a paper mill in New York, until he caught gold fever and joined the stampede to California in 1849. He booked passage on a boat sailing to Chagres, Panama, on the east coast of Central America, and then crossed the Isthmus of Panama by canoe, mule and on foot. In Panama City, on the Pacific coast, he obtained passage to San Francisco on the Dutch sailing ship Alexander Humbolt. During the voyage, which took one hundred and one days, he and his fellow passengers consumed "hard beans and hardtack, mahogany beef and bilge water daily." Among his traveling companions were Collis P. Huntington and Dr. Benjamin Flint, and it was this latter association that eventually led to the creation of the Irvine Ranch.

Upon his arrival in California, my great-grandfather set out for the gold fields, where he worked for a time as both merchant and miner. In 1854, he bought an interest in a San Francisco commission house on Front Street. As large profits came in from the business, he invested them in income-producing San Francisco real estate. Then, in 1864, after many of the largeranchero holdings had been devastated by the Great Drought of 1863–64, my great-grandfather joined with Llewellyn Bixby and Benjamin and Thomas Flint to purchase three Mexican land grants in Los Angeles County: the Rancho San Joaquin, the Rancho Lomas de Santiago (hills of St. James), and a portion of the Rancho Santiago de Santa Ana. Covering roughly 115,000 acres and reaching from the Pacific Ocean to the San Bernardino County line, twenty-three miles long and eight miles wide, these three tracts of land—known then as Rancho San Joaquin—would eventually become the Irvine Ranch, comprising one-fifth of what is today Orange County.

By 1866, James Irvine I had become a very prominent citizen in San Francisco. Some years earlier, his father and mother had come from Belfast to live in Cleveland, Ohio, and my great-grandfather was well acquainted in that city. That same year, he married Henrietta Maria ("Nettie") Rice of Cleveland. The couple made their home at the corner of Folsom and Eleventh streets, and the house with its furnishings cost more than $25,000, "But it is a very comfortable one," my great-grandfather wrote, "with a beautiful yard filled with shrubbery, flowers and clover, and there I take solid enjoyment."

Nettie Rice came from a distinguished family. Her father, Harvey Rice, was an educator, lawyer, real estate salesman, and prolific author, and he served in the Ohio legislature. As a state senator, he took an active part in badly needed prison reform and sponsored the bill that established Ohio's public school system and school libraries. His fellow citizens gratefully knew him as the "father of the common school system of Ohio."

On October 16, 1867, my grandfather James Harvey Irvine was born. His father's happiness at the birth of a son and heir was cut short, however, as Nettie contracted puerperal fever, the dreaded curse of childbirth in that pre-antiseptic age. For a while, it was uncertain whether my great-grandmother would live or die. When the crisis passed, my great-grandfather could hardly find words to express his relief and gratitude. To Nettie's mother, he wrote: "I am going to do all in my power to benefit or make her happy, I love her too dearly to do otherwise, and daily I feel grateful to you and her father for the wife you gave me, for I think a sweeter nature and lovelier spirit than hers, God never breathed into human form."

Archibald Willard, *Harvey Rice*, The Irvine Museum

21

MUCH OF MY GREAT-GRANDFATHER'S PURCHASE OF LAND had originally been held by the Mission San Juan Capistrano, the seventh mission to be built in Alta California. In 1769, by edict of King Carlos III, Spain had moved to establish permanent colonies in California, owing to the apprehension that England and the Russian Empire were expanding into California from colonies in Canada and the Pacific Northwest. The task of setting up a chain of missions in California fell to Father Junípero Serra, and the series of presidios that would protect them became the responsibility of Captain Gaspár de Portolá.

Portolá had been appointed governor of Baja California in 1767. When the order came to colonize the north, he relished the adventure. In order to scout, identify and map potential sites for the construction of missions and presidios, Portolá set out on an expedition from San Diego and charted a series of locations throughout California, going as far north as present-day San Francisco. There he was forced to turn back, owing to the poor health of several members of his group and his inability to cross the estuary now called the Golden Gate. During his journey, he and his chief scout, Sergeant José Francisco Ortega, became the first Europeans to set foot in what are now the major cities of California.

Anna Hills, *The Vespers Hour*, Courtesy of DeRu's Fine Arts, Laguna Beach

Elizabeth Borglum, *Facade of San Juan Capistrano*, c. 1895, The Irvine Museum

The California missions came into existence with the founding of a presidio and mission in San Diego in 1769. The second mission, and indeed the headquarters of the entire California mission system, was founded in Monterey in 1770 and later moved to Carmel. The earliest recorded use of a water system for the irrigation of crops in southern California was at the Mission San Gabriel, in 1771.

Mission San Juan Capistrano, founded in 1776, became the seventh in a series of twenty-one missions that would reach as far north as Sonoma. According to historian Don Meadows, the original mission site was in San Juan Canyon, on the old Lacouague Ranch, about two miles up San Juan Creek. Father Francisco Palóu, who had never visited the original site, quotes Father Serra as saying, "The site of the mission is very pleasant and it has a good view. From the buildings, the ocean can be seen and the ships when they cruise there; for the beach is only about half a league distant (about a mile and a half)."

Duncan Gleason, *The San Carlos Entering the Golden Gate*, Courtesy of the estate of the artist

Alexander Harmer, *Mission San Juan Capistrano*, 1886, Private Collection, Courtesy of The Irvine Museum

On October 4, 1778, all work on the mission was abandoned, and it was moved to ensure a constant supply of fresh water for the growing community. The new site was located between San Juan Creek and Trabuco Creek.

At one time, the Mission San Juan Capistrano took in some 300,000 acres, extending from the Santa Ana River south to San Mateo Creek, just below present-day San Clemente, and from the Pacific Ocean inland to the top of the Santa Ana Mountains. Almost all of the acreage was grazing land except for a small number of acres devoted to field crops, vineyards and orchards.

The mission complex was vast in design, including a small adobe chapel (now called the Serra Chapel), granaries, a winery and brandy distillery, tallow vats, hide tanning pits, shops for harness- and shoe-making, weaving, dyeing, candle- and soap-making, as well as forty adobes where the Indian neophytes were housed. Moreover, the Mission San Juan Capistrano had the only known foundry and iron forge in Alta California.

Lloyd Harting, *Scenes of Mission Life*,
Courtesy of the Mission San Juan Capistrano Museum

Cattle Drive at Mission San Gabriel, Courtesy of the
Mission San Juan Capistrano Museum

Californios Throwing the Lasso, Courtesy of the California History Section,
California State Library

The mission maintained vast herds of cattle as well as horses, sheep, goats and pigs, and it was the Indian converts' job to tend them. The Spanish rule that neophytes must not learn to ride was ignored, and the Indians, who had never seen horses or cattle, were taught to be cowboys. They were also instructed how to scrape and tan hides and how to fashion leather into harnesses and shoes. They learned to render fat into tallow, which they used to make soap and candles. They were taught to shear sheep from the mission flocks, process the wool and then dye and weave the yarn into rough cloth. Much of this instruction was done outside the mission quadrangle.

The mission thrived with activity, and more than 1,200 people lived and worked there. Because of the area's mild climate, fertile soil and good water supply, agricultural production flourished. In 1811, the mission records show 500,000 pounds of wheat, 190,000 pounds of barley, 202,000 pounds of corn, 20,600 pounds of beans, 14,000 cattle, 16,000 sheep and 740 horses. Thriving vineyards produced wine and brandy, and olives from the orchards were pressed for valuable oil. Pomegranates and figs were also important produce from the mission orchards.

Fred Behre and J. Gutzon Borglum, *Mission San Juan Capistrano*, (reconstructed view) Courtesy of the Mission San Juan
Capistrano Museum

Because of this abundance, ships frequently stopped at Capistrano Bay to conduct trade. Some ships came to purchase supplies for their voyages, such as grain, wine, olive oil and hemp rope, while others came bearing manufactured goods and exotic items to trade for mission hides and tallow. Among the most desirable items these ships offered to the mission were books, bells, special utensils and ornaments for the church, and long-awaited news from the rest of the world.

In 1797, the cornerstone was laid for the greatest and most ambitious building at the Mission San Juan Capistrano, the Great Stone Church. This edifice, made of sandstone quarried from a local site, would become the largest structure in California. The plan called for a Spanish-style cruciform church, with the main doors facing south, a central aisle, a large dome over the crossing, six smaller domes and a tall bell tower. The large labor force needed for the construction was composed of Indians, as the soldiers found any type of heavy labor unacceptable. A master stonemason named Isidro Aguilar was brought in from Mexico to supervise construction.

While the church was being built, religious services continued as before, in the small adobe chapel. In 1803, Aguilar died; without his guiding hands, the padres took more than eight years to complete the church, much longer than expected.

Finally, in 1806, the Great Stone Church was completed and personally dedicated by Father Serra. Many dignitaries attended the ceremony. Governor José Arrillaga arrived accompanied by soldiers in glittering uniforms, from San Diego and Santa Barbara. The cathedral-like church was crowded with neophytes from distant rancherías. The rows of magical, flickering tapers, made of tallow mixed with native beeswax, excited the mystical side of the Indians. Many had even agreed to be baptized primarily so they could attend the alluring candlelit ceremonies. The fiesta that followed became a legend in southern California, with feasting and praying lasting for several days.

For the next six years, the Mission San Juan Capistrano had the largest and grandest church in California. It could be seen from throughout the Capistrano Valley and its bells heard at least ten miles out to sea.

Tragically, on the summer-like morning of December 8, 1812, a severe earthquake shook the region just as Indian converts were in the church celebrating mass. Walls swayed, the domes fell in and the bell tower collapsed on the main part of the church, killing forty people. What had been the most imposing edifice of its time had become California's most beautiful ruin.

Alson Clark, *Ruins of the Chapel,* Private Collection, Courtesy of The Irvine Museum

In 1821, Mexico won its independence from Spain and claimed the provinces of California (Alta and Baja) and New Mexico (made up of the present-day states of Arizona and New Mexico). Twelve years later Mexico passed a general secularization law: All mission lands, livestock, tools and supplies were to be confiscated and divided, half to resident Indians and the other half to be administered "for the public good." By law, the missions were to become Indian pueblos, but in reality, most of the best pieces of former mission land ended up going to wealthy Californios, usually friends or relatives of the governor.

In fact, the last Mexican governor of California—the notoriously corrupt Pío Pico—gave out 87 grants in the last six months of his two-year term (1845–46), and almost all at the maximum allowable size of 11 square leagues (approximately 50,000 acres). Pico was not just a benefactor to his friends: he had himself often been the beneficiary of other governors' largesse and had thereby built his own tremendous fortune. Among the Pico family landholdings were the former lands of the Mission San Fernando, at approximately 117,000 acres, and the Rancho Santa Margarita y las Flores (Saint Margaret and the Flowers), which measured 133,000 acres in northern San Diego County and was formerly part of the Mission San Luis Rey. The Rancho Santa Margarita y las Flores later became the property of Pico's brother-in-law Don Juan Forster and was eventually sold to James C. Flood and Richard O'Neill, Sr.

Richard Henry Dana, Jr. in 1892, photograph, Courtesy of The Bancroft Library, University of California, Berkeley

During the period of Mexican rule, the only commercial outlet for Californios was the hide and tallow trade, which furnished much of the raw materials for New England's developing leather industry. This trade was to become a powerful factor in arousing American interest in the province and in California's eventual annexation by the United States.

One of the major accounts of the hide and tallow trade was written by Richard Henry Dana, a student of Harvard University who had been compelled to take a leave from his studies after a serious case of measles affected his eyesight. Wanting to go to sea, Dana declined the chance to travel as a passenger and instead chose to sign on as an ordinary seaman on the *Pilgrim*, which sailed from Boston in August 1834, destined for California by way of Cape Horn, around the southern tip of South America. He spent nearly two years on the voyage, loading a full cargo of hides, tallow and horn, which were sent back to Boston and made into shoes and other manufactured goods. Dana returned on the *Alert*, again as an ordinary seaman, arriving in Boston in September 1836. He reentered Harvard, graduated in 1837 and went on to earn a law degree. In his career as a lawyer, Dana specialized in cases brought by seamen against the cruel and oppressive treatment they had received on board merchant ships.

Frank W. Thompson, *The Brig Pilgrim*, Courtesy of Santa Barbara Historical Society

Describing the long and dangerous voyage to California, Dana wrote in his diary: "Here we were, in a little vessel, with a small crew, on a half-civilized coast at the ends of the earth, and with a prospect of remaining an indefinite period, two or three years at the least...We were in the remote parts of the earth, on an almost desert coast, in a country where there is neither law nor gospel, and where sailors are at their captain's mercy."

Dana used the diaries he had kept on his voyage to write *Two Years before the Mast*, "to present the life of a common sailor at sea as it really is." The book gained wide popularity and led to long-needed reforms in the shipping industry. In 1841, Dana published *The Seaman's Friend*, a book that included a summary of laws pertaining to ships and seamen.

Dana tells that, along the California coast, the arrival of a trading ship was a major event. Just before the ship's long-awaited arrival, a messenger-agent would visit all of the ranchos, pueblos and missions in the area to spread the news. When a ship was due in Capistrano Bay, for instance, notice was given as far away as the San Gabriel and San Fernando missions, and entire families from those distant areas would journey to Capistrano to partake of trading.

After waiting onshore, groups of eager Californios—including wives and children of wealthy rancheros—would be rowed out to the ship. Once on board, they proceeded below deck, where they found row upon row of merchandise. Ladies could choose from fine cotton fabric, silk, lace, shawls from the Orient, jewelry, perfume, shoes and porcelain dishes. For the men, there were guns, knives, iron tools, boots and saddles made from the very same leather that had been secured on previous voyages. These "floating department stores" also stocked furniture, musical instruments, books, toys and window glass, and they offered, as Dana relates, "everything under the sun, in fact everything that can be imagined, from Chinese fireworks to English cart wheels, of which we had a dozen pairs with their iron tires on."

When fully loaded, each ship carried a cargo of approximately 40,000 hides. The number of hides exported during the rancho period was extremely large, perhaps upward of one million or more. The largest number went to Boston, the center of New England shoe manufacturing. As described in Dana's book, a typical voyage from Boston might last two years, with frequent stops along the California coast to unload goods and pick up hides.

Duncan Gleason, *Hides being Loaded into the Hold of a Trading Ship*, Courtesy of the Estate of the Artist

Tallow and horn were also valuable commodities. Tallow was used in the production of soap and, above all, candles—an important necessity in the days before kerosene lamps and electric lights. Horn was used much like our modern plastics, such as for shoe buttons and small utensils.

In describing the hide and tallow trade, Dana's *Two Years before the Mast* had an unexpected effect in that it brought California, a distant and unknown region, to the attention of a large number of Americans. His depiction of the land, its people and the romantic way of life they followed was the only basis for forming an understanding of California for many years to come. And of all the ports and places he had visited, Dana found San Juan Capistrano the most beautiful: "the only romantic spot in California…there was a grandeur in everything around, which gave solemnity to the scene: a silence and solitariness…no sound heard but the pulsations of the great Pacific…as refreshing as a great rock in a weary land." The message Dana proclaimed about California was clear and convincing. It was "a country embracing four or five hundred miles of sea coast, with several good harbors; with fine forests in the north; the waters filled with fish, and the plains covered with thousands of head of cattle; blessed with a climate than which there can be no better in

Dana Point, photograph, Courtesy of First American Title and Trust Historical Collection

the world; free from all manner of diseases, whether epidemic or endemic; and with a soil in which corn yields from seventy to eighty fold. In the hands of an enterprising people," he wrote, "what a country this might be!"

Elmer Wachtel, *San Juan Bluffs*, Courtesy of Joseph Ambrose and Michael Fedderson

FROM LEFT: Maraneta Alvarado, Ignacia Alverado de Pico. Pio Pico, Trinidad de la Guerra, photograph, Courtesy of Southwest Museum, Los Angeles

IN 1845, THE MISSION SAN JUAN CAPISTRANO was auctioned for $710 by Governor Pico to the highest bidders: John Forster, his brother-in-law, and James McKinley, who was later bought out by Forster. Because the mission was still a parish church, Forster's purchase included all the buildings at the mission except for the old adobe church and an adjoining room where the resident padre lived. Forster moved into the old mission, walling off a portion of the front building into comfortable living quarters, where he and his family settled into the Californio way of life.

Through Pico's influence, Forster became a land baron. In another grant, he received the Potreros de San Juan Capistrano (the pastures of the old mission) and Rancho Trabuco (musket), on Trabuco Creek, which was near the Mission San Juan Capistrano. He moved to San Juan Capistrano and purchased the adjoining Rancho Mission Vieja (now called Rancho Mission Viejo, or the old mission) and the Rancho Desechos (rough terrain), now part of the city of San Clemente. By age thirty-two, Forster owned an estate of more than 100,000 acres. The Mission San Juan Capistrano remained Forster's home until 1865, when a Federal Land Patent issued in the name of President Lincoln returned the mission to the Catholic Church.

In 1864, a severe drought brought many California landowners to bankruptcy. The Pico brothers—Pío, the former governor, and Andrés, the victorious general at the Battle of San Pasqual

LEFT: John "Juan" Forster, c. 1860, photograph, Courtesy of San Juan Capistrano Historical Society; RIGHT: Mrs. Juan Forester, photograph, Courtesy of San Juan Capistrano Historical Society

Colin Campbell Cooper, *Mission Courtyard*, Private Collection, Courtesy of The Irvine Museum

and the last Californio commander to surrender to American forces—were in debt and desperately feared losing their vast holdings. Among their many ranches was the Rancho Santa Margarita y las Flores, situated along the coast between what are now San Clemente and Oceanside. The property was originally an Indian pueblo called Santa Margarita y San Onofre. Pío Pico maneuvered title to the rancho in 1844, in part through a grant from Governor Juan Bautista Alvarado. The Pico ranch house is now the commandant's quarters at the U.S. Marine base Camp Pendleton.

The Pico brothers' great debt, the result of years of high living and unrestrained gambling, threatened to ruin them. Pío convinced Juan Forster to take the Rancho Santa Margarita in exchange for assuming a debt of $37,000. The Picos could not raise this large amount, and they feared that a foreclosure action against them would bring about the loss of their other properties. To legalize the transfer, Pío signed a deed, which of course was written in English. In 1865, Forster moved his family from the Mission San Juan Capistrano to the Rancho Santa Margarita y las Flores. Years later, the Pico brothers maintained that the agreement had been for only half of the ranch, and that Forster had, in Spanish, verbally confirmed this when Pío signed the deed.

Alfred Sully, *Monterey, California Rancho Scene*, c. 1849, Courtesy of Oakland Museum of California, The Oakland Museum Kahn Collection

Rancho Santa Margarita ranch house, photograph, Courtesy of San Juan Capistrano Historical Society

Henry Chapman Ford, *Rancho Santa Margarita*, Courtesy of the Mission Inn Foundation and Museum, Riverside, California

William Wendt, *Mission Viejo*, 1908, Private Collection, Courtesy of The Irvine Museum

John Gamble, *Wild Buckwheat Near Capistrano*, Courtesy of Bonhams and Butterfields Auction

Frank L. Heath, *Landscape at Dana Point*, 1887, Courtesy of Dr. and Mrs. Edward H. Boseker

To clear his title to the ranch, Forster sued the Pico brothers in 1873. In the trial, the Picos claimed that the ranch was then valued at $75,000 (this appears to be an exaggerated figure, as in 1864, James Irvine and his partners had bought the Rancho San Joaquin at about the same price per acre that Forster had paid for the Rancho Santa Margarita), and that the debt of $37,000 represented half the value of the ranch. Forster, in turn, produced the deed and offered notes that he had paid an additional $24,000 of Pío's ever-increasing debts. He further showed that, as sole owner, he had paid the annual taxes on the entire ranch. He called witnesses to testify that he had conducted business at the ranch as sole owner. The jury took less than thirty minutes to find in favor of Forster. With clear legal title to the Rancho Santa Margarita, Forster now held more than 250,000 acres.

At the time, San Juan Capistrano had the only Mexican administrative office and justice court between San Gabriel and San Diego. The San Juan justice, Emigdio Vejar, was granted the 6,600-acre Rancho Boca de la Playa (mouth of the beach), which included modern-day Capistrano Beach, Doheny State Park and northern San Clemente. As beach property had no value to the Spanish and Mexicans, the bluff lands on either side of Boca de la Playa, such as modern-day Dana Point and southern San Clemente, remained in the public domain. Other coastal lands that were left in the public domain included those of modern-day Arch Beach, South Laguna and Laguna Beach, which were homesteaded in the 1870s.

Rancho Niguel, named for an Indian village, lay north of Dana Point. It had been granted to Juan Ávila in 1842. Lewis Moulton, who had come to California in 1874 and become a sheepherder for the Irvine Ranch, partnered with Jean-Piedra Daguerre to increase the original Ávila land grant to 22,000 acres, calling it the Moulton Ranch. It was operated as a cattle ranch until 1959, when it was sold to a syndicate that developed the land into the communities of Aliso Viejo, Laguna Niguel, Laguna Hills and Leisure World.

William Wendt, *Vibrant Coast, Dana Point*, c. 1903, The Irvine Museum

Ivan Summers, *Salt Creek*, Courtesy of Dr. and Mrs. Edward H. Boseker

Joseph Kleitsch, *Laguna Shoreline*, Courtesy of Mr. and Mrs. Thomas B. Stiles, II, photograph, Courtesy of Redfern Gallery, Laguna Beach

William Wendt, *Moonrise, Moulton Ranch*, Courtesy of Mr. and Mrs. Thomas B. Stiles II

Henri Pénélon, *Don José Sepúlveda*, c. 1856, Courtesy of Bowers Museum of Cultural Art, Santa Ana, California

Another local landholder was José Andrés Sepúlveda, son of Francisco Sepúlveda, the owner of the Rancho San Vicente, which occupied what is now most of the western part of Los Angeles. In 1837, young José Andrés was granted a large tract of former Mission San Juan Capistrano land called Cerrito de las Ranas (small hill of the frogs), which stretched along the coastline from the present-day city of Newport Beach to the city of Laguna Beach, and inland to the foothills of the Santa Ana Mountains. The coastal acreage included the present-day site of Crystal Cove State Park.

In 1842, Sepúlveda was granted a second, adjoining tract of land known as the Bolsa de San Joaquin (pocket or area of dry land in a swamp). He combined the new grant with his existing one, the Cerrito de las Ranas, and formed the Rancho San Joaquin, encompassing 48,803 acres of land and reaching from Newport Bay to Laguna Canyon and northward to the foothills of the Santa Ana Mountains. At the rancho he built a large adobe house for his family, developed part of the tract into fields and gardens and used the remainder for grazing approximately 14,000 head of cattle, 3,000 horses and 8,000 sheep.

Sepúlveda became one of the most picturesque figures in southern California, known for his great landholdings, fast racehorses, reckless wagers, openhanded hospitality and elegant costumes. His extravagant lifestyle soon put him into a slough of debt from which he never escaped; ultimately, he was forced to sell the Rancho San Joaquin, which would later become the lower half of the Irvine Ranch.

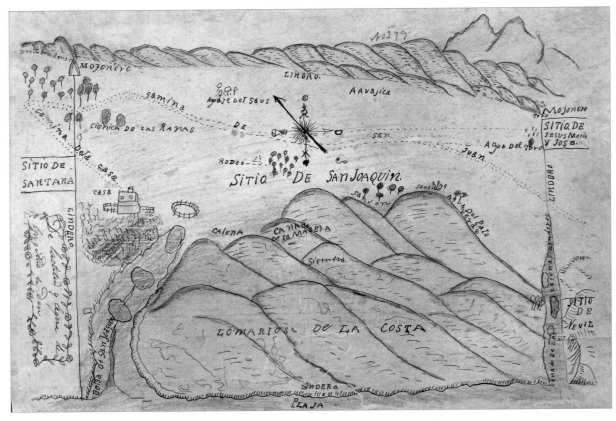

Diseño of Rancho San Joaquin, 1842, Courtesy of Sherman Library and Gardens, Corona del Mar, California

William Hahn, *Mexican Cattle Drivers in Southern California*, Courtesy of Santa Cruz Island Foundation

William Hahn, *Mexican Cattle Drivers in Southern California*, Courtesy of Dr. and Mrs. Edward H. Boseker

Cattle on the Irvine Ranch, photograph, Irvine Historical Society

William Wendt, *Santa Ana River*, 1928, Private Collection, Courtesy of The Irvine Museum

Another part of the future Irvine Ranch was the 62,516-acre Rancho Santiago de Santa Ana, given to José Antonio Yorba and his nephew Juan Pablo Peralta in 1810 as the first Spanish land grant in what is now Orange County. This rancho lay on the east bank of the Santa Ana River and extended from the Santa Ana Mountains to the sea. It included the lands around the confluence of the Santa Ana River and Santiago Creek, an area that now encompasses the city of Santa Ana. The land grant allowed the use of the flows of the Santa Ana River adjacent to the land and the groundwater beneath the land. The first irrigation diversion from the Santa Ana River was made by Yorba and Peralta in 1810 or 1811. Some 3,800 acres of the Rancho Santiago de Santa Ana, adjacent to the Santa Ana River, later became part of the Irvine Ranch.

The third grant that would make up the Irvine Ranch was the Rancho Lomas de Santiago, or the Ranch of the Hills of St. James. In 1846, Governor Pico issued this private grant of four square leagues (about 17,000 acres) to Teodosio Yorba. Falling within the grant was the magnificent grove of ancient coastal oaks that may still be seen in present-day Irvine Park, in Santiago Canyon. Like his older brother Don Bernardo Yorba, whose longhorns grazed west of the oak grove on the Rancho Santiago de Santa Ana, Teodosio devoted the Rancho Lomas de Santiago to cattle.

Granville Redmond, *California Oaks*, 1910, The Irvine Museum

William Wendt, *Ranch in the Valley*, Private Collection, Courtesy of The Irvine Museum

Cattle on Rancho San Joaquin, photograph, The Irvine Family Archives

The First Ranch House, Rancho San Joaquin, photograph, The Irvine Family Archives

SHORTLY AFTER MY GREAT-GRANDFATHER'S 1864 purchase from these three ranchos, he found that wool was in great demand, owing to the disruption of the cotton industry in the South caused by the Civil War. Consequently, he and his three partners brought in 20,000 sheep from Iowa and imported 25 merino rams from the Sandwich Islands, now known as the Hawaiian Islands, to stock their newly acquired ranchos. In addition to raising sheep, the Rancho San Joaquin also ran a substantial number of cattle. These were the descendants of the vast herds that had grazed there during both the mission and rancho periods.

In the summer of 1867, my great-grandfather visited the properties and returned to San Francisco more enthusiastic than ever. "We rode about a good deal," he wrote, "sometimes coming home in the evening after a thirty or forty mile ride, pretty thoroughly tired out, but we had to do it in order to see much of the ranch and the flock. We have been making further purchases of land adjoining ours. Now our tract contains about 101–115,000 acres. On one side, the line is nearly 23 miles long and the average width is nearly eight miles. So you can see there is considerable riding to be done, if one is to see much of it."

In order to have a suitable place to stay and conduct business while he visited the Rancho San Joaquin, my great-grandfather commissioned a home to be built in 1868. The two-story frame house, also intended to be the headquarters for the ranch superintendent, cost $1,300 and was constructed near the old Sepúlveda compound. The finest house for miles around, and the first wooden one to be erected between Anaheim and San Diego, the San Joaquin Ranch house had a kitchen, dining room, parlor, four bedrooms and a porch that ran around most of the building. It was staffed with Chinese household help.

As early as three years before, the 105-ton, stern-wheeled river steamer Vaquero was paying regular visits to San Joaquin Bay, known today as Newport Bay, mainly to collect hides, meat and tallow from the nearby ranchos. In 1868, the Vaquero brought the lumber that was used to construct the San Joaquin Ranch house, and the partners began shipping their wool to San Francisco, and then on to New York or Boston.

The following year, the San Joaquin Ranch produced 70,000 pounds of wool that brought around 30 cents a pound in Boston and New York. In spite of these satisfactory returns, my great-grandfather found the property a constant source of irritation. Squatters began moving in onto the ranges, and the conflicts between the landowners and the intruders became increasingly bitter, with the quarrels often leading to violence and bloodshed. Wages and ranch costs were rising; taxes on some of the property were getting out of hand; a trusted employee had taken to whiskey and gambling; and the business of the ranch "was being greatly neglected."

In 1876, my great-grandfather acquired his partners' interest in the Rancho San Joaquin for $150,000. As soon as he secured full ownership of the ranch, the historic drought of 1876–77 dried up the ranges and devastated the sheep-grazing industry of southern California, just as the drought of the mid-1860s had destroyed the range cattle industry.

That same year, my great-grandfather instructed the ranch superintendent to find a more suitable place for a ranch headquarters, one that was closer to civilization. The location that they decided on was near Tustin City and the stage depot. Construction soon began on the country-style Georgian frame house that would serve as both the Irvine family home and the ranch office on Rancho San Joaquin.

Sheep Shearing on Rancho San Joaquin c. 1890, photograph, Courtesy of San Juan Capistrano Historical Society

Irvine home near Tustin and Rancho San Joaquin office, photograph, Courtesy of First American Title and Trust Historical Collection

Carl Schmidt, *Sheep Grazing*, Courtesy of Bonhams and Butterfield Auction

James Harvey Irvine, photograph, The Irvine Family Archives

Frances Anita Plum, photograph, The Irvine Family Archives

By the mid-1880s, the semi-frontier conditions of the Santa Ana Valley were rapidly giving way to a more advanced social and economic order. The completion of the Southern Pacific Railroad to Los Angeles in 1876, and the coming of the Santa Fe Railway nine years later, changed the agricultural outlook for the Los Angeles–Santa Ana Basin, brought about a large influx of population, stimulated the subdivision of many large landholdings and ushered in the great boom of 1886–88. But my great-grandfather, founder of the Irvine Ranch, was not able to participate to any degree in these new developments, as he died in San Francisco on March 15, 1886. Three years later, on August 1, 1889, the citizens of the Santa Ana Valley broke off from Los Angeles County and created the County of Orange.

According to the provisions of his father's will, my grandfather James Irvine II, who was then eighteen years old, had to be twenty-five before he could receive his inheritance. The trustees of my great-grandfather's estate included, among others, his older brother George Irvine, who oversaw the management of the Irvine Ranch. As squatters were a constant problem, George Irvine had encouraged tenant farmers to sharecrop the land in order to keep it productive.

One of the earliest tenant farmers was James Sleeper, the grandfather of historian Jim Sleeper. He began farming on the ranch in 1888, leasing 1,400 acres. His house and barns were located on the old Laguna Road (Highway 101) three miles southwest of Tustin and became a local landmark known as "Sleeper's Corner."

The previous year, the trustees of the estate had put the Irvine Ranch up for public auction. On April 16, 1887, the trustees "offered and agreed to sell" at least 100,000 acres of the Irvine Ranch in Los Angeles County at public auction. The bidding began at $1,300,000 and had reached $1,385,000 when the timekeeper became confused as to which of the two bidders had made the final bid. When the decision was challenged in court, the judge ruled that neither bidder was entitled to the land.

William Wendt, *Oaks and Sycamores*, Private Collection, Courtesy of The Irvine Museum

William Wendt, *Foothill Ranch*, Private Collection, Courtesy of The Irvine Museum

The trustees continued their efforts to sell the ranch, but negotiations dragged on and time ran out. In 1893, James Irvine II came into full possession of the property. He retained complete control and direction over the ranch until his death well over half a century later, on August 24, 1947.

Under the Irvine-Flint-Bixby Partnership, the property had been used almost entirely for pasturing sheep, but by 1878, a small amount of the land had begun to be devoted to tenant farming. Although raising sheep continued to be an important business long after the death of James Irvine I, the large flocks of earlier years had dwindled and been replaced by a substantial number of cattle. Much of the rangeland was leased to outsiders, as the Irvine Ranch underwent its radical transition from a grazing and pastoral economy to a farming-based one, a reflection of the general agricultural development of most of southern California.

By the close of 1888, more than 5,000 acres of the Irvine property had been leased in relatively small tracts for hay and grain. In addition to grain farming, more and more land was being cultivated for beans and other crops. A small vineyard was set out, chiefly for home use, and the trustees made a strong effort to establish an olive industry as one of the major interests of the ranch, without success. A walnut orchard, irrigated at first by tank wagon, was also set out, and more than 11,000 eucalyptus or "gum trees" were planted for both wood and windbreaks; a few orange trees were also propagated but used only for home consumption.

In 1892, James Irvine II married my grandmother, San Francisco socialite Frances Anita Plum. Two years later, on June 4, 1894, he incorporated his holdings as The Irvine Company under the laws of the state of West Virginia, an action that would prove vital to the future development of the Irvine Ranch.

Cattle on the Irvine Ranch, photograph, Courtesy of Irvine Historical Society

Thresher and mule team on the Irvine Ranch, photograph, Courtesy of Irvine Historical Society

Granville Redmond, *Tending the Flocks*, Private Collection, Courtesy of The Irvine Museum

Edgar Payne, *Sycamores, Orange County Park*, Private Collection, Courtesy of The Irvine Museum

Frances Anita Plum Irvine at Irvine Park, photograph, The Irvine Family Archives

My grandfather's Scottish frugality was legendary—less well known, perhaps, was his great love of nature, a sentiment not held by most of his contemporaries. If an oak tree intruded upon a projected road widening, my grandfather would reroute the road rather than remove the tree. It was no surprise when a beautifully wooded parcel of land in Santiago Canyon, which early settlers had called the "Picnic Grounds," became the pride of his great ranch.

It was the personal retreat of my grandfather and grandmother and the private playground of their two eldest children, my father, James Harvey Irvine, Jr., known as "Jase," born on June 11, 1893, and my aunt Kathryn Helena, born on September 29, 1894. My grandparents' youngest child, my uncle Myford, was not born until April 25, 1898. All three children were born at home in San Francisco.

In spite of my grandfather's fondness for the site, in April 1897 he gave Orange County 160 acres in Santiago Canyon, including the "Picnic Grounds," for a public park. The new park, originally called Orange County Park and now called Irvine Regional Park, totaled 477 acres and was the first county park in California. It became the envy of the state.

The gift came with a few conditions: a road that had bisected the grove was to be relocated on the north side, thus becoming the park's first entrance; the grounds were to be fenced and an "inspector" appointed to keep out sheepherders and woodchoppers; no intoxicating liquors were to be sold on the premises; admission was to be free; and, above all, my grandfather stipulated that the trees were to receive good care and the grounds be kept as natural as possible.

Dogs are still welcome in the park, and this would certainly please my grandfather, as he was particularly fond of them. An avid bird shooter, my grandfather kept more than a dozen Irish Setters and English Pointers for hunting the vast number of quail and dove that populated the ranch and the swarms of ducks and geese that migrated through the property each fall on their way south. My grandfather even kept a large aviary behind the ranch house in Tustin, where injured game birds were kept until they had recovered and could be released into the wild.

From his childhood, my father would accompany my grandfather when he went hunting. He loved the ranch just as his father did, and had been groomed from childhood to take over the management of The Irvine Company.

James Harvey Irvine Jr., known as Jase, Kathryn Helena Irvine and Myford Irvine, photograph, The Irvine Family Archives

Irvine family San Francisco home, photograph, The Irvine Family Archives

Jase and Kathyrn at Irvine Park, photograph, The Irvine Family Archives

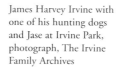

James Harvey Irvine with one of his hunting dogs and Jase at Irvine Park, photograph, The Irvine Family Archives

James Harvey Irvine with one of his hunting dogs, photograph, The Irvine Family Archives

Mule-drawn harvester, Irvine Ranch, photograph, The Irvine Family Archives

Walnut shipment at the train yard, photograph, The Irvine Family Archives

After San Francisco's 1906 earthquake and fire, my grandfather and his family moved their residence to the new San Joaquin Ranch house in Tustin. Three years later, my grandmother died, leaving a deep and abiding hurt in my grandfather's life. Something went out of him forever, and he became more and more involved in hunting and fishing, and less and less dependent on the society and companionship of others.

The Irvine Company, nevertheless, continued to prosper and expand in both the magnitude and the variety of its operations. During the first ten years of my grandfather's administration, the ranch continued to evolve from a pastoral to a farming operation, but its development was limited to field crops such as beans and barley, rather than garden vegetables or orchards. Eventually, however, my grandfather, who always described himself as "just a farmer," transformed his property into one of the great agricultural empires of the world.

Irvine Ranch house and agricultural headquarters, photo by Eddie Martin, Courtesy of historian Judy Gauntt

William Griffith, *The Bean Ranch*, 1931, The Irvine Museum

William Wendt, *Plowed Fields*, Private Collection, Courtesy of The Irvine Museum

George Gardner Symons, *Southern California Coast*, The Irvine Museum

Frank Cuprien, *The Golden Hour*, Private Collection,
Courtesy of The Irvine Museum

FROM THE 1880S TO THE 1920S, LAGUNA BEACH was a mecca for plein air artists from the United States and Europe because its unique California light was like that of southern France. For more than a century, Crystal Cove and the Irvine Coast have been favorite locations for artists such as Guy Rose, William Wendt, Edgar Payne, Jack Wilkinson Smith, Frank Cuprien, Raymond Nott, Hanson Puthuff, Anna Hills, Donna Schuster, Granville Redmond, Joseph Kleitsch and many others.

Indeed, the glorification of nature has been a universal theme throughout the history of art. In the United States, landscape painting is a time-honored tradition that is inseparable from the spirit of American art. In the early 1800s, at the time of the Industrial Revolution, a group of dedicated landscape painters known as the Hudson River School ventured into what was then the wilderness of the Hudson River Valley. Lamenting the destruction of the natural environment, they painted scenes of virgin and unspoiled countryside. These artists were in awe of the beauty and grandeur of nature and developed a popular and long-lived style that centered on landscape as primary subject. In their own way, they were the first environmental activists.

In California, a similar group of spiritually aware painters working in the early 1900s recorded the beauty of nature. One of the most prominent of these artists, William Wendt, believed that nature was a manifestation of God and viewed himself as nature's faithful interpreter. His feelings for the land were so profound that he rarely included people or animals in his landscapes.

Guy Rose, *Laguna Rocks, Low Tide*, Private Collection,
Courtesy of The Irvine Museum

According to Janet Blake in *The Laguna Beach Art Association, 1918–1928*, the first artist of note to visit Laguna Beach was the English-trained watercolorist Norman St. Clair, who reportedly painted sketches there around 1900, later exhibiting them in San Francisco. Shortly thereafter, Wendt and George Gardner Symons arrived in Laguna for the first time and quickly succumbed to its charms. Symons built a studio home in Arch Beach (South Laguna) in 1903 and visited periodically throughout his career. In August 1906, when *Los Angeles Times* art critic Antony Anderson visited Laguna Beach, he reported that Symons was living there year-round, and that Wendt, St. Clair and William Swift Daniell were each obtaining land to build a studio. Anderson also noted that Elmer Wachtel, Granville Redmond, Benjamin Brown, William Lees Judson and Gottardo Piazzoni had painted in Laguna Beach "in recent years."

Anderson returned in 1915 and made "the rounds of the new studios, which are strung along the high shore like jewels, from Arch Beach to Laguna Cliffs." He wryly observed that "today, there must be a hundred canvases that bear the alluring title 'Rocks at Laguna.'" He then reported at length on a visit to the studio of Frank Cuprien and also on visits to William Swift Daniell, Anna Hills and Xarifa Hamilton.

William Wendt, *Houses Along the Coast*, Private Collection,
Courtesy of The Irvine Museum

Laguna Beach, c. 1910, vintage postcard, Private Collection

William Lees Judson, *Hills at Laguna (The Old Coast Road)*, The Irvine Museum

William Wendt, *The Old Coast Road*,
Private Collection

Blake states that in a span of less than ten years, the number of artists living permanently or part time in Laguna Beach had increased to about thirty or forty. In 1918, Edgar Payne, who had first painted there in 1911, recognized the need for a gallery in which artists could display and sell their works. Payne persuaded the city council to allow the artists to use the abandoned town hall, a single-room frame structure situated in a eucalyptus grove near the Laguna Beach Hotel. The transformation into a viable gallery was accomplished by the conversion of side windows into a skylight, the addition of electric lights, the preparation of the walls, and the installation of a new roof.

Laguna Beach Art Gallery, c. 1918, photograph, Courtesy of Laguna Art Museum

On July 27, 1918, the first exhibition opened with nearly a hundred paintings in both oil and watercolor. Twenty-five artists participated: Mabel Alvarez, Charles Percy Austin, Franz A. Bischoff, William V. Cahill, R. Clarkson Colman, Frank Cuprien, Lillian Ferguson, Alice V. Fullerton, Conway Griffith, Abby Williams Hill, Anna Hills, Katherine Kavanaugh (Cahill), Marie B. Kendall, Beulah May, Helen Norton, Evylina Nunn Miller, Edgar Payne, Elsie Palmer Payne, Hanson Puthuff, Granville Redmond, Jack Wilkinson Smith, George C. Stanton, William Wendt, Emily White and Celeste Withers.

The exhibition was an immediate success. After just three weeks, nearly 2,000 people had signed the guest book. The artists quickly recognized the need for an organization that would support the activities of the gallery. The Laguna Beach Art Association was officially founded that August, with a membership roster of 150; 34 of the members were artists and the rest were patrons. Edgar Payne was elected as the first president. The stated purpose of the association was to advance the knowledge of and interest in art, creating a spirit of cooperation and fellowship between painter and public, while maintaining an art gallery that was open every afternoon of the year. In 1919, the association became a chapter of the American Federation of Arts, and the following year it was incorporated as a non-profit corporation.

According to Blake, during the first few years, the juried exhibitions changed monthly. Admission was free, and there was a paid custodian who received a small salary plus commission on sales. On Saturday nights, there was an open house, with the artists acting as hosts to the visitors in an informal atmosphere. The regular Saturday night get-togethers proved extremely popular.

Anna Hills, *The Spell of the Sea*, Private Collection, Courtesy of The Irvine Museum

Joseph Kleitsch, *Glenneyre Street*, Private Collection, Courtesy of The Irvine Museum

Edgar Payne, *Eucalyptus Trees*, Private Collection,
Courtesy of The Irvine Museum

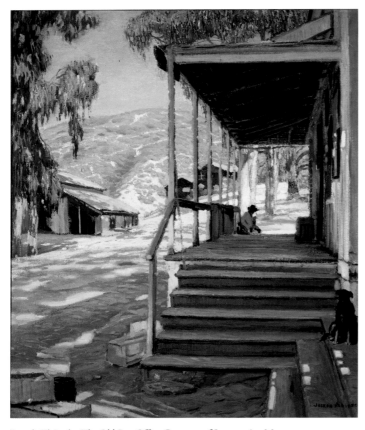

Joseph Kleitsch, *The Old Post Office*, Courtesy of Laguna Art Museum

It soon became clear that "even though Laguna Beach is a small place, it is destined to play a large part in the art development, of an art appreciation not only in California but throughout the whole United States." That the association had brought the Laguna Beach art colony a national reputation was reflected in an article published in International Studio in March 1920. The writer, Neeta Marquis, in noting that many nationally famous artists were active members of the association, observed, "France has the imperishable glory of the Barbizon; the eastern United States has its Gloucester; and the Southwest has its Laguna Beach…so this settlement, old, quaint, remote, on the southern California coast, is already synonymous with landscape art as developed in the land of perpetual sun."

In July 1920, it was announced that a special annual exhibition would be established in August, and would thereafter mark the anniversary of the founding of the association. Over the next few years, the Laguna Beach Art Association became even more prominent, and it attracted to its programs and exhibitions such noted artists as Maurice Braun, George Brandriff, Benjamin Brown, Colin Campbell Cooper, Sam Hyde Harris, Thomas L. Hunt, William Lees Judson, Joseph Kleitsch, Jean Mannheim, Arthur G. Rider, Guy Rose, Walter Elmer Schofield, George Gardner Symons and Karl Yens.

Eventually, the Laguna Beach Art Association outgrew the temporary gallery in the old town hall, and a series of exhibitions was held to raise money to purchase a piece of land and construct a permanent gallery space. In 1926, the association purchased a lot on the southwest corner of Coast Highway and Cliff Drive, and on February 16, 1929, the association's new gallery was officially opened to the public. Over the years, it became the Laguna Beach Museum, and in 1986, the building, now known as the Laguna Art Museum with Bolton Colburn as director, was expanded to the size it is today.

Guy Rose, *Lifting Fog, Laguna*, The Irvine Museum, Gift of Mrs. and Mrs. James Ries

Thomas L. Hunt, *The Cannery*, The Irvine Museum

Thomas Hunt Painting Class, photograph,
Courtesy of Laguna Art Museum

Franz A. Bischoff, *When Golden Sunbeams Shimmer*, Private Collection,
Courtesy of The Irvine Museum

Green Bay, Laguna Beach, vintage postcard, Private Collection

Emerald Bay from North Point, photograph, Courtesy of
First American Title and Trust Historical Collection

AS MY GRANDFATHER'S PRIMARY INTEREST was the agricultural development of the ranch in the Santa Ana Valley, he would from time to
time sell parcels of land along the coast to pay real estate taxes.
According to noted historian Robert Glass Cleland, "The
Townsend-Dayman Investment Company of Long Beach bought
400 acres at Newport for $200 an acre, and 1,280 acres less favor-
ably situated at $100 an acre. The purchase included 20 acres of
water-bearing land. In 1904, George E. Hart acquired the site now
known as Corona del Mar."

North of Laguna, my grandfather sold 148.6 acres with a
fine beach, sometimes called "Green Bay" and now called "Emerald
Bay," to William Miles and his partner Harry Callender for
$26,000, about $175 an acre. Included in this 1906 sale were a
windmill and a watering trough, located in what is today Swanson
Park. Miles built a house on a bluff overlooking the beach and a
beach cabana at the foot of the bluff. The new owner also built a
road to Laguna to get supplies, and my grandfather gave him per-
mission to dig for water in Niguel Canyon, now called Emerald
Canyon. In those days, the acreage was bare of trees, but cactus, poison oak, white and blue elderberries and wild roses grew in abundance. The following year Miles planted thousands of eucalyptus
trees, which had to be watered by hand during the summer, and he
fenced in the property to keep my grandfather's cattle from returning to the watering trough.

In 1907, my grandfather considered selling from "a mile to
a mile-and-a-half" on the oceanfront between Newport and Laguna
Beach for $200 an acre. Although the perennial problem of squat-
ters had subsided since my great-grandfather's time, people would
still come and camp on the beaches along the coast, such as Crystal
Cove and Morro Cove, located north of Abalone Point.

George Spangenberg, *Eucalyptus Trees*, The Irvine Museum

Emerald Bay Camp, vintage postcard, Private Collection

William Griffith, *Laguna Landscape*, The Irvine Museum

William Wendt, *Crystal Cove*, 1912, Private Collection, The Irvine Museum

Crystal Cove, c. 1917, photograph, Courtesy of
Crystal Cove Alliance

Silent film set at Crystal Cove, photograph,
Courtesy of Crystal Cove Alliance

Thatched-roof huts at Crystal Cove, photograph,
Courtesy of Crystal Cove Alliance

Arthur G. Rider, *Near Laguna* (Crystal Cove), Private Collection,
Courtesy of The Irvine Museum

In fact, during the late 1910s and early 1920s, Crystal Cove attracted the attention of the booming silent film industry. Good weather and sandy beaches provided a tropical South Seas backdrop for many early movies. Small cottages were built and thatched with palm fronds, giving the cove the exotic appearance of Hawaii and Tahiti. Palm trees and thatched huts are shown in photographs as early as 1917, and a "Paradise of the South Seas" was created for the benefit of filmmakers who leased the property from The Irvine Company. The early versions of *Sadie Thompson* (based on *Rain* and starring Gloria Swanson and Lionel Barrymore) and *Treasure Island* were shot at this location, as were *Half a Bride*, starring Esther Ralston and Gary Cooper, *White Shadows in the South Seas* and *Return to Bora-Bora. The Sea Wolf* was filmed there in 1920, and *Storm Tossed* was shot in 1921 at Table Rock, located at the southernmost end of the cove. For years, the cottages built at the cove kept their palm thatching because the needs of the filmmakers were considered foremost.

The coastal shelf above the beach was leased out by The Irvine Company for agricultural purposes, and there were many citizens of Japanese origin engaged in truck farming there. Growing conditions were ideal, and the farmers produced peas, corn, tomatoes and other vegetables. Strawberries were also grown in abundance. I will always remember those meticulously tended green fields that ran from along the Coast Highway down to the cliffs overlooking the sea, and the golden San Joaquin Hills that rose on the inland side of the road, which the company used for grazing cattle.

Donna Schuster, *On the Beach*, 1917, The Irvine Museum

Crystal Cove, c. 1920, hand-colored vintage postcard, Private Collection

Michael Obermayer, *Crystal Cove*, Courtesy of the artist

Crystal Cove, c. 1950, hand-colored vintage postcard,
Private Collection

Abalone Point, Coast Highway, Looking towards Laguna Beach,
hand-colored vintage postcard, Private Collection

Barse Miller, *Road to Capistrano*, Courtesy of The Buck Collection

Because of the large number of persons involved in the farming operation, The Irvine Company built a schoolhouse for the Japanese children on the bluffs above Crystal Cove. When the United States entered World War II in December 1941, the Japanese tenants were put off the land and sent to internment camps. Thereafter, the Marines took over the school and stationed guards there.

The community of Crystal Cove developed over a number of years. While its first residents were squatters, my grandfather eventually encouraged his employees and friends to build shelters and cottages there and to pitch tents along the beach close to the creek that flowed from Los Trancos Canyon.

When road-building bond acts were passed in the 1920s, the Pacific Coast Highway was extended southward from Los Angeles. In 1924, The Irvine Company deeded the right-of-way of its old coast road between Corona del Mar and Laguna Beach to the State Highway Department. My father laid out the first paved road along the Irvine Coast. It had been his dream to create a public park on the ocean side of the highway, between Corona del Mar and Abalone Point, north of Laguna Beach. The Coast Highway was officially opened in 1926, when Mary Pickford and Douglas Fairbanks tied together two ribbons, uniting the beach communities of Corona del Mar and Laguna Beach.

In 1927, Robert Windolph, who provided propane to the coastal farmers, secured a lease from The Irvine Company and established Tyron's Camp on the beach at El Morro Cove north of Abalone Point; there he added a restroom and opened a market that offered fresh abalone to campers. Tent camping grew in popularity on the beaches of California during the 1930s; Tryon's Camp eventually was renamed El Morro Camp, after the beach it represented. Trailers and recreational vehicles replaced tent camping in the 1940s, and parking spaces were made available for trailers on the beach as well as on the inland side of the Coast Highway. In 1954 the facility was renamed El Morro Trailer Park.

Irvine Cove, located south of Abalone Point, was where my grandfather and his family enjoyed the beach and entertained their friends. My father suffered from tuberculosis, which he had contracted as a child from exposure to an infected housekeeper. When he was in the service in World War I, he experienced the first severe effects of the disease. With treatment, the illness came under control. Although he wanted to build a home at the cove, he was not sure that he could tolerate the constant dampness of the beach environment. Nevertheless, he had two small green tenant houses that stood across the old coast road moved to the cliff above the beach.

Construction of Pacific Coast Highway, photograph, Courtesy of First American Title and Trust Historical Collection

Tyron's Camp, c. 1927, photograph, Courtesy of First American Title and Trust Historical Collection

Aerial view of Irvine Cove, showing the little green house, garage and bathhouse, photograph, The Irvine Family Archives

The little green house at Irvine Cove, photograph, The Irvine Family Archives

The little green house and bathhouse at Irvine Cove, photograph, The Irvine Family Archives

Frank Cuprien, *Evening Iridescence*, Private Collection, Courtesy of The Irvine Museum

James Irvine, Jr.(Jase) and Athalie Irvine at the bathhouse at Irvine Cove c. 1929, photograph, The Irvine Family Archives

FRONT ROW: Unidentified guest with Athalie Irvine and Mort and May Plum
BACK ROW: : Jase. and Zelpha and Randall Hood at Irvine Cove c. 1929, photograph, The Irvine Family Archives

Guests at a Fourth of July party at Irvine Cove, photograph, The Irvine Family Archives

James Harvey Irvine taking photographs at a Fourth of July party at Irvine Cove, photograph, The Irvine Family Archives

Matteo Sandona, *In Her Kimono*, Private Collection,
Courtesy of The Irvine Museum

My mother, who was born in Los Angeles on February 3, 1903, was trained as a commercial artist and became quite successful in that field, keeping an office in downtown Los Angeles in the Walter P. Story Building at the corner of Broadway and Sixth. She created fashion drawings for Bullock's and Robinson's, fashion covers for the *Los Angeles Times*, furniture designs for Barker Brothers, and even the menu for the Coconut Grove, which featured a group of monkeys with coconut bottoms. She would tell me how she would go to the big department stores that displayed clothes by top-flight designers and then sketch the mannequins in the windows so that the patterns could be made and copied by local manufacturers.

To further her technique in fashion design, she applied for admission as a student at the Wolfe School of Costume Design, which was the leading institution of design in Los Angeles. After submitting her portfolio, however, she was hired as a teacher instead. The school offered classes in fashion illustration and pattern making, as well as designing for the movie industry.

Among the students there were Edith Head and "Irene," one of my mother's pupils, who later became one of the top fashion designers in the country and made quite a name for herself in Hollywood as a film costume designer. I remember vividly, as a teenager, going to the Tea Room at Bullock's Wilshire with my mother for the "Irene" fashion shows. We always had a wonderful time. Afterward my mother and I would go to the second floor, where I could try on the designs that had been modeled that day; sometimes she would buy one for me.

Cinelandia covers by Athalie Richardson Irvine, The Irvine Family Archives

58

Irvine Ranch House, Tustin, photograph, The Irvine Family Archives

My mother first met my father at the Irvine Ranch in Tustin in 1926. They were married three years later on January 10, 1929, and lived at the ranch house in Tustin. Although they loved the little green house at the cove, my father found that he could not tolerate the damp coastal air. They still enjoyed going there during the summer months, and my mother would often tell stories about the Fourth of July parties at the cove, which my grandfather particularly enjoyed. Frank Cuprien, one of the foremost seascape painters of that time, was a close friend of my father. He was a frequent visitor at the cove and painted many of his beautiful opalescent seascapes there and along the Irvine Coast.

My mother also told stories about the Prohibition-era rumrunners who used to moor their boats off Crystal Cove at night while their cargoes were being smuggled ashore. Sometimes she accompanied my father while he was assisting the sheriff in intercepting and arresting the bootleggers and confiscating their contraband.

Frank Cuprien painting *en plein air*, Courtesy of Laguna Art Museum

Frank Cuprien, *Tranquil Evening*, Courtesy of The James Irvine Swinden Family Collection

Colin Campbell Cooper, *The Rustic Gate*, The Irvine Museum

James Harvey Irvine,
photograph, The Irvine
Family Archives

Shortly after my parents returned to the ranch house from their honeymoon in Hawaii, the housekeeper became ill. My grandfather, who lived in San Francisco, was there at the time and asked my mother if she would supervise the household. This meant planning the meals, managing the staff and taking care of the needs of his guests. My mother talked it over with my father, and he said he knew she could handle it.

The ranch house was not very attractive when my mother first went there to live. My grandfather's room badly needed refurbishing, and he agreed to let my mother redo it. He was very pleased with the results and said she could remodel the entire house if she would do as good a job as she had with his room and bath. This task my mother undertook with the help of Mr. Baxter, the head carpenter.

During each of his visits to the ranch, my grandfather would ask my mother to accompany him on his morning walks. This he enjoyed doing before he went to the company office, which was near the ranch house. He told my mother about his life and a great deal about the ranch. With sadness, he told my mother the story of each of the Irvine women and said that they had not fared very well. He did not remember his mother, he said, as she had died when he was a small child. His beautiful wife, Frances Anita, had died when his three children, Jase, Kathryn and Myford, were still young. His daughter, Kathryn, had died during the birth of her only child, Kathryn Anita Lillard. It was the story of a very sad life.

He told my mother how he and my grandmother had planted the holly trees on both sides of Myford Road. He also told her how they had loved the Matilija poppies and how they used to ride out on the ranch to find these beautiful plants and carefully bring them back and place them in their garden at the ranch house.

He was very knowledgeable about agriculture and would describe, in detail, the origin of every tree that was growing on the ranch. My mother always remembered the beautiful walnut trees behind the tenant houses on Irvine Boulevard. He used the tall eucalyptus trees, which are native to Australia, for windbreaks between the rows and rows of citrus trees. They stood like sentinels along Irvine Boulevard.

Myford, Jase, Kathryn and James Harvey Irvine, c.1910, photograph,
The Irvine Family Archives

Armin C. Hansen, *The Farmhouse*, The Irvine Museum,
Gift of James and Linda Ries

James Irvine Jr. and Atahlie Irvine in a pony cart in the driveway of the ranch
house, photograph, The Irvine Family Archives

Mule shed at the corner of Myford Road and Irvine Boulevard, photograph,
The Irvine Family Archives

Albert R. Valentien, *Matilija Poppies*, Private Collection

Ben Foster, *Irvine Orange Grove*, The Irvine Museum

Irvine Ranch house and headquarters, photo by Eddie Martin, Courtesy of historian Judy Gauntt

Orange trees on the Irvine Ranch, photograph, The Irvine Family Archives

Walnut trees on the Irvine Ranch, photograph, The Irvine Family Archives

The original office building at the Irvine Ranch, photograph, Courtesy of historian Judy Gauntt

Irvine Ranch headquarter office, 1929, photograph, The Irvine Family Archives

He enjoyed telling her about his travels to foreign lands. He said he always brought back some kind of plant or tree that he hoped would grow in its new environment. That was why we had so many varieties of fruit and unusual plants in the gardens around the ranch house. They would walk, mile after mile, through the extensive Valencia orange, navel orange, grapefruit and lemon groves. The walnuts, citrus and avocados totaled about five thousand acres of trees. This left an indelible impression on my mother's memory— the beauty and nobility of these magnificent trees, planted so precisely in countless rows of beautiful groves, as far as the eye could see.

My grandfather would show my mother where they planned to bring in water for irrigation, and she would watch as my father "witched" for wells. Once they found water, she was shown how they drilled the wells. My father was responsible for much of the development and conservation of the water resources on the ranch, including the Santiago Canyon Dam that forms Irvine Lake. This structure allowed The Irvine Company to become one of the largest single landholdings under cultivation in the United States, maintaining one of the largest Valencia orange groves in the world. All the agricultural knowledge and experience my mother acquired from my grandfather was later put to use when she purchased and farmed ranches of her own.

One of the highlights that my mother recalled during her years at the ranch was being present at one of the series of experiments that were conducted there by Dr. Albert Michelson, measuring the speed of light. She vividly remembered that she was the only woman given the privilege to look into the mile-long tube that had been especially built for the experiments.

While my grandfather was on a trip to Australia in 1929, my father had a white stucco building with a red tile roof built on the east side of Myford Road, opposite the driveway to the ranch house, and designated it as the new Irvine Ranch headquarters office. When my grandfather returned, he was extremely upset and insisted that his rolltop desk be taken back to the old office building next to the house. Not long after that, however, he moved his office across the street.

Well drilling on the Irvine Ranch, photograph, The Irvine Family Archives

My grandfather mourned the loss of a magnificent grove of sycamore trees that were destroyed when the Santiago Dam was built, photograph, The Irvine Family Archives

Santigo Dam, photo by Eddie Martin, Courtesy of historian Judy Gauntt

Irvine Lake, photograph, The Irvine Family Archives

Marion K. Wachtel, *Sunset*, Private Collection, Courtesy of The Irvine Museum

Sam Hyde Harris, *Barn in the Fog*, c. 1925, Courtesy of Jean and Linda Stern

On January 31, 1931, my grandfather married his second wife, Katherine Brown White. The new Mrs. Irvine was very antagonistic toward my father. Some months prior to the wedding, my mother recalled, "Father Irvine phoned us one evening to please come to San Francisco right away, as he was in trouble. We left and drove all night, not knowing what to expect. We arrived in time for breakfast. He told us that Mrs. White was going to sue him for breach of promise. He was very upset because Mrs. White had engaged a Mr. James Cantillon in Los Angeles as her lawyer." Mr. Cantillon was an expert on divorce law and was considered the Marvin Mitchelson of his day.

My mother further recalled, "Mr. Irvine said, 'Jase, we will have to fight fire with fire.' He asked Jase to find out everything he could about Mrs. White as quickly as possible. After Jase gathered considerable information, he gave it to his father. In turn, Father confronted Mrs. White, and in a moment of weakness, revealed to her who his source had been. Mrs. White was furious. Father hated publicity and Mr. Cantillon was notorious for trying his cases in the newspapers. I told Jase that I was afraid his father had met his Waterloo. From that time forward, 'Big Kate,' as she was called, continually found reasons to criticize Jase on every pretense she could think of."

In May 1931, my mother accompanied my father and my grandfather's accountant and tax advisor N. Loyall McLaren to Washington, D.C., as my grandfather had asked my father to confer with the legal counsel representing The Irvine Company in a case before the Board of Tax Appeals. The case was decided in the company's favor on my father's birthday, June 11, when he reached a compromise by agreeing to make the land that extended from Corona del Mar to Crystal Cove a federal park.

Of the last family gathering at the ranch house, in 1931, my mother recalled, "On the first of December, Father Irvine returned to the ranch for the quail season. It was cold and rainy. Jase and his father would leave at 6 a.m. and return at 6 p.m. Both of them would be soaked. I worried about Jase, as he had caught cold but still went every day. He started coughing. Father said there was nothing wrong with him and would be annoyed if I suggested Jase should stay at home."

Kate came down the week before Christmas and provoked a bitter argument between my father and my grandfather. After she took the car and headed back to San Francisco, my grandfather stated that he would not be staying for Christmas but would return to San Francisco that day. During the drive to the train station in Santa

Ana, my father tried to explain that he was not at fault, but his father did not believe him. My grandfather told my father, "You accept her! If you don't, get out!"

On New Year's Day, my father told my mother that he felt he had picked up some kind of bug. He coughed most of the night and the following day suffered a massive pulmonary hemorrhage. Dr. Pottinger, who had treated my father earlier for tuberculosis, came to the ranch, examined him and diagnosed pneumonia. He believed that the sealed-off tubercular bacilli had been activated, and that this was the cause of the hemorrhage. He called an ambulance and had my father taken to his sanatorium in Monrovia.

My mother was devastated. She called my grandfather in San Francisco to inform him that they had left the ranch, but not in the way they had expected to leave. My mother recalled of that phone call, "I simply said, 'Jase is in Pottinger's Sanatorium, and I am going to stay there with him.' Father Irvine seemed as stunned as I had been when I first learned of Jase's condition. Mr. Irvine told me he would return to the ranch the following day. This he did and came to the sanatorium. His whole demeanor had changed, and he looked like a man who was facing something he did not know how to accept. He saw Jase and how very ill he was. As he stood at Jase's bedside, his face registered both remorse and regret. It was like he had realized, for the first time, how wrong he had been."

My father never returned to the ranch and never saw his vision of a park on the Irvine Coast become a reality. He died on June 23, 1935, at forty-two years of age, owing to an accident during a surgical procedure in treating his tuberculosis. His death was a great blow to my grandfather, not only because of the close relationship that existed between them, but also because my grandfather had depended upon my father for the management of the Irvine Ranch and had expected that my father would succeed him as president of The Irvine Company.

The only memories I have of my father are of seeing him in a bed, in a garden or on a hospital sundeck, wrapped in a blue shawl and wearing a gray felt hat. After my mother died, when I was going through a box of her old cards and letters, I found a small white envelope containing a lock of light brown hair tied with a blue thread. The envelope was identified in my mother's handwriting as "Jase's hair, June 23, 1935." Not a thread of gray marred the silken strands, which were as fine as a child's. At that moment, I was suddenly deeply moved by the great tragedy of my father's untimely and unnecessary death.

Paul Grimm, *Landscape with Cloudy Sky*, Private Collection, Courtesy of The Irvine Museum

Frank Cupien, *Dream Ship*, Private Collection, Courtesy of The Irvine Museum

Cinelandia cover,
The Irvine Family Archives

Jeanne Richardson Ziebe,
The Irvine Family Archives

My mother continued to publish my father's Spanish-language magazine, *Cinelandia*, with the assistance of her sister Jeanne Richardson. In 1936, President and Mrs. Franklin D. Roosevelt invited my mother to a luncheon at the White House to receive a posthumous award for my father's participation in Latin American affairs.

During the years that she lived on the Irvine Ranch, my mother became very interested in farming. One of the first investments she made after my father's death was the old Simms Ranch in Visalia, in the San Joaquin Valley. She acquired the property in 1937. The ranch was the setting for *The Grapes of Wrath*, and John Steinbeck had lived there while writing his novel.

Two years after my father's death, Loyall McLaren convinced my grandfather to sign the indenture of trust that became the basis for the holding by the James Irvine Foundation of the controlling fifty-one percent interest in The Irvine Company. My uncle Myford Irvine served as president of the foundation from its inception until his death, when he was succeeded by Loyall McLaren.

In about 1937, my grandfather gave the city of Newport Beach one mile of bayfront property along the Coast Highway between Bay Shores and the Arches for a public park and dockage. Although this property was deed-restricted for park and recreation purposes, shortly after my grandfather died in 1947, the city leased the property for a number of different uses, including the Balboa Bay Club, which was of course private.

After my father's death, nothing was ever done with respect to his commitment to make a portion of the Irvine Coast a federal park. When my uncle Myford succeeded my grandfather as president of The Irvine Company in 1947, for years he would not attend any events at the Balboa Bay Club because he was so incensed at what Newport Beach had done with his father's gift of parkland.

Thomas Craig, *California*, The Irvine Museum

Pacific Coast Highway, Newport Beach, c. 1935, photograph, Courtesy of First American Title and Trust Historical Collection

Jeff Horn, *Pelican Point*, 2001, Courtesy of the artist

Jeff Horn, *Solitary Path, Crystal Cove*,
Courtesy of the artist

The Irvine Bowl, photograph, Courtesy of First American Title and Trust Historical Collection

IN 1941, MY GRANDFATHER GAVE THE CITY OF LAGUNA BEACH the land for the Irvine Bowl, the amphitheater in Laguna Canyon that is used for the Pageant of the Masters, part of the Festival of Arts. This popular event has been held annually since 1932, except for four years during World War II.

When Pageant Director Diane Challis Davy selected artworks to be transformed into "living pictures" for the "Portrait of the Artist" pageant in the summer of 2004, she had an opportunity to take a closer look at the lives and legends of some of the world's great artists. Lurking behind some of the world's most memorable artworks are stories of artists equally famous for their vanity, chauvinism, insecurity and egotism. "Portrait of the Artist" shed light on the public and private lives of such larger-than-life artists as Picasso, Manet, Matisse and Cellini.

Also included in the living pictures were artworks by Leonardo da Vinci, Diego Velázquez, Caspar David Friedrich, Anton Otto Fischer, Frederic Remington and Anna Hyatt Huntington. One particular painting entitled "William Wendt at Work," by William Alexander Griffith, shows Wendt painting in Laguna Canyon.

Also located in Laguna Canyon, in a magnificent stand of majestic sycamores, is the Art Institute of Southern California. Constructed on land given by The Irvine Company in 1974, the Art Institute, under the direction of Dennis Power, has risen to one of the best art schools in California. The college is committed to offering its curriculum through accredited degree programs that imaginatively combine studio work with academic studies.

William Griffith, *William Wendt at Work*, Courtesy of Joseph Ambrose and Michael Fedderson

William Wendt, *Pasture Land*, Private Collection, Courtesy of The Irvine Museum

Michael Obermeyer, *Crystal Cove Cottages*, (2001 Festival of Arts poster), Courtesy of Festival of Arts, Laguna Beach

The Art Institute of Southern California, photo by Jean Stern

Each year at the Festival of Arts, thousands of art lovers, from the serious collector to the weekend enthusiast, meet at California's oldest and most respected outdoor art show. The Festival displays and offers for sale original works of art by a select group of the area's most accomplished artists working in a multitude of media, such as painting, sculpture, pastel, drawing, serigraphy, photography, ceramics, jewelry, weaving, fiber art, etched and stained glass, hand-crafted furniture, model ships and even classical scrimshaw.

For several years, there was an unsuccessful effort on the part of certain of the Laguna Beach Art Festival's board members to move the festival to San Clemente. Luckily, it has remained in Laguna Beach, where it was founded in 1932 and where it belongs.

An article by Stanley Allison entitled "Transformed Casa Romantica Offers New Elegance, Purpose" appeared in the *Los Angeles Times* on September 6, 2004, stating: "When they set out to restore Casa Romantica, the picturesque but decaying estate of San Clemente founder Ole Hanson, the goal was to bring back the seaside villa's splendor and elegance and make it a cultural center for the community."

The house, built in 1928, was on a five-acre estate, and it had seven bedrooms and seven bathrooms. It was designed by Carl Lindbom, who also designed La Casa Pacifica, which was the former Nixon Western White House, and the Santa Barbara City Hall. Difficult financial circumstances caused Hanson to lose his home in 1934. Since then, the house passed through various owners until it was purchased by the San Clemente City Redevelopment Agency in 1989 and listed on the National Register of Historic Places in 1991.

Casa Romantica is not yet ready for full-time use. The gardens, which are currently incomplete, were designed by internationally noted landscape architect Isabelle Greene, and will make the Casa a showplace for the entire region. Isabelle Greene is the granddaughter of Henry Mather Greene, who with his brother Charles was one of the pioneers of the early Craftsman movement in southern California.

Alexey Steele, *Irvine Cove*, 1996, Courtesy of the artist

Anna Hills, *Gulls at Play*, Private Collection, Courtesy of The Irvine Museum

Athalie Irvine and baby Athalie Anita at Irvine Cove c. 1935, photograph,
The Irvine Family Archives

The little green house and bathhouse at Irvine Cove c.1935, photograph,
The Irvine Family Archives

MY MOTHER AND I ALWAYS SPENT OUR SUMMERS in the little green house at Irvine Cove, and my mother's sister, my aunt Jeanne, would frequently stay with us. As soon as we arrived, my grandfather Irvine would come to see me and stay for dinner and bridge by gaslight, as the house had no electricity. He always brought Charlie Cogan, the Irvine Company purchasing agent, so that there would be enough people to play bridge after I went to bed. They kept a running score, and before my grandfather would leave, he would want to know about the next night. My mother and Aunt Jeanne always loved to have him visit, as he enjoyed himself so much.

   I loved our summers at the cove. At low tide, my mother would take me to search for seashells and starfish in the rocks and tide pools around Abalone Point or in the caves at the other end of the beach. She showed me how to press my fingers against the moss-green sea anemones that covered the rocks until they squirted streams of saltwater, and how to catch the tiny sand crabs that scurried into the wet sand when the waves receded into the sea. When the tide came in, she would hold my small hand tightly in hers, and we would splash in the frothy white water that swirled along the edge of the pounding waves. Sometimes in the evening, she would read me stories about the seashells and creatures we had encountered during the day. My room would become filled with many of these treasures as the summer wore on.

Elliot Torrey, *Golden Reflections*, c. 1930, Courtesy of Jean and Linda Stern

71

One evening, when my grandfather came for dinner and bridge, I told him that I had found lots of shells on the cliffs above the rocks at Abalone Point, and could not understand how they had gotten there. He told me that once there had been a large Indian encampment there, and that the Indians had eaten shellfish. He said that there had been Indian encampments like that one on the ranch, along the coast and in Newport Bay and the Back Bay.

On occasion, my mother would pack a picnic lunch, and she, my grandmother Richardson, my nurse Dear Dear and I would go to Irvine Park, where I loved to feed candied popcorn to the deer through the fence at the zoo. I also liked to play on the "giant iron whirler," better known as the merry-go-round, and the metal slide under the sycamores at the children's playground.

In the mid-1930s, Orange County added a much taller slide, swings, rings and monkey bars. Although my mother had forbidden it, I always wanted to slide down that big slide. One day when she wasn't looking, I quickly climbed up the steps to the top and slid down. Before I even got to the bottom, I was whisked away, severely scolded and taken home. The next time my mother took me to Irvine Park, much to my disappointment, both of the slides were gone. My mother told me my grandfather had had them removed because I had disobeyed her.

In reality, three adult women who should not have been on the slides in the children's park in the first place had landed rather recklessly on the hard ground. They immediately sued the county, claiming "grievous bodily injury" and "mental anguish." After that, the county had the slides removed.

Acagchemem Village, Courtesy of the Mission San Juan Capistrano Museum

Anna Hills, *Under the Sycamores, Orange County Park*, Courtesy of Mr. and Mrs. Thomas B. Stiles II, photograph, Courtesy of Redfern Gallery, Laguna Beach

Anna Hills, *Fall, Orange County Park*, Private Collection, Courtesy of The Irvine Museum

William Wendt, *Oaks and Sycamores*, Private Collection, Courtesy of The Irvine Museum

Joan Irvine and Athalie
Richardson Irvine in front of the
Beverly Hills house, photograph,
The Irvine Family Archives

Tom Mitchell, Joan Irvine,
Athalie Irvine Mitchell at the
Beverly Hills house, photograph,
The Irvine Family Archives

Joan Irvine with her mother and
grandparents Dr. and Mrs.
George H. Richardson on a trip
to Yosemite, photograph,
The Irvine Family Archives

When I was four years old, my mother, Dear Dear and I moved from my grandparents' home to a new home in Beverly Hills. My mother continued to devote a great deal of time to my father's estate and to the publication of *Cinelandia*. It was at that time that I became very taken with a Mother Goose nursery rhyme that went:

"Here I am, little jumping Joan,
When nobody's with me, I'm always alone."

I told my mother that I wanted to be called Joan instead of Athalie Anita.

My mother always insisted that I wear my hair in shoulder-length sausage curls that were secured with a large bow on the right side of my head. How I hated standing in front of the bathroom mirror each morning while my nurse brushed in each of those sausage curls! In looking through old photographs of my mother as a young girl, I can see where she got the idea for those curls and that big bow I hated; I was of course the proverbial tomboy.

Grandfather Irvine would often drive up from the ranch to visit my mother and me at our new home. He played the piano by ear and loved to sit and improvise at our grand piano in the corner of the living room. My grandfather wore high-top shoes that always fascinated me. As soon as he'd sit down, I would get down on my hands and knees to inspect the laces on his shoes. When I did this, he would put his heavily shod foot on my hand so that I couldn't get away. The harder I tried to get free, the more pressure he would put on my fingers. My mother would wince visibly at this performance, but I would never cry. As a child, I knew instinctively that he was just playing a game with me. After dinner, he would sit with my mother and talk, long after my nurse had put me to bed.

On April 12, 1938, my mother married Thomas Hampton Mitchell, manager of Radio Corporation of America (RCA) in Southern California and a graduate of the U.S. Naval Academy at Annapolis. In the beginning, Tom was a good husband and stepfather. We went to Yosemite and Catalina and spent happy summers at Irvine Cove. When my mother would go to visit her cotton ranch in Visalia, she and Tom and I would picnic among the wildflowers that covered the hillsides along the Ridge Route. We would often go to Sequoia National Park, where Tom would spend hours sitting with me while we fed the chipmunks and deer.

Alson S. Clark, *Catalina*, Courtesy of Ruth Westphal

Scott Burdick, *Shadow and Light, Avalon*, 2002, Courtesy of Jean and Linda Stern

John Gamble, *Joyous Spring*, Private Collection, Courtesy of The Irvine Museum

Lodgepole Chipmunk,
© Dr. Lloyd Glenn Ingles, California Academy of Science

Maurice Braun, *Yosemite Falls from the Valley* (detail), 1918, The Irvine Museum

James Harvey Irvine with his hunting dogs, photograph, The Irvine Family Archives

Unknown artist, *Irish Setter*, hung in the ranch house, The James Irvine Swinden Family Collection

Paul Grimm, *Country Road*, Private Collection, Courtesy of The Irvine Museum

Jessie Arms Botke, *Beau Brummels*, Private Collection, Courtesy of The Irvine Museum

After I began school at Marymount, across from UCLA in West Los Angeles, my mother allowed me to go with my nurse to visit my grandfather at the ranch house in Tustin on weekends and during my school vacations. Every morning, my grandfather and I had our breakfast promptly at 8 a.m. At that time, Dulin Grant, the kennel man, would bring two of my grandfather's four favorite Irish setters over to the house to spend the day. The dogs were named Tubby, Rough, Rex and Mike.

Mike was so old that his face was completely white, and he had a white bandage on the end of his tail. He moved so slowly that he had lost the tip of his tail by getting it caught in the swinging door between the dining room and the pantry. One morning, when I came out of the ranch house, I saw my grandfather and several of the men who worked on the ranch standing at the edge of the gold-fish pond across the driveway. When I went over to my grandfather, I noticed a tear on his cheek. One of the men told me that Mike had tried to get a drink of water at the pond and then fallen in and drowned. Later, when I went home, I told my mother what had happened, and she told me that Mike had been my father's dog. It was the only time in my life I ever saw my grandfather show such tender emotion.

During my visits to the ranch, I would often accompany my grandfather to his office in the morning and play on the floor with his Irish setters while he worked at his rolltop desk. I would then go with him and the dogs when he drove around the ranch to inspect his wells, irrigation ditches and lakes, field crops, orchards, packing houses, sugar beet factory, the salt works and coastal property. Sometimes he would take me fishing at Peter's Lake. He, Dulin and I and the setters would all pile into a 1923 Packard touring car that had belonged to my father and drive to the lake. The three of us and the two dogs would then get into a small rowboat, which was kept in a boathouse there, and Dulin would row us around the lake until we found a spot to fish. My grandfather, who always insisted that I bait my own hook, brought the fish that we caught back to the ranch house in buckets of water and put them in the swimming pool so that he could have fresh fish for breakfast. Near the pool he had a large aviary where he kept a variety of birds including injured game birds until they recovered and could be released back into the wild.

Peters Lake, photograph, Courtesy of First American Title and Trust Historical Collection

Myford Road at Irvine Boulevard, photograph, The Irvine Family Archives

High Line Canal, photograph, Courtesy of First American Title and Trust Historical Collection

Field workers picking peppers, photograph, The Irvine Family Archives

Picking oranges in the orchards, photograph, The Irvine Family Archives

Orange packing house interior, vintage postcard, Private Collection

Orange packers, Frances Packing House, photograph, The Irvine Family Archives

Orange crate labels used by Irvine Company packing houses, The Irvine Family Archives

The bean warehouse in Irvine, photograph, The Irvine Family Archives

Frances Packing House, photograph, The Irvine Family Archives

Lima bean sorters c. 1939, photograph, Courtesy of Irvine Historical Society

Sugar beet factory, photograph, The Irvine Family Archives

Salt works, photograph, The Irvine Family Archives

View of Newport Bay from the Castaways Restaurant, photograph, The Irvine Family Archives

Standard Gas Station and Bay Shore Cafe, photograph, The Irvine Family Archives

View of the Back Bay looking towards the Castaways Restaurant, photograph, The Irvine Family Archives

Indian mortar and pestle, photograph, Courtesy of First American Title and Trust Historical Collection

On the steps leading to the front door of the ranch house, there was a large Indian stone pestle and mortar that my grandfather had found on the ranch. He also had a collection of Indian baskets, some of which he kept in a bookcase in the parlor next to the fascinating objects he had collected on his many trips abroad. In the evenings, my grandfather and I would sit with the dogs in front of the living-room fireplace while he read the newspaper. He always kept a tennis ball with a long string tied to it in his pocket and would suddenly throw the ball across the room. Much to my great delight, the dogs would scramble over the furniture to retrieve it.

My grandfather taught me how to play dominos and hearts, as I was not old enough to learn to play bridge. After dinner, he and I would play dominos, or he would invite Irvine Company Vice President Paul Dinsmore, who lived across the street, to play hearts with us.

Christmas at the Irvine Ranch House, Tustin, photograph, The Irvine Family Archives

Paul de Longpré, *Poppies in an Indian Basket*, Private Collection, Courtesy of The Irvine Museum

William Wendt, *Shady Canyon*, Private Collection, Courtesy of The Irvine Museum

William Wendt, *Barns and Water Troughs*, Private Collection, Courtesy of The Irvine Museum

William Wendt, *Laguna Hills*, Private Collection, Courtesy of The Irvine Museum

I loved riding a wonderful gray horse named Eagle with Ray Serrano and the other cowboys on the ranch when they moved cattle through the majestic oaks and sycamores in the San Joaquin Hills and the Santa Ana Mountains. At that time, I had the unique opportunity to see the land as Captain Gaspár de Portolá and the first Spanish explorers must have seen it, over two centuries ago, and I loved it as my grandfather did.

Louise Moulton at a cattle round-up on the Moulton Ranch, photograph, Courtesy of Saddleback Area Historical Society

Branding calves, photograph, Courtesy of San Juan Capistrano Historical Society

Ray Serrano, photograph, Courtesy of San Juan Capistrano Historical Society

Every spring, my grandfather held a roundup on the ranch to brand and castrate the calves—an event that was reminiscent of the rodéos held a century before on the early ranchos. One day, my grandfather took me to a roundup and barbecue on the neighboring Moulton Ranch. Ray and some of the other cowboys from the Irvine Ranch were there, helping with branding and cutting the calves. After that was over, they roped a spirited brown colt that was running with some of the other horses in the field where we were. The colt was thrown to the ground, cut and then released. Although as a child I did not understand exactly what had occurred, I never forgot how subdued the colt was when he walked away.

Ray Serrano, whose family dated back to the early Spanish settlers, taught me to ride a stock horse when I was a little girl. Don Francisco Serrano, his great-great-grandfather, was Alcalde, or mayor, of Los Angeles in 1799, and his son Don José Serrano was Juece del Campo, or "judge of the plains" in that district. Don José was the arbitrator of all disputes between landholders, and he had jurisdiction over the rodéos, an equally important matter during a time so devoted to cattle ranching and the breeding and training of fine horses.

Mr. and Mrs. Dwight Whiting at the Serrano Adobe before restoration, photograph, Courtesy of Saddleback Area Historical Society

Serrano Adobe after restoration, 1935, The Serrano Adobe Historical Site, photograph, Courtesy of Saddleback Area Historical Society

William Wendt, *Rocky Ascent*,
Private Collection, Courtesy of The Irvine Museum

Marion K. Wachtel, *Old Adobe*, Private Collection, Courtesy of The Irvine Museum

William Wendt, *Oaks and Sycamores*, Private Collection,
Courtesy of The Irvine Museum

Anna Hills, *Near the
Roadside, El Toro*,
The James Irvine Swinden
Family Collection

In 1842, Don José was granted Rancho Cañada de Los Alisos (Canyon of the Sycamores), which consisted of 10,668 acres where modern-day El Toro is located. In 1863, Don José's family built the Serrano adobe on the rancho, and in 1885, Dwight Whiting bought 10,000 acres of the property and encouraged the development of El Toro.

The Serrano adobe was first restored by George and Dwight Whiting, Jr. in 1932, when it was made State Historical Landmark No. 199. It is now part of Heritage Hill Historical Park, which was opened in 1981 as Orange County's first historical park.

In 1959, the Whiting properties were sold to a developer, and in July 1988, approximately 1,200 acres were dedicated to Orange County to be preserved as Whiting Ranch Wilderness Park. Since then, additional acquisitions have enlarged the park to approximately 4,300 acres.

Paul Grimm, *Beverly Hills*, The Irvine Museum

Paul Grimm, *Bel Air*, Private Collection, Courtesy of The Irvine Museum

Paul Grimm, *Shady Glade*, Private Collection, Courtesy of The Irvine Museum

My mother allowed me to have an assortment of pets, such as dogs (including a female Dalmatian named Spottie who I loved dearly and who always went to the cove with us), cats, pigeons, rabbits and a mouse. On one of my visits to the ranch, I found an orphaned baby coyote that I of course wanted to take home. My grandfather said I couldn't have it because it was a wild animal and would bite me. But I wanted the coyote anyway. So, I pleaded with my mother and Tom and, unbeknownst to my grandfather, we took the coyote home with us to Beverly Hills. I named him Buster. The next day, I remember, my mother was ill when I left for school. When I returned from school, I found her in bed with Buster beside her. She had been feeding him warm milk with an eyedropper. As time passed, Buster grew quite large and eventually ran away. I'm sure he had a good life living in the mountains above Sunset Boulevard and rummaging through all the garbage cans in Beverly Hills.

My mother continued to publish *Cinelandia*, and it was at about that time that she presented the Pan American Award to Bette Davis at our home in Beverly Hills. I remember having my picture taken with the famous actress. Eventually my mother sold *Cinelandia* to a young French entrepreneur.

Athalie Irvine Mitchell and Buster the coyote, photograph, The Irvine Family Archives

Bette Davis receiving the First Cinelandia Pan-American Award, as Hollywood's outstanding contributor to the cause of Pan-Americanism, at a reception given in Athalie Irvine Mitchell's home. FROM LEFT: Mona Maris, Rita Hayworth, Edgar Bergan, Bette Davis, Athalie Irvine Mitchell, Jane Wyman and Ronald Reagan, photograph, The Irvine Family Archives

Bette Davis and Joan Irvine, photograph, The Irvine Family Archives

When I was growing up, I was often subject to colds. Because of this, my mother bought a small house in La Quinta, near Palm Springs, and she and Tom and Spottie and I would go there on weekends during the winter. On the drive out to the desert, we always stopped and had dinner at a diner in Banning, where my mother and father had lived for a time during his illness. In later years, my mother's great love of the desert prompted her to buy the house that President Eisenhower had used as the Winter White House, at the El Dorado Country Club in Palm Desert.

When I was about six, my mother took me for English riding lessons at the Riviera Country Club in West Los Angeles. One day after my lesson, my riding instructor Snowy Baker took me for a ride on the bridle trail around the polo field. When my horse stumbled, I fell off and knocked out my four front teeth. When my mother came to pick me up and saw my bloody shirt and toothless grin, she was horrified. Although my enthusiasm for riding lessons was not dampened, my mother's certainly was. After that, Tom would take me riding at a stable near our house. He also taught me to shoot during our summers at the cove. He, my mother and I would practice shooting with a .22 at cans that we would set up along the edge of one of the cliffs next to the little green house.

Paul Grimm, *Hacienda*, Private Collection, Courtesy of The Irvine Museum

Anna Hills, *San Gorgonio from Beaumont*, The Irvine Museum

Anna Hills, *Cherry Blossoms*, Private Collection, Courtesy of The Irvine Museum

John Frost, *Studio, Palm Springs*, Courtesy of Bonham and Butterfield Auction

Paul Grimm, *Palm Canyon*, Private Collection, Courtesy of The Irvine Museum

Paul Grimm, *Smoke Trees*, Private Collection, Courtesy of The Irvine Museum

Paul Grimm, *Desert Flowers*, Private Collection, Courtesy of The Irvine Museum

Marion K. Wachtel, *Summer Afternoon, Santa Monica,* 1916, Private Collection, Courtesy of The Irvine Museum

Tustin Lighter-than-air base hanger at upper left, photograph, Courtesy of historian Judy Gauntt

THE MILITARY FIRST CONSIDERED ORANGE COUNTY as a site for a Lighter-Than-Air Station in 1928. The Chief of Naval Aviation, Rear Admiral W. A. Moffett, flew over the area and found a suitable site on the Irvine Ranch. After the bombing of Pearl Harbor in 1941, the Navy contacted my grandfather about acquiring two sites for military bases on the ranch. One was the site near Tustin that had been selected by Admiral Moffett, and the other, at the urging of the Santa Ana Chamber of Commerce, was located near the mouth of Cañada del Toro (Canyon of the Bull), right in the center of the largest lima bean field in the world, the 17,000-acre pride of the Irvine Ranch. Although my grandfather offered to lease them other sites for a dollar a year, the Marines wanted the bean field. In early 1942, the Navy purchased 1,600 acres of land for the Tustin Lighter-Than-Air Base and approximately 2,400 acres for the El Toro Marine Corps Air Station for $1 million.

Airship at Tustin Lighter-than-Air base, Private Collection

Officers and crew at Tustin Lighter-than-Air base, Private Collection

El Toro Marine Corps Air Station, photograph, Courtesy of historian Judy Gauntt

In 1944, The Irvine Company bought the 82,000-acre Flying D Ranch in Bozeman, Montana. My grandfather purchased it with the money the government had paid the company for the two military bases, in order to avoid paying capital gains tax. The Flying D was bounded by the Madison River on the west and the Gallatin River on the east and lay at the base of the Spanish Peaks, 75 miles north of the west gate to Yellowstone National Park. The ranch had some of the best grazing land in the world, and its rivers and streams contained an abundance of trout. It was operated by a resident tenant, and my grandfather liked to visit the property during the summer to enjoy the fishing. In later years, I also visited the ranch with family and friends in the summer to fish, and in the fall to hunt deer and elk.

Flying D. Ranch, Bozeman, Montana, photograph, Courtesy of Irvine Historical Society

James Irvine II died while fishing at his Flying D. Ranch in Bozeman, Montana on August 24, 1947, photograph, The Irvine Family Archives

Paul de Longpré, *Orange Blossoms*, Private Collection

Franz Bischoff, *Grapes*, The Irvine Museum

After the war began, my trips to the Irvine Ranch became less frequent because my mother didn't have the gasoline coupons that were necessary to drive that distance. Those who were engaged in farming were entitled to more gasoline, so she felt that if she could find a ranch close enough to where we lived, I could keep a horse and she would have more gasoline coupons, which would enable me to make more trips to the ranch to see my grandfather.

Due to the gasoline shortage, grandfather Irvine came to Beverly Hills to visit us less frequently. His driver would bring him in, and he would have dinner and spend the night with us. In the morning, he would have my mother drive him to the Chancellor Hotel, which he owned. By doing this, he could save his gasoline.

It was during one of his visits in 1942 that my mother told my grandfather she had seen an ad in the *Los Angeles Times* regarding a ranch in the San Fernando Valley. The property was located on the corner of Tampa and Nordhoff Avenues and was planted with Valencia and navel oranges and walnuts. The owner had told her that the ranch was in a probate estate, so he had to have all cash. Since she was $10,000 short of the asking price, she was hoping that my grandfather would loan her the money. My mother always remembered how he twisted and puffed, and then his face turned crimson red when he said, "With a war going on, you should not be buying a ranch. How do you think you could operate one with thousands of men going into the service?" My mother responded by telling him that the ranch manager was not that young and would not be drafted. Nevertheless, he felt that she should know better than to think that this man would work for a woman. He seemed very concerned and told her in a very positive manner she should not make that kind of deal.

Later, when my mother informed my grandfather that she had gone ahead and purchased the ranch, he was quite displeased and said that she had paid too much; the price was $500 an acre, which came to $40,000. After she told him that her Federal Land Bank loan was approved for twenty years at three percent, he told her he would come up and take a look at the ranch.

I remember my mother packed a picnic lunch, and she and my grandfather and I drove out to the San Fernando Valley to see the ranch. The property had a barn and an old house that must have been built before the turn of the twentieth century. Adjacent to the back of the house was a wide pergola covered with Concord grape vines. My grandfather was very fond of those grapes, and we had a wonderful picnic. He was very impressed with my mother's purchase and said that she had a very fine ranch.

My grandfather's cousin Percy Rice remodeled the ranch house. He also built stalls in the barn and an adjoining paddock where I could keep a couple of horses.

Joan Irvine and her horse Donna at the San Fernando Valley Ranch, c. 1945, photograph, The Irvine Family Archives

Conrad Buff, *Orange Grove*, The Irvine Museum

Sam Hyde Harris, *California Mist*, Private Collection, Courtesy of The Irvine Museum

Franz Bischoff, *Arroyo Seco Bridge*,
The Irvine Museum

Benjamin Brown, *The Joyous Garden*,
Private Collection,
Courtesy of The Irvine Museum

Wedding of Atahlie Richardson Irvine and Judge Thurmond Clarke, September 11, 1944, Joan Irvine at left, and Frances Clarke at right, photograph, The Irvine Family Archives

Anita Jeanne Ziebe and Athalie Irvine Clarke, photograph, The Irvine Family Archives

After the war, my aunt Jeanne, her husband Richard Ziebe and my cousin Anita Jeanne Ziebe, who was born in 1946, lived at the San Fernando Valley ranch house. With my mother's support, Anita completed a Master of Science in Nursing and began a career in nursing administration at the UCI Medical Center in 1987. Eventually she became Associate Director of Adult Acute Services there. Today she remains a part of the UCI health care system.

My mother eventually sold the ranch in various parcels. One part was traded in 1969 for Byrnely, her farm in The Plains, Virginia. Another part of the property was sold to a Dr. Gladstone, who developed it into a major shopping center. He had devised a plan whereby all of the income was to be given to medical research. My mother assisted him in accomplishing his goal, and as a result of their generosity, the University of California Medical School, San Francisco, today has one of the largest cardiovascular research centers in the United States.

Although Tom was a good stepfather to me, he did not remain faithful to my mother, and their marriage ended in divorce in 1944. I was very sad when he left and did not understand until years later what their differences had been.

On September 11, 1944, my mother married Judge Thurmond Clarke. At that time, Thurmond sat on the Superior Court bench in Los Angeles. In 1955, he was appointed a U.S. District Judge for the Southern District of California by President Eisenhower, a position he held until he retired.

Thurmond did not like Beverly Hills. He said he drove into the sun going to work in Los Angeles in the morning and had the sun in his eyes coming home. He preferred Pasadena, so we moved to a new home there on Landor Lane. His fourteen-year-old daughter Frances attended Miss Branson's School in Marin County, north of San Francisco. I remained at home and attended Polytechnic and later Westridge School for Girls in Pasadena.

Russell Iredell, *Joan Irvine*, 1944, The Irvine Family Archives

Alson Clark, *Medora on the Terrace,*
Courtesy of the Rose Family Collection

Franz Bischoff, *Amidst the Cool and the Silence,*
Private Collection, photo Courtesy of George Stern Fine Arts

Thurmond belonged to the California Club in Los Angeles, and my mother and I would often join him there for lunch. The club is where I first saw and fell in love with California plein air art, as there was always a significant collection of this art on display.

When we moved to Pasadena, my parents joined the Flintridge Riding Club, where I kept my horses and was able to ride after school and on weekends with my classmates Suzanne Schirm and Althea Milbank. At that time, I resumed my English riding instruction and learned to jump. It was not long before my instructor Jimmy Scarborough told me that I needed a new horse. A few days later, a dealer he knew brought a handsome chestnut gelding to Flintridge for me to try. I jumped him around the course in the ring, and he went perfectly. After begging my mother for days to buy him for me, she finally gave in. When I went up to the club to ride my new horse, which I had called Golden Boy, I discovered that he had an Irvine Company brand. And, although he was beautiful and a lovely ride, he did not jump.

One day when Golden Boy and I were having a jumping lesson on the Flintridge outside course, he ran out between the standard and a tree, and I ended up in the hospital with a concussion. Even though Golden Boy was not a gifted jumper, I loved him anyway and spent many happy hours riding him at Flintridge and also at the Irvine Ranch, where he had been bred and born and was finally retired. Years later, I learned from my friend Howard Magor that the dealer had substituted Golden Boy for the horse I had first been shown and had tried.

LEFT: Althea Milbank and Joan Irvine at the Flintridge Riding Club for a horse show benefiting the Arthritis Foundation, photograph, Courtesy of Althea Milbank Brimm. RIGHT: Joan Irvine on Golden Boy at the Irvine Ranch, photograph, The Irvine Family Archives

George Gibson, *Soledad Shade*, Private Collection, Courtesy of The Irvine Museum

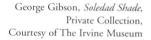

Emil J. Kosa, Jr., *The Sun Was Everywhere*, Private Collection, Courtesy of The Irvine Museum

Linda Irvine with a calf, her horse Red Cloud and the Irvine Ranch cattle foreman Bascom Edwards, photograph, The Irvine Family Archives

View of Newport Bay from Swales Yacht Landing, photograph, The Irvine Family Archives

Sheep in pens on the Irvine Ranch, photograph, The Irvine Family Archives

Emil J. Kosa, Jr., *The Road to Yesterday*, Private Collection, Courtesy of The Irvine Museum

Katrina Lance Lutge on her pony Elky holding her horse Relanpago in Newport Bay, photograph, The Irvine Family Archives

Phil Dike, *Corona del Mar*, also known as *Newport Harbor*, 1932, The Irvine Museum

Joan Irvine on Mascus at The Flintridge Riding Club 1951, photograph, The Irvine Family Archives

Joan Irvine competing on Hunter Champion Mascus at Keith Spalding's property in Flintridge, photograph, The Irvine Family Archives

Maurice Braun, *Spring Landscape*, Private Collection, Courtesy of The Irvine Museum

Ferdinand Kaufmann, *Flintridge in the Spring*, Private Collection, Courtesy of The Irvine Museum

My uncle Myford Irvine, his wife Thelma and daughter Linda, who is seven years younger than I am, lived in Burlingame. In the mid-1940s, they began sharing the little green house at Irvine Cove with us during the summer months. When Linda was about six, she started taking riding lessons from Katrina Lance Lutge at Lionel Harris's barn, which was located on Irvine Company property overlooking Newport Bay. One day, I accompanied my uncle and Linda to Harris's barn; there I met Lionel and Katrina, who would become my lifelong friend. There was a large field between the barn and the Coast Highway where Lionel had built a brush course. Linda, Katrina and I loved to ride our horses around that course or ride them over the hills behind Corona del Mar. Katrina and I would also jump in and out of the sheep pens in Big Canyon and sometimes ride down the cliff to the beach and swim our horses in the bay.

In 1947, my mother took me on a trip to the East Coast to look at preparatory schools and to find a suitable show horse. Foxcroft School in Middleburg, Virginia, was on the list. When we visited, Miss Charlotte Noland, the founder and headmistress of the school, showed me her field hunter, a lovely brown mare that she rode sidesaddle with the Middleburg Hunt. I, of course, wanted to find a horse just like hers. She said she had purchased the mare from her friend Morton W. "Cappy" Smith, and she set up an appointment for my mother and I to visit his barn the following day. When we arrived, Cappy brought out a beautiful chestnut gelding named Mascus, which I tried and loved. After much begging, I convinced my mother to let me have the horse, and she made arrangements for my trust to purchase him. I showed him successfully in the Junior and Amateur Hunter divisions and at hunter trials on Keith Spalding's property, which was across the street from the club at that time. Eventually, I loaned Mascus to a young girl named Peggy Ostercamp, who showed him very successfully in Junior/Amateur Hunters for many years.

Myford and Thelma Irvine, photograph,
The Irvine Family Archives

Linda Irvine, photograph,
The Irvine Family Archives

Wedding of Myford and Gloria Irvine,
Linda Irvine at left and Gay and Billy
White at right, photograph, The Irvine
Family Archives

Myford with Katie and Charlie Wheeler,
photograph, The Irvine Family Archives

The Wheeler house in Newport Beach, photograph, The Irvine
Family Archives

Myford Irvine's family visiting
the redwoods, photograph,
The Irvine Family Archives

My grandfather suffered a heart attack and died on August 24, 1947, at the Flying D Ranch in Montana while on a fishing trip with Irvine Company manager William Bradford Hellis and his friend, real estate broker Walter S. Tubach. At that time, my uncle Myford Irvine became president of The Irvine Company and he and his family moved from Burlingame in northern California to the ranch house in Tustin. Then, in 1949, Myford separated from Thelma, his wife of many years, and he and his daughter Linda came to live with my mother and stepfather and me in Pasadena. The following year, Myford married Gloria Wood White. Gloria was the former wife of William Thornton White II, the son of my grandfather's second wife, Katherine Brown White Irvine. Gloria had two children from her former marriage: a son, William Thornton White III, and a daughter, Gay White. Soon after the marriage, Myford and Linda and his new family moved back to the ranch house in Tustin. In 1953, a son, James Myford Irvine, was born.

When Katherine Brown White Irvine died in 1950, my cousin Kathryn Anita ("Katie") Lillard Wheeler succeeded her as a trustee of the James Irvine Foundation. Shortly thereafter, Katie and her husband, Charles S. Wheeler, who lived in northern California, moved to a house that "Big Kate" had built in 1931, just south of Harris's barn, overlooking Newport Bay.

I always looked forward to the annual spring roundup in Bommer Canyon. All of the Irvine family members would attend and often brought friends. Working as a team in one of the corrals, the cowboys would brand, castrate, dehorn and inoculate each calf in less than a minute. As the company ran 4,500 head of cattle, there were always a large number of calves each spring, and this procedure could take at least half the day. Afterward, we all enjoyed a western-style barbecue in the shade of a nearby grove of magnificent sycamore trees that grew near the creek on the canyon floor.

This was one of my grandfather's favorite spots, not only because of the beautiful sycamore trees that he loved, but also for the fact that the hills between Bommer Canyon and Shady Canyon were full of quail. He and my father had frequently hunted there, and in later years Dulin Grant often took me quail hunting there with the same twenty-gauge L C Smith shotgun my father had used as a boy.

Bommer Canyon, photograph, Courtesy of historian Judy Gauntt

California quail, ©Joyce Green, California Academy of Science

Aaron Kilpatrick, *Sycamores and Oaks*, Private Collection, Courtesy of The Irvine Museum

Kennelman Dulin Grant, photograph, The Irvine Family Archives

Cattle camp in Bommer Canyon, photograph, The Irvine Family Archives

Cattle on the Irvine Ranch, photograph, The Irvine Family Archives

Roundup, Bommer Canyon, photograph, Courtesy of Irvine Historical Society

Family ride in Bommer Canyon, FROM LEFT Thurmond Clarke, Gloria Irvine, Athalie Irvine Clarke, Joan Irvine, Dixie Gramatky, Linda Irvine, photograph, The Irvine Family Archives

Joan Irvine Burt with a bull on the Irvine Ranch, photograph, *The American Weekly*, October 1961

Athalie Irvine Clarke on family ride in Bommer Canyon, photograph, The Irvine Family Archives

Charles L. Swinden and Joan Irvine Swinden, photograph,
The Irvine Family Archives

James Harvey Irvine
and Glenn L. Martin,
photograph, The
Irvine Family Archives

IN 1951, I BRIEFLY ATTENDED THE University of California at
Berkeley, and later Marymount College. In October 1952, I married
Charles L. ("Chuck") Swinden, a student and track star at Santa Ana
City College. On July 31, 1953, my eldest son, James Irvine
Swinden, was born. His godfather was aviation pioneer Glenn L.
Martin, a close family friend. In 1909, my grandfather had allowed
Martin to use a small part of the ranch to fly an airplane he had
designed and built. Martin took off in a bean field, climbed eight
feet and stayed airborne for twelve seconds, long enough to cover a
distance of 100 feet. It was the first successful airplane flight in
California. Four years later, Martin convinced my grandfather to fly
over the ranch with him. Although my grandfather enjoyed seeing
his land from the air, he never flew again.

Also in 1951, my mother had introduced my uncle
Myford to Henry Grandin, head of the Boy Scouts for the western
United States. That introduction led to Myford bringing the 1953
National Boy Scout Jamboree to the Irvine Ranch. I attended the
opening ceremonies on July 17, when he welcomed 52,000 boys to
the event. It was the first international gathering of Boy Scouts held
in the western United States, and it made history in Orange County.

ABOVE: Boy Scout
Jamboree site, 1953,
vintage postcard,
Private Collection

RIGHT: Map and
memorabilia from Boy
Scout Jamboree,
Private Collection

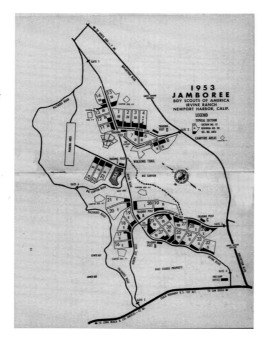

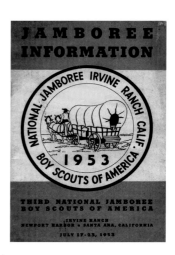

LEFT: Hill between Bommer Canyon at left and Shady Canyon at right, photograph, Courtesy of historian Judy Gauntt
RIGHT: Sand Canyon reservoir in Shady Canyon, photograph, Courtesy of historian Judy Gauntt

One day, Chuck wanted to take his track coach, John Ward, quail hunting on the ranch, in Bommer Canyon. I had brought my two golden retrievers, Goldy and Gamble, and my Dalmatian, Spottie, with us. After I had driven through the gate between Shady Canyon and Sand Canyon Reservoir, Chuck let the three dogs out to run in the field along the right-hand side of the car. I had not gone far when I felt a bump against the front right wheel. I immediately stopped, jumped out of the car, and to my horror found that I had hit Spottie. As she was badly hurt and bleeding internally, John, who was very experienced with guns, took her where I couldn't see and shot her to put her out of her misery. I was devastated. Even though I knew it was an accident, I never got over it.

In 1955, I began taking flying lessons with my close friend Mimi Honeyman Magor at the Orange County Airport. The following year, I married longtime friend Russell S. Penniman, a Navy pilot. We spent our eight-month honeymoon flying around South America in a single-engine Cessna 180, hunting and fishing. During the trip, we took pictures for *Time-Life* magazine that were published in *Sports Illustrated*. On August 16, 1957, my second son, Russell S. Penniman, was born. His father and I were divorced shortly thereafter. Later I married Richard D. Burt, a Laguna Beach builder, but he and I were divorced in 1963.

Eddie Martin Airport, later Orange County Airport, photo by Eddie Martin, Courtesy of historian Judy Gauntt

Eddie Martin, a pioneer aviator and photographer who took many aerial photographs of the Irvine Ranch, photograph, Courtesy of historian Judy Gauntt

Russell S. Penniman and Joan Irvine Penniman, photograph, The Irvine Family Archives

Richard D. Burt and Joan Irvine Burt at Irvine Cove, photograph, *The American Weekly*, October 1961

Jean Mannheim, *Salton Sea*, Courtesy of DeRus' Fine Arts, Laguna Beach

Paul Grimm, *Purple Hues*, Private Collection, Courtesy of The Irvine Museum

Little green house at Irvine Cove, photograph, Courtesy of historian Jim Sleeper

IN 1953, THE IRVINE COMPANY PURCHASED 2,400 acres of prime agricultural land in the Imperial Valley. This acquisition was the first of many to follow under the direction of ranch manager Brad Hellis, who by that time had become a foundation trustee and a member of the board of directors. For some time, my mother and I had heard reports that Hellis and his real estate broker and friend Walter Tubach had been cutting themselves in with The Irvine Company on these Imperial Valley land deals. Later, when we visited those properties, we found that this was indeed true.

When I succeeded my mother on The Irvine Company's board of directors in 1957, the company had 93,000 acres in Orange County, 11,000 acres in the Imperial Valley and about 100,000 acres in Montana. At that time, we had our legal counsel, Loeb & Loeb of Los Angeles, begin an investigation of the company books, as we believed that certain improper land deals had taken place in the Imperial Valley between The Irvine Company, Hellis and Tubach. After a lengthy investigation conducted by our counsel, Howard I. Friedman, my mother and I instituted legal proceedings against The Irvine Company, Hellis and Tubach. When we served subpoenas on Hellis and Tubach demanding that they produce their tax records and books, they both immediately agreed to a partition of the properties they held with The Irvine Company in the Imperial Valley. Hellis resigned from the Irvine Foundation and the Irvine Company board of directors. However, he continued his role in the company's management until May 1959.

This was the first in a series of legal actions that my mother and I were forced to bring in order to protect our stock interest in The Irvine Company. My stepfather, Judge Thurmond Clarke, had vast legal knowledge and excellent counsel that proved invaluable to us during the long years of litigation that followed, a process that was ongoing for thirty-two out of the next thirty-four years.

For many years, I had tried in vain to either lease or buy the land where the little green house at the cove was located. In spite of that, in October 1957, after I had removed my belongings, the company management burned the house to the ground, as they considered it inferior to the quality of homes that were to be built in an adjoining subdivision. I was, of course, heartbroken.

Thomas Van Sant, *Irvine Cove*, Courtesy of the James Irvine Swinden Family Collection

The Irvine Ranch House, photograph, The Irvine
Family Archives

Firetruck at the house, June 5, 1965, photograph, The Irvine
Family Archives

Demolition of the house in 1968,
photograph, The Irvine Family Archives

Urban sprawl in El Segundo, Los Angeles County, Courtesy of Susan Jordan,
www.californiacoastline.org

Ten years earlier, my mother and I had asked to lease and
restore the original San Joaquín Ranch house and have a small
amount of acreage there where I could keep my horses. The Irvine
Company management denied our request, and had the main section of that historic house destroyed in 1961 in order to accommodate Sam Barnes, a local attorney who developed the San Joaquín
Golf Course on adjacent company property. At that time, my mother and I also requested to lease the ranch house in Tustin in order to
restore the home and grounds to the way they were when my mother and father had lived there in the late 1920s and early 1930s.
Again, our request was denied. After a minor fire there in 1966, the
Irvine Company management had the house torn down in 1968
and collected the insurance.

By the time I became a director of the company, the blight
of urban sprawl had already begun to overrun Los Angeles County.
As the development of the Irvine Ranch was not only timely but also
inevitable, I continually urged my fellow directors to adopt a master
plan for the property in order to avoid the mistakes that had
occurred in Los Angeles and other areas. The plan I envisioned
would combine residential, commercial and industrial development
with greenbelts, parks and large, natural, open spaces that would
preserve the beauty of the land and the native plants and animals
that existed there—in other words, a plan that would balance economic growth and environmental preservation. My request, unfortunately, but not unexpectedly, always fell on deaf ears.

William Wendt, *A Clear Day*, 1903, The Irvine Museum

UC President Clark Kerr,
photograph, Courtesy of UCI

Joan Irvine Burt riding in the San Joaquin hills overlooking the future site of the
University of California at Irvine, photograph, *The American Weekly*, October 1961

Harvey Rice, photograph, The Irvine Family Archives

In October 1957, the Regents of the University of California, under the leadership of UC President Clark Kerr, retained the firm of William L. Pereira & Associates to study possible locations for a new university in southeast Los Angeles or Orange County. When the firm identified three sites on the Irvine Ranch as potential locations for a new campus, the foundation trustees were not receptive. When foundation trustee A. J. McFadden, who was also a Regent, was asked to donate 1,000 acres to the university, he told the Regents, "The Irvine Company will not give one nickel to the richest university in the world."

Other communities and landowners, like the Diamond Bar Ranch near Pomona, had already offered to donate 1,000 acres of land to the university for a campus. My mother and my uncle Myford and I wanted the university on the ranch, but Myford thought it would be impossible to convince the board to make a gift of 1,000 acres. He felt he would not be able to convince them that such a gift would be of future benefit to The Irvine Company. However, being aware of what UCLA had done for the Janss property in Westwood, I knew what the university would mean for the development of the Irvine Ranch and the surrounding communities.

In 1927 my grandfather James Irvine, who was a very astute businessman, had given 100 acres and sold an additional 300 acres of his Moraga Ranch in Contra Costa County to Saint Mary's College to bring culture and people to the area. He took great pride in the fact that the college was located on the ranch. His maternal grandfather, Harvey Rice, was known as the "Father of the Common School System in Ohio." At a time when education was a luxury reserved for the wealthy, my great-great grandfather sought to make the common schools "the colleges of the people—"cheap enough for the poorest, and good enough for the richest"—and thereby create "a democracy of knowledge" that would encourage true brotherhood and equality among men.

After my uncle Myford died on January 11, 1959, the James Irvine Foundation gained absolute control over The Irvine Company. N. Loyall McLaren succeeded my uncle as president of the foundation and was elected vice president of The Irvine Company. A. J. McFadden became vice president of the foundation and was elected president of the company. I was to be the only stockholder of record to sit on the Irvine Company board of directors for the next fifteen years.

Shortly thereafter, McLaren brought a proposal to the board to set up a separate development company in which The Irvine Company would put up $12.5 million in land, and Roger Stevens of New York, one of the shrewdest real estate developers in the country, would invest $5 million. Individual Irvine Company shareholders could invest in the Stevens group, as could the foundation trustees. Furthermore, the Stevens Development Company had the right of first refusal on the balance of all Irvine Company property.

As my mother and stepfather were on a trip in Russia at the time, I immediately took the Stevens Development proposal to our counsel, Loeb & Loeb. Walter Hilborn of that firm researched the Irvine Company corporate charter and discovered that, as the company was a West Virginia corporation, not a California corporation, a shareholder with 20 percent of the stock (rather than 51 percent) could sue for liquidation. As I held 20 percent of the stock, I advised McLaren that if he moved forward with the Stevens proposal, I would sue to liquidate the company. Eventually, he and the other foundation trustees abandoned the idea.

Subsequently, McLaren and McFadden met with the Irvine Company shareholders and advised us that they had received a proposal from Sam Barnes, former State Senator Dennis Carpenter and local developer Don Koll to form a company to develop the Irvine Ranch. The individual shareholders could invest in this company, as could, I suspected, the foundation trustees as individuals. Sensing another Stevens deal in the offing, I did not support the proposal. I suggested instead that The Irvine Company create its own subsidiary corporation to develop the Irvine Ranch lands. Eventually, the company did just that when it created the Irvine Pacific Development Company.

Joan Irvine Burt, photograph, Courtesy of *Newport Harbor Pilot*, December 16, 1959

IN MARCH 1959, MY ATTORNEY HOWARD FRIEDMAN told me that his client Walter Burroughs, the owner, publisher and editor of the *Newport Harbor Pilot,* a community newspaper that serves coastal Orange County, was very interested in bringing the University of California to Orange County. When Mr. Burroughs and I met on March 10, he advised me to retain his public relations consultant Chip Cleary and explained how much it would mean to the people of Orange County if the company gave the university a site. A master organizer, Burroughs suggested that all county residents who favored the university be invited to a mass meeting. I agreed to the suggestion but insisted that the event take place before the next meeting of the Irvine Company board of directors; we settled on the following Tuesday. Walter and Brick Power, a fellow UC Berkeley graduate, organized a very large luncheon meeting at a Newport Beach restaurant, where attendees overflowed into the parking lot. That day, the participants organized a support group called the Friends of the University of California in Orange County. Ultimately, nearly 50,000 people gave their support.

I worked on persuading the company directors, and eventually, they reluctantly agreed to give 650 acres of the preferred site on a hill above Corona del Mar, overlooking the ocean. At the same time, community leaders tried to influence the Regents, who weren't convinced that the Irvine Ranch land was the most advantageous location for a campus. However, by the time enough progress had been made with the Regents to secure the site, the Irvine Company management had sold it for $5,000 an acre to a group headed by their friend Sam Barnes, for use as a cemetery. I immediately proposed another site for the cemetery with a beautiful view and agreed to supply both water and a road. The cemetery group refused the offer and quickly brought in some bodies from paupers' graves in Santa Ana and buried them to secure their hold on the first site.

Residential construction on the Irvine Ranch, photograph, Courtesy of Irvine Historical Society

Paul Grimm, *Old Road*, Private Collection, Courtesy of The Irvine Museum

Urbanus Square, William Pereira's office, photograph, Courtesy of Irvine Historical Society

That month, the Regents selected an inland site on the ranch for the university, which William Pereira believed would be very acceptable. However, the Irvine Company board members continued to drag their feet on giving the university the land and adopting a master plan for the ranch property. Fed up with their stalling, I had Mr. Cleary send my open letter to McFadden of April 12, 1960, to the media, demanding that he "either give the company the vigorous and alert leadership which is the obligation of the president, or step aside." The following day, the Irvine Company board of directors voted to establish a master plan for the urban development of the ranch. Within a few days, The Irvine Company announced that it had retained J. Stanley Ott, a nationally recognized planner, to direct development of The Irvine Company's Orange County landholdings. Later that year, Ray Watson joined the company's planning staff.

In July 1960, The Irvine Company offered to gift 1,000 acres of land and to sell an additional 500 acres to the University of California. The selection of the Irvine site for the university would make it possible for an entire community to develop around the campus.

Charles S. Thomas, a former Secretary of the Navy and president of TWA, assumed the presidency of The Irvine Company on October 1, 1960. He had attended high school in Los Angeles with my mother and stepfather and was also a friend of Loyall McLaren. Thomas was very familiar with the southern California coast and the Irvine Ranch, having flown the mail for the Navy in World War I between San Diego and San Pedro. An avid duck hunter, he had from the 1930s been a member of both the San Joaquín Gun Club and the Bolsa Chica Gun Club, where he shot ducks in the sloughs and marshes of the Irvine Ranch and the Bolsa Chica.

About that time, The Irvine Company hired the Pereira firm to create a master plan for the Irvine Ranch. Pereira and his planning staff, headed by Jack Bevash, his resident partner, moved into the ranch house in Tustin, which had been converted into offices for them.

Pereira later moved to the site of the former Buffalo Ranch, at MacArthur Boulevard and Ford Road, where he established one of his seven offices nationwide. Renaming the site "Urbanus Square," Pereira and his staff produced the plan for the UCI campus and also the master plan for the Irvine Ranch lands and Irvine Center. Although he had wanted Jack Bevash to become the head of planning at The Irvine Company, the management gave the position to Ray Watson instead.

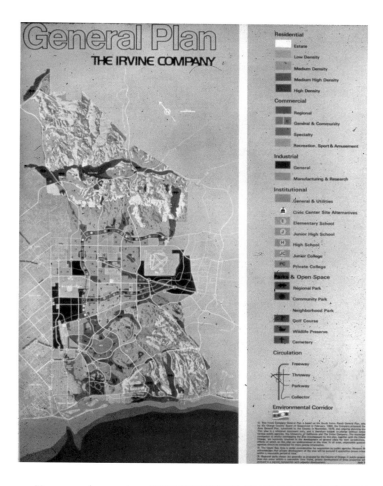

Pereira's plan divided the ranch into three planning areas—north, central and south. The least priority was given to the remote, mountainous areas to the north, as the topographical restraints would make development of the infrastructure there difficult and expensive. The central section, which contained the best agricultural land on the ranch, received second priority. The highest priority went to the southern section of the property, from the coast to the alignment for the San Diego Freeway. It included the new university and its surrounding communities.

Martin Schiesl, a history professor at California State University, Los Angeles, writes that the Irvine Ranch property sat at a central point in the state's network of roads. In 1959, the legislature approved plans for three major freeways that would link the Irvine property with the Los Angeles metropolitan area. Schiesl states: "Pereira's plan for the new campus promised permanent assurance against encroachment by outside developments and pointed the way to the avoidance of uncontrolled suburbanization of ranch property."

Schiesl further writes that each planned community was to contain residential districts with a sense of place and identity, to which inhabitants could relate on a more intimate level. Each district, or village, would have its own schools, churches and shopping centers.

The Master Land Use Plan for the ranch proposed the development of major industrial areas, including The Irvine Company's industrial complex near the airport. Newport Center was envisioned as "a downtown for the South Coast of Orange County." This site, which comprised 700 acres, was to contain high-rise office buildings, medical centers, service businesses and a regional shopping center.

Pereira's master plan for the university campus was created in the shape of a giant wheel, with six principal quadrangles radiating from a sixteen-acre central park. The park was to contain an amphitheater, and was to be "the focus of university life." "Among the advantages of the circular campus plan," Pereira wrote, "is the fact that all major academic buildings as well as The Irvine Company facilities, will be within a ten minute walk of each other. Wherever possible, the natural topography of the terrain will be followed, with the building areas designed and all the other land preserved for all time as open space." Pereira's plan for the new campus included developing a master plan for the entire Irvine Ranch, in order to enhance both the importance of the fledgling university and the coffers of The Irvine Company. Pereira spoke several times

Newspaper photograph showing William Pereira, Joan Irvine Burt and Charles Thomas examining plan for Newport Center by Charles Luckman

Fashion Island, Newport Center, originally designed by Charles Luckman was later redesigned by The Irvine Company management, photograph, Courtesy of Irvine Historical Society

University of California at Irvine under construction, photograph, Courtesy of Irvine Historical Society

of his vision for the Irvine campus as the focal point for "A City of Intellect." At other times, he referred to the campus and its surrounding community as "The City of Tomorrow," one that he projected would reach a population of 100,000 by 1990—without the blight of urban sprawl.

The suggestion to master-plan the future community triggered a bitter two-year battle among the Irvine Company's board of directors, but in the end, the board finally agreed to Pereira's plan. "Few large organizations," writes Schiesl, "have played a greater role in the post-war economic and social evolution of Orange County than The Irvine Company." By 1993, the master-planned city of Irvine had reached a population of some 120,000 people, although Pereira's complete plan has never been fully carried out.

With the site selected, an architect chosen, and community support assured, the next step was to appoint a chancellor. Once again, Clark Kerr exhibited particularly astute judgment. He selected just the right person for the job: Daniel G. Aldrich, Jr., the university's statewide Dean of Agriculture. The appointment was made in January 1962. Kerr's judgment was subsequently affirmed many times by the outstanding leadership of Chancellor Aldrich throughout his twenty-two years at UCI.

Daniel Aldrich, William Pereira and Charles Thomas and the UCI plan, photograph, Courtesy of UCI

William Pereira at UCI, photograph, Courtesy of Irvine Historical Society

On April 14, 1963, the Irvine Company board of directors adopted a resolution for the implementation of a master plan for the Irvine Ranch. On October 10, Pereira outlined to the company board what steps would be taken in general land development planning for the Irvine Ranch lands. When the first section of the company's master plan was presented to the Orange County Planning Commission in 1963, the commissioners and the spectators who crowded the room rose to their feet and applauded.

The Irvine Ranch, photograph, Courtesy of Irvine Historical Society

President Lyndon Johnson at the dedication of UCI, June 20, 1964, photograph, Courtesy of UCI historian Sam McCullough

The University of California at Irvine was dedicated on June 20, 1964. President Lyndon B. Johnson gave the dedication address. Classes began in September 1965. An advertisement purchased by The Irvine Company in the Daily Pilot's Dedication Issue stated, "We feel privileged to have donated the 1,000 acre campus to the university. In this, our centennial year [sic], we are additionally engaged in an era of magnificent developments, encompassing space-age facilities, residential communities, unlimited recreational opportunities, commercial centers and agricultural expansion to nourish a growing population. Our neighbors may be assured that our Master Plan for developing our properties also includes adequate provisions for educational institutions and cultural endeavors."

Pereira became known as the father of the largest master-planned area on the North American continent. Famous for his other accomplishments, such as the landmark Transamerica Pyramid in San Francisco and the Los Angeles County Museum of Art, Pereira counted the development of the Irvine Ranch, together with the University of California campus and Newport Center, as one of the most challenging projects of his career.

The South Irvine Ranch General Plan was approved by the Orange County Board of Supervisors in 1964. At that time, company president Charles Thomas said that The Irvine Company was undertaking the "finest land development in the world" and that it expected to see "enormous progress and prosperity" for the local area.

Joan Irvine Smith and Athalie Irvine Clarke, c. 1964, photograph, The Irvine Family Archives

The Irvine Ranch, photograph, Courtesy of Irvine Historical Society

Even after the adoption of the master plan for the Irvine Ranch lands, self-dealing, conflicts of interest and acts of mismanagement persisted within the company. Although the Irvine Ranch lay directly in the path of urban development, former company management allowed a major "opportunity to achieve our golden destiny" to pass us by for more than ten years. In 1965, the California legislature passed the Williamson Act, which enabled agricultural land to be placed in a ten-year preserve and be subject to lower property taxes based on land use. The company management took full advantage of the act, placing 49,000 acres in the preserve in 1969. But as urban development leapfrogged over the ranch, developments like Mission Viejo in the southern part of Orange County reaped the rewards, and The Irvine Company remained a sleeping green giant.

Morton W. "Cappy" Smith competing at The Warrenton Horse Show in Virginia, c. 1960, photograph, The Irvine Family Archives

Joan Irvine Smith and Cappy Smith, c. 1963, photograph, The Irvine Family Archives

IN 1962, I HAD A HANDSOME CHESTNUT Irish Thoroughbred gelding named Rossmore that I had purchased from Neal McCarthy and had in training with Jimmy Williams at Flintridge. Jimmy was to show the horse in the hunters at Del Mar in July, and Peggy Ostercamp asked me if she could also take Mascus, who had been retired for several years, to the show. When I asked her why, she said because Cappy Smith is judging. The evening that Mascus was to show, Katrina Lance Lutge and I went to the event. I went up to Cappy before the class and asked if he remembered me, to which he replied that he not only remembered me, but my mother as well. He said that Mascus had been the most difficult horse sale he had ever made, as he had to deal with all those lawyers. Peggy laid down a perfect round and won the class handily.

After the show, as Katrina and I were leaving, Cappy caught up with us and asked if we would like to go to C. Arnold Smith's house for a party. We accepted. Cappy remained in California for the next three weeks. Before he left, he told me that he was coming back to marry me. He and I were married in September 1963. I moved to Middleburg, Virginia, with my two sons, Jim and Russell, and purchased my 230-acre horse farm, The Oaks.

At that time, I began collecting British and French sporting art, which went on display at the Middleburg Sporting Library on April 12, 2006, and will remain there for one year. I also collected American and English antiques and Chinese porcelain for my new home in Middleburg. For years, my mother and I spent many enjoyable days ferreting through various shops searching for Oriental porcelain, pottery and screens to decorate our homes in California.

The Orange County Hunt at Bernley Farm, The Plains, Virginia 1969, photo by Marshall Hawkins

As I had always loved gardening, shortly after moving to Middleburg I planted tulips, daffodils and crocuses throughout the woods on both sides of the driveway leading to the house. When my mother and I found an azalea nursery in the area that was going out of business, I purchased a number of large plants and landscaped the house and surrounding grounds with pink and white azaleas and native dogwood trees. Eventually, I expanded the garden and planted a number of native Virginia plants in order to naturalize the woods leading to the house.

Six years later, my mother purchased Byrnely Farm in The Plains, not far from Middleburg. Both The Oaks and Byrnely Farm are located in the best fox-hunting country in America. Although they did not ride, my mother and Thurmond enjoyed the colorful spectacle of the hunt as well as the hunt breakfasts and other social events that were part of our community life. Cappy, who had dominated the horse show scene for three decades beginning in the 1930s, became Master of the Orange County Hunt, and the rest of the family rode to the hounds as well.

Our years in Middleburg were very happy for my mother and me. My sons Jim and Russell, as well as my youngest son, Morton Irvine Smith, who was born on August 12, 1965, and my stepdaughter Alletta Morris Smith, lived on the farm and were in school on the East Coast. Cappy and I were breeding, training and selling horses on the farm.

During the 1950s, I had partnered with Louis Rowan breeding and racing Thoroughbreds in California. When I married Cappy, he and I bred, sold and raced Thoroughbreds in the United States and Ireland and also raced in France. It was at that time that I began looking for a Selle Français stallion to cross on some of my Thoroughbred mares, but I was unable to find the right horse. Years later, when I saw the legendary Holsteiner stallion Livius compete for the West German team in the 1984 Olympics, I knew I had found the type of horse I wanted.

The Oaks, Middleburg, Virginia, photo by Morton Irvine Smith

Joan Irvine Smith and Morton W. "Cappy" Smith with the Orange County Hunt at The Oaks, Middleburg, Virginia, photo by Howard Allen

Jim Swinden, Russ Penniman and Morton Smith, Orange County Hunt, Middleburg, photo by Howard Allen

Diana, Tracey, Keith and Linda Irvine Gaede, Orange County Hunt, Middleburg, 1969, photo by Marshall Hawkins

Cappy Smith and Joan Irvine Smith on Incomparable and Chocolate Soldier, Orange County Hunt, Middleburg, Virginia, photo by Howard Allen

Joan Irvine Smith on Brown Jack, Orange County Hunt, Middleburg, Virginia, photo by Marshall Hawkins

After moving to Middleburg in 1963, I flew back to California monthly for Irvine Company board meetings. I was becoming increasingly dissatisfied with the James Irvine Foundation's actions as majority shareholder in The Irvine Company and its modest pay-out to individual stockholders and for charitable purposes each year. In 1964, my mother and I retained Lyndol L. Young and C. Ray Robinson to file suit against the company and the foundation in federal court in Los Angeles. At the conclusion of the trial, the judge indicated that the matter belonged before the Congress rather than before the court.

In the mid-1960s, Loyall McLaren brought a project called the Upper Bay Development Company to the company's board of directors. Under this plan, The Irvine Company would have a third, the individual shareholders would have a third, and the James Irvine Foundation would have a third of the new company, which would develop about 175 acres of residential property in the Back Bay. McLaren further explained that as this was to be a very speculative venture, the foundation would give up its one-third interest and give it to the trustees as individuals instead. It was necessary for my mother and I to engage the law firm of Jackson, Kelly, Holt and O'Farrell in Charleston, West Virginia, and file suit in order to enjoin the Irvine Company management from going forward with the project.

About that time, Charlie Thomas sent members of the management team, including its planning staff, abroad to study famous coastal resorts. Upon their return, they designed the Promontory Point development in Newport Beach as well as a development plan for the Irvine Coast that included the three and one-half miles of coastline and coastal hills stretching from Newport to Laguna Beach. This plan, a larger version of the Promontory Point project, included resort hotels and 12,000 homes. It called for an ocean walk along the bluffs connecting Newport and Laguna Beach, a golf course on the coastal shelf, moving Pacific Coast Highway up on top of the coastal hills, dredging out Los Trancos Canyon at Crystal Cove inland for a quarter of a mile to create a harbor and coastal village like Portofino in Italy, plus building a reef offshore to allow boats to sail into the harbor to visit the inns, restaurants and shops planned along its cobblestone-lined banks.

When the Irvine Company management presented its plan for the Irvine Coast to the shareholders, the new Irvine Company president William R. Mason told me that my father "had really been stupid when he placed the Pacific Coast Highway where he did." I reminded Mr. Mason that my father had wanted all of the land on the beach side of the highway, from Corona del Mar to Abalone Point, to be a public park. I further stated that in 1931, my father had resolved a case before the Board of Tax Appeals in Washington by agreeing to give the land for a federal park. McLaren, who was attending the meeting and who had participated in the resolution of that tax case said, "We do not want to talk about that." My mother and I would never support The Irvine Company's management plan for the Irvine Coast.

In order to protect both my mother's and my own vested interest in the company as well as the financial well being of my grandfather's charitable legacy, I lobbied for six years in Washington, D.C., and testified before both the House Ways and Means Committee and the Senate Committee on Finance in support of the Tax Reform Act of 1969. This landmark legislation, which impacted all charitable foundations, required the James Irvine Foundation to diversify its investments by disposing of its controlling interest in The Irvine Company, and to increase its charitable grants to at least five percent of asset value each year. On December 20, 1969, it was signed by President Richard Nixon and became law in 1970. Nevertheless, the foundation trustees refused to relinquish their control of the company and in 1973, I testified before the House Ways and Means Committee concerning their efforts to circumvent the law.

Upper Newport Bay, Photo by Jean Stern

Raymond Nott, *Laguna Coast*, Private Collection, Courtesy of The Irvine Museum

Jack Wilkinson Smith, *Crystal Cove State Park*, Private Collection, Courtesy of The Irvine Museum

On December 28, 1971, after a vigorous campaign by The Irvine Company management, the city of Irvine was incorporated, encompassing an area of more than 40 square miles. Within the city's sphere of influence were the three and one-half miles of Irvine Coast property. At that time, the new city council voted a temporary moratorium on all future construction in the city while it studied The Irvine Company's master plan for major revisions. The council created a planning commission and hired a consulting firm

Joan Irvine Smith after testifying before the House Ways and Means Committee in Washington, D.C. in 1973, photograph, The Irvine Family Archives

to help prepare the 1973 City of Irvine General Plan, which set goals and policies for future growth.

In the meantime, in 1972, under Governor Ronald Reagan's administration, California voters approved the Coastal Act. President Nixon signed the Clean Water Act that year as well; two years before, he had created the Environmental Protection Agency and approved the Clean Air Act. The environmental movement had become a force to be reckoned with.

In 1973, the Irvine Company's management attempted to sell 1,800 acres of coastal land between Corona del Mar and Laguna Beach to the state of California for $7.5 million, or approximately $4,000 an acre, for park and recreation purposes. Fearing a recurrence of what had happened to my grandfather's gift of parkland to the city of Newport Beach, my mother and I filed suit in Charleston, West Virginia, to enjoin the sale. At that time, it was discovered that, under Governor Reagan's administration, State Parks had purchased two and one-half acres just north of the pier at Huntington Beach for more than $600,000, or $250,000 an acre. A private gated condominium project known as the "Huntington Pacific" was constructed on this oceanfront park property.

My mother and I had hoped that The Irvine Company would go public. However, during the State Park litigation, we learned from our West Virginia counsel James K. Brown, of the law firm of Jackson, Kelly, Holt and O'Farrell, that he had heard that the Foundation trustees had secretly made a "sweetheart" deal to sell the company to Mobil Oil Corporation for $200 million. Believing that the price was unreasonably low, my mother and I immediately retained a Washington, D.C. law firm and filed litigation in California to enjoin the proposed $200-million merger between Mobil and The Irvine Company. Shortly thereafter, we substituted in as counsel the law firm of Loeb & Loeb, with Howard Friedman as lead counsel, and were joined in the suit by the California Attorney General. After a preliminary injunction was granted, we became embroiled in the bidding war and public controversy that followed.

In 1977, in an effort to stem the takeover of The Irvine Company by Mobil, my mother and I joined a group of financial giants to outbid Mobil and buy the company for $337 million. Our group, Taubman-Allen-Irvine, Inc., included shopping center magnate A. Alfred Taubman; investment bankers Charlie Allen and his brother Herbert Allen, senior members of Allen & Co.; Max Fisher, chairman of United Brands; Milton Petrie of Petrie Stores; and automotive heir Henry Ford II. Also part of the team was local homebuilder Donald Bren, and Howard Marguleas, chairman of Sun World International, a prominent Coachella Valley produce firm. After a friendly merger, The Irvine Company was incorporated under the laws of the state of Michigan. When the James Irvine Foundation was forced to give up its controlling interest in the company and diversify its investments, its charitable grants increased from $1 million to $10 million per year.

My mother had been a member of the board of directors of the Irvine Industrial Complex from the time of its inception in the early 1960s, until the company was sold to eastern investors in 1977. The 2000-acre complex, located east of the El Toro Marine Corps Air Station, together with the airport area Irvine Industrial Complex West, made The Irvine Company the owner of the largest industrial development in the United States. The 1980s brought recognition for the City of Irvine as a "national model of comprehensive development that provided for all aspects of working and living," according to Schiesl.

During the Crystal Cove State Park litigation, a well-known real estate developer who had been a close friend of my mother's since high school, visited her at her home in Corona del Mar. He told her that if she and I would drop our lawsuit blocking the sale of the Irvine coastal land to State Parks, he would give her the finest condominium that he intended to build on that property. When my mother related the conversation to me, she said, "You know, dear, I believe they really do intend to develop the park!"

The Irvine Industrial Complex West c.1970, photograph, Courtesy of Irvine Historical Society

View Toward Laguna Beach—Irvine Open Space Reserve, © Harold Malde

Joan Irvine Smith at the Orange County Courthouse during the trial with Mobile Oil in 1976, photograph, The Irvine Family Archives

stal Ridges—Irvine Open Space Reserve, 1991, © Stephen Francis Photography

Costal Ridges—Irvine Open Space Reserve, 1991, © Stephen Francis Photography

In 1976, the Friends of the Irvine Coast (now called the Friends of the Newport Coast) was founded by its current president, Fern Pirkle, for the primary purpose of preserving the maximum possible public open space and natural wildlife habitat on the Irvine Coast. At that time, the property consisted of 9,432 acres of undeveloped land located between the cities of Laguna Beach and Newport Beach, and included three and one-quarter miles of coastline and coastal hills. Since the formation of the Friends, a great deal has been accomplished in cooperating with other environmental organizations to ensure the protection of more than 77 percent of the Irvine Coast for the public's enjoyment as well as for wildlife habitat.

That same year, the Orange County Board of Supervisors approved The Irvine Company's plans for the construction of resort hotels and 12,000 homes along the Irvine Coast. These plans would have permitted an increase in population on the coast of approximately 38,000 people. Because of the Coastal Act, the development plans became subject to approval by the South Coast Regional Coastal Commission.

In 1979, with the Friends and other environmental organizations vigorously opposing its approval, the proposed plan for the coast was flatly rejected by the Commission. My mother and I also resolved our litigation in 1979, when The Irvine Company agreed to sell approximately 2,300 acres of coastal land to the state of California for $32.6 million, or about $14,000 per acre.

California Gnatcatcher, © Bruce Farnsworth

William Griffith, *In Laguna Canyon*, 1928, The Irvine Museum, Gift of Josephine N. Milnor

Joseph Kleitsch, *Laguna Canyon*, Courtesy of Mr. and Mrs. Thomas B. Stiles II

Kevin Macpherson, *Mustard Field, Laguna Canyon*, Courtesy of Redfern Gallery, Laguna Beach

In the early 1970s, Laguna Beach bookstore owner and visionary James Dilley dreamed of a 3,000- to 5,000-acre greenbelt around Laguna Beach. In 1972, the Orange County Board of Supervisors endorsed Dilley's concept. In 1978, Laguna Beach purchased the area now known as the James Dilley Preserve, in the Laguna Coast Wilderness Park. This was the start of the South Coast Wilderness area, which today includes 17,000 acres of parks and open space as well as 2,000 acres of marine preserves. In 1979, the development agreements for the Aliso Viejo Development Project gave Orange County most of the land for the Aliso and Wood Canyons Wilderness Park.

Benjamin Brown, *Laguna Canyon Road*, Courtesy of Nick Alexander

William Wendt, *Rushing Onward*, Private Collection,
Courtesy of The Irvine Museum

William Wendt, *The New Bridge*, Private Collection, Courtesy of The Irvine Museum

The Laguna Coast Wilderness Park involved three major land transactions—Sycamore Hills, The Irvine Company's Laguna Laurel development and the San Joaquín Hills toll road. The park's evolution was also intertwined with the Irvine/Newport Coast and Aliso Viejo developments.

In November 1990, the residents of Laguna Beach demonstrated their commitment to the Laguna Laurel preservation campaign with a historic $20 million bond measure vote. The tax increase was approved by nearly 80 percent, the highest vote for a bond measure in California since 1956. Laguna Coast Wilderness Park was dedicated to the public in an inspiring ceremony on April 10, 1993. By October 1993, four out of the five Laguna Laurel options had been purchased for parkland at a cost of $45 million. The city of Laguna Beach, Orange County, the state of California and the Laguna Canyon Foundation provided the purchase funding, which included the $20 million tax bond.

As the purchase agreement ended in 1995 without the fifth and final Laguna Laurel purchase, Michael Pinto and Mary Fegraus of the Laguna Canyon Foundation initiated a series of meetings from 1994 to 2001 with neighbors to the new park. Attending the meetings were representatives from the cities of Irvine, Laguna Beach, Laguna Woods and Laguna Hills, along with the community of Leisure World, the County of Orange and interested individuals.

William Griffith, *Sycamores in Laguna Canyon*, The Irvine Museum

Maria del Carmen Calvo, *Laguna Sycamores*, Private Collection, Courtesy of The Irvine Museum

Laguna Laurel, © Kay Ogden 1991

William Wendt, *Sermons in Stone*, Private Collection, Courtesy of The Irvine Museum

Irvine Company cattle in Laguna Canyon, 1952, photo by Horace H. Fritz III, The Irvine Family Archives

Maria del Carmen Calvo, *Sycamores*, Private Collection, Courtesy of The Irvine Museum

Maria del Carmen Calvo, *Hillside Bushes*,
Private Collection, Courtesy of The Irvine Museum

John Cosby, *Tribute to Crystal Cove*, Courtesy of the artist

John Cosby, *Seaside Morning, Crystal Cove*, Courtesy of Meriam Braselle

Anita Hampton, *Grey Day, Crystal Cove*, Private Collection, Courtesy of
The Irvine Museum

Dan Goozeé, *House at Crystal Cove*, Courtesy of the artist

Sunset at Crystal Cove, © John Connell, Courtesy of Crystal Cove Alliance

California Sea Lions, © Rhea Sax

California Brown Pelican, © Joyce Gross

IN JUNE 1979, THE RESIDENTS of Crystal Cove succeeded in listing their community on the National Register of Historic Places as the area's last remaining example of a 1920s- and 1930s-era California beach colony. This was done as a means to extend their stay on the property; they understood that once listed, the cottages could not be torn down.

In 1981, the Orange County Board of Supervisors approved a modified plan submitted by The Irvine Company for the Irvine Coast. This plan proposed 200,000 square feet of office space in high-rise towers, 1,500 hotel rooms and 2,600 residences. While open space dedications were included in the plan to offset the impact of the development, the complex dedication program was considered unworkable by the Friends of the Irvine Coast. At about that time, the Orange County Board of Supervisors approved an increase of 9,400 residential units in the Aliso Viejo development plan.

The Crystal Cove State Park General Plan was approved by the State Parks and Recreation Commission in March 1982 and certified by the California Coastal Commission two months later. The plan recommended maintaining the 12.3-acre Crystal Cove Historic District and its 46 wood-frame cottages and providing access for recreation, culture and education. It listed several potential uses for the cottages, such as for a hostel and visitor center, rental units and education. The plan also included a 1,140-acre underwater park extending the entire three-and-one-quarter-mile length of the park shoreline and reaching from the mean high tide line to a 120-foot depth offshore. It also called for an ecological marine preserve, located at Pelican Point.

The cottage tenants, who had been on a month-to-month lease, won a court fight in July 1983 and received a ten-year lease. In return, they agreed to waive relocation rights and received a two-year extension that allowed them to remain until 1995. In fact, the residents did not leave Crystal Cove until July 8, 2001.

Athalie Irvine Clarke and Joan Irvine Smith at the 1991 Oaks Classic, photo by Tish Quirk

In 1983, Donald Bren advised my mother and me of his intention to take over The Irvine Company. At that time, he offered to acquire half of our shares in the corporation and allow us to exchange the balance of our stock for shares in his new company. Because of my great love for the ranch, I seriously considered his offer. However, due to my concern that he might abandon the master plan for the development of the property and break up and sell off the land, we did not accept his proposal.

In November 1983, Bren bought out the other Irvine Company shareholders and gained control of the company. My mother and I rejected his offer and became engaged in lengthy litigation to establish the value of our Irvine Company stock. As the case was tried in Michigan, Howard Friedman associated with Bruce Donaldson of the Detroit law firm of Dykema & Gosset. When we resolved the litigation in 1991, we were required to sign an agreement that we would in no way impede the company's development of the ranch.

ABOVE, FROM LEFT: Russ Penniman, Athalie Irvine Clarke, Morton Smith, Jim Swinden and Joan Irvine Smith having lunch at The Oaks, July, 1991
BELOW: Pepper tree next to the porch

Albert R. Valentien, *California Pepper Tree*, Courtesy of The Lodge at Torrey Pines

Frank Cuprien, *A Glorious Evening*, The Russell and Carol Penniman Collection

After years of litigation, the Friends and The Irvine Company finally reached an agreement in 1988 that allowed limited development to occur on approximately 2,200 acres of the coast, while preserving in permanent open space uses approximately 7,200 acres of the coast. The improved plan included additional open space, reduced building heights and hotel development, prompt dedication of open space, controls on open space land uses, wildlife protection and runoff control measures. Under the plan, the proposed population would be reduced from 38,000 people to about 8,000 people.

Nevertheless, in 1996, The Irvine Company proposed a major amendment to the Irvine Coast Local Coastal Program that would have intensified development without providing mitigation by the dedication of additional open space. The Friends, led by its founder and president, Fern Pirkle, filed lawsuits against the Coastal Commission, Orange County and The Irvine Company; these were settled in June 1997. The settlement agreement provided for the conversion of 70 acres of land slated for intensive development into permanent open space adjacent to Crystal Cove State Park. Other improvements included wildlife corridors, a reduction in the number of residential units that could be built in sensitive areas and a requirement of at least a 100-foot setback from the Coast Highway for the commercial center.

Emil J. Kosa, Jr., *Late Fall*, Private Collection, Courtesy of The Irvine Museum

William Wendt, *Along the River*, Private Collection, Courtesy of The Irvine Museum

William Wendt, *San Juan Creek, Near the Mission*, Private Collection, Courtesy of The Irvine Museum

126

The Oak Grove at The Oaks, photograph, Alexey Steele

Alain Vaillancourt placed second on Stand Alone in a $25,000 Showpark Grand Prix in 1990

Laura Kelly on Jumper Champion Excalibur

In 1985, my mother and I began acquiring the property that today comprises The Oaks, my 22-acre private equestrian training facility in San Juan Capistrano. It is located directly across San Juan Creek from the Lacouague Ranch, the original site of the Mission San Juan Capistrano from 1776 to 1778. A beautiful oak grove on my property was once an Acagchemem Indian campground that existed centuries before the arrival of Portolá and the padres.

At the time that I purchased the property, I had a number of hunters and jumpers in training with Jimmy Kohn, who rented a barn there. Eventually I put some hunters in training with Ron Kennedy, who later also rented a barn on the property. Although I had been divorced from my former husband, the legendary horseman Cappy Smith, since 1976, and Cappy had remarried in 1979, we remained close friends and business partners. He always came to California for Christmas and at other times to help me with my horses, as many of them had come from him and because he was the event coordinator for the horse shows we held at The Oaks.

Joan Irvine Smith, Cappy Smith and Leslie Vaillancourt at Showpark in 1990

Diana, Tracy, and Linda Irvine Gaede and Keith Gaede at the
Santa Barbara Horse Show, photo by Fallaw 1974

Cappy Smith and Joan Irvine Smith on Hunter Champion Idle Hour at The Oaks 1990

Cappy Smith and Joan Irvine Smith

Leslie Vaillancourt on Hunter Champion Patch at Griffith Park

Cappy Smith and Ron Kennedy on Hunter Champion After Hours at Griffith Park

Joan Irvine Smith on Hunter Champion Stars and Bars at The Oaks

FROM LEFT: Grand Prix placed Hermes, Alain Vaillancourt, Monty Fisher, German Olympic Equestrian Team Captain Hans Winkler, Mrs. Winkler, Laura Kelly and Cappy Smith

FROM LEFT: U.S. Olympic Equestrian Team Captain Bill Steinkraus, Joan Irvine Smith and Cappy Smith

The Oaks' first Grand Prix-placed horses included: Last Laugh, Hermes, Kontiki, Break Away and Heros. Hunter and jumper champions included: Patch, Full Cry, Idle Hour, Ocean Blue, Big John, Memphis Belle, Carte Blanche, After Hours, White Gloves, The Little Prince, Golden Boy, My Turn, American Express, Magnum, Parkmore, On the Cuff, Excalibur, Stars and Bars and Redskin, among others.

Joan Irvine Smith on Grand Prix placed Heros at The Oaks

Jimmy Kohn on Last Laugh at Spruce Meadows, Canada, photo by Tish Quirk

Alain Vaillancourt on Hermes in Tucson, Arizona, photo by Dennis

Alain Vaillancourt on Break Away at Phoenix, Arizona, photo by Tish Quirk

Leslie Vaillancourt with Magnum, Grand Champion Adult/Amateur Hunter Phoenix, Arizona, photo by James Leslie Parker

129

Athalie Irvine Clarke
at The Oaks in 1990

I would go to The Oaks almost daily, not only to watch my horses work, but also to oversee the improvements that had to be made on the property. My mother would often join me for lunch, as she enjoyed seeing what progress had been made. My children and grandchildren came to ride, play tennis and swim, and the family always celebrated Christmas and Thanksgiving in one of the houses there. At Easter I had a very large Easter egg hunt for my grandchildren and my friends' children.

FROM LEFT: Joan Irvine Smith, Athalie Irvine Clarke, Cappy Smith, Leslie Vaillancourt and Russ Penniman at The Oaks

Russ Penniman on Captain

Jim Swinden at The Oaks

Carol, Rex and Elizabeth Penniman at The Oaks

Jim Swinden on Captain at The Oaks, 1990

Madeline and Jim Swinden at The Oaks

Russ and Carol Penniman at The Oaks

Elizabeth and Rex Penniman with Jase Swinden, Christmas at The Oaks 1994

Madeline Swinden, Joan Irvine Smith and Anita Ziebe

Jim Swinden, Joan Irvine Smith, Morton Smith, Russ Penniman

LEFT: Marianne and Virginia Rose Smith
BELOW: Paige Dendiu with Santa Claus on Apple

Carol, Elizabeth, Russ and Rex Penniman

Toni and Charlotte Smith for Christmas at The Oaks 2001

Russ Penniman, Jim Swinden and Morton Smith at The Oaks, Easter 1990

Family and Friends at an Easter egg hunt at The Oaks

Rex Penniman

Presley Van Brow, Toni Smith, Jase Swinden and Charlotte Smith

Charlotte, Toni and Virginia Rose Smith

ABOVE: Family and Friends at an Easter egg hunt at The Oaks
RIGHT: Easter egg hunt at The Oaks
LEFT: Virginia Rose and Charlotte Smith with Blackie

In 1989, when Ron Kennedy and my trainer Alain Vaillancourt were showing some of my hunters and jumpers at Showpark in Del Mar, I got a Jack Russell terrier puppy named Skippy and two golden retriever puppies named Buck and Berkeley at the horse show. I put the three dogs in the care of Debbie Mallard, who worked for Ron Kennedy at The Oaks. However, when Skippy was hit by a van and almost killed, I took him home, where he became my devoted and constant companion for more than fifteen years. That same year, I got Skippy's brother Sport, who stayed at The Oaks. The following year, I found Skippy a female companion named Sissy, who came to live with Skippy and me. I also got four courgi puppies named Teddy, Simba, Poppy and Wendy, who stayed at the farm.

For years, Skippy and Sissy accompanied me everywhere, even joining me and my attorney Alden Pierce of Loeb & Loeb at water board meetings, which both amused and on occasion irritated some board members. Over the years, there were many puppies, some of which I still have. This summer, while I was writing this text, I lost Skippy. After a seven-month battle with kidney failure, he died in my arms on July 17, 2004, at 12:15 in the morning, on the same day and at the same time that my former husband Cappy Smith had passed away two years before.

Skippy

Sport, Blanche, Skippy with the Corgis, and Blue and Berkley at The Oaks

Athalie Irvine Clarke with Skippy

Joan Irvine Smith with Skippy at The Oaks

Sissy and puppies

Sissy and Skippy

Jase Swinden with a puppy at The Oaks

Simba

Everyone in my family loves dogs. When they come to visit me at The Oaks, they often bring their dogs along with them, even from as far away as Newport, Rhode Island, where my stepdaughter Alletta Smith Cooper and her three children, Alletta, Nathalie and Willem, live.

Skippy

Sport

Berkeley

John Costanza with Skippy
and Sissy at The Oaks

Carol Penniman with Rex and
Skippy at The Oaks

Anita Ziebe with Buck, Gracie, and Hunter Champion
Let's Dance

Joan Irvine Smith with Skippy, Athalie Irvine Clarke,
Jim Swinden and baby Jase by the tennis court at The Oaks

Toni Smith with Blackie

FROM LEFT: Charlotte, Morton, Toni, Marianne and Virgina
Rose Smith with Blackie

FROM LEFT: Carol, Rex, Elizabeth and Russ Penniman with Tigger, Duchess and Beau

Madeline, Jim and Jase Swinden with Cinco

133

The Oaks Indian Hill Ranch, Valley Center, California 1993

Eventually, I acquired a rottweiler named Bretta, who stayed at The Oaks Indian Hill Ranch, the 42-acre stud farm I acquired in Valley Center, California, in 1992.

Bretta the Rottweiler was the guarddog at The Oaks Indian Hill Ranch.

Carol Penniman making friends with the horses

Ranch Manager Lou Lake showing Elizabeth Penniman's fourth-grade class the Indian grinding stone on the ranch

Nancy Lake showing Elizabeth's class the horses

Broodmare Melony J and her foal Southern Swell by South Pacific

Yearlings at The Oaks Indian Hill Ranch

Alexey Steele, *Oaks and Sycamores at The Oaks*, Private Collection

Joan Irvine Smith and Last Laugh on the cover of the May 8, 1986 edition of "Newport Beach [714]" magazine which contained an article on the first annual Oaks Classic held in June 1986

THE 1986 OAKS CLASSIC, CONTINUED ON NEXT PAGE

THE FIRST WEEKEND IN JUNE 1986, my mother and I hosted the first Oaks Classic, an Olympic-style Grand Prix jumping competition, at The Oaks in San Juan Capistrano. The event benefited the UCI College of Medicine, headed by our good friend Dr. Walter Henry, who was dean at the time, and featured The Oaks Classic Grand Prix Luncheon and $50,000 Grand Prix. Larry Langer was the show manager, and my former husband Cappy Smith was the event coordinator. Jenny Iverson won the Grand Prix on her Dutch Warmblood gelding Delfsen.

Behind the Marine color guard are Morton W. "Cappy" Smith, event coordinator, Linda Allen, course designer, Larry Langer, show manager.

Jenny Iverson and Delfsen winners of the 1986 $50,000 Oaks Classic Grand Prix receives award from Joan Irvine Smith and Athalie Irvine Clarke with Deborah Swinden, Liz Penniman, Jim Swinden, Carol Penniman and Morton Smith. Mrs. Smith and Mrs. Clarke received certificates of merit from the Orange County Board of Supervisors and the City of San Juan Capistrano "in recognition of the great success of the First Annual Oaks Classic"

ABOVE LEFT: Big tent at The Oaks Classic Grand Prix
ABOVE RIGHT AND RIGHT: Guests seated around the Grand Prix field

Susie Hutchison on Livius winner of the 1987 $50,000 Oaks Classic Grand Prix receives award from Joan Irvine Smith with Atahlie Irvine Clarke, Jim and Deborah Swinden Carol Penniman with Elizabeth, Alletta Cooper with Little Alletta and Nathalie, Morton Smith and Bill Cooper.

Martin Cohen managed The Oaks Classic for the next four years, and it continued to benefit the UCI College of Medicine. In 1987, we added the House of Hermès $10,000 Acorn Junior/Amateur Grand Prix and the Thoroughbred Spread Barbecue, which was held in The Oak Grove the night before the event. The following year, we added the $10,000 Dash for Cash speed class and presented the first perpetual Mayor's Trophy for the City of San Juan Capistrano. Susan Hutchison won the 1987, 1988, 1989 and 1990 $50,000 Grand Prix on Livius and Samsung Woodstock.

FROM LEFT: Athalie Irvine Clarke, Joan Irvine Smith and Mr. and Mrs. Jean-Louis Dumas in front of the House of Hermes tent, photo by Tish Quirk

LEFT, FROM LEFT: Jenna Mikas on Crusader winner of the $10,000 House of Hermes Acorn Junior/Amateur Grand Prix, Patrick Guerrand, Jean-Louis Dumas, Joan Irvine Smith and a Hermes Representative, photo by Tish Quirk
RIGHT, FROM LEFT: Patrick Guerrand, Francine Bardo, Athalie Irvine Clarke, Joan Irvine Smith and Cappy Smith in front of the House of Hermes tent, photo by Tish Quirk

LEFT: Luncheon guests under the big tent watch Susie Hutchison and Livius clear a fence in The Oaks Classic Grand Prix, photo by Tish Quirk
RIGHT:Alain Vaillancourt on Hermes in The Oaks Classic Grand Prix, photo by Tish Quirk

Susie Hutchison on Livius winner of the 1998 $50,000 Oaks Classic Grand Prix receives winning trophy from Joan Irvine Smith and Athalie Irvine Clarke with Morton Smith, Jim Swinden, Carol and Russ Penniman, Anita Ziebe and Alletta and Bill Cooper, photo by Tish Quirk

FROM LEFT: Chrysler Fisher, Cynthia Edmondson, winner of the $ 10,000 House of Hermes Acorn Junoir/Amateur Grand Prix, Zas Zsa Gabor, Joan Irvine Smith, Laurent Mommeja, photo by Tish Quirk

The $10,000 Dash For Cash winner Jennifer Newell on Gleason receives the Mayor's Trophy from San Juan Capistrano Councilman Bill Jones, Joan Irvine Smith, and Mayor Gary L. Hausdorfer, photo by Tish Quirk

Alan Balch center with Mr. and Mrs. Montgomery Fisher, photo by Tish Quirk

Morton W. "Cappy" Smith, photo by Tish Quirk

Athalie Irvine Clarke, Joan Irvine Smith with trophy, photo by Tish Quirk

Alain Vaillancourt on Kontiki in the Grand Prix, photo by Tish Quirk

Alain on Hermes in the Grand Prix, photo by Tish Quirk

139

THE 1989
OAKS CLASSIC,
CONTINUED ON
NEXT PAGE

Dr. Walter Henry,
Dean of the UCI
College of
Medicine, with his
wife, Maria del
Carmen Calvo, and
Athalie Irvine
Clarke at the 1989
Oaks Classic, photo
by Tish Quirk

My mother always organized the seating arrangements for The Oaks Classic Grand Prix Luncheon. She would spend hours with my cousin Anita Ziebe working out the diagram that placed our more than 1,500 complimentary and paying guests at the round tables under the big white tent or at the umbrella tables around the ring. In addition, she would insist on having handwritten place cards at each of the brightly colored tables. Rococo catered both the Grand Prix Luncheon on Sunday and the Thoroughbred Spread Barbecue in the oak grove the night before. Hermès never failed to have an elegant booth with its beautiful scarves, purses, belts, ties and riding tack and accessories. Over the years, in addition to Hermès, we had various sponsors, including Budweiser, Mercedes-Benz, Land Rover, Tiffany & Co., Rolex and Jaguar, to name only a few.

Guests under the big tent and around the field at the Grand Prix luncheon

Joan Irvine Smith and Athalie Irvine Clarke, photo by Tish Quirk

Guests under the big tent at The Oaks Grand Prix luncheon, photo by Tish Quirk

FROM LEFT: Dr. Howard House, Mrs. Clarke, Morton I. Smith, Albert and Regina Grassellie and Cappy Smith and Joan Irvine Smith at Saturday luncheon with Mayor's Trophy, photo by Tish Quirk

Guests visiting the House of Hermes tent, photo by Tish Quirk

Susan Hutchison and Samsung Woodstock winner of the 1989 $50,000 Oaks Classic Grand Prix receives trophy from Joan Irvine Smith, accompanied by Morton Smith, Alletta and Bill Cooper, Carol and Russ Penniman, Jim Swinden, Athalie Irvine Clarke, and Anita Ziebe, photo by Tish Quirk

Claudia O'Farrell on Tanagra winner of the $10,000 House of Hermes Acorn Junior/Amateur Grand Prix with Joan Irvine Smith, Francine Bardo and Chrysler Fisher, photo by Tish Quirk

Dash for Cash winner Bernie Traurig on Maybe the One receives the Mayor's Trophy from San Juan Capistrano Mayor Gary L. Hausdorfer and Joan Irvine Smith, photo by Tish Quirk

Seafood bar catered by Rococo, photo by Tish Quirk

Sunflowers by Maria del Carmen Calvo, Private Collection

FROM LEFT: Susan Hutchison winner of the 1990 $50,000 Oaks Classic Grand Prix on Samsung Woodstock, Jimmy Williams, Joan Irvine Smith, Morton Smith, Carol and Russell Penniman, Anita Ziebe, Madeline and Jim Swinden, and Frances and John Rae, photo by Tish Quirk

Susie Hutchison on Samsung Woodstock winner of the Oaks Classic Grand Prix, photo by Tish Quirk

Joan Irvine Smith, Course Designer Linda Allen, Cappy Smith, and Regina Grassellie, photo by Tish Quirk

Lauren Hough on Carone winner of the $10,000 House of Hermes Acorn Junior/Amateur Grand Prix with Joan Irvine Smith, Francine Bardo and Chrysler Fisher, photo by Tish Quirk

Alain Vaillancourt on Hermes in the Grand Prix, photo by Tish Quirk

Center, Event Coordinator Morton W. "Cappy" Smith with other horse show officials including course designer Linda Allen and show manager Martin Cohen, far right, photo by Tish Quirk

Joan Irvine Smith, Jim Swinden, Russ Penniman, and Morton Smith, Trish Quirk photo

Mrs. Conrad Hilton, Mrs. David Bricker, Hal Roach, and Mrs. Charles Howard, photo by Tish Quirk

In the early 1960s, the German Holsteiner breeders adopted the policy of using Thoroughbred, Anglo-Arab and Selle Français stallions to establish their riding and sport horse model. The stallions used were Anblick, Cottage Son, Frivol, Manometer, Marlon and Ladykiller. Three other sires used were Ramses, an Anglo-Arab, and Cor de la Bryère and Silbersee, both Selle Français. Already a devoted and long-time breeder of Thoroughbreds, my interest was now sparked by the Holsteiners, which were being bred to look like Thoroughbreds and to have similar qualities.

In 1989, I began buying well-bred Holsteiner geldings, stallions and mares here in the United States through Arsia Ardalan of Caspian Farms. When these horses consistently performed well in competition, I had Arsia find young stallions and mares of the same bloodlines abroad and import them. The Oaks' Grand Prix winners and Grand Prix–placed horses have included: South Pacific, Alitalia, Contender, Reveur, Marco, Luganda, Atlas, Challenger, Balderdash, Rofino, Ocean I, Landstorm, Orlando, Cheer, Sydney, Stand Alone, Surprise and Carolus Magnus. Jumper champions have included, among others: Lybelle, Canaletto, Cobbler, Witch Broome Wizard, Chaka Kahn, Casanova, Lapaloupe, Ocean II, Esmerelda, Batik, Royal Ballet, Lennox, Casper and Lonford. Hunter champions have included: Land Baron, Chamois, Silver Sea, Coco, Amerens, Let's Dance and Chanel.

Arsia Ardalan on Alitalia by Argentinus out of Gesa by Godehard winner of the $50,000 Pulsar International Challenge at the North American Horse Show at Spruce Meadows in 1994

Alain Vaillancourt on Landstorm in a Grand Prix at Indio, photo by Tish Quirk

Alain Vaillancourt on Lybelle by Lord out of Heitere by Benedictus winner of two speed classes at the World Cup in Del Mar, California in 1992, photo by Tish Quirk

Alain Vaillancourt on Rofino in a Grand Prix at The Oaks, photo by Tish Quirk

Alain Vaillancourt on Orlando placed second in a Grand Prix at Flintridge, photo by Tish Quirk

Alain Vaillancourt on Balderdash in the Queen's Cup at Spruce Meadows, Canada, placed 3rd in the EMO Agency, Inc. 1994 PCHA Grand Prix Horse of the Year Standings.

Alain on Contender the American Holsteiner Horse Association's NGL Award Winner for 1994 and the EMO Agency, Inc. PCHA Grand Prix Horse of the Year

Alain on Grand Prix placed Surprise by South Pacific out of a Fasolt daughter, photo by Jumpshot

Kerry Bernay on Jumper Champion Sydney by South Pacific out of a Fasolt daughter, photo by Jumpshot

Lauren Dendiu on Hunter Champion Let's Dance, photo by Tish Quirk

Leslie Vaillancourt on Hunter and Jumper Champion Amerens by Nimmerdor

Arsia Ardalan on South Pacific, 5th in the 1987 Oaks Classic Grand Prix

Alain Vaillancourt on South Pacific placed 6th in the $100,000 Grand Prix of the Desert at Indio in 1993

The great International Grand Prix winner and sire, South Pacific by Silvester out of Kamera by Cor de la Bryère, was born in West Germany on February 27, 1982; he combined the two legendary Grand Prix jumping bloodlines of Silbersee and Cor de la Bryère.

His breeder, Peter H. Johannsen, sold South Pacific as a two year old to Emil Jung, who brought him to his farm Locksley in Millwood, Virginia, in 1984. That year South Pacific was the Champion Stallion of the North American Holsteiner Breeding Program and the only stallion ever to have received a score of 10 for his type from the American Association of Breeders of Holsteiner Horses, Inc.

South Pacific began his breeding career in 1985. Two years later he was purchased by Arsia Ardalan of Caspian Stables for Ian Abrams, as an investment. The first time I saw the beautiful seal brown stallion was when he placed fifth in The Oaks Classic Grand Prix in 1987 as a five year old. I later purchased South Pacific and brought him to The Oaks in San Juan Capistrano in 1990.

In 1993 South Pacific placed in eight major Grand Prix jumping competitions, including second in the $50,000 Oaks Fall Classic Grand Prix and the $40,000 Samsung Grand Prix at the Flintridge Amateur Horse Show, and sixth in the $100,000 Grand Prix of the Desert at Indio, California.

South Pacific won the $20,000 ESSO Grand Prix at Spruce Meadows in 1994 and placed in sixteen other national and international jumping competitions, including fifth in the $100,000 Grand Prix of Indio that year. He ranked seventh in the EMO Agency, Inc. 1994 Grand Prix Horse of the Year standings.

In 1995 South Pacific placed in six Grand Prix during the Desert Circuit Series at Indio, and in 1996 placed fifth in the $50,000 Oaks Classic Grand Prix, shortly before he was retired to stud.

South Pacific's sons and daughters have won and consistently placed in all levels of jumper competition, the Hunter divisions, and the International Jumper Futurity.

Alain and South Pacific won the $20,000 ESSO Grand Prix at Spruce Meadows and placed in sixteen other national and international jumping competitions, including fifth in the $100,000 Grand Prix of Indio in 1994

The great International Grand Prix winner and sire South Pacific by Sylvester out of Kamera by Cor de la Bryere at The Oaks in 1993
photo by Joan Irvine Smith

South Pacific with Alain Vaillancourt placed 2nd in the 1993 $50,000 Oaks Fall Classic Grand Prix. FROM LEFT: Joan Irvine Smith, Morton Smith, Francis and John Rae, Carol Penniman, Anita Ziebe, Rex Penniman, Jim Swinden, Russ Penniman, Elizabeth Penniman, and Alletta Cooper with Little Alletta, Willem, and Nathalie Cooper, and horn blower J. Vincent Wholey, photo by Tish Quirk

South Pacific, by Silvester out of Kamera by Cor de la Bryére, photo by Jumpshot

Today I stand my world-class Holsteiner stallions at The Oaks Indian Hill Ranch in Valley Center, California. I also maintain a frozen semen bank from my stallions, including The Oaks' flagship stallion South Pacific, who died on April 15, 1998. My stallions currently available for breeding include the following:

*South Pacific, by Silvester out of Kamera by Cor de la Bryère—Private Treaty
*Cheer, by Caletto I out of Hetaere by Sable Skinflint
*Challenger, by Cor de la Bryère out of Paria by Leander
*Canaletto, by Caletto II out of Sedan by Lord
 Champagne, by Chin-Chin out of Autholocity by Authenticity
 Ocean I, by South Pacific out of René by Ramses
*Lennox, by Landgraf I out of Rike by Calypso II
*Luganda, by Labrador out of Wiga by Caletto II
*Solomon, by Silvester out of Optik by Ladykiller
 Fahrenheit, by Fargo out of J-Conga by Condus
*Southern Showtime, by South Pacific out of Amerens by Nimmerdor
*Southern Crown, by South Pacific out of E'Coronada by Corrado
(*American Holsteiner Horse Association–approved stallions)

Cheer, by Caletto I out of Hetaere by Sable Skinflint

Challenger, by Cor de la Bryére out of Paria by Leander

Canaletto, by Caletto II out of Sedan by Lord

Champagne, by Chin-Chin out of Autholocity by Authenticity

Solomon, by Silvester out of Optik by Ladykiller, photo by Jumpshot

Ocean I, by South Pacific out of René by Ramzes, photo by Jumpshot

Fahrenheit, by Fargo out of J-Conga by Condus, photo by Jumpshot

Lennox, by Landgraf I out of Rike by Calypso II

Southern Showtime, by South Pacific out of Amerens by Nimmerdor

Luganda, by Labrador out of Wiga by Caletto II, photo by Jumpshot

Southern Crown, by South Pacific out of E'Coronada by Corrado

In both Virginia and California, I currently have more than three hundred Warmblood and Thoroughbred brood mares and young horses by these stallions, some of which are hunters and jumpers, and hunter and jumper prospects in training at The Oaks. I personally supervise all levels of The Oaks' breeding and training programs.

The Oaks' breeding program is considered ideal. Not only does it produce exceptional Holsteiner foals, but it also combines the stature, temperament and athletic ability of some of the top jumping bloodlines from Europe with the elegance, heart and stamina of the American Thoroughbred, which Cappy Smith believed produced the perfect combination of size, mind and muscle in a horse.

As with most modern breeding operations, the stallions' semen is fresh-cooled or frozen and then delivered to mares for artificial insemination in the United States, Canada and Mexico. This prevents infections and injuries during breeding and enables each stallion to inseminate many more mares. It also allows the stallion to continue competing and carry on its regular life. Much newer and more unusual is The Oaks' move toward the use of surrogate mares and implanted embryos. My son Russell Penniman has assisted me in many aspects of The Oaks' breeding operation.

Jumper Champion Superman, by South Pacific out of the Hanoverian mare Alitalia by Argentinus out of Gesa by Godehard, was produced by having both frozen semen and a frozen embryo implanted in a surrogate mare

The Oaks Indian Hill Ranch, Valley Center, California

The jumper champion Superman, by South Pacific out of the Hanoverian mare Alitalia by Argentinus out of Gesa by Godehard, was produced by having both frozen semen and a frozen embryo implanted in a surrogate mare. According to Dr. Matthews of Matthews Equine Services of Valley Center, who performed the procedure, this was the first time this had ever been accomplished in equine fertilization technology. As The Oaks is on the cutting edge of this technology for horses, at Russell's suggestion, representatives from the San Diego Zoo came for a fact-finding tour of The Oaks Indian Hill Ranch, where this process takes place. The Joan Irvine Smith & Athalie R. Clarke Foundation supports the Zoo's program on the reproduction of endangered species, including California condors and native plants.

ABOVE: California Condor, © Anthony Mercieca
BELOW: Coastal Sage Scrub, © Moose Peterson

150

Alexey Steele, *In the Shadow of an Old Oak*, Private Collection

Alexey Steele, *Misty Morning* , Private Collection

Alexey Steele, *On the Ranch—Oaks*, Private Collection

In October 1996, I leased 60 acres of land from Rancho Mission Viejo on the northwest corner of Ortega Highway and La Pata Avenue, in order to have pastures for my yearlings and two and three year olds. As the Antonio Parkway bridge had not yet been built across San Juan Creek, there was a magnificent view from the property all the way to the Santa Ana Mountains to the east.

ABOVE: : 60 acres of land on the northwest corner of Ortega Highway and La Pata Avenue leased by The Oaks from Rancho Mission Viejo for horse pastures in 1996, photo by Charlie Adermatt

Horse Pastures, photo by Charles Adermatt

I put in a water system, roads, and five-foot pipe fencing, and seeded the paddocks with pasture grass. It was a tranquil idyllic spot nestled in the surrounding hills, and I would go there in the late afternoons, not only to see my horses but also to watch for the various wild animals that frequently appeared.

Joan Irvine Smith and young horses, photo by Terry Gleason

FROM LEFT: Loretta, La Bamba and Love Boat, photo by Terry Gleason

153

Doe and fawn

Coyotes

Bobcat

Wildlife photographs © Richard Jackson

A badger that lived in the field had to relocate his hole when we began disking the land. A bobcat had her den in a bank on the west end of the property and raised cubs there each year, while a golden eagle had her nest in a majestic eucalyptus tree next to the entry road. A pair of coyotes, which had cubs in a nearby den, would go there to hunt for the rodents that thrived in the new pastures. Many birds, including hawks, herons, egrets and other species, also went there to hunt for food. A covey of quail often scurried along the road beside the creek, and deer occasionally grazed on the grass between the sage scrub and willows that grew there. Ducks and other waterfowl went to the creek to feed on frogs and other amphibians. On several occasions, I even saw mountain lion tracks on the property.

Badger

Coyote pup

Bobcat cub

California quail, photo by Joan Irvine Smith

Mallard ducks, photo by Joan Irvine Smith

Least Bell's Vireo nesting, © Anthony Mercieca

Pacific tree frog, © Richard Jackson

Great Blue herons, © John Modesso, Jr.

Golden eagle, © Terry Spivey

Mountain lion track, © Richard Jackson

Susan Hutchison on Samoan Chief by South Pacific out of the Hanoverian mare Alitalia, by Argentinus, was the National PHR Sliver Stirrup Champion Six-Year-Old Jumper, Reserve Champion in the West Coast Young Jumper Championship for Six-Year-Olds and received first place IJF Western prize money in 2003. Samoan Chief received second place IJF Five-Year-Old Western prize money in 2002, photo by Jumpshot

Susie on Sail Away by South Pacific out of Helium, by The Scriber, A TB, was the National PHR Sliver Stirrup Reserve Champion Six-Year-Old Jumper and received fourth place IJF Western prize money in 2003. He won first place IJF Five-Year-Old Western prize money in 2002, photo by Jumpshot

In the early 1990s, I supported Alan Balch in his efforts to have the Jockey Club recognize both Thoroughbred and half-Thoroughbred sport horses in its registry. Today, the Jockey Club's Performance Horse Registry (PHR) not only recognizes Thoroughbred and half-Thoroughbred, but Warmblood sport horses as well.

In 2004, I received the U.S. Equestrian Federation–PHR Silver Stirrup Leading Hunter Breeder Award for 2003. I also won the Leading Breeder Award for 2002, and was the Leading Jumper Breeder and runner-up in the Hunter Breeding category in 2001 and 2002. The Oaks' stallions and The Oaks' breeding program are producing young horses of outstanding quality, exceptional jumping ability and excellent temperament. These horses have won and consistently placed in competitions of the U.S. Equestrian Federation, the Performance Horse Registry, the International Jumper Futurity, the Pacific Coast Horse Show Association, the American Holsteiner Horse Association and others. The horses include, among others: South Shore, LuLu Belle, Samoan Chief, Sail Away, Superman, El Campeon's Shamrock, Cherokee Chief, Challenger's Pride, Southern Showtime, Ocean Flyer, Captain Courageous, Cheer's Challenge, Offshore, Shaman, South Bay, South Beach, Tasman Bay, Saveur de Cour, Southern Breeze, Cantina, Falcon, Moscow Ballet, Cheer's Playboy, Miniver, Southern Lights, Sea Spray, Chase, Cimarron, Cheer Me On, Crimson Cheer, Can't Touch This, Cheer's Jubilee, Kenda, Night Light, Mikasa, Macarena, Castle Rock, Chieftain, Lady Bug, Johanna, Gabreal, Irish Cheer, Solomon's Wisdom, Good & Plenty, Ondine, Oahu, Neona, Pashmina, Polynesia, Romantic Affair and Reef Point.

Susie on Ocean Flyer by Ocean I out of the French Thoroughbred mare Sleeping by Lightning was the Best Type and Most Grand Prix Potential Champion and Reserve Best Performance Champion in the IJF Western Regionals for Four-Year-Olds in 2003, photo by Tish Quirk

Tanya Levorchick on Solomon's Pride by Solomon out of Cessy J by Caletto I was the Most Grand Prix Potential, Best Type and Best Performance Champion in the IJF Western Regionals for Four-Year-Olds, with Jorge Gonzalez and Joan Irvine Smith, photo by Jumpshot

Susan Hutchison on Jumper Champion LuLu Belle by South Pacific out of Lybelle by Lord, photo by Jumpshot

Tanya Levorchick on Jumper Champion Cherokee Chief by Challenger out of Canada Girl, photo by Jumpshot

Tanya on Captain Courageous by Challenger out of E' Lovely Girl by Lombard, was the Best Performance Champion in the IJF Western Regionals for Four-Year-Olds in 2003, photo by Jumpshot

Tanya on Cheer's Challenge by Cheer out of Batik by Challenger was the Reserve Best Type Champion in the IJF Western Regionals for Four-Year-Olds in 2003, photo by Jumpshot

Tanya on Hunter Champion Night Light by Canaletto out of the Thoroughbred mare Crystal Garnett, photo by Jumpshot

Tanya on Challenger's Pride by Challenger out of E' Lovely Girl by Lombard was the IJF Western Regional Four-Year-Old Most Grand Prix Potential and Best Type Champion in 2002, photo by Jumpshot

Susie on Jumper Champion Falcon by Farenheit out of Soraya by South Pacific, photo by Jumpshot

Tanya on Offshore by Ocean I out of Ikon by Cheer was Reserve Champion Best Performance in the IJF Western Regionals for Four-Year-Olds in 2004, photo by Jumpshot

Patricia Okura on Hunter Champion Kenda by Cheer out of Brillance by Largo, photo by Jumpshot

Hunter and Jumper Champion Castle Rock by Challenger the Thoroughbred mare Me & Melissa, 1996 AHSA National Champion in Three Year Old Hunter Breeding.

Tanya Levorchick on Hunter Champion Cheer's Jubilee by Cheer out of the Thoroughbred mare My Silver Girl, photo by Tish Quirk

Tanya on Hunter Champion Macarena by Cheer out of the Thoroughbred mare Only one Conniver, photo by Jumpshot

According to world-renowned horseman and teacher George H. Morris, co-Chef d'Equipe of the U.S. Olympic Team, "The Oaks is leading the American show horse world toward solving one of its biggest problems, and that is coming up with an American sport horse capable of meeting the Europeans head on. For years, Americans have gone to Europe to try to buy quality horses, only to wind up with leftovers or inferiors that the Europeans try to slough off on them. As a result, Americans wind up competing well with Americans in this country but fall short in international competition. Europeans over centuries have established some superior bloodlines, but they jealously guard them to preserve their own dominance in equestrian sports. The problem has always been how to tap into those bloodlines. This is exactly what The Oaks has done."

Emily Trowbridge on Hunter Champion Ingrid by Cheer out of the Thoroughbred mare Norma Jean P., photo by Jumpshot

Tanya on Hunter Champion Can't Touch This by Cheer out of the Thoroughbred mare White Gloves, photo by Flying Horse Photography

Patricia on Hunter Champion Mikasa by Lennox out of the Thoroughbred mare Favorite Daughter, photo by Jumpshot

Elizabeth Penniman competing in 2005 on the 1997 IJF Four-Year-Old Reserve Champion Southern Breeze by South Pacific

The Oaks 1995 Premiere Sporthorse Auction

Bidders under the tent

A horse being shown under the tent

The Oaks held its first Premiere Sport Horse Auction with Eurosport Auctions of Culpepper, Virginia, at The Oaks in San Juan Capistrano on August 20, 1995. A large crowd gathered to view and bid on an outstanding group of hunters, jumpers and hunter and jumper prospects, many of which were Oaks' homebreds by Holsteiner stallions out of Thoroughbred and Warmblood mares. Also offered was a select group of horses from other prestigious consignors.

Topping the sale was The Oaks Jumper Champion Lapaloupe, an own son of Landgraf I out of a Lamour daughter. This nine-year-old gelding had an outstanding show record as a Junior Jumper in both Germany and the United States. He reached a bid of $72,000, selling to Tami Semler of Malibu, California.

National Amateur/Owner Hunter Champion Full Cry, a Thoroughbred gelding by Ayes Turn, was purchased from The Oaks by Mimi Edwards of New Hope, Pennsylvania, for $50,000. Ron Roth of North Oaks, Minnesota, purchased Jumper Champion Cheerio by Cheer in 1995, and then Hunter Champions Sebastian by South Pacific and Chandelle by Champagne in 1996.

The Oaks sale offering in 1995 reached an overall average of $23,000. The consignor horses' average was $20,366. The overall average of horses sold was $22,725.

Mimi Edwards of New Hope, Pennsylvania on National Amateur/Owner Hunter Champion Full Cry, photo by Pennington Galleries

Hunter Champion Sebastian by South Pacific out of the Thoroughbred mare Only One Conniver

Tami Semler of Malibu, California, on Jumper Champion Lapaloupe by Landgraf I

Lannie Deboer of North Oaks, Minnesota, on Jumper Champion Cheerio by Cheer out of Rohagani by Marlon

Francie Steinwedell-Carvin and Holsteiner Jumper Champion Atlas by Antaras, winners of the $50,000 Grand Prix of Tampa in 1997, photo by James Leslie Parker

Hunter Champion Sea Spray by South Pacific out of Daisy II by Prinz Gaylord

Hunter Champion Chaka Khan by Cor de la Bryere, photo by Jumpshot

Hunter Champion Solomon's Wisdom by Solomon out of the Thoroughbred mare Jan

Jumper Champion Atlas, a Holsteiner gelding by Antares out of a Marlon daughter, was purchased from The Oaks by Arsia Ardalan for $86,000 at The Oaks Premiere Sport Horse Auction in 1996. Atlas was later purchased by Francie Steinwedell-Carvin and won the $50,000 Grand Prix of Tampa in 1997. In 1996, R. J. Brandes of Newport Beach purchased International Jumper Futurity Champion and Grand Prix–placed Orlando from The Oaks for $60,000.

The Hunter Champion Sea Spray, an Oaks homebred gelding by South Pacific out of the Oldenburg mare Daisy II by Prinz Gaylord, sold as a two-year-old for $43,000 to McKenna BMW, Huntington Beach, California, at The Oaks Third Annual Premiere Sport Horse Auction in August 1997.

Chaka Khan, an eight-year-old Oaks Holsteiner stallion by Cor de la Bryère out of a Ramiro granddaughter, topped the auction when he was sold to former pro football player Joe Montana and his wife, Jennifer, for $75,000. The Montanas later purchased Grand Prix–placed Landstorm and Hunter Champion Chamois by Champagne from The Oaks. That same year, Mr. and Mrs. Joseph Schieszler of Illinois, purchased two-year-old Hunter Breeding Champion Solomon's Wisdom, an Oaks homebred gelding by Solomon out of a Thoroughbred mare.

The Oaks Fourth Annual Premiere Sport Horse Auction, held August 15, 1998, in San Juan Capistrano, California, hosted leading sport horse enthusiasts from the United States, Mexico and Canada, and broke auction sales records. Thirty-one horses were sold, grossing $800,000 to average $25,806, establishing a Eurosport Auctions record. Many of the buyers that year were return customers who had purchased Oaks' horses at the prior auctions.

The success of the sale was due primarily to The Oaks' high quality imported Holsteiner horses and home breds from our nationally acclaimed breeding program, which is producing young horses of outstanding quality, exceptional jumping ability and excellent temperament that have won and consistently placed in Hunter and Jumper competitions.

Kerry Bernay on Contender by Caletto II out of a Mentor daughter, the American Holsteiner Horse Association's NGL Award Winner for 1994 and the EMO Agency, Inc. PCHA Grand Prix Horse of the Year, photo by Jumpshot

Lauren Dendiu on Hunter Champion Land Baron by Landlord, photo by Jumpshot

Alain Vaillancourt on Jumper Champion Cobbler at Spruce Meadows, Canada

Saltador by South Pacific out of Alitalia by Gesa

Jumper Champion Superman by South Pacific out of Alitalia

The Oaks' Grand Prix Winner Contender, a thirteen-year-old Holsteiner gelding by Caletto II out of a Mentor daughter, the American Holsteiner Horse Association's NGL Award Winner for 1994 and the EMO Agency, Inc. PCHA Grand Prix Horse of the Year, topped the sale in 1998 when he sold for $110,000 to Richard Mulhall of Bradbury, California. Close behind at $97,000 was Hunter Champion Land Baron, a nine-year-old Holsteiner gelding by Landlord out of a Montevideo daughter, when he was sold by The Oaks to Alletta Cooper of Newport, Rhode Island. She later purchased The Oaks Holsteiner Jumper Champion Ocean II, a full brother to Grand Prix–placed Ocean I, by South Pacific out of Rene by Ramses for $20,000, and Jim and Jill Mooney purchased Jumper Champion Cobbler for $20,000.

Oaks homebred Saltador, by South Pacific out of the Hanoverian mare Alitalia, was the highest-selling two year old in the history of Eurosport Auctions when he was sold by The Oaks for $50,000 to Mr. and Mrs. Joseph Schieszler. Ocean Pacific II, a three-year-old Holsteiner gelding by Ocean I out of a Landgraf I daughter, was sold by The Oaks for $17,000 to Ron Roth of North Oaks, Minnesota.

The Oaks' Jumper Champion Superman, a colt by South Pacific out of Alitalia, shattered the record for the highest-selling four year old in the history of Eurosport Auctions when he sold for $80,000 at The Oaks Fifth Annual Premiere Sport Horse Auction in 1999. He was purchased by Richard Mulhall of The Thoroughbred Corporation.

Sea Star by South Pacific out of T' Romana by Rodrigo

Arielle Raveling on Jumper Champion Shamu by South Pacific out of Amerens by Nimmerdor, photo by Lili

Sea Star, a two year old Holsteiner Oaks homebred colt by South Pacific out of T'Romana by Rodrigo, was purchased for $25,000 by Pat Raveling, now of Perrieta Farms, Reddick, Florida. Ms. Raveling later purchased Amateur/Owner Jumper Champion Shamu by South Pacific out of Amerens by Nimmerdor from The Oaks as a three year old. The Amateur/Owner Hunter Champion Southern Lights, a full brother to Sea Star, was sold by The Oaks as a two year old colt to Joie Gatlin Show Stables for $16,000 at the auction in1999.

That same year Hunter and Jumper Champion Challenge Me a two year old Holsteiner gelding by Jumper Champion Challenger out of Jumper Champion Lybelle by Lord was sold at the auction to Lauren Vogel for $15,000. Miss Vogel later purchased Hunter and Jumper Champion Chances Are (Cornelius), a five year old Holsteiner gelding by Challenger out of Holly Golightly by Lugar, an own son of Lord, and Jill Humphrey purchased Hunter Champion Big John. The Oaks also sold Jumper Champion Lullaby, a three year old Holsteiner filly by Ocean II out of a Chin-Chin grand daughter to Holly Dietz, Horses Unlimited, Albuquerque, New Mexico and Jumper Champion Lady Bug, a three year old Holsteiner filly by Jumper Champion Solomon out of a Chin-Chin daughter to Southern Nevada Racing, Las Vegas, Nevada at the auction in1999.

That same year, Jumper Champion Can We Dance by Jumper Champion Canaletto out of a South Pacific daughter was sold by The Oaks as a two-year-old colt to Mr. and Mrs. Blair Cudmore of Omaha, Nebraska. The following year, Jumper Champion Southern Pride by South Pacific out of a Caretino mare was purchased from The Oaks by Arsia Ardalan as a two-year-old colt and sold to Mr. and Mrs. Cudmore.

Hunter Champion Chase by Challenger was sold as a two year old by The Oaks to Dan Tsujioka for $30,000 at The Oaks Premiere Sport Horse Auction held in July 2000. Also sold were a group of hunter and jumper prospects, many of which were Oaks homebreds by Holsteiner stallions out of Thoroughbred and Warmblood mares, as well as a select group of horses from other prestigious consignors.

Hunter Champion Southern Lights by South Pacific out of T' Romana by Rodrigo

Lauren Vogel on Hunter and Jumper Champion Challenge Me by Challenger out of Lybelle by Lord, photo by Jumpshot

Lauren Dendiu on Hunter Champion Big John, photo by Jumpshot

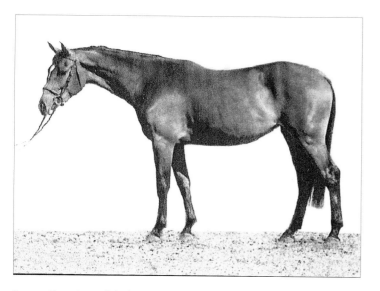

Jumper Champion Lullaby by Ocean II out of Caroline by Champagne

Carly Ow-Wing on Hunter and Jumper Champion Chase by Challenger out of the Thoroughbred mare Chalk Mark, photo by Flying Horse Photography

Jumper Champion Can We Dance by Canaletto out of Hula Dancer by South Pacific

Kathy Lombardo on Jumper Champion Latigo II by Luganda out of Capri by Caligula, photo by Jumpshot

Grand Prix winner Southern Pride by South Pacific out of Coco by Caretino

Lauren Wenz on Jumper Champion La Port au Prince by Luganda out of Greta by Churchill

Will Simpson on International Grand Prix Winner Shamrock by South Pacific out of Carmel by Errigal Flight, photo by Jumpshot

Jumper Champion Shamrock, a colt by South Pacific out of an Errigal Flight daughter, was sold by The Oaks as a two year old to El Campeon Farms following The Oaks Premier Sporthorse Auction held in August 2001. The Oaks continues to hold its Sport Horse Auctions yearly at either The Oaks in San Juan Capistrano or The Oaks Indian Hill Ranch in Valley Center, California.

In 2002, 2003 and 2004, The Oaks held their auctions at The Oaks Indian Hill Ranch and Blenheim Farms adjacent to The Oaks in San Juan Capistrano. They featured a number of homebred hunter and jumper prospects by The Oaks Hosteiner stallions out of our Thoroughbred and Warmblood mares, as well as a select group of horses from prestigious consignors.

The most recent Oaks Premiere Sport Horse Auction and Inventory Reduction Sale was held on August 13, 2005 at Blenheim Farms. The Oaks homebred filly, Solomon's Treasure, a three year old by Solomon out of I'Loreal by Lennox, an own son of Landgraf I, out of a Thoroughbred mare, topped the sale at $37,500. She was purchased by Adel Melson of Irons Lane Farms, Dagsboro, Delaware. Other Oaks homebreds purchased by Mrs. Melson were Fair and Plenty, a two year old Holsteiner gelding by Farenheit out of Good and Plenty by South Pacific, for $20,000; Lennoko, a two year old Holsteiner gelding by Lennox out of Kona by Cheer, for $20,000; Ocean Cheer, a two year old Holsteiner gelding by Ocean I out of Fontana by Cheer, for $30,000; Shining Star, a three year old Holsteiner filly by Champagne out of L'Etoile by Cheer, for $20,000; and Lumiro, a three year old Holsteiner gelding by Luganda out of Bonita by Merano, for $30,000.

Jennie Martin on Jumper Champion On The Town, by Castle Rock out of the Thoroughbred mare White Gloves, photo by Ed Moore

Solomon's Treasure by Solomon out of I'Loreal by Lennox

Oaks homebred Life of the Party, a four year old Holsteiner gelding by Luganda out of Irish Cheer by Cheer, was sold to Monique Redmond of Scottsdale, Arizona for $24,000 and another Oaks homebred Star Gazer, a two year old Holsteiner gelding by Southern Crown out of Black Cat by Gibramino, was sold to Lisa Miles of Hidden Hills, California for $10,000.

Shining Star by Champagne out of L'Etoile by Cheer

Fair & Plenty by Farenheit out of Good & Plenty by South Pacific

Lumiro by Luganda out of Bonita by Merano

Lennoko by Lennox out of Kona by Cheer

Life of the Party by Luganda out of Irish Cheer by Cheer

Ocean Cheer by Ocean I out of Fontana by Cheer

Star Gazer by Southern Crown, an own son of South Pacific, out of Black Cat by Gibramino

1987 UCI Medal recipients: Athalie Richardson Irvine Clarke(Lower Left), Frederick Reines (Upper Left), Arnold Beckman (Upper Right), photograph, Courtesy of UCI

Joan Irvine Smith speaking at the UCI 25th anniversary celebration in1990, photograph, Courtesy of UCI

1990 UCI Medal recipients Jean (Mrs. Daniel) Aldrich, Ed Carter, Joan Irvine Smith, Governor Edmund G. Brown and Clark Kerr, photograph, Courtesy of UCI

UC President Clark Kerr, Joan Irvine Smith and Governor Edmund G. Brown each received a UCI Founders Medal in 1990, photograph, Courtesy of UCI

IN 1991, AFTER MY MOTHER AND I resolved our litigation with Donald Bren over the evaluation of our stockholding in The Irvine Company, we created the Joan Irvine Smith & Athalie R. Clarke Foundation. She and I were staunch supporters of the University of California at Irvine (UCI), even before the dedication of land for its campus. In 1987, my mother had received the UCI Medal, the university's honorary degree and its highest award, from Chancellor Jack Peltason. I received my medal in 1990, on the occasion of the twenty-fifth anniversary of UCI's founding. Identifying me as a "Founder Recipient," the award recognizes the key role that I played, and continue to play, in the development of the campus.

Our foundation provided the primary grant for the acquisition of the first building in the new Center of Health Sciences.

Athalie Irvine Clarke and Joan Irvine Smith, a 1990 UCI Founders Medal recipient, photograph, Courtesy of UCI

University of California, Irvine, 1990, photograph, Courtesy of UCI

Irvine Hall, the first building in the new Center for Health Sciences, photograph, Courtesy of UCI

LEFT TO RIGHT: Louise Turner Arnold, Mary Roosevelt, Suzie Peltason, Jean Aldrich and former UCI Chancellor Jack Peltason, Medal Dinner 1993, photograph, Courtesy of UCI

ABOVE: Joan Irvine Smith, Donald Bren and Arnold Beckman, UCI Trustees Emeriti, Medal Dinner 1999, photo by Yana Bridle
FAR LEFT: UCI Chancellor Ralph Cicerone and Joan Irvine Smith, Medal Dinner2000, photo by Laurel Hungerford
RIGHT: Joanne and Dr. F. Sherwood Rowland, a 1995 UCI Nobel Laureate for his world-renowned atmospheric chemistry research efforts, photograph Courtesy of UCI

FRONT ROW, LEFT TO RIGHT: Joan Irvine Smith, Madeline Swinden, Chancellor Jack Peltasen, Suzie Peltason and guest, BACK ROW LEFT TO RIGHT, Donald Bren, Dean of Claire Trevor School of the Arts, Jill Beck and other guests, UCI Medal Dinner 2002, photo by Laurel Hungerford

FRONT ROW, LEFT TO RIGHT: Laura Davick, Katrina Lutge, R.J. Brandes and Russell Penniman, BACK ROW, LEFT TO RIGHT: Russ and Joan Allen, Morton and Marianne Smith and Diana Atkins, UCI Medal Dinner 2002, photo by Laurel Hungerford

The foundation also supports the UCI Research Associates, which was founded by my mother when Dr. Stanley van den Noort was dean of the medical school. Among other things, the foundation has supported UCI's world-renowned atmospheric chemistry research efforts, including those of Dr. F. Sherwood Rowland, winner of the 1995 Nobel Prize in Chemistry and the Donald Bren Research Professor of Chemistry at UCI.

In June 2003, the foundation began supporting Dr. Rowland's research in the development of an ultra-high sensitivity device for volatile chemicals as a tool for the diagnosis of pathological chemical imbalances in humans. The present system of analysis—designed for ambient atmospheric analysis—is very useful in that regard and will promote the development of non-invasive techniques in medical applications.

The Joan Irvine Smith & Athalie R. Clarke Foundation has also committed a major pledge to the establishment of a law school that would compliment UCI's existing business, engineering and medical schools. My mother and I always wanted to have a law school there; in her words, it would "complete the vision of the university as one of the great institutions of learning in the country."

UCI College of Medicine Dean, Tom Cesario and Research Associates President Anita Ziebe, photo by Brian Cummings

UCI Research Associates luncheon FROM LEFT Marianne Smith, Joan Irvine Smith, Anita Ziebe, Jan McDonnell, Madeline Swinden, and Etta Hatfield, photograph, Courtesy of UCI

UCI Deans Walter Henry, Tom Cesario and Stanley van den Noort, with Dr. Ted Quilligan, photo by Brian Cummings

Joan Irvine Smith and first Research Associates President Barbara Ficker, photo by Brian Cummings

Joan Irvine Smith and second Research Associates President Mary Roosevelt, photo by Brian Cummings

Granville Redmond, *California Landcape with Flowers*, The Irvine Museum

Maurice Braun, *Road Through the Canyon*, Private Collection, Courtesy of The Irvine Museum

ALSO IN 1991, I BEGAN PURCHASING historic California plein air paintings like the ones I had so admired at the California Club over fifty years before. I created Joan Irvine Smith Fine Arts, Inc., in December 1991. Eventually, I opened an art gallery in San Juan Capistrano, and then another one in Laguna Beach. One day, when my mother and I were looking at California paintings that we were considering purchasing, she turned to me and said, "Now, dear, you must be very careful when you are buying this plein air art, as it could become addicting."

In 1992, my mother and I founded The Irvine Museum, which is dedicated to California Impressionism. I wished to show our paintings—not only for their merit and beauty—but also to make people aware of how much of our fragile California environment has been lost and how necessary it is for us to protect what remains. Our first board of directors consisted of my mother and I, my three sons, James Irvine Swinden, Russell S. Penniman and Morton Irvine Smith, as well as my cousin Anita Ziebe and my attorney Russ Allen. Our executive director, Jean Stern, has held that position since the museum was founded.

Through its thirteen books accompanying national and international exhibitions, its series of lectures and its videotapes, The Irvine Museum, under the guidance of my son James Irvine Swinden and of Jean Stern, has become the most active institution in the country educating people about this genre. The Joan Irvine Smith & Athalie R. Clarke Foundation provides financial support for the museum.

Guy Rose, *Laguna Eucalyptus*, The Irvine Museum

Jean Stern and Joan Irvine Smith at The Irvine Museum, photo by Lori Bryston

Guy Rose, *Incoming Tide*, Private Collection, Courtesy of The Irvine Museum

William Wendt, *There Is No Solitude Even in Nature*, Private Collection, Courtesy of The Irvine Museum

Joan Irvine Smith and the Duke of Edinburgh discuss water reclamation at a luncheon for The Duke Of Edinburgh's Award World Fellowship at the Bel Air Hotel in Beverly Hills

The foundation has also been active in helping to care for and develop the world's precious water resources. I developed a keen appreciation for protecting and replenishing water supplies from my grandfather. When I was a child, I remember him taking me on tours of his water projects on the Irvine Ranch. My mother's interest in water came from her early days on the ranch as well, and her own farming experiences.

With encouragement from my mother and me, and with financial support from the Joan Irvine Smith & Athalie R. Clarke Foundation, five southern California water and sanitation agencies formed the National Water Research Institute (NWRI) in 1991. The NWRI is a public-private partnership devoted to water-related research. Its mission is to "create new sources of water through research and technology and to protect the freshwater and marine environments."

On February 15, 1992, the National Water Research Institute held its first event, a planning workshop for the purpose of developing a framework for its research program. Executive Director Ronald Linsky invited key persons from the water and wastewater utility community in Southern California as well as state and federal legislators who were members of important water-related committees.

The late Senator Paul Simon (D. Illinois) was the only legislator to attend, and he remained for the entire day-long workshop, contributing significant suggestions to assist NWRI in achieving its mission. His insights were especially appreciated when he encouraged NWRI to plan not only for the short term but to think long term and to remember that water issues are global in nature and not necessarily only local.

In the opening chapter of his book *Tapped Out*, published in 1998, Senator Simon states the following:

By the gift of water you nourish and sustain us and all living things." These are the words used in the baptismal rite in Lutheran services. But in our world increasing numbers of people cannot assume they will be nourished and sustained, and within a few years, a water crisis of catastrophic proportions will explode on us—unless aroused citizens in this and other nations demand of their leadership actions reflecting vision, understanding, and courage. Political leadership on water issues—as in every other

William Wendt, *Santa Ana River*, Private Collection, Courtesy of The Irvine Museum

field—tends to be shortsighted. But on water, shortsightedness could be cataclysmic. It is no exaggeration to say that the conflict between humanity's growing thirst and the projected supply of usable, portable water will result in the most devastating natural disaster since history has been accurately recorded, unless something happens to stop it.

The world's population of 5.9 billion will double in the next forty to ninety years, depending on whose estimates you accept. Our water supply, however, is constant. Compounding those grim realities is the fact that per capita world water consumption is rising twice as fast as the world's population. You do not have to be an Einstein to understand that we are headed toward a potential calamity.

Nations fight over oil, but valuable as it is, there are substitutes for oil. There is no substitute for water. We die quickly without water, and no nation's leaders would hesitate to battle for adequate water supplies.

The NWRI is unique: its core funding from the Joan Irvine Smith & Athalie R. Clarke Foundation is matched at more than a one-to-one ratio by funds from federal, state and local governments, private industry, public utilities and university partners. Since the institute's inception, a total of $13.7 million contributed by the Joan Irvine Smith & Athalie R. Clarke Foundation has been matched with $15 million from NWRI partners. With a total investment of $28.7 million devoted to water research, NWRI is the fourth-largest research organization in the United States.

More than 119 NWRI partners have provided funds to support more than 158 projects in 14 states, on 29 campuses and in 28 utility and/or industrial laboratories. More than 110 peer-reviewed technical publications have been produced as well as 160 conference presentations. Three U.S. patents have been granted from NWRI research investigation.

Research projects focus on water-quality assessment, knowledge management, exploratory research and treatment and monitoring. For example, projects with the U.S. Department of the Interior's Bureau of Reclamation have focused on membrane research and desalination/water purification processes. Projects with the Environmental Protection Agency have focused on the fate and transport of viruses related to water wells and the risks associated with water distribution systems.

Under Ronald Linsky's direction, NWRI has developed partnerships with several international entities, including the University of New South Wales in Australia; the Institute Armand-Frappier in Quebec, Canada; the Sultanate of Oman; and the Ministry of Water Resources of the People's Republic of China. Finally, NWRI and American Oceans Campaign have identified a common interest in storm water management.

The centerpiece of NWRI's institutional design is the concept of an "institute without walls." NWRI operates by facilitating, coordinating and supporting deserving research projects wherever the best people and facilities are found. The organization maximizes its financial resources by minimizing the cost burdens of supporting its own facilities, equipment and staff.

After my mother's death in 1993, in order to honor her vision of the importance of careful stewardship and development of water resources, NWRI established the Athalie Richardson Irvine Clarke Prize in 1993 to recognize outstanding individuals who have implemented better water science research and technology. The Prize—a gold medallion and an award of $50,000—is presented annually. As part of the award ceremony, the recipient is invited to present the Clarke Prize Lecture. The Clarke Prize has been designated by the International Congress of Distinguished Awards as one of the most prestigious in the world.

Athalie Richardson Irvine Clarke and the National Water Research Institute Clarke Prize Medal

FRONT ROW CENTER: 2005 Clarke Prize winner Dr. Menachem Elimelech with prior winners Dr. Vernon Snoeyink at left and Dr. Joan Rose at right. BACK ROW: Joan Irvine Smith with prior winners FROM LEFT: Dr. Bruce Rittmann, Dr. Walter Weber, Dr. George Tchobanoglous, and Dr. Charles O'Melia

Ronald B. Linsky, Executive Director of the National Water Research Institute from 1991 until his untimely death in 2005 when he was succeeded by Jeffery J. Mosher

Arthur G. Rider, *Mission Garden*, Private Collection, Courtesy of The Irvine Museum

Arthur Rider painting at Mission San Juan Capistrano, photograph, Courtesy of Robert Mc Chesney Bethea

Scaffolding near the garden, Photo by Christopher Bliss

ALSO IN 1993, JEAN STERN AND I were invited on a special tour of the Mission San Juan Capistrano by Gerry Miller, the mission administrator; our tour included an extensive survey of the ongoing restoration efforts in the mission's Great Stone Church. While we were inspecting the ruin, Gerry explained that the mission had been contacted by the managers of the "Three Tenors"—Jose Carreras, Placido Domingo and Luciano Pavarotti. They had wanted to do an event in the Great Stone Church but later declined because of the supporting scaffolding. Soon afterward, through the Joan Irvine Smith & Athalie R. Clarke Foundation, my mother and I made our first in a series of donations toward completing the preservation of the historic ruin and in particular having the scaffolding removed from the church wall that adjoins the Sacred Garden.

The Mission San Juan Capistrano, known as the "Jewel of the Missions," is certainly the most important historical and cultural monument in the state of California. Ever since the early twentieth century, it has been the most frequently painted structure in the western United States, and to this day, still attracts artists from throughout the world.

Scaffolding of Mission wall, Photo by Christopher Bliss

Joan Irvine Smith and Jean Stern with a Charles Austin painting at the Mission

In 1995, Joan Irvine Smith Fine Arts, Inc., along with the California Art Club and the Mission San Juan Capistrano, initiated an outdoor painting competition called the Mission San Juan Capistrano Annual Plein Air Art Festival. Held in August each year, it featured about 100 invited artists who painted at the mission for one week and then submitted a painting that was judged by a noted panel. The $10,000 in prize money offered by Joan Irvine Smith Fine Arts—consisting of $5,000 for first place, $3,000 for second and $2,000 for third—was the highest amount awarded in any California plein air art competition. Every year, we purchased the first-place painting and donated it to the mission's art collection.

In 1997, I joined with my daughter-in-law Madeline Swinden and Gerry Miller in founding the support group Friends of the Mission, which provides advice and counsel for mission programs and fundraising. The first fundraising dinner hosted by the Friends of the Mission, called "Romance of the Bells" and held in September 1998, was an elegant black-tie event in the mission courtyard. The goal was to raise funds for the completion of the preservation of the Great Stone Church. Subsequent dinners have continued to the present time.

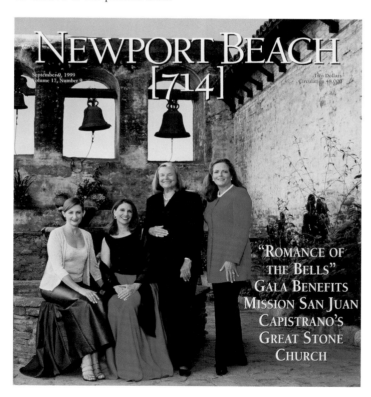

FROM LEFT: Gloria Brandes, Melissa Holmes Snyder, Joan Irvine Smith and Madeline Swinden on the cover of the September 9, 1999 edition of "Newport Beach [714]" magazine which contained an article on the second fundraising gala, "Romance of the Bells" benefiting the Mission San Juan Capistrano's Great Stone Church, hosted by the Friends of the Mission in September 1999.

PAINTINGS FROM
MISSION SAN JUAN CAPISTRANO
PLEIN AIR ART FESTIVALS

Anita Hampton

West Fraser

Dan Gozee

Dan Gozee

Peter Adams

Wang

Ruo Li

Ruo Li

Anita Hampton

Mian Situ

177

Franz Bischoff, *San Juan Capistrano Yard*, Private Collection, Courtesy of The Irvine Museum

Alson Clark, *Cloisters, Mission San Juan Capistrano*, Private Collection, Courtesy of The Irvine Museum

Joseph Kleitsch, *San Juan Capistrano*, Private Collection, Courtesy of The Irvine Museum

Also in 1998, Orange County business and community leaders joined to form the Mission Preservation Foundation in order to preserve the mission's Great Stone Church. The president of the foundation is longtime mission friend and supporter Anthony R. Moiso, president and chief executive officer of Rancho Mission Viejo. When the foundation was formed, Moiso remarked, "Mission San Juan Capistrano is the true birthplace of Orange County. Its history is our heritage. Its story is our legacy. It belongs to everyone."

The initial preservation work on the church ruins was started in 1895 by the Landmarks Club and continued by Father St. John O'Sullivan, resident priest from 1910 to 1933. The modern preservation of the Great Stone Church began in 1987, according to John Loomis, the project lead architect. The ruin was placed in supporting scaffolding in 1989. My son Russell S. Penniman, a Captain in the Naval Reserve and also a member of the Mission Preservation Foundation, took an active role in the design of the mission's earthquake retrofit program, which allowed the scaffolding to be removed.

Joseph Kleitsch, *Red and Green*, The Irvine Museum

FROM LEFT: Richard O' Neill, Joan Irvine Smith and Michael Amante, photograph, Courtesy of Mission San Juan Capistrano

On July 28, 2004, the mission held a community celebration under the direction of Mechelle Lawrence, mission administrator, marking the completion of the preservation of the Great Stone Church. An internal support structure was created to prevent further erosion of the ruin and to make it safe for visitors to approach and enjoy. It cost a total of $9.6 million, more than half of which was raised through private funding sources. The completion of the church preservation project enables the mission to focus on new areas of restoration and preservation, which include among other things: the Serra Chapel, the mission museum, the historical native industrial area, along with the "basket weave" chimneys, walkways, fountains and lighting and the addition of landscaping to the Great Stone Church.

On September 17, 2004, the Romance of the Great Stone Church fundraising dinner, hosted by the Mission Preservation Foundation and myself as honorary chair, celebrated the completion of the stabilization of this magnificent ruin. The gala was held in the Great Stone Church and featured a concert by tenor Michael Amante, who sang in front of the historic altar. It honored the past, celebrated the present and looked forward to the future, when generations to come will benefit from this national treasure.

Romance of the Great Stone Church concert by Michael Amante 2004, photograph, Courtesy of Mission San Juan Capistrano

The Serra Chapel, photograph, Courtesy of the Mission San Juan Capistrano

Joan Irvine Smith and Richard O' Neill, photo by Carla Rhea

The following year on September 16, the Mission Preservation Foundation and Honorary Chair, Mr. Richard O'Neill, hosted the Romance of Serra Chapel, featuring a concert by Michael Feinstein in the ruins of the Great Stone Church. It was followed by an elegant candlelight dinner in the Mission Main Courtyard. The event was held to raise funds for the restoration and preservation of the historic Serra Chapel, for which Mr. O'Neill has given a generous leadership gift of $250,000.

Romance of Serra Chapel concert by Michael Feinstein 2005, photo by Carla Rhea

Entrance to the Serra Chapel from the Mission courtyard, photo by Carla Rhea

Table settings, photo by Carla Rhea

FROM LEFT: Art and Gay Birtcher with Michael Feinstein, photo by Carla Rhea

FROM LEFT: Madeline and Jim Swinden with Mission San Juan Capistrano Executive Director, Mechelle Lawrence, photo by Carla Rhea

FROM LEFT: Joan Irvine Smith, Tony Moiso, Father Arthur A. Holquin, and Mechelle Lawrence, photo by Carla Rhea

FROM LEFT: Russell Penniman, Alletta Cooper, Katrina Lutge, Michael Feinstein and Carol Penniman, photo by Carla Rhea

FROM LEFT: Father Art with Ann and Tony Forster, photo by Carla Rhea

Father Art and Bishop Todd D. Brown, photo by Carla Rhea

FROM LEFT: Brett and Gretchen Thomson, Wylie and Bettie Aitken, Joan Irvine Smith and Tony Moiso, photo by Carla Rhea

FROM LEFT: Mechelle Lawrence, Bob and Simone Mc Donough and Father Art, photo by Carla Rhea

FROM LEFT: Father Art, Morton Smith, Alletta Cooper, and Mechelle Lawrence, photo by Carla Rhea

Our Beloved Monsignor Paul M. Martin, 1930–2005, photograph, Courtesy of the Mission San Juan Capistrano

Msgr. Martin was appointed Pastor of the Mission Church in 1978 and was conferred the title of Monsignor by Pope John Paul II in 1990. With much devotion of time and energy Msgr. Martin worked to preserve the historic mission, build a magnificent new church and a state of the art elementary school. Like Saint Francis, he tended his flock with humility, love and selflessness and also his beloved abandoned cats and dogs. A beautiful garden has been designed as a loving tribute to Msgr. Martin and will be created next to his home, the Rectory, photo by Tom Baker

FACING PAGE AND ABOVE:

THE MISSION GALA, ROMANCE OF SERRA CHAPEL, 2005

FROM LEFT: Myron and Mozelle Sukut, and Eden and George O'Connell, photo by Carla Rhea

Michael and Arlene Hagan and Father Art, photo by Carla Rhea

In 1991, Arthur Hawkins began managing The Oaks Classic, and we added The Oaks Fall Classic, also benefiting the UCI College of Medicine. The September event offered more than $180,000 in prize money and included The Oaks Fall Classic $101,000 Grand Prix, which at that time was the largest purse presented in a jumping competition in the United States. The event also included the $10,000 Oak Leaf Junior/Amateur Grand Prix, hunter classes and the International Hunter Futurity West Coast Finals. That year Susie Hutchison won The Oaks Classic Grand Prix on Samsung Clover Mountain. Bernie Traurig and Flying Scott galloped away with The Oaks Fall Classic Grand Prix for Albert Court Ltd.

The 1991
Oaks Classic

The 1991 Oaks Classic show manager, Arthur Hawkins, and Joan Irvine Smith, photo by Tish Quirk

Susie Hutchison on Samsung Clover Mountain winner of the 1991 $50,000 Oaks Classic Grand Prix, photo by Tish Quirk

Wilder Di Santo on Karachi winner of the 1991 $10,000 House of Hermes Acorn Junior/Amateur Grand Prix FROM LEFT, Francine Bardo, Joan Irvine Smith and Maria del Carmen Calvo, Robert Drennan and Robin Serfass, photo by Tish Quirk

Joan Irvine Smith and Maria del Carmen Calvo, photo by Tish Quirk

Athalie Irvine Clarke, Cappy Smith and Joan Irvine Smith, photo by Tish Quirk

Mrs. Clarke and Dr. Howard House, photo by Tish Quirk

Roger and Louise Williams, photo by Tish Quirk

FROM LEFT: Bill Ficker and Mary and James Roosevelt with other guests at the Grand Prix luncheon, photo by Tish Quirk

San Juan Capistrano Mayor Gary L. Hausdorfer and his wife Debora, photo by Tish Quirk

Bernie Traurig on Flying Scott winner of the 1990 Memorial Day Classic Grand Prix at Griffith Park receives award from Joan Irvine Smith. Bernie and Flying Scott also won the 1991 $101,000 Oaks Fall Classic Grand Prix, photo by Tish Quirk

Dr. Walter Henry, Dean of UCI College of Medicine, and his wife Maria del Carmen Calvo present a gift to Joan Irvine Smith, photo by Tish Quirk

Alexander M. Groos and Say You Will winners of the $10,000 Oak Leaf Junior/Amateur Grand Prix with Dr. Walter Henry and Maria del Carmen Calvo, photo by Tish Quirk

FROM LEFT: Cappy Smith, Joan Irvine Smith, Morton Smith and Alletta Smith Cooper, photo by Tish Quirk

Conformation Hunters being shown in hand in The Oaks Grove at The Oaks, photo by Joan Irvine Smith

Hugh Mutch on S&L Ballet winner of the 1992 $50,000 Oaks Classic Grand Prix trophy presented by FROM LEFT: Joan Irvine Smith Anita Ziebe, Madeline Swinden, Morton Smith, James Swinden, Liz Schmidt, Russell and Carol Penniman with Rex and Elizabeth Penniman, Lori Penniman, and Bob Schmidt, with Calli, Max, Libby, Jesse and Sam Edelman, photo by Tish Quirk

In 1992, The Oaks Classic began benefiting the National Water Research Institute, and The Oaks Fall Classic benefited UCI College of Medicine. Both events offered more than $150,000 in prize money, including a $50,000 Grand Prix, and featured an exhibition of historic California plein air paintings from The Irvine Museum as well as from prominent art dealers from across the country. At the fall event my mother and I received commendations from Thomas F. Riley, chairman of the Orange County Board of Supervisors, and from Gary Hausdorfer, mayor of the city of San Juan Capistrano. That year, Hugh Mutch won The Oaks Classic Grand Prix on S&L Ballet for owners Sam and Libby Edleman. Susie Hutchison and Samsung Woodstock won The Oaks Fall Classic Grand Prix.

Francisco Cardenas on Rangoon, winner of the $10,000 House of Hermes Acorn Junior/Amateur Grand Prix with J. Vincent Wholey, Loretta Swift and Francine Bardo, photo by Tish Quirk

San Juan Capistrano Mayor, Jerry Harris with Arthur Hawkins present the Mayors trophy to Susie Hutchison on Fleetwood for the Dash for Cash, photo by Tish Quirk

Joan Irvine Smith and Jim Swinden present a check to Don Owen, President of the National Water Research Institute, photo by Tish Quirk

Ron Linsky, Executive Director of the National Water Research Institute, second from left: describes the mission of the institute to guests

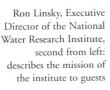

FROM LEFT: Madeline Swinden, Joan Irvine Smith, Cappy Smith, and Jean Stern select paintings to be exhibited in The Irvine Museum tent

The 1992 Oaks
Fall Classic

Susie Hutchison and Samusung Woodstock winners of the 1992 $50,000 Oaks Classic Grand Prix with Joan Irvine Smith , Morton Smith , Russell and Carol Penniman with Elizabeth and Rex Penniman, Hermes representative, Jim and Madeline Swinden with Jase Swinden, Anita Ziebe, Liz and Bob Schmidt with Caroline Schmidt, photo by Tish Quirk

FROM LEFT: Supervisor Thomas F. Riley, Maria del Carmen Calvo, UCI Chancellor Jack Peltason and Dr. Walter Henry, Dean of UCI College of Medicine, present commendations to Joan Irvine Smith and Athalie Irvine Clarke, photo by Tish Quirk

Joie Gatlin on Reveur in The Oaks Fall Classic Grand Prix, photo by Tish Quirk

Joie on Stand Alone winner of the Dash for Cash with Robin Serfass and Arthur Hawkins, photo by Tish Quirk

Cappy and Joie holding Dash for Cash Prize, photo by Tish Quirk

Elizabeth Penniman's first lead line class on Coventry Meadow Mouse (Chevy), photo by Tish Quirk

Brad and Dana Connors on Chevy with Sue Connors and Elizabeth, photo by Tish Quirk

Exhibition of California plein air paintings from The Irvine Museum

Plein air art dealers

FROM LEFT: Athalie Irvine Clarke, Dr. Howard House and Joan Irvine Smith tour The Irvine Museum tent, photo by Tish Quirk

187

Meta Cressey, *Under the Pepper Tree*, Private Collection, Courtesy of The Irvine Museum

Flowers at Athalie Irvine Clarke's house at The Oaks

That summer, my mother began using a wheelchair and we would have lunch under the pepper tree next to the patio beside the tennis court. One day our contractor Charlie Adermatt was working on a project across the driveway next to the wall that separated the adjoining subdivision from The Oaks. I borrowed his ladder and climbed up to look over the wall into our neighbor's yard, discovering that the house was empty and most of the plants in the yard were dead, except for two very large bougainvillea vines, one of coral and the other of fuchsia. On closer inspection, we found out that the house was handicapped accessible and available for sale.

Shortly thereafter, my mother purchased the property. The first thing I did was to have most of the cinderblock wall torn down and replaced with a wrought iron fence. Then I enlarged the patio and the trellis above it and put in three oak trees, trumpet vines, ferns, clivia, star jasmine, pink roses, gardenias, begonias and impatiens in pots and geraniums in hanging baskets. From her patio and garden, my mother could watch us riding horses on the road and playing tennis. I also decorated the interior of the house, where the family celebrated Thanksgiving, Christmas, Easter and many other happy occasions.

CLOCKWISE FROM TOP LEFT: Athalie Irvine Clarke's house at The Oaks at the time of purchase; beginning of remodeling; 4 views of the house and garden after completion of remodeling

Paul de Longpré, *Wild Roses*, Private Collection, Courtesy of The Irvine Museum

Athalie Irvine Clarke with Dr. Howard House on the patio of her house at The Oaks, photo by Charles Adermatt

That same year, I retained the internationally renowned architect Robert Jolicoeur of International Equestrian Design of Montreal, Canada, to design a derby field on a portion of The Oaks' property that was held in trust by my mother. She would often join me for lunch to see what progress had been made. Two-thirds of the field was sand, with two grass islands, where I planted three very large oak trees. A grass bank was built around half of the field, on the north side, where I also planted a number of very large oaks. I later put in large and small birds of paradise, cactus, agave and roses at various locations. Jasmine and honeysuckle were used as ground-cover and on the fence surrounding the field. I then planted a number of large sycamore trees around the fence enclosing the field.

When we settled our lawsuit with Donald Bren, my mother told me, "I have helped you all I can. Now you must let me go. I want to join your father." She had specified to have her ashes placed next to my father's at Fairhaven Cemetery in Santa Ana. Years before, she had arranged to relocate my father's ashes from Forest Lawn in Los Angeles to Fairhaven, as she had always intended to be with him. We completed construction on the derby field in May 1993, and held a memorial service for my mother there during The Oaks Classic in June, as she died just two weeks before the event, on May 22.

Paul de Longpré, *Wild Roses*, Private Collection, Courtesy of The Irvine Museum

Views of the Derby Field at The Oaks designed by internationally renowned
architect Robert Jolicoeur of International Equestrian Design of Montreal, Canada

191

My mother's close friend Dr. Robert Schuller conducted
the memorial service. Another close friend, noted pianist Roger
Williams, played two of her favorite pieces, *Autumn Leaves*, and
Somewhere My Love (from the movie *Doctor Zhivago*), on a grand
piano that I had placed under a bougainvillea-covered gazebo that
was used as the judges' stand during competition. The day was over-
cast and still; however, when the service began, a sudden wind blew
across the field. When the service was over, the wind died away as
suddenly as it had come.

The 1993
OAKS CLASSIC,
CONTINUED ON
NEXT PAGE

The 1993 Oaks Classic began the following day and my
family and many of our friends attended the event. Susie Hutchison
won The Oaks Classic Grand Prix on High Heels.

Roger Williams at the piano in the gazebo on the Derby Field playing two of
Mrs. Clarke's favorite songs, *Autumn Leaves* and *Somewhere My Love*

Joan Irvine Smith and Dr. Robert Schuller at the Athalie Richardson Irvine Clarke
memorial service held on the Derby Field at The Oaks

Family and friends at
the memorial service

192

Susie Hutchison on High Heels winner of the 1993 $50,000 Oaks Classic Grand Prix with FROM LEFT: John Fleckenstein, Jimmy Williams, Jimsey Fleckenstein, Joan Irvine Smith, Jim and Madeline Swinden with Jase Swinden, Carol Penniman, Alletta Cooper, Morton Smith, Liz Schmidt, Anita Ziebe, Bob Schmidt, Lori Penniman, Pam Ziebarth and Russell Penniman, Photo by Tish Quirk

FROM LEFT: J. Vincent Wholey, Francine Bardo and Jennifer O'Neill with Acorn winner Steve Harris on Giacomo, photo by Tish Quirk

Joan Irvine Smith and Jim Swinden present a check to Ron Linsky of NWRI, photo by Tish Quirk

Dash for Cash winner Will Simpson on Atem with Arthur Hawkins and Mrs. Smith, photo by Tish Quirk

Russ and Carol Penniman with Rex in the lead line class followed by Jennifer Patterson with Tasha Ardalan, Elizabeth Penniman and Jessica Vaillancourt, photo by Tish Quirk

Russ Penniman with Rex on Poco Juan who receives his lead line class award from Joan Irvine Smith, photo by Tish Quirk

Jim and Madeline Swinden with Jase on Rosinate who receives his lead line class award from Mrs. Smith, photo by Tish Quirk

Joan Irvine Smith with Clyde Tritt and Cappy Smith, photo by Tish Quirk

FROM LEFT: Rev. Robert and Arvella Schuller with Lillian Fluor and Peter Fluor, photo by Tish Quirk

Mrs. Smith with Rev. Robert Schuller, Jr. and Donna Schuller, photo by Tish Quirk

The 1993 Oaks
Fall Classic,
continued on
next page

That year, we added the International Jumper Futurity West Coast Finals and the Pacific Coast Horse Show Association/Jimmy Williams Futures Finals to The Oaks Fall Classic. At that time, I engaged Dan Wyan of Tri-Crown Productions to televise The Oaks' jumping events for Horse World. Hap Hansen and Henzo won The Oaks Fall Classic Grand Prix, with Alain Vaillancourt and South Pacific placing second for The Oaks.

Alan Waldman and Running Fleet the 1993 IJF Western Regional Four-Year-Old Champion with Course Designer Linda Allen, photo by Tish Quirk

Dan Wyan of Tri-Crown Productions photographs an interview by World Champion Cowboy Larry Mahan with Joan Irvine Smith for Horse World at The Oaks Fall Classic in 1993, photo by Tish Quirk

Cindy Brooks with International Hunter Futurity Grand Champion Frisky Trucker receives award from Robin Serfass, photo by Tish Quirk

Jennifer Preletz on All Heart receives the award for the Jimmy Williams Futures Finals from Mrs. Smith, John French, Jimmy Williams and Larry Mayfield, photo by Tish Quirk

Tara Ardalan and Witch Broome Wizard, five time Young Rider Gold Medal winners, won the $10,000 Oak Leaf Junior/Amateur Grand Prix with FROM LEFT: Diana Gates, Joan Irvine Smith, Rick Pickney and Course Designer, Robert Jolicoeur, photo by Tish Quirk

John French with Champion Regular Working Hunter Ten Downing, photo by Tish Quirk

Lauren Dendiu and Hunter Champion Memphis Belle receive award from Elaine Gleason, photo by Tish Quirk

Hap Hansen on Henzo winner of the 1993 $50,000 Oaks Fall Classic Grand Prix receives award from Joan Irvine Smith with Morton Smith, John and Frances Rae, Carol Penniman with Rex, Jim Swinden, Russ Penniman with Elizabeth, Alletta Copper with Nathalie, Willem, and Little Alletta Cooper, photo by Tish Quirk

Alain Vaillancourt and South Pacific placed second in The Oaks Fall Classic Grand Prix, photo by Tish Quirk

Dr. Walter Henry, Dean of UCI College of Medicine, Tricia Nichols, Executive Committee Chairman of The Oaks Fall Classic, Maria del Carman Calvo, Supervisor Thomas F. Riley and Councilman Gary Hausdorfer present Joan Irvine Smith with a gift from UCI and commendations from the Orange County Board of Supervisors and the City of San Juan Capistrano, photo by Tish Quirk

Alain Vaillancourt on Lybelle receives the Dash for Cash award from Mrs. Smith, photo by Tish Quirk

FROM LEFT: Course Designer Robert Jolicoeur of International Equestrian Design of Montreal, Canada, who designed The Oaks Derby Field, Cappy Smith and Joan Irvine Smith, photo by Tish Quirk

Guests viewing paintings in the Irvine Museum tent

Redfern Gallery tent

FROM LEFT: Sheriff Brad Gates unidentified guest, Gary Cambell and San Juan Capistrano Mayor Colleen Cambell, photo by Tish Quirk

195

ABOVE AND BELOW: Views of Joan Irvine Smith's residence at The Oaks

Alexey Steele, *Joan's House*, Private Collection

Alexey Steele, *Katrina's House*, Private Collection

Although I spent a great deal of time at The Oaks, I had never spent the night there. One month after my mother's death, my son Russell and I stayed there. The following day, I moved from my home in Corona del Mar to the farm where I live with my dogs in a modular house that reminds me very much of the little green house at Irvine Cove.

I have a view of the Capistrano hills from my porch where morning doves make their nests in the baskets that hang from the pergola. Their cooing at dawn brings back vivid memories of my childhood visits with my grandfather at the ranch house in Tustin. Hawks, barn owls and kites have also built nests in the trees on the property and great blue herons nest in the sycamores along San Juan Creek where coyotes often howl in a chorus after dark.

My gardens have attracted a large variety of smaller birds as well as skunks, opposums, raccoons and many cottontail rabbits. Late one afternoon, a handsome young male bobcat came over the fence along the creek and sat beside a pepper tree in front of my porch. He sat for about fifteen minutes watching the rabbits eat the grass and then left as quietly as he had come.

Cooper's Hawk, photo by Sharon Groth, courtesy of the artist

Mourning Dove, © Alden M. Johnson, California Academy of Science

Great Blue Herons Nesting in Tree, ©Richard Jackson

Barn Owl, Courtesy of U.S. Fish and Wildlife Service

Black-Shouldered Kite, ©George Morris MacDonald

Opossum with Young, © Alden M. Johnson California Academy of Science

Skunk, ©Richard Jackson

Raccoon, © Robert Potts, California Academy of Science

Jack Rabbit, ©Tom Geer

Bobcat, © Gerald and Buff Corsi, California Academy of Science

Earlier that year, I had underwritten a number of improvements at the Creekside Equestrian Center located on the other side of San Juan Creek and operated by Diana and Brad Gates. These included, among other things, the lights for the existing covered arena and five riding rings for both English and Western competition on 40 acres of land that Creekside leased from Rancho Mission Viejo. Perlow Equestrian Productions (PEP) put on its first series of horse shows, Harvest Festivals I & II, there in October 1993. The PEP shows continued until the Creekside property fell into such disrepair that the shows were moved to The Oaks in August 1994.

At that time, my sons James Swinden and Russell Penniman were competing successfully in the jumper and hunter divisions and my daughter-in-law Carol Penniman began competing in Adult Amateur Hunters. Russell also began assisting me with The Oaks' events.

ABOVE: Creekside Equestrian Center

Richard O'Neill and other guests at Creekside barbeque, 1993

LEFT: Sam Perlow presents award to Lauren Dendiu and Hunter Champion Coco
RIGHT: Carol Penniman and Sam Perlow present award to Jennifer Patterson and Hunter Champion The Little Prince, Harvest Festival II 1993

LEFT: Sam Perlow and Cornelia Guest present award to Arsia Ardalan on Corazone for the Jimmy Williams Futures Class, Harvest Festival II 1993
RIGHT: Sam Perlow and Diana Gates present the award to Cornelia Guest on Parkmore for Adult/Amateur Jumpers, Harvest Festival II 1993

Jim Swinden with Jase on Casper, Del Mar 1994

Linda Irvine Gaede on Hunter Champion Magic Spell, Del Mar 1974

Jim Swinden on Jumper Champion Casper, The Oaks Classic 1994

Russell and Elizabeth Penniman, Show Park 1994

Carol Penniman on Hunter Champion Stands to Reason, The Oaks Classic 1994, photo by Tish Quirk

Carol on Stands to Reason with Russ, Elizabeth, and Rex Penniman, Showpark 1994

FROM LEFT: Tasha Ardalan, Alletta Cooper, Nathalie Cooper and Elizabeth Penniamn compete in a walk/ trot class at The Oaks

Russ Penniman on Parkmore winner of the Marshall and Sterling Adult/Amateur Jumper Classic at Showpark 1994

Russ Penniman on Jumper Champion Stand Alone at The Oak

Russ Penniman on Jumper Champion Parkmore at The Oaks

Tony Font on Hendrix winner of the 1994 $50,000 Oaks Classic Grand Prix with FROM LEFT Joan Irvine Smith, Carol and Russ Penniman, Jim and Madeline Swinden with Jase and John and France Rae, photo by Tish Quirk

Acorn winner Tara Ardalan on Witch Broome Wizard with FROM LEFT Mrs. Smith, Larry Mahan and Francine Bardo, photo by Tish Quirk

LEFT TO RIGHT: Bill and Katie Shattuck, Nathalie Cooper, Marie Mainz, Cappy Smith, Tully Rector and Robert Jolicoeur walk the Grand Prix course, photo by Tish Quirk

Alain Vaillancourt and Balderdash placed second in both The Oaks Classic and The Oaks Fall Classic Grand Prix in 1994, photo by Tish Quirk

ABOVE, FROM LEFT: Nathalie and Alletta Cooper, Tasha Ardalan and Elizabeth Penniman display walk/trot class ribbons in the pony cart with driver Steve Cataina and Rick Pickney holding Tara's Yes Sir, photo by Tish Quirk
LEFT: Joan Irvine Smith Fine Arts tent, photo by Tish Quirk
BELOW LEFT: Russ Allen and Joan Irvine Smith looking at paintings, photo by Tish Quirk

Joan Irvine Smith, Cappy Smith and Course Designer, Robert Jolicoeur, photo by Tish Quirk

Mrs. Smith with artist Wally Noll, photo by Tish Quirk

In 1994, Tony Font won The Oaks Classic Grand Prix on Hendrix, with Alain Vaillancourt and Balderdash placing second for the Oaks. Elizabeth Alexander and Macho Man won The Oaks Fall Classic Grand Prix, with Alain Vaillancourt and Balderdash placing second. Elizabeth and Macho Man won the Oak Leaf Junior Amateur Grand Prix in 1992.

Elizabeth Alexander on Macho Man winner of 1994 $50,000 Oaks Fall Classic Grand Prix with FROM LEFT: Joan Irvine Smith, Rick Pickney, UCI Associate Chancellor, Paul Silverman, Elizabeth Penniman, Alletta and Nathalie Cooper in front of Anita Ziebe, Madeline Swinden, Dr. Tom Cesario, Dean of UCI College of Medicine, Staurt W. Martin, Willem Cooper and Rex Penniman in front of Jim Swinden, Carol and Russ Penniman, Alletta and Bill Cooper, and Frances and John Rae. Elizabeth and Macho Man also won the 1992 $10,000 Oak Leaf Junior/Amateur Grand Prix at The Oaks, photo by Tish Quirk

Robin Serfass and Cece Younger with Damian Gardner on Fleet's Queen, the 1994 IJF Four-Year-Old Champion, photo by Tish Quirk

Oak Leaf winner Kerry Bernay on Jimbob with Mrs. Smith, J. Vincent Wholey and a Land Rover Representative

International Hunter Futurity Champion Magistrate and owner Sandy Aston with rider Darren Dilin at left, photo by Tish Quirk

Russ Penniman on Jumper Champion Royal Touch

Megan Johnstone on Marco placed 5th in the Oaks Fall Classic Grand Prix. Megan purchased Marco from The Oaks, photo by Tish Quirk

Alain Vaillancourt on Cheerful, winner IJF Western International Five-Year-Old Finals Stake

Jase with Jim Swinden during the lead line class, photo by Tish Quirk

Dr. Tom Cesario presents a gift to Mrs. Smith, photo by Tish Quirk

The Thoroughbred Spread Barbecue tent, photo by Tish Quirk

Francie Steinwedell on Sylvia winner of the 1995 $50,000 Oaks Classic FROM LEFT: Madeline Swinden, Joan Irvine Smith with Jim and Jase Swinden behind Willem, Little Alletta, Alletta and Nathalie Cooper, and Russ, Elizabeth, Carol and Rex Penniman with horse show staff, photo by Tish Quirk

Jamie Schmidt on Mojave winner of the $10,000 House of Hermes Acorn Junior/Amateur Grand Prix with FROM LEFT: Tawney Little, Francine Bardo and Robert Drennan, photo by Tish Quirk

FROM LEFT: Cappy Smith, Tully Rector and Elizabeth Penniman with Russ Penniman on Jumper Champion Stand Alone at The Oaks, photo by Tish Quirk

Jim Swinden on Jumper Champion Casper at The Oaks

Russ Penniman on Jumper Champion Stand Alone at The Oaks

Jim Swinden on Jumper Champion Casanova at The Oaks

Jim Swinden on Jumper Champion Lonford at The Oaks

Russ Penniman on Jumper Champion Parkmore at The Oaks

Russ Penniman on Jumper Champion Lonford at The Oaks

Joie Gatlin on Reveur winner of
the 1995 $50,000 Oaks Fall
Classic Grand Prix for The Oaks
FROM LEFT: UCI Chancellor Laura
Wilkening, UCI Associate
Chancellor Paul Silveman, Robert
Drennan, Joan Irvine Smith Carol
and Russ Penniman with
Elizabeth and Rex Penniman,
Anita Ziebe, Alletta and Nathalie
Cooper, Marie Mainz and Jim and
Madeline Swinden with Jase,
photo by Tish Quirk

In 1995, Francie Steinwedell won The Oaks Classic Grand
Prix on Sylvia. Joie Gatlin and Reveur captured The Oaks Fall
Classic Grand Prix for The Oaks.

Joie Gatlin on Idle Hour, the 1995 AHSA National Grand Champion Regular
Hunter and Champion Conformation Hunter, photo by Joan Irvine Smith

Joie Gatlin on Land Prince, the1995 International Jumper Futurity Western
International Four-Year-Old Champion

Will Prieto on Damascus won the $10,000 Oak Leaf

Darren Dilin on Southshore by South Pacific, the 1994 IJF Western Regional Four-
Year-Old Champion and 1995 Western Regional Five-Year-Old Champion owned
by Sandy Aston

George Morris on Golden Boy demonstrates a riding technique to his students during his clinic at The Oaks in 1993

I had long dreamed of bringing the Olympic Jumping Trials to The Oaks in San Juan Capistrano. In 1993, I spoke about my vision to Richard J. O'Neill, the patriarch of the O'Neill family, which owns Rancho Mission Viejo. Mr. O'Neill thought it was a great idea, and he said that he and the ranch would work with me on the project.

When the famous instructor George Morris came to conduct a clinic at The Oaks in January 1995, I told him of my idea to bring the Olympic Trials there and showed him the Rancho Mission Viejo property that I thought would be an ideal location for the event. George was very enthusiastic and said that he would help me with the Olympic Committee.

Joan Irvine Smith on Idle Hour in the George Morris Clinic at The Oaks in 1991

Students with George Morris at his clinic on the Derby Field at The Oaks in 1993

Tara Ardalan on Latigo in the George Morris Clinic on the Derby Field at The Oaks in 1993

Joan Irvine Smith on Kontiki at the George Morris Clinic at The Oaks in 1990

Cornelia Guest on Parkmore in the George Morris Clinic on the Derby Field in 1993

204

Edgar Payne, *Capistrano Canyon*, Private Collection, Courtesy of The Irvine Museum

THE IRVINES AND O'NEILLS have been both neighbors and friends for more than a century. Richard O'Neill's grandfather, Richard O'Neill, Sr., immigrated to the United States in 1849. After arriving in San Francisco, he established the California Meat Company and joined with James C. Flood to purchase real estate along the Embarcadero, where he opened several meat markets. Flood, a former carriage-maker turned saloonkeeper, opened a bar called the Auction Lunch Saloon across the street from the Mercantile Exchange, where he traded gold and silver. Eventually, Flood went to Virginia City, Nevada, where he struck it rich at the Comstock Lode, America's most famous and richest silver deposit. He then founded the Bank of Nevada.

In 1882, in a deal struck with a handshake, Flood and O'Neill became equal partners in three properties: the Rancho Santa Margarita y las Flores, the Rancho Mission Viejo, and the Rancho Trabuco, with O'Neill to work out his half as resident manager. These lands, originally owned by John ("Juan") Forster, were in both Orange and San Diego counties. Under O'Neill's management, the 230,000-acre combined rancho was improved and the cattle herd upgraded. In addition, a tourist hotel was built at San Juan Hot Springs, and the ranch became home to Orange County's biggest wheat fields.

Richard O'Neil, Sr., photograph, Courtesy of San Juan Capistrano Historical Society

Rancho Santa Margarita y las Flores, photograph, Courtesy of San Juan Capistrano Historical Society

Rancho Santa Margarita Ranch House, photograph, Courtesy of San Juan Capistrano Historical Society

Rancho Santa Margarita Ranch House courtyard, photograph, Courtesy of San Juan Capistrano Historical Society

Rancho Santa Margarita roundup, photograph, Courtesy of San Juan Capistrano Historical Society

Richard O'Neill Jr., Richard O'Neill Sr., with grandson Jerome Baumgartner, Mr. Harding and Jerome O'Neill at the Rancho Santa Margarita Ranch House, photograph, Courtesy of San Juan Capistrano Historical Society

French Hotel, San Juan Capistrano 1890s, photograph, Courtesy of San Juan Capistrano Historical Society

Jerome O' Neill at the San Juan Capistrano train station in 1899, photograph, Courtesy of San Juan Capistrano Historical Society

Yorba Adobes and French Hotel 1930s, photograph, Courtesy of San Juan Capistrano Historical Society. The adobe at the left is now Richard J. O'Neill's El Adobe Restaurant

As Rancho Mission Viejo's historical records indicate:

In 1907, James L. Flood, son of the "Silver King," made good on his father's promise and conveyed half of the ranch to Richard O'Neill, Sr. Four months later, declining health forced O'Neill to deed his interests to his son Jerome, under whom the rancho continued to flourish. Agricultural operations were greatly expanded and the cow herd grew to 15,000 head. In 1923, Jerome O'Neill and James L. Flood solidified a second-generation friendship and consolidated their interests under the name "Santa Margarita Company." Three years later, both men died, just two days apart. The O'Neill beneficiaries included Jerome's sister Mary O'Neill Baumgartner and her family, his younger brother Richard, Jr., and Richard's wife, Marguerite, as well as their two children, Alice and Richard Jerome O'Neill.

Mary O'Neill Baumgartner was married to John Jay Baumgartner, a San Francisco artist who was very active in the California art community. On a number of occasions, Baumgartner and his family visited the Rancho Santa Margarita, where he painted wonderful views of the ranch and the Orange County coast.

The rancho records continue:

During the 1930s, approximately 17,500 acres of the rancho were sold, including parcels today known as Coto de Caza, Dove Canyon, Caspers Regional Park, the Audubon Wilderness and the Thomas Riley Wilderness Park. In 1939, the Santa Margarita Company was dissolved, with the Floods and Baumgartners taking the San Diego County portion (Rancho Santa Margarita y las Flores) and Richard O'Neill, Jr. retaining the Orange County parcels (Rancho Mission Viejo and Rancho Trabuco). Just two years later, the Marine Corps absorbed the entire San Diego property for the establishment of Camp Joseph H. Pendleton.

John J. Baumgartner, *Rancho Santa Margarita*, Private Collection, Courtesy of The Irvine Museum

Rancho Santa Margarita cattle drive 1916, photograph, Courtesy of San Juan Capistrano Historical Society

Rancho Santa Margarita cattle herd 1916, photograph, Courtesy of San Juan Capistrano Historical Society

FROM LEFT: Alice O'Neill Avery, Richard J. O'Neill, and Marguerite "Ama Daisy" O'Neill, ABOVE FROM LEFT: Mrs. Avery's sons Jerome and Tony Moiso, photograph, Courtesy of San Juan Capistrano Historical Society

What remained of the family's historic rancho were the 52,000 acres in Orange County, now known as Rancho Mission Viejo. Despite several attempts by banks, which held the lands in trust, to liquidate during the mid-1940s, Marguerite "Ama Daisy" O'Neill, Richard, Jr.'s widow, was able to keep the remaining land in the family. In 1950, the O'Neill family established the first of its open space dedications to the people of Orange County with the establishment of 278 acres as O'Neill Regional Park.

Edgar Payne, *Canyon Mission Viejo*, Private Collection, Courtesy of The Irvine Museum

ABOVE AND BELOW: The City of Mission Viejo surrounding Lake Mission Viejo,
Courtesy of The Mission Viejo Company

Forced to modify its pastoral ways in the mid-1960s by
Orange County's population explosion, the ranch established the
Mission Viejo Company in 1964 and embarked on its first residen-
tial venture, the 10,000-acre planned community of Mission Viejo.
Serving as officer of Mission Viejo Company was Anthony R.
("Tony") Moiso, son of Alice O'Neill Avery and great-grandson of
Richard O'Neill, Sr. In 1972, Mission Viejo Company was sold to
Philip Morris, and Moiso accepted the responsibility of managing
the remaining 40,000 acres.

Rather than liquidate the ranch on a piecemeal basis in
response to development pressures, the O'Neill family, led by
Moiso, decided to retain family ownership and develop portions of
the land through master plans intended to accomplish important
goals: 1) help solve housing and transportation issues facing South
Orange County; 2) meet needs for residential, light industrial,
office, recreational and essential support services in a balanced community; 3) create additional value for the community at large
through the dedication of permanent open space to enhance the
regional park and trail system; and 4) serve the community that has
blessed the family.

William Wendt, *Mission Viejo*, Private Collection, Courtesy of The Irvine Museum

William Wendt, *Saddleback Mountain, Mission Viejo*, Private Collection, Courtesy of The Irvine Museum

Gabino Canyon, Rancho Mission Viejo, © Stephen Francis Photography

Richard J. O'Neill and Donna O'Neill at the Rancho Mission Viejo Ranch House on Rancho Mission Viejo, photograph, Courtesy of Rancho Mission Viejo

Alexey Steele, *Sunrise in the Valley, Mission Viejo*, 2005, Private Collection

In 1981, the O'Neill and Moiso families continued the tradition of open space dedications through a 600-acre addition to O'Neill Regional Park followed by another 1,026 acres just a year later. In 1982, the families also added 2,200 acres to Caspers Regional Park.

In 1983, Moiso re-established Santa Margarita Company and began developing the 5,000-acre Rancho Santa Margarita community, now recognized as one of the nation's most innovative new communities. Over the next ten years, the O'Neill and Moiso families dedicated another 1,500 acres of open space to the people of Orange County. Those dedications included 177 acres of key pasture land originally zoned for development, the 1,200-acre Rancho Mission Viejo Land Conservancy (renamed the Donna O'Neill Land Conservancy on January 28, 2003, in memory of Richard O'Neill's late wife, who was indeed an environmental icon), and 105 acres of agricultural land transformed into the successful Cañada Gobernadora Ecological Restoration Area.

William Wendt, *Gobernadora Canyon, Rancho Mission Viejo*, Private Collection, Courtesy of The Irvine Museum

Cattle, Chiquita Canyon 1929, photograph, Courtesy of San Juan Capistrano Historical Society

Cowboys at roundup, Rancho Mission Viejo, photograph, Courtesy of San Juan Capistrano Historical Society

A barbeque under the sycamore, photograph, Courtesy of San Juan Capistrano Historical Society

In the early days, the Irvines and O'Neills shared the yearly rituals of the cattle roundups, brandings and barbecues that were common to large cattle operations. Although The Irvine Company no longer runs any cattle, the 30,000-acre Rancho Mission Viejo continues to maintain a herd of 500 head, making it one of the last operating cattle ranches in California.

Vice President of Ranch Operations Gilbert Aguirre on horseback and Ranch CEO Tony Moiso at right during a Rancho Mission Viejo cattle roundup, c. 1980, photograph, Courtesy of Rancho Mission Viejo

Tony Moiso and friends riding on Rancho Mission Viejo, © Richard Jackson

Cattle, Rancho Mission Viejo, © Richard Jackson

Mexican longhorns, Rancho Mission Viejo, © Richard Jackson

Conceptual plan of The Oaks/Rancho Mission Viejo Riding Park produced by Robert Jolicoeur of International Equestrian Design, September 1995

Moving the indigenous trees from the ditch on the south edge of the Grand Prix field at The Oaks/Rancho Mission Viejo Riding Park, photos by Charlie Adermatt

In January 1995, I signed a lease with Rancho Mission Viejo for the 80 acres that was to become The Oaks/Rancho Mission Viejo Riding Park. Once again, I retained Robert Jolicoeur to design the facility and then brought in my contractor, Charles Adermatt, who worked with Fred Vorhees from the ranch and my Oaks personnel to construct the project.

At the time, there was a large man-made ditch that carried water from a nursery located east of La Pata Road and ran along the base of the bank at the southern edge of the Grand Prix field. Our first project was to move the ditch and reroute the water to the perimeter of the property along Ortega Highway.

After that was accomplished, I had all of the indigenous trees that were growing in the ditch, such as the wild willows, boxed and moved to the edge of the property along the highway. The personnel at the ranch thought I had lost my mind, but when California Fish and Game approved the project, they decided that I wasn't really crazy after all. At that time, I created a nursery for the indigenous shrubs and trees that we had removed from various locations on the property, and maintained them until they could be relocated. My counsel Andy Culbertson was of great assistance to me on environmental matters at that time and on other occasions.

I also purchased several hundred large oak, sycamore and elder trees that were at a nursery on Rancho Mission Viejo that was going out of business. Some of the trees were already boxed, but others had to be dug out and boxed and then brought over to the riding park. I placed all of the trees in the nursery I had created on the east end of the property, where they could be maintained until I needed them for landscaping.

ABOVE AND BELOW: Clearing, grading and watering The Oaks/Rancho Mission Viejo Riding Park

ABOVE AND BELOW: The Santa Ana Bermuda grass on the Grand Prix field, photos by Charlie Adermatt

We began grading in March 1995. After that was completed, I personally supervised the placing and planting of every tree on the property and, at the suggestion of Olympian Bernie Traurig, planted Santa Ana Bermuda grass on the field to ensure that we would have the best footing for jumping competition. I completed The Oaks/Rancho Mission Viejo Riding Park, including all of the landscaping, in May of 1996.

At that time, I began holding The Oaks Classic and The Oaks Fall Classic, which became The Oaks International, at both The Oaks/Rancho Mission Viejo Riding Park and The Oaks. The events offered more than $150,000 in prize money, including a $50,000 Grand Prix, and continued the tradition of featuring an exhibition of historic California plein air paintings from The Irvine Museum as well as from prominent art dealers from across the country.

Anna Hills, *Summer in the Canyon*, Private Collection, Courtesy of The Irvine Museum

James Irvine II with one of his hunting dogs, photograph,
The Irvine Family Archives

ON APRIL 25, 1993, MY COUSIN Linda Irvine Gaede married Harvey A. Smith. Two years later, Orange County Harbors, Beaches & Parks staff, headed by Eric Jessen, began planning a series of events to celebrate the Irvine Park Centennial. At Eric's request, in order to develop a program that celebrated the centennial of our grandfather's gift, my cousins the late Katie Wheeler, James Myford Irvine and Linda Irvine Smith, agreed to share their private photographic archives of stills and movies with the county so that they could be reproduced and put in the public domain. The Irvine Company gave a grant of $10,000 to the Academy of Motion Picture Arts and Sciences to reproduce the movies and store the originals in its archives.

At that time, my cousin Bill White told Eric that the Irvine family was interested in having a statue of James Irvine II placed in Irvine Park. Funding for the project came from the Joan Irvine Smith & Athalie R. Clarke Foundation as well as from Katie Wheeler, Linda Irvine Smith, James Myford Irvine, Bill White and his sister Gloria White Bryant.

The county commissioned sculptor Deborah Copenhaver Fellows of Big Fork, Montana, to produce a larger-than-life-size bronze statue of James Irvine II with two of his Irish setters. The statue, entitled "The Winds of Change," was based on a photograph of him that was taken around 1918, while he was hunting in the Newport Back Bay. The statue was placed near the Pavilion in Irvine Park, where the Irvine family photos were exhibited during the Centennial Celebration.

The grand finale of the Irvine Park Centennial Celebration was a gala dinner held on October 3, 1997, under the stars in front of the band shell at the park. The two hundred attendees included members of the Irvine family, various public officials, representatives from many prominent Orange County families as well as Eric's parents, whose family had built and supplied the Irvine Ranch with farm equipment and machinery starting in the 1880s. The guest of honor was my cousin Katie Wheeler, the then-matriarch of the Irvine family and the only family member to be born and raised in the Irvine ranch house. After dinner and the showing of Irvine family historic films, Supervisor Todd Spitzer and Eric escorted Katie up to the statue for the installation. When the statue was unveiled, Katie dedicated "Winds of Change" with fireworks in the background.

Deborah Copenhaver, *The Winds of Change*,
© Christopher Bliss

Dedication of statue of James Irvine II, *The Winds of Change*, at the Irvine Park Centennial Celebration on October 3, 1997. BACK ROW FROM LEFT: James Myford Irvine, Gay White Bryant, sculptress, Deborah Copenhaver, Katie Wheeler, Joan Irvine Smith, Linda Irvine Smith, James I. Swinden, William Thornton White III and Ryan and Paul White with Gorine and Jeremy Irvine. FRONT ROW FROM LEFT: Monica Haefelfinger Kelly, Sasha Connelly Borland, Nita Connelly, Tanya Rohr and Robert James Haefelfinger, photo by Eric Jessen

Christopher and Dana Reeve at the 1996 Oaks International at The Oaks/Rancho Mission Viejo Riding Park, photo by Yana Bridle

IN MAY 1995, ACTOR Christopher Reeve, famous for his role as Superman, shattered two neck vertebrae and became paralyzed when he was thrown from his horse during the cross-country phase of a three-day event in Culpepper, Virginia. After seeing several of his interviews on television, I was very impressed with the courage and perseverance shown by him and his wife, Dana, and with Christopher's exceptional ability to communicate with people. I also took notice that in his interviews, he never blamed his horse for the accident.

Because of my longtime involvement in equestrian jumping competition and fox hunting, I was certainly aware that this type of accident could happen to anyone who rides. Although the principal causes of spinal cord trauma are violent crime, traffic accidents and sports injuries, such as occur in diving, surfing, cycling and football, I kept thinking, "There but by the grace of God go I or my children or my grandchildren."

Kevin Short, *The Real Deal, Tony Forster and Jim Severson Surfing*, Courtesy of Tony Forster

Joan Irvine Smith and Kontiki at the George Morris clinic at The Oaks 1990, photos by John Moroney

Frank H. Myers, *Football Players*, The Irvine Museum, Gift of the Estate of Patricia C. Myers and the Brian Myers Trust

On October 20, 1995, when I attended the groundbreaking of the William J. Gillespie Neuroscience Research Facility at UCI, I told Dr. Tom Cesario, dean of the medical school, and then Chancellor Dr. Laurel Wilkening that I thought Christopher Reeve would be a terrific spokesperson for the research that UCI was doing with regard to spinal cord injuries and disease. I also told them that the Joan Irvine Smith & Athalie R. Clarke Foundation would put up $1 million toward a Reeve-Irvine Research Center at UCI.

Shortly thereafter, Dan Wyan of Tri-Crown Productions, who did the Horse World television coverage for the equestrian jumping events at The Oaks, contacted me and told me he wanted to get an introduction to Christopher Reeve. Horse World wanted to do a television interview with him in which he could reassure children not to be afraid to ride just because of his accident. At that time, I told Dan that our foundation was going to put up $1 million toward a Reeve-Irvine Research Center at UCI for spinal cord injuries. Dan said that this was the "hook" he needed, and he gave me the name of Christopher Reeve's secretary Michael Manganello, who was at the Kessler Institute for Rehabilitation in New Jersey with Christopher while he was undergoing physical therapy there.

About that time, Dr. Carl W. Cotman, a professor of neurobiology and behavior in the School of Biological Sciences and a professor of neurology in the College of Medicine at UCI, was vis-

iting Christopher at the institute to confer with him and his doctors. Dr. Cotman's landmark studies at UCI since 1968 have advanced the understanding of Alzheimer's, Parkinson's and other age-related disorders. He is currently a member of the Christopher Reeve Paralysis Foundation and Director of the UCI Institute for Brain Aging and Dementia.

I then wrote to Christopher and indicated that the Joan Irvine Smith & Athalie R. Clarke Foundation wished to give $1 million for a spinal cord injury research center at UCI if he would be our spokesperson. About ten days later, I received a call from Michael, who told me that Christopher had received my letter, but because he didn't know me or of the University of California at Irvine, had placed it in the pile that he termed "kook mail." A few days later, Michael told him that he should take a look at that letter from Mrs. Smith, as it was for a $1 million donation. When Christopher did read the letter, he asked Michael to call me. It took a number of phone calls and a trip by Michael and Mitchell Stoller of the American Paralysis Association to see the campus in order to convince Christopher that although the University of California at Irvine was on the West Coast, it was nevertheless a very prestigious institution and a national leader in neurological research. At first, Christopher was not sure that he could physically handle the task; however, after I told him, "Yesterday, you played Superman, now you can be Superman," he decided that he would try to do it.

Dr. Oswald Steward, Christopher Reeve and Joan Irvine Smith at the Reeve-Irvine Research Center at UCI, photograph, Courtesy of UCI

On January 10, 1996, we held a joint press conference at UCI announcing that I was joining with actor Christopher Reeve, the American Paralysis Association and the UCI College of Medicine in forming the Reeve-Irvine Research Center for spinal cord injuries and disease, with the goal of finding a cure for paralysis. Dr. Cesario further announced that the center would be housed at UCI's developing center for health sciences. Christopher Reeve, who spoke to the gathered media by speaker phone from his home on the East Coast, said, "I want to express my thanks to Joan Irvine Smith for this amazing and stunning act of generosity. It's proof of what can be accomplished by the private sector."

I spoke briefly to Christopher during the event, saying, "Horse people stick together," and further stating that I was overwhelmed by his tremendous courage when I saw him interviewed after the accident. "Providence dealt you a terrific blow," I told him, "but she gave you the gift to touch the heart. Yesterday, you played Superman; today you are Superman."

My good friend, the late Dr. Howard House, founder of the House Ear Institute in Los Angeles, advised me on both the past and the then current treatment of spinal cord injury. As his son Dr. John House, who now heads up the institute, had broken his neck in a surfing accident, Howard had a personal interest in this type of research. My mother had been both a close friend and a patient of Howard's for more than fifty years and was a major supporter of the House Ear Institute. The Joan Irvine Smith & Athalie R. Clarke Foundation supports the House Ear Institute.

Most of the research being done on spinal cord injuries in 1996 was focused on preventing and limiting neurological damage at the time of injury. Little had been done to explore ways of mitigating and reversing the damage once it had occurred. In contrast, treatment of the chronically afflicted patient was the initial area of research conducted at the center. This research also benefited individuals struggling with multiple sclerosis, Alzheimer's disease, Lou Gehrig's disease and other diseases involving neurological dysfunction.

Dr. Howard House and Athalie Irvine Clarke at The Thoroughbred Spread Barbecue in The Oak Grove at The Oaks Fall Classic, 1991, photo by Tish Quirk

THE 1996
OAKS CLASSIC,
CONTINUED ON
NEXT PAGE

Marine color guard and the Portola Riders open the 1996 Oaks Classic at The Oaks/Rancho Mission Viejo Riding Park, photo by Jumpshot

The Thoroughbred Spread Barbecue in The Oak Grove at The Oaks

Monsignor Paul M. Martin of Mission San Juan Capistrano gave the invocation, photo by Jumpshot

Portola Rider Buck Bean proudly carries our flag, photo by Jumpshot

Richard and Donna O'Neill at the Good Times Bar, barbecue catered by El Adobe

IN JUNE 1996, The Oaks Classic benefited the National Water Research Institute and was held at both The Oaks/Rancho Mission Viejo Riding Park and The Oaks. The event featured The Oaks Classic Grand Prix Luncheon and $50,000 Grand Prix, the House of Hermès $10,000 Acorn Junior/Amateur Grand Prix, the $10,000 Dash for Cash, The Oaks $10,000 Hunter Derby, the Thoroughbred Spread Barbecue and an exhibition of historic California plein air paintings from The Irvine Museum as well as from prominent art dealers from across the country. Richard Spooner won the Grand Prix on Kirk for owners Dave and Tracey Kenley.

Richard Spooner on Kirk winner of the 1996 $50,000 Oaks Classic Grand Prix receives award from Joan Irvine Smith with FROM RIGHT: National Water Research Institute Executive Director Ron Linsky, Col. John Foley, Ted Dansen of the American Oceans Campaign and far left Robert Sulnick of the AOC photo by Jumpshot

Renee Bondi sang the Star Spangled Banner, photo by Jumpshot

FROM LEFT: Jim Swinden, Robert Sulnick, Ted Dansen, Ron Linsky, the 1996 Clarke Prize recipient Dr. Walter Webber, Joan Irvine Smith with Russ Penniman at far right, photo by Jumpshot

Will Simpson and Sandstone Landsman winners of the Mayor's Trophy for the Dash for Cash with Joan Irvine Smith and San Juan Capistrano Mayor Wyatt Hart, photo by Jumpshot

Kerry Potter and Call me in the Morning winners of the $10,000 House of Hermes Acorn Junior/Amateur Grand Prix with Robert Drennan and Robin Serfass, photo by Jumpshot

Willem Cooper on Glenmore's Dixieland with Nathalie Cooper receives the lead line class award from Robert Drennan, photo by Jumpshot

Larry Mahan and Ted Dansen, photo by Jumpshot

LEFT: Joan Irvine Smith and Cappy Smith present award to Nathalie Cooper on Glenmore's Dixieland, photo by Jumpshot RIGHT: Lauren Dendiu on Ocean Blue, the 1997 AHSA National Grand Champion Regular Hunter and the 1997 and 1996 AHSA National Champion Regular Conformation Hunter, in the $10,000 Open Hunter Classic, photo by Jumpshot

THE 1996 OAKS INTERNATIONAL, CONTINUED ON NEXT THREE PAGES

In September, we held The Oaks International for the benefit of the Reeve-Irvine Research Center at UCI. On Friday, September 13, we held the Thoroughbred Spread Barbecue in the Oak Grove at The Oaks. The following night, Christopher Reeve's cachet brought Robin Williams, Jane Seymour, Joan Rivers and 560 other guests to the Mission San Juan Capistrano for the Evening Under the Stars dinner and auction. The event raised $80,000 for the center.

Marine color guard opens the 1996 Oaks International at The Oaks/Rancho Mission Viejo Riding Park, photo by Jumpshot

Richard Spooner on Robinson winner of the 1996 $50,000 Oaks International Grand Prix receives trophy from Joan Irvine Smith with FROM RIGHT: UCI Chancellor Laurel Wilkening, Budweiser representatives, Robert Drennan, and Dr. Tom Cesario, Dean of UCI College of Medicine, photo by Jumpshot

Megan Johnstone on Bonius winner of the $10,000 Tiffany & Co. Oak Leaf Junior/Amateur Grand Prix with Robert Drennan and a Tiffany & Co. representative, photo by Jumpshot

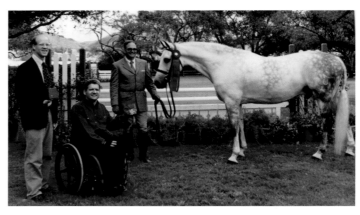

Jim Swinden with Hunter Champion Casper at The Oaks, photo by Jumpshot

LEFT: Leslie Vaillancourt on Hunter Champion Chanel at The Oaks, photo by Jumpshot
RIGHT: Lynn Obligado on Southern Flight by South Pacific, the 1996 IJF Western Regional Four-Year-Old Champion, photo by Jumpshot

FROM LEFT: Joan Irvine Smith, Dr. Tom Cesario, Dean of UCI College of Medicine, Dr. Martin Schwab, first Reeve Research Medal and $50,000 prize recipient, Christopher and Dana Reeve, photo by Yana Bridle

Dr. Tom Cesario, Dr. Martin Schwab with the Reeve Research Medal and UCI Chancellor Laurel Wilkening, photo by Yana Bridle

Russ Penniman on Parkmore, in the $10,000 Open Hunter Classic, photo by Jumpshot

Dr. Howard House, Tully Rector, Cappy Smith and Robert Jolicoeur at The Oaks Grand Prix luncheon, photo by Yana Bridle

Jane Seymour giving an interview regarding the Reeve-Irvine Research Center at UCI, photo by Yana Bridle

At the Grand Prix Luncheon, on Sunday, September 15, we presented the first Christopher Reeve Research Medal and $50,000 prize to Dr. Martin Schwab from the University of Zurich, Switzerland, the outstanding international scientist in the field of spinal cord research. The event included The Oaks International $50,000 Grand Prix, the $10,000 Oak Leaf Junior/Amateur Grand Prix, The Oaks $10,000 Hunter Derby and an exhibition of historic California plein air art. Richard Spooner won the Grand Prix on Robinson for HMB Enterprises.

Alexey Steele with his painting of The Oaks/Rancho Mission Viejo Riding Park, photo by Yana Bridle

Jim Swinden on Casper, in the $10,000 Open Hunter Classic, photo by Jumpshot

Ted Dansen seated at left and other guests at The Oaks Grand Prix luncheon, photo by Yana Bridle

THE EVENING UNDER THE STARS GALA AT MISSION SAN JUAN CAPISTRANO BENEFITING THE REEVE-IRVINE RESEARCH CENTER AT UCI, CONTINUED ON NEXT PAGE

Evening Under the Stars Dinner, Mission San Juan Capistrano, benefiting the Reeve-Irvine Research Center at UCI, 1996 FROM LEFT: Tom and Elizabeth Tierney, Jane Seymour, and UCI Chancellor Laurel Wilkening, photo by Yana Bridle

Fish pond in the courtyard at Mission San Juan Capistrano, photo by Yana Bridle

Dining tables in courtyard, photo by Yana Bridle

The Lacouague Sisters FROM LEFT: Denise Loyatho, Renee Bondi, and Michelle Smith, at the Evening Under the Stars Dinner, photo by Yana Bridle

FROM LEFT: Suzie Peltason, Mary Roosevelt, and Linda White Peters, photo by Yana Bridle

Joan Irvine Smith and Laura and David Dukes with Christopher Reeve, photo by Yana Bridle

Joan Rivers and guest, photo by Yana Bridle

FROM LEFT: Robin Williams, Christopher Reeve, Dr. Martin Schwab, Joan Irvine Smith, Louise and Roger Williams and Jane Seymour, photo by Yana Bridle

FRONT ROW FROM LEFT: Dr. Walter Henry, Tracey Gaede, Diana Gaede, Harvey and Linda Smith. BACK ROW FROM LEFT: Maria del Carmen Calvo, Dr. Howard house, Roger and Louise Williams, Charles and Maureen Swinden, Katrina Lutge and Carol Penniman, photo by Yana Bridle

FRONT ROW FROM LEFT: Marie Mainz, Cappy Smith, Joan Irvine Smith and Jim Swinden. BACK ROW FROM LEFT: Tully Rector, Alletta and Bill Cooper, Russ Penniman, Anita Ziebe and Madeline Swinden, photo by Yana Bridle

Nicole Shahinian and El Campeon's Jo Jo winners of the 1997 $30,000 Oaks Classic Grand Prix receives trophy from Joan Irvine Smith and Fran Steinwedell at left with Mercedes Benz Mission Viejo Imports Representatives, Ron Linsky, Executive Director of the National Water Research Institute, and owners, Lou, Jonathan and Eva Gonda, at right, photo by Jumpshot

Jill Prieto and Free Styling, winners of the 1997 $10,000 House of Hermes Acorn Junior/Amateur Grand Prix, with Francine Bardo and Bill Whitehead of Hermes at right, photo by Jumpshot

Will Simpson on Sandstone Landsman receives the Mayor's Trophy for the Dash for Cash from San Juan Capistrano Mayor David Swerdlin and Joan Irvine Smith, photo by Jumpshot

In June 1997, we held The Oaks Classic for the benefit of The National Water Research Institute. The event featured, among other things, The Oaks Classic $30,000 Grand Prix and USET Regional Show Jumping Championship. Nicole Simpson won the Grand Prix on El Campeon's Jo Jo.

Jennifer Patterson and Carte Blanche winners of the $10,000 Open Hunter Classic receives trophy from Alletta Cooper and Elaine Gleason, photo by Jumpshot

THE 1997 OAKS
INTERNATIONAL,
CONTINUED ON
NEXT TWO PAGES

FROM LEFT: Dr. Tom Cesario, Dean
of UCI College of Medicine, UCI
Chancellor Laurel Wilkening, Joan
Irvine Smith, Christopher Reeve,
Dana Reeve, and second
Christopher Reeve Research Medal
and $50, 000 prize winner Dr. Fred
Gage, photo by Yana Bridle

Dr. Tom Cesario, Jerry Mandel,
Director of Development at UCI,
and Mary Roosevelt, photo by
Yana Bridle

In September, we held The Oaks International benefiting
the Reeve-Irvine Research Center. On Saturday, September 13, we
held the Thoroughbred Spread Barbecue in the Oak Grove at The
Oaks to benefit the center. At the Grand Prix Luncheon the following day, we presented the second Christopher Reeve Research Medal
and $50,000 prize to Dr. Fred Gage, professor of genetics at the Salk
Institute for Biological Studies in La Jolla. The event featured,
among other things, The Oaks International $50,000 Grand Prix
and also an exhibition of historic California plein air art from The
Irvine Museum and original photographs from the Nature
Conservancy. Kerry Bernay and The Oaks' stallion Luganda, a
grandson of Landgraf I, won the Grand Prix.

Kartina Lutge, Jim Swinden, Marie Mainz and other guest at the Grand Prix
luncheon, photo by Yana Bridle

Linda White Peters, Peggy Goldwater Clay and Louise Turner Arnold with other
guests at the Grand Prix luncheon, photo by Yana Bridle

LEFT: Dr. Fred Gage seated with
his family AT LEFT and Suzie
Peltason at right. SECOND ROW
FROM LEFT: Godfrey Sill, UCI
Chancellor Laurel Wilkening
and former Chancellor Jack
Peltason, photo by Yana Bridle
RIGHT, FROM LEFT: Trent McGee,
Santa Ana Mayor Miguel Pulido
and David Dukes, photo by
Yana Bridle

Joan Irvine Smith presents trophy to Kerry Bernay on Luganda winner of the 1997 $50,000 Oaks International Grand Prix for The Oaks with Budweiser representative Pam Ziebarth and Mercedes Benz Mission Viejo Imports representatives, photo by Jumpshot

LEFT: Marine color guard
RIGHT: Jill Prieto on Free Styling winner of the $10,000 Oak Leaf Junior/Amateur Grand Prix sponsored by Body Wise with Tom and Elizabeth Tierney and their granddaughters, photo by Jumpshot

Jessica Vaillancourt, Elizabeth Penniman and Sue Connors with Dana Connors on Night Light in the lead line class, photo by Jumpshot

Elizabeth Penniman on Hunter Champion Top Drawer (Cowboy)

Monsignor Paul M. Martin of Mission San Juan Capistrano, Dana Reeve and Russ Penniman on the Grand Prix Field after Father Martin gave the invocation, photo by Jumpshot

Dana Reeve with Will on Coventry Meadow Mouse in the lead line class, photo by Jumpshot

Jase on Apple with Jim and Madeline Swinden in the lead line class, photo by Jumpshot

The Oaks Thoroughbred Spread Barbeque on Saturday September 13, during the 1997 Oaks International in The Oak Grove at The Oaks benefiting the Reeve-Irvine Research Center, photo by Yana Bridle

San Juan Capistrano Mayor Wyatt Hart and Richard O'Neill, photo by Yana Bridle

Joan Irvine Smith, photo by Yana Bridle

Elizabeth and Tom Tierney, photo by Yana Bridle

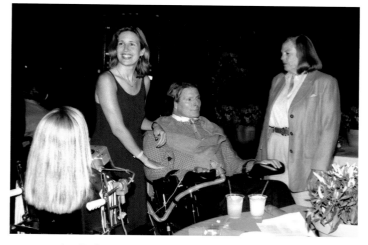

FROM LEFT: Ann Ruth, Dana and Christopher Reeve with Joan Irvine Smith, photo by Yana Bridle

David Dukes and Trent McGee, photo by Yana Bridle

FROM LEFT: Linda White Peters, Mr. Peters, Elizabeth Tierney and David and Laura Dukes, photo by Yana Bridle

FROM LEFT: Madeline and Len Zuckerman with Peggy Goldwater Clay and Bob Clay, photo by Yana Bridle

233

Today, the Reeve-Irvine Research Center (RIRC), chaired by Dr. Oswald Steward, is housed in the William J. Gillespie Neuroscience Research Facility in the UCI Biomedical Research Center. In order to stimulate and encourage research efforts, from 1996 through 2002 our foundation funded the Christopher Reeve Research Medal with a $50,000 cash prize that is presented annually to the researcher who makes the most gains in the field. In 2003, I asked Christopher if he would mind if we renamed the award the Reeve-Irvine Research Medal, and he told me that he would be honored.

In addition to Dr. Steward, two additional faculty members were recruited to the center in 2000 and 2001, Dr. Hans Keirstead and Dr. Aileen Anderson.

William J. Gillespie Neuroscience Research Facility in the UCI Biomedical Research Center where the Christopher Reeve Research Center is located, photo by Yana Bridle

Dr. Tom Cesario, Dean of UCI College of Medicine, addressing the audience, photo by Yana Bridle

FROM LEFT: Christopher Reeve, William J. Gillespie, Chancellor Laurel Wilkening and Dr. Tom Cesario, photo by Yana Bridle

FROM LEFT: Dr. Howard House, Joan Irvine Smith, Arnold Beckman and Jim Moore, Esq. at the opening of the facility, photo by Yana Bridle

FROM LEFT: Dr Tom Cesario, Dean of UCI College of Medicine, UCI Chancellor Laurel Wilkening, Peggy Goldwater Clay and James Asp, Associate Vice Chancellor of the University Foundation with Ken Waldrop, photo by Yana bridle

Dr. William E. Bunney, photo by Yana Bridle

FROM LEFT: Elizabeth and Tom Tierney, Jessica Behrens, and Janice and Roger Johnson

Former UCI Chancellor Jack Peltason and Suzie Peltason, photo by Yana Bridle

Arnold Beckman and Pat Beckman, photo by Yana Bridle

Dr. Howard House and Joan Irvine Smith, photo by Yana Bridle

Mary and Tom Cesario, photo by Yana Bridle

FROM LEFT: Dr. Howard House, Joan Irvine Smith, Chancellor Laurel Wilkening, Jim and Madeline Swinden and Dr. Carl Cotman, photo by Yana Bridle

FROM LEFT: Carol and Russ Penniman, Dr. Howard House, Chancellor Wilkening and Mrs. Smith, photo by Yana Bridle

FROM LEFT: Morton Smith, Russ Penniman, Anita Ziebe, Dana and Christopher Reeve, Joan Irvine Smith, Jim and Madeline Swinden, photograph, Courtesy of UCI

According to Dr. Steward:

Recent scientific accomplishments have provided a basis for hope for new therapies to reduce the level of disability, promote recovery of function and stimulate actual nervous system regeneration, even in individuals with long-standing injuries. To capitalize on this potential, the goals of the RIRC were to create a research enterprise that bridged across disciplines, promoted collaborations and allowed a fusion of the host of biomedical approaches that offer promise. Research related to spinal cord injury ranges from molecular and cellular studies, including studies with stem cells, studies on synthetic biological compounds, tissue and bioengineering, gene therapy and molecular modeling. In the end, all new therapeutic approaches must be tested in animal models of spinal cord injury, yet it is not efficient, or for that matter even possible, for every lab to undertake the full range of studies. Accordingly, spinal cord injury research, perhaps more than any other clinically relevant research focus, requires cooperation and coordination across individual investigators and laboratories.

In the five years since its establishment, the RIRC has developed research programs that focus on basic cellular and molecular mechanisms that underlie the response of the nervous system to injury, focusing especially on mechanisms underlying axon regeneration and the use of human stem cells for therapeutic applications. The three principal investigators (Drs. Steward, Keirstead and Anderson) have attracted grants that now total more than $1.5 million per year for basic research funding. Grants to Dr. Steward support basic research to discover ways to promote nerve regeneration following spinal cord injury. Grants to Dr. Keirstead and Dr. Anderson focus on the use of stem cells for nervous system repair. These projects are collaborative ventures with biotechnology companies that are developing either human embryonic stem cells (in the Keirstead project) or human fetal stem cells (in the Anderson project) for potential use in treating disorders resulting from spinal cord and brain injury. The strategy may also prove to be useful for treating neurodegenerative disorders, including Alzheimer's disease, Parkinson's disease and Huntington's disease.

Dr. Tom Cesario, Dean of the UCI Medical School, explains:

Stem cells are special cells that retain the characteristics of very basic cells found in early states of the embryo that can differentiate into a variety of different tissues and different organs. As such, they offer an enormous potential to reconstitute damaged organs. Stem cells can be safety prepared, without crossing ethical barriers, from a variety of sources, including human blood, the placenta, or from fetal tissues used at the time of in vitro fertilization that have been declared unwanted. These cells, when properly prepared, can be used to repair key damaged organs. For example, they can be used in the bone marrow if, for some reason, disease has damaged the ability to produce red cells or white cells. In this situation, they could conceivably be lifesaving. Additionally, they could permit aggressive use of chemotherapy in treating cancer patients. Many chemotherapeutic drugs are toxic and therefore limited in their use because of their potential to damage the bone marrow. If ways were available to reconstitute bone marrow with stem cells, it would allow us to more aggressively treat cancer patients in a simpler way than now-used bone marrow transplantation.

Similarly, diseases of the central nervous system such as Alzheimer's disease, possibly Parkinson's disease or traumatic diseases, including those brought out by damage to the blood vessels such as stroke, could potentially be ameliorated by the use of stem cell transplants. Additionally, damaged hearts that have been injured through the process of myocardial infarction, or better known as a heart attack, could be repaired through the use of appropriate injections of stem cells.

With all of these various considerations in mind, it is key to move forward to investigating the potential of stem cells to know where they may be of benefit and where their application would be of limited or no value. Much of the stem cell studies to date have been done in other animal systems. What are badly needed now are further studies on human stem cells. Again, appropriately collected stem cells, collected under the strictest of moral and ethical guidelines, can and must be studied to determine their value in treating diseases such as those mentioned above. Indeed, given the potential of stem cells, it seems that it would be immoral and unethical not to better understand what the potential is in easing human suffering. In order to accomplish this, we will need both private and public support.

My good friend Christopher Reeve died on October 10, 2004, at his New York home from heart failure due to complications from an infection. His relentless efforts to find a cure for spinal cord injury and disease truly made him a legend in his own time.

A prominent and forceful advocate for expanding embryonic stem cell research, Christopher was a critic of President Bush's 2001 decision to limit federal funding to existing stem cell lines. In his testimony before the U.S. Senate, Christopher said, "While we prolong the stem cell debate, millions continue to suffer. We must harness the power of the government and go forward."

Although Christopher is gone, he will not die, for he will live in the hearts of those he loved and left behind and through the UCI Reeve-Irvine Research Center's pursuit of his dream to find a cure for spinal cord injury and disease.

After Christopher's death, my dear and courageous friend, Dana Reeve, continued her late husband's campaign for stem cell and other medical research to treat spinal cord injuries. During the 2004 campaign, she publicly endorsed Senator John F. Kerry, who cited Christopher's efforts for more stem cell research during a debate with President Bush, who continues to limit the use of federal funds for that research. Last August, Dana was diagnosed with lung cancer and died seven months later on March 6, 2006.

An editorial in the *New York Times* on November 5, 2004, entitled "California to the Rescue," states the following:

When California voters enacted Proposition 71, a lavishly financed stem cell program, on November 2 they performed a valuable service that should help keep this nation in the forefront of one of the most promising areas of biomedical research. It was especially important given the big role that religious conservatives, who are strongly opposed to embryonic stem cell research, played in re-electing President Bush. There seems to be little chance that Mr. Bush will retreat from his limits on federal support for such research, and a Congress that has shifted rightward may try, once again, to ban therapeutic cloning, the most promising area of embryonic stem cell research. Now that California has enshrined stem cell research and therapeutic cloning in its Constitution and state law, it may be the engine that keeps the nation moving.

The ballot measure won almost 60 percent of the vote, thanks in part to strong support from Gov. Arnold Schwarzenegger, who agrees with many moderate Republicans that the research holds enormous potential for treating intractable diseases. California is now authorized to borrow up to $3 billion over a decade for research in the state's universities, nonprofit institutions and private companies. The money would be doled out at a rate that could reach $300 million a year. This is a staggering sum of money, 12 times as much as the federal government spent last year on embryonic stem cell research under the president's restrictive policies.

Christopher and Dana Reeve at the 1996 Oaks International, photo by Yana Bridle

The new gusher of support is apt to tilt the playing field toward California in the race to attract top scientists and expand the biotechnology industry. California's universities are already plotting to lure top scientists from other states or even other nations with newly built laboratories and hefty research budgets. States that aspire to scientific preeminence may soon find themselves under pressure to spend to avoid losing top talent.

An article entitled "Defection Bares Stem Cell Rifts, The majority leader's break with Bush to back federally paid research provokes angry rebukes," which appeared in the *Los Angeles Times* on July 30, 2005 indicates the following:

Abandoned by his most prominent Senate ally, President Bush moved closer July 29 to a confrontation with fellow Republicans over his opposition to expanded federal backing for embryonic stem cell research, as one of the most explosive moral issues of his presidency reignited in Congress.

Senate Majority Leader Bill Frist (R-Tenn.) announced that he would support the Senate version of the Castle bill, legislation allowing the federal government to finance research using a broader range of embryonic stem cells. His decision substantially raised the odds that the bill would win approval in Congress and face a presidential veto, which White House strategists had hoped to avoid.

Frist's announcement, in a speech in the Senate on July 29, exposed deep rifts within the GOP hierarchy that controls the Capitol and the White House. The issue pits social conservatives, who view the research as immoral because human embryos are destroyed in the process, against people who say the research is warranted because it may lead to cures for diseases.

In his speech, Frist broke from conservatives who say the potential of the research is overstated. "Cure today may be just a theory, a hope, a dream," he said. "But the promise is powerful enough that I believe this research deserves our increased energy and focus."

Stem cells from human embryos have drawn interest because many scientists believe they might one day be fashioned into brain cells for Parkinson's disease patients, insulin-producing cells for diabetics, and other replacements for cells and tissues that go awry in disease.
Under rules set by Bush, the federal government only finances research on cells drawn from human embryos before he announced the policy on Aug. 9, 2001. Bush said his goal was to allow the research to move forward without using taxpayer money to cause additional embryos to be destroyed. The rules do not prohibit privately funded research on new stem cell groups.

On July 29, Frist sided with scientists, patients' groups and lawmakers who have said Bush's policy is too restrictive, leaving federally backed scientists unable to work with newer and apparently more versatile cell groups.

"The limitations put in place in 2001 will, over time, slow our ability to bring potential new treatments for certain diseases," Frist said. "Therefore, I believe the president's policy should be modified."

Frist said he would back legislation allowing the government to fund research using embryonic stem cells no matter when they were created. As under current policy, the cells could come only from embryos that couples created at fertility clinics but that were no longer needed and would otherwise be destroyed.

Frist's position is significant because he is the Senate's majority leader as well as a physician who carries clout with his colleagues on health issues. He is also one of several lawmakers who oppose abortion because it destroys embryos but who, under certain restrictions, favor research that entails destroying embryos.

In California, officials said that even if a broader federal policy became law, the federal government still could not finance research allowed under Proposition 71, which created the state's $3-billion embryonic stem cell agency.

Bob Klein, chairman of the agency, the California Institute for Regenerative Medicine, said a broader federal policy would still leave a "massive gap" that California could fill. For example, Proposition 71 funds a procedure that aims to use cloning techniques to create stem cells that exactly match an individual's genetic makeup.

Stem cells created this way would presumably be easier to transplant into a patient. But the technique, sometimes called therapeutic cloning, is controversial and would not be funded under the legislation moving through Congress. The House has voted twice to criminalize it.

In Congress, Republican supporters of stem cell research said they were optimistic that Frist's support would persuade other Republicans to switch their position.

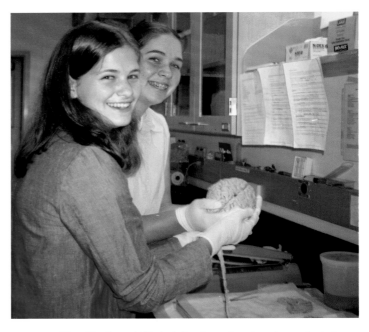

FROM LEFT: Kerry Vaughn and Elizabeth Penniman observing a human brain in Dr. Carl W. Cotman's laboratory at UCI, photograph, Courtesy of UCI

The 2005 Reeve-Irvine Research Medal was awarded to Drs. Carl W. Cotman from UCI and Geoffrey Raisman from Oxford for discoveries related to sprouting and synapse reorganization in the central nervous system. Their findings led to breakthroughs in the understanding of adult neuroplasticity, the natural ability of the brain and spinal cord to form new connections to compensate for injury. Carl W. Cotman, Ph.D. is a professor of neurobiology and behavior in the School of Biological Sciences and professor of neurology in the College of Medicine. He is also Director of the UCI Institute for Brain Aging and Dementia.

The Joan Irvine Smith & Athalie R. Clarke Foundation recently made a gift of $10,000 to the Reeve-Irvine Research Center for research to improve the functionality of prosthetic hands and arms. I made the gift soon after reading a commentary by Gordon Dillow entitled "Helping Hand for Maimed Veterans" which appeared in The Orange County Register on October 30, 2005 about a 19-year-old UCI student, Ryan Langan, who had initiated a project to advance prosthetic technologies at the campus's Reeve-Irvine Research Center.

For a long time I've wanted to do something for our wounded veterans from the war in Iraq. When I read Mr. Dillow's commentary I felt I had found a way to be helpful that would also advance research at UCI and recognized it as the perfect opportunity to open the door for new breakthroughs in the development of prosthetic hands.

Current upper-limb prosthetic devices do not simulate the function and appearance of a real arm efficiently. Even myoelectric prostheses, which have active-motion capabilities controlled by sensors, do not offer the kind of realistic action that the research team hopes to develop. The team has identified the following advances that would significantly improve upper-extremity prostheses: full range of motion, including articulating fingers; light-grasping capability for opposing fingers and thumbs; tactile sensors; and the ability to control a prosthetic hand by signals from the nervous system. The work is being carried out primarily by three UCI researchers: William C. Tang and Abraham Lee, professors of biomedical engineering; and James Fallon, professor of anatomy and neurobiology. According to Dr. Oswald Steward, director of the Reeve-Irvine Research Center, my gift was key to getting the project started. With this seed funding, they can begin to establish collaborative links that will eventually lead to a new "arm" of the Reeve-Irvine Research Center—advanced prosthetic hand research.

Science Lecture Hall, 1996, photograph, Courtesy of UCI

Biological Sciences Unit II, McGaugh Hall, 1993, photograph, Courtesy of UCI

Panoramic view of Physical Sciences Units I, Rowland Hall, and II, Reines Hall, 1993, photograph, Courtesy of UCI

William Wendt, *San Juan Capistrano Hot Springs*, Private Collection, Courtesy of The Irvine Museum

Eric Jessen head of Orange County Harbors, Beaches and Parks assisting with the installation of the exhibition, *A Silent Testament: Nature and Humankind in the Balance* at the Bowers Museum of Cultural Arts in Santa Ana in1998

Silent Testament exhibition at the Bowers Museum

As part of The Oaks International held in 1997, The Irvine Museum joined with the Nature Conservancy of California in an exhibition of California plein air paintings and original photographs with the objective of raising public awareness of the necessity of protecting our threatened California environment. The success of this remarkable exhibition led me to ask Peter Keller, president of the Bowers Museum of Cultural Art in Santa Ana, who attended the event, if the Bowers had an opening where we might continue the exhibition and make it available to a larger audience. Peter offered us a gallery from mid-March through mid-April 1998. We called the exhibition *A Silent Testament: Nature and Humankind in the Balance.*

Conserving the environment and preserving the imperiled diversity of life on our planet are two of the most important issues facing humankind today. The exhibition A Silent Testament linked natural history, environmental science and fine art in order to raise public awareness of critical environmental issues.

California Gnatcatcher, © Richard Jackson

Murals commissioned by Donna O'Neill, by Rebecca Jo Morales © 1993

To achieve this remarkable exhibition, I brought together the following organizations and corporations: the Friends of the Nature Reserve of Orange County, the Nature Conservancy, The Irvine Company, the County of Orange, the Orange County Natural History Association, The Irvine Museum, the Bowers Museum of Cultural Art, the American Oceans Campaign, UCI, the National Water Research Institute, the Joan Irvine Smith & Athalie R. Clarke Foundation, the Archaeological Conservancy, the Audubon Society, the Hubbs-Sea World Research Institute, the Irvine Ranch Water District, the Laguna Canyon Foundation, Laguna Greenbelt, Inc., LSA Associates, Inc., the Metropolitan Water District of Southern California, the Orange County Water District, the Rancho Mission Viejo Company, the Rancho Mission Viejo Land Conservancy (now known as the Donna O'Neill Land Conservancy) and the Scripps Institution of Oceanography.

From left: Joan Irvine Smith, Dr. Peter Keller, President of the Bowers Museum, and his wife Signe Keller at The Oaks Classic, 1993, photo by Tish Quirk

On the evening of March 24, 1998, Peter Keller opened the *Silent Testament* exhibition with the following comments:

It is a great pleasure for the Bowers Museum to open its special exhibition gallery to a consortium of prestigious organizations that share the common goal of preserving our delicate ecology and our precious environment. This exhibition, *A Silent Testament: Nature and Humankind in the Balance*, portrays our county as a designated environmental "hot zone," a region particularly rich in biodiversity of species and in danger of encroachment by human population.

Other designated hot zones include places like the Amazon Basin, the Himalayas and Madagascar. The big difference that sets Orange County and coastal Southern California apart is a very intelligent approach that we have taken to being respectful of our environment while developing one of the most vibrant economies in the world.

This is the first time in the history of the renovated Bowers Museum that we have allowed an outside group to use our exhibition facilities. I want to take this opportunity to thank Mrs. Joan Irvine Smith for conceiving this idea and for bringing a dynamic team together to produce this important exhibition. Hopefully, this exhibition and its organizing team will stimulate the interest necessary to develop and successfully maintain a natural history museum in Orange County with a mission to preserve the past, and through programming, help guarantee the future of our very delicate environment.

FROM LEFT: Mark Sanderson of The Nature Conservancy, Joan Irvine Smith, Jean Stern, Dr. E. O. Wilson, Graham Chisholm of The Nature Conservancy and Nancy Golden of the Natural Resources Defense Council, at the San Diego Zoo

That same year, The Irvine Museum began working with Mark Sanderson of The Nature Conservancy of California to produce an art exhibition entitled *Native Grandeur: Preserving California's Vanishing Landscapes*, in order to raise public consciousness of the need to preserve California's natural environment. The companion book, which was jointly published in 2000, included paintings from not only The Irvine Museum but also from other prominent museums.

In his introductory essay, "California…A Land Apart," Donn B. Miller, Chairman of the Board of The Nature Conservancy of California, states the following:

> One way to understand the scope and grandeur of this state's lands and waters is to think of California as its own world, isolated on the edge of the continent by alpine peaks and shimmering deserts. Within its borders are vast grasslands, rugged foothills, lush forests, oak woodlands, teeming marshes and sloughs, billowing dunes. California's natural landscapes are so rich and diverse that they harbor more native species of plants and animals—and more native species at risk—than any other state.

Yes, many of California's unique lands, rivers, streams, coastal waters and the native species they support are at risk of being lost forever. The clock is ticking. Imagine all the present inhabitants of New York State deciding to settle in California. Growth of that magnitude is forecast; our population is expected to mushroom from 32 million to 50 million people by the year 2025.

Safeguarding California's landscapes and native species is essential—right now, before it's too late. That is the mission of our California chapter of The Nature Conservancy, a private, non-profit organization and one of the world's leading conservation groups.

We believe that growth does not need to overwhelm California's natural areas. We also believe that a robust economy and healthy natural landscapes must go hand in hand in the twenty-first century. We invited farmers, ranchers, and business people to be our partners. They, along with public agencies, local conservation organizations, universities, foundations and individual donors, join with us to achieve mutual conservation goals. Basing our work on sound science and careful planning, we use non-confrontational, market-based economic solutions to protect the best examples of every vital natural community represented in the state.

The effort to save our wildlands, open spaces and native species is being made on multiple fronts. One of them is this book, Native Grandeur. In it we celebrate California's natural wonders and survey conservation successes and challenges, but the book's message includes a call to action. The evocative nineteenth- and early twentieth-century landscape paintings that illustrate this volume enhance our appreciation of California's natural beauty, deepen our concern about the fate of its marvelous landscapes and strengthen our determination to safeguard them for future generations.

Santa Rosa Plateau, © Tupper Ansel Blake

Cosumnes Tundra Swans, © Timothy Wolcott

Professor Edward O. Wilson wrote the foreword to *Native Grandeur*. In his incisive essay, entitled "California's Living Landscapes," he states the following:

Like few other places in the world, the natural landscapes of California invite celebration by the visual arts. In topographic and climatic diversity, the state resembles a small continent: edged by the Pacific on its western border, high mountains to the east, and the Mojave Desert to the south. Each latitudinal transect taken at 200-mile intervals from the Klamath Mountains south to San Diego traces a separate journey of exceptional beauty.

It has been said that the human species evolved to live where citruses grow. California is one of only five regions of the world with a Mediterranean climate, sharing that blessing with central Chile, the Western Cape of South Africa, southwestern and south-central Australia and the Mediterranean basin itself. Each has a rich assemblage of animal species, but the flora is in each case the crown jewel. Africa south of the Cunene and Zambezi rivers, for example, has about 30,000 species of flowering plants, 60 percent endemic to the region, to which the Western Cape is a disproportionate contributor. California, or more precisely the California Floristic Province stretching from southern Oregon to Baja California, has a comparable distinction in relation to the rest of North America. Its approximately 4,300 species of flowering plants make up one-fourth of all those occurring in the United States and Canada combined, and half are endemic to the California Province—in other words, found nowhere else. Its major vegetation types, including redwood forest, coastal scrub, oak woodland, chaparral and desert, differ strikingly in appearance and species composition one from the other.

Californians have awakened, unfortunately too late for a few of the living landscapes, to the extraordinary value of their ancient wild heritage. Scientists who study biological diversity offer strong practical reasons for conserving all of it, including especially the economic and medical potential in products from wild species, and the free but vital services natural ecosystems provide in building soil, cleansing water and, indeed, generating the very air we breathe. But they also agree that the aesthetic and spiritual value wildlands provide, and California possesses in fortunate abundance, are equally important to human welfare. To capture and give immediacy to this important part of our lives is one of the great and unique roles of the visual arts. To depict biodiversity as it most powerfully strikes the eye is to unite science and the humanities in a common purpose.

Paul Grimm, *Mount San Gorgonio*, Private Collection,
Courtesy of The Irvine Museum

243

The Oaks 1996
Premiere Sport
Horse Auction
held in
The Oak Grove
at The Oaks

I FIRST MET R. J. BRANDES AT THE PEP Jumper Futurity Preview horse show at The Oaks in August 1996. We were standing at the derby field watching a jumper class when he struck up a conversation, saying how much The Oaks reminded him of the Upperville horse show grounds near Middleburg, Virginia. I remarked on how that was a coincidence, as I had a farm called The Oaks in Middleburg. He then told me that he was related to the Averell Harriman family. His aunt Phyllis Harriman Mason was the daughter of Edward Roland Harriman, who for many years was the head of the American Red Cross. E. Roland Harriman is the brother of William Averell Harriman, former U.S. Ambassador to the United Kingdom and Governor of New York. R. J. indicated that he had visited many times at their home in Middleburg as a boy. He further told me that he had lived in Argentina and played polo there, and that his eleven-year-old daughter Katy had tried polo, but wanted to ride jumpers.

As our second Oaks Premiere Sport Horse Auction was to be held that week on August 18, he asked me if I had a horse in the auction that would suit Katy. I thought my Grand Prix jumper Orlando might be a good horse for Katy, so I let her try him in a jumper class. It was a match made in heaven, for Orlando cantered around the course like a big hunter, and Katy was thrilled. R. J. bought Orlando and two young jumper prospects at the auction.

It was at that time that R. J. told me he was looking for horse property in Rancho Santa Fe; I took him over to Creekside, which I knew was for sale. When he complained that it didn't have trees like The Oaks, I told him I had a number of large boxed oaks and sycamores, some of which he could have, at The Oaks/Rancho Mission Viejo Riding Park next door. I gave him a tour of the Riding Park and told him of my dream to bring the Olympic Trials there, and that I was working with George Morris on the project. As Katy Brandes' enthusiasm for hunter, jumper and equitation competition grew, R. J.'s interest in horse shows developed as well. In January 1998, he purchased the 17 acres owned by Creekside and began making a number of improvements to the property, including building a lovely home and barn, constructing a seating area inside the indoor arena, adding a derby field and planting all of my oak trees. In September 1998, I entered into a lease with Rancho Mission Viejo for the Creekside property adjoining the grand prix field and rebuilt all of the rings.

In a letter dated August 5, 1998, George Morris indicated to my show manager, Arthur Hawkins, "The next Olympic Games will be held in Sydney, Australia, September 15–October 1, 2000. Show Jumping riders and the Show Jumping Selection Task Force (which is responsible for the development of selection procedures) have held many discussions concerning where these trials should be held, and are interested in determining your interest in hosting one or more. Trials will take place between June and mid-August. Because of the importance of these trials, the United States Equestrian Team (USET) requires that Show Management must have organized at least one major competition (offered a Grand Prix with $25,000 or more in prize money) within the past two years."

In conclusion the letter states, "On behalf of the Team, thank you for your interest. We encourage you to submit an application, even if you are not able to meet all the enclosed requirements, as it is possible that a compromise can be reached.

"So that decisions regarding the Trials can be made in a timely manner, we respectfully ask you to complete and return the enclosed form to the USET by August 28, 1998, if you are interested in hosting a Trial. We look forward to working with you toward our goal of Olympic medals in Australia." At that time, Arthur and I put in an application to bring the 2000 U.S. Show Jumping Olympic Selection Trials to San Juan Capistrano.

On November 11, 1998, R. J. and I entered into an operating agreement to form The Oaks/Blenheim Exhibitions LLC. His participation was extremely important as he completed the negotiation for the Olympic Trial, brought many additional sponsors to support our events and also made some important improvements on the 120-acre Oaks/Rancho Mission Viejo Riding Park. These improvements included, among other things, converting a large shed into an office, placing decomposed granite in the stall and parking areas, purchasing portable wooden stalls and installing wash racks. He also purchased the same type of natural rail fencing that I had used on the grass field and around the hunter rings, placing it around two new lunging rings that he had built and at other locations. He then added two food stands, extended several hunter rings, added a sand warm-up ring and a grub in the grass field and eventually built a stone gate at the main entrance.

The great International Grand Prix winner and sire South Pacific by Sylvester out of Kamera by Cor de la Bryere at The Oaks in 1993, photo by Joan Irvine Smith

In the spring of 1998, The Oaks' flagship stallion, South Pacific, appeared to be in excellent physical condition, with good muscle tone and a beautiful, shiny coat. On March 16, however, while I was involved in organizing the *Silent Testament* exhibition at the Bowers Museum, South Pacific's groom, Javier Moncada at The Oaks Indian Hill Ranch in Valley Center, noticed he was partially off his feed following a series of yearly immunizations, which had been administered to all of my horses. Dr. Matt Matthews had South Pacific's blood analyzed, and the results revealed alterations consistent with kidney dysfunction. The results of the blood work were immediately sent to San Luis Rey Equine Hospital in Bonsall, California. South Pacific was referred to the clinic for treatment of kidney disease by Drs. Barrie Grant and Joe Cannon. Enlarged, abnormal kidneys were identified with ultrasound by Dr. Norman Rantanen.

By April 2, South Pacific had lost the sight in his right eye. On April 10, a biopsy of the right kidney was performed by Dr. Grant under ultrasound guidance by Dr. Rantanen. By April 13, complete blindness had occurred in both of South Pacific's eyes.

South Pacific at the San Luis Rey Equine Hospital in Bonsall

The final result of the kidney biopsy report was returned at 2 p.m. on April 14. Diagnosis of a very rare parasitic infestation by the nematode *Halicephalobus deletrix*, formerly known as *Micronema deletrix*, was made. Infestation with this parasite in horses and humans had resulted in fatalities in all previously documented cases. The life cycle and reservoir of this organism remain a mystery to science. Infection with the parasite is presumed to be through the mouth, lungs or an open wound.

At that time, only thirteen cases of this parasite had been reported and confirmed through necropsy on horses in the United States in more than twenty-three years, with approximately five to eight additional cases ever having been reported in the entire world. Three cases of human deaths had also been reported.

When I entered South Pacific's stall on the morning of April 15, he was lying on the shavings with his head elevated. I called his name, and he raised his head slightly and nickered softly in response. I told him that we must say goodbye for now, but I knew that we would meet again someday. His great heart never faltered until he was euthanized at 9:30 that morning. I remained beside him until his life drifted away.

At that time, I directed Dr. Matthews to have a necropsy performed, as I believed South Pacific could be our "silent witness" to the circumstances surrounding his death. The postmortem examination performed by Dr. Hailu Kinde at the California Veterinary Diagnostic Lab in San Bernardino showed extensive parasitic infestation of the kidneys, optic nerves and brain, with 85 percent of

Horses at The Oaks Indian Hill Ranch in Valley Center

South Pacific in The Oaks International Grand Prix in 1993

South Pacific with his second place ribbon from The Oaks International Grand Prix in 1993

both kidneys destroyed. Further examination revealed no evidence that the organism had entered his system through his nasal passage or mouth.

South Pacific was always supervised by his groom when he left his stall to exercise or breed, and he had had no cut or abrasion in more than a year; therefore, it is believed that the parasite did not enter his system through an open wound. None of South Pacific's stable mates, or the other 160 horses on my Valley Center farm, has shown any signs of infection with *Halicephalobus deletrix*. Nor did any of the fourteen sites tested on the property by Dr. James Bishop of The University of California at Riverside show any evidence of the parasite. In light of the foregoing, it would appear that South Pacific may have been given an injection of the fatal parasite.

Dr. Howard House with the yearlings at The Oaks Indian Hill Ranch in Valley Center

Not only was South Pacific a great show jumping stallion and sire, he was also a wonderful friend and truly a part of my family. All those who knew and loved him grieved at his passing. Although the barn seems empty without him, we are consoled by the fact that his great legacy will live on through his beautiful and talented progeny, and also through the medical research that will stem from the circumstances surrounding his death.

After South Pacific died, I wanted to have a bronze statue created, both as a memorial to South Pacific and as a perpetual trophy to be awarded to the winner of The Oaks International Grand Prix. Although I had painted since childhood and also done some sculpture, I did not feel up to the task of doing it myself. Therefore, at the suggestion of my friend Ray Redfern of the Redfern Gallery in Laguna Beach, I commissioned and collaborated with internationally renowned sculptor Mark Rossi to do the South Pacific bronze.

South Pacific Memorial Award Bronze by Mark Rossi and Joan Irvine Smith

South Pacific, 1995, painted by Arellano

In 1998, The Oaks Classic benefited the National Water Research Institute and Richard Spooner won the Grand Prix on Robinson. That year, The Oaks International benefited the Reeve-Irvine Research Center and Richard and Robinson also won the Grand Prix and received the first South Pacific Memorial Trophy.

In 1999, The Oaks Classic again benefited the National Water Research Institute and Nicole Simpson won the Grand Prix on El Campeon's Jo Jo. That year, R. J. and I hosted The Oaks International and $50,000 Oaks International Grand Prix at the riding park that we had now called The Oaks/Blenheim/Rancho Mission Viejo Riding Park. This event benefited the Drug Use is Life Abuse support group, the Reeve-Irvine Research Center at UCI, the Fran Joswick Therapeutic Riding Center, the Mission San Juan Capistrano, the National Water Research Institute, the Rancho Mission Viejo Land Conservancy and The Boys and Girls Club of Capistrano Valley.

Tara Ardalan and Starlet winners of the 1998 $10,000 Oak Leaf Junior/Amateur Grand Prix sponsored by Treatwells with FROM LEFT: Robert Drennan, Kent Moeller, Treatwell's representative and Joe Lombardo, photo by Jumpshot

Richard Spooner and Robinson won the 1998 $50,000 Oaks Classic Grand Prix. That year they also won the $50,000 Oaks International Grand Prix and received the first South Pacific Memorial Trophy presented by Joan Irvine Smith with second from left: Dr. Tom Cesario, Dean of UCI College of Medicine and UCI Chancellor Ralph Cicerone, photo by Jumpshot

Nichole Shahinian and El Campeon's Jo Jo winners of the 1999 $50,000 Oaks Classic Grand Prix received the award FROM LEFT: Joan Irvine Smith, R.J. Brandes, Katy Brandes and Robert Ridland, photo by Jumpshot

Richard Spooner and South Pacific's son Southshore received the South Pacific Memorial Trophy when they won the 1999 $50,000 Oaks International Grand Prix for owners Pat and Jim Iverson from left: Joan Irvine Smith, R.J. Brandes, Linda Blair and Robert Drennan. In 2000, Richard and Southshore won the $150,000 Grand Prix of the Desert at Indio and received a second South Pacific Memorial Trophy when they won the Oaks International Grand Prix. In 2001, Mary Tyng and Southshore won the $150,000 Grand Prix of the Desert for China Blue Farms, photo by Jumpshot

In 1999, Richard Spooner and South Pacific's son Southshore received the South Pacific Memorial Trophy when they won The Oaks International Grand Prix for owners Jim and Pat Iverson. In 2000, Richard and Southshore won the $150,000 Grand Prix of the Desert at Indio and received a second South Pacific Memorial Trophy when they won The Oaks International Grand Prix. In 2001, Mary Tyng and Southshore won the $150,000 Grand Prix of the Desert for China Blue Farms and on April 1, 2005 I acquired Southshore for The Oaks. That same year, Gabriella Salick and Sandstone Laurinn received the South Pacific Memorial trophy when they won the $50,000 Oaks Blenheim Fall Classic Grand Prix, a World Cup qualifier, sponsored by HBO.

ABOVE: Richard Spooner on Southshore
LEFT: In 2005, Gabriella Salick and Sandstone Laurin received the South Pacific Memorial Trophy when they won the $50,000 Oaks/Blenheim Fall Classic Grand Prix, a World Cup qualifier, sponsored by HBO. FROM LEFT: Joan Irvine Smith, Lance Walters, Melissa Mullins, Robert Ridland with Misti and Derrick Cassar, photo by Jumpshot

Jessica Steward with Hunter Champion Golden Boy at The Oaks, photo by Joan Irvine Smith

Elizabeth Penniman with Hunter Champion The Little Prince at The Oaks, photo by Joan Irvine Smith

Elizabeth Penniman on Jumper Champion Lonford at The Oaks/Blenheim/Rancho Mission Viejo Riding Park, 2005, photo by Jumpshot

Nathalie Cooper on Jumper Champion Ocean II by South Pacific out of Rene by Ramzes at the Fairfield Hunt Club in Fairfield, Connecticut

FAR LEFT: Nathalie Cooper on Hunter Champion Lord of the Manor at the Fairfield Hunt Club in Fairfield, Connecticut
LEFT: Nathalie Cooper with Hunter Champion Lord of the Manor at Mount Holyoke, South Hadley, Massachusetts

FROM LEFT: Russ, Elizabeth, Rex and Carol Penniman, Joan Irvine Smith, Toni, Morton and Marianne Smith with Charlotte Smith, Jase, Madeline and Jim Swinden at The Oaks, photograph, Courtesy of *Coast Magazine*

In 2001, South Pacific ranked third among American-Based Jumper Sires and sixteenth on the list of Leading International Jumper Sires. The Leading Jumper Sire list is based on total money earned by offspring of a sire during the competition year in recognized U.S. Equestrian competition. In 2002, I created the South Pacific Memorial Award, in which a South Pacific bronze statue is presented to a Performance Horse Registry stallion based in the United States with at least 75 percent of the progeny earnings from offspring born in North America. That year, the Selle Français Galoubet by Almé won the South Pacific Memorial Award for the top-ranked U.S.-based sire of show jumpers, with Ocean II by South Pacific the runner-up, and South Pacific ranking fourth. The Thoroughbred Aly Dark by Alydar was named as the recipient of the 2003 South Pacific Memorial Award, with Ocean II ranking seventh. The Dutch Warmblood Consul by Nimmerdor received the award for 2004. In 2005, Ocean II won the South Pacific Memorial Award.

South Pacific

Mares and foals at The Oaks Indian Hill Ranch in Valley Center

One of three Navy Seals who parachuted into the arena at the 2004 U.S. Show Jumping Olympic Selection Trials at The Oaks/Blenheim/Rancho Mission Viejo Riding Park, photo by Tish Quirk

My partner in The Oaks/Blenheim Exhibitions LLC R. J. Brandes' involvement in bringing the 2000 U.S. Show Jumping Olympic Selection Trials to San Juan Capistrano was crucial to holding them here. He is CEO of Blenheim EquiSports, the management group headed by Olympian Robert Ridland, which hosted the event at the very successful Oaks/Blenheim Exhibitions venue The Oaks/Blenheim/Rancho Mission Viejo Riding Park. Blenheim EquiSports has also hosted the 2004 U.S. Show Jumping Olympic Selection Trials, four Cargill International CSI-A trials and trials for the last two World Cups. The group also manages the Del Mar Horse Park.

Governor Arnold Schwarzenegger, R.J. Brandes, San Juan Capistrano Mayor Joe Soto and Joan Irvine Smith, photo Tish Quirk

Orange County Sheriff's color guard, photo by Tish Quirk

Bezzie Madden on Authentic, winner of the $175,000 Cargill Grand Prix of the United States at the 2004 U.S. Show Jumping Olympic Selection Trials held at The Oaks/Blenheim/Rancho Mission Viejo Riding Park in San Juan Capistrano. FROM LEFT: Cargill Representatives, John Long, CEO of the USA Equestrian Federation, Gloria Brandes, Joan Irvine Smith, Melissa Brandes Mullins, Vice Admiral Michael D. Malone, R.J. Brandes, Bill Whitehead of Hermes and Robert Ridland, photo by Jumpshot

Blenheim Cottage at Blenheim Farms serves as a second home for R. J. and his lovely wife, Gloria, as their main residence is in Newport Beach. Designed after an Argentinean estancia, the house is built entirely from compressed hay bales that have been covered with stucco, in the manner of some early California houses. The cottage, which doubles as a conference center, and its beautiful garden have been made available by R. J. and Gloria for a number of charitable fundraisers, including the St. Margaret's Episcopal School Home Tour and events for the National Water Research Institute, the Mission San Juan Capistrano and the U.S. Equestrian Federation.

R. J. and Gloria also hold many gatherings of both family and friends at the cottage, as he has always told me that the farm was a way of keeping his family together. Katy, who rode there almost daily, won the Silver Medal at the Young Riders in Chicago in 2004, and is now studying at Princeton University. His older daughter Melissa Brandes Mullins is essential to the success of his events, as she has become an excellent marketing director.

R. J. is on the board of the Mission Preservation Foundation of Mission San Juan Capistrano and has assisted in underwriting several events at the mission. He is also head of the Circle of Friends of the National Water Research Institute, a support group that assists students throughout the United States in the pursuit of their master's and doctoral degrees in water-related sciences. As another mark of his environmental consciousness, R. J. is the CEO of Belgravia Capital, a privately held investment group that focuses on renewable energy technologies. He has invested in photovoltaic technology and has his team working on making this resource available in the residential marketplace. To that end, he has installed solar panels in the roof of the indoor arena in order to produce electricity. R. J. is also becoming actively involved in the production of hydrogen-powered cars that emit water instead of pollutants.

Gwendolyn Myer of Cargill and Melissa Brandes Mullins, Marketing Director for Blenheim Equisports, photo by Tish Quirk

Gloira and R.J. Brandes at the 2004 U.S. Show Jumping Olympic Selection Trials at The Oaks/Blenheim/Rancho Mission Viejo Riding Park, photo by Tish Quirk

Katy Brandes on Jumper Champion Orlando, photo by Rick Osteen

FROM LEFT: Madeline, Jase and Jim Swinden, Joan Irvine Smith with Rex, Elizabeth, Russ and Carol Penniman at the opening of the Athalie Richardson Irvine Clarke Wildflower Garden at the UCI Arboretum in Irvine in 1998, photograph, Courtesy of UCI

FROM LEFT: Jim Swinden, Joan Irvine Smith, Anita Ziebe and Russ Penniman at the Wildflower Garden opening, photograph, Courtesy of UCI

Former UCI Chancellor Laurel Wilkening and Joan Irvine Smith at a luncheon benefiting the Athalie Richardson Irvine Clarke Wildflower Garden at the UCI Arboretum in Irvine, photograph, Courtesy of UCI

IN TRIBUTE TO MY LATE MOTHER'S LOVE of California wildflowers, the Joan Irvine Smith & Athalie R. Clarke Foundation funded the Athalie Richardson Irvine Clarke Wildflower Garden, which opened on April 25, 1998, at the UCI Arboretum in Irvine. A rustic path welcomes one to hillsides resplendent with lupine, golden poppy, Indian paintbrush, owl's clover and other California wildflowers. The dedication of the garden, hosted by UCI Chancellor Laurel Wilkening, was coordinated with an exhibition entitled Of Springtimes Past at The Irvine Museum, featuring historic paintings of California's wildflowers.

I first met UCI's current chancellor, Ralph Cicerone, when he was dean of UCI's School of Physical Sciences. He and his colleague Dr. Sherry Rowland met with the Joan Irvine Smith & Athalie R. Clarke Foundation board to explain their research on the earth's ozone layer. I later had the opportunity to know Ralph and Carol Cicerone when UCI joined with The Irvine Museum, the Nature Conservancy, The Irvine Company, the County of Orange and a number of other organizations to produce the *Silent Testament* exhibition. Through our common interest in the environment, Ralph and Carol and I became good friends, and I was elated when I learned that Ralph was selected to be the new chancellor at UCI.

UCI Chancellor Ralph Cicerone and Carol Cicerone, photograph, Courtesy of UCI

On May 13, 1999, in a short speech welcoming Ralph Cicerone as chancellor at his inaugural dinner, I took the opportunity to commend Donald Bren for placing more than 21,000 acres of Irvine Company land with the Nature Conservancy. Today, this land is the cornerstone of Orange County's Natural Community Conservation Planning program, which grew out of the uncommon alliance of government, industry and public interest groups, held together by the common goal of finding a better way to integrate conservation and land use.

FROM LEFT: Roger Stanton, Chairman of The Orange County Board of Supervisors, Doug Wheeler, California Resources Secretary under Governor Pete Wilson and a former member of The Nature Conservancy's California Board, Bruce Babbit, Secretary of the Interior under President Bill Clinton, and Donald Bren of The Irvine Company, executing the documents creating Orange County's Natural Community Conservation Plan in 1996. At that time Donald Bren placed more than 21,000 acres of Irvine Company land with The Nature Conservancy. Today this land is the cornerstone of Orange County's NCCP program, photograph, Courtesy of The Irvine Company

Alexey Steele, *Wildflowers and the San Joaquin Hills*, Private Collection

ABOVE AND BELOW; Coastal Sage Scrub near UCI, © Moose Peterson

The article by Dwight Holing entitled "The Coastal Sage Scrub Solution" which appeared in the July/August 1997 *Nature Conservancy* magazine indicates the following:

Back when the Beatles were releasing a new album each year, surfboards were long, not short, and there were more citrus groves than people in Orange County, California. I could hike from my house in South Laguna to my best friend's in San Juan Capistrano, three miles away as the red-tailed hawk flies, without walking on pavement or across anybody's backyard. Nothing lay between us but sun-dappled canyons and rolling hills covered by sage and chaparral.

There was no end to what I could see as I made the trek. Harriers, black-shouldered kites and turkey vultures glided effortlessly on swirling thermals. Cactus wrens perched atop prickly pears, easily identifiable by their curved beaks, upturned tails and distinctive calls of chug-chug-chug-chug. Deer grazed openly. Bobcat tracks and coyote scat marked every trail. And in spring, when white-blossomed popcorn flowers and yellow-petalled beach primroses dotted the otherwise verdant hillsides, the minty smell of coastal sage filled the salt air.

It's been 25 years since I called that part of California home, but I can still recall the pungent aroma as if it were yesterday. What I can't do is retrace the footsteps of my youth. Thousands of houses, dozens of shopping centers and miles upon miles of asphalt now cover the hillsides and fill the canyons where I once roamed.

What happened to this once-sleepy corner of the state is not unique. But no other place in the country has experienced more explosive growth over the past 40 years than the coastal corridor between Los Angeles and the Mexican border. And if any place is ground zero for the Southern California boom, it is Orange County. Over the past 30 years the population has skyrocketed from 700,000 people to more than 2.5 million. Another 600,000 are expected by 2010.

Orange County's growth has come at a steep environmental price. Wholesale development has led to wholesale habitat destruction. Entire ecosystems have been fragmented almost beyond recognition, and many species have been pushed perilously close to the brink of extinction.

Thus was the case of a now-famous songbird, the California gnatcatcher, which six years ago was at the center of a showdown between developers and conservationists. It is no surprise that this clash occurred in Southern California. But what is remarkable is the cooperative program—Natural Community Conservation Planning (NCCP)—that has enabled all sides to plan collaboratively for both development and conservation in the coastal sage scrub ecosystem between Los Angeles and San Diego. Beginning in Orange County and now spreading to San Diego, Los Angeles, San Bernardino and Riverside counties, NCCP promises to be remarkable in another sense, too: a model that has been hailed as the future of habitat conservation in the United States.

Orange County

In 1991, Southern California was on the verge of becoming the latest and perhaps greatest battleground over the Endangered Species Act. Conservationists had petitioned the U.S. Fish and Wildlife Service (USFWS) to add the California gnatcatcher to federal endangered species list. The gnatcatcher is a tiny bluish-gray songbird whose call sounds like the soft mew of a kitten. It depends on coastal sage scrub habitat for survival. The trouble is, all but between 10 percent and 20 percent of the unique mix of sagebrush and chaparral that once ranged from Ventura County to San Diego has been destroyed; the remaining 250,000 acres are highly fragmented, and much is degraded. USFWS surveys indicate gnatcatcher populations have declined dramatically in the last 20 years.

Landowners opposed listing the bird, as they were determined to build on some of the most valuable unbuilt real estate in the United States. (Some parcels in Orange County with ocean views are valued at $4 million an acre.) Once the gnatcatcher fell under federal protection, land owners would have a difficult time obtaining permission to build there. Local governments worried their land-use authority would be reduced or even taken away. But this would be only the tip of the iceberg: With many other protected species in the region, and more certain to be listed as habitat is further reduced, the conflict would surely escalate.

Mounting tensions over the coastal sage scrub threatened to make the Pacific Northwest timber wars over the northern spotted owl pale in comparison. But NCCP, a state program in which the federal government is participating, averted what could have been the biggest environmental

California Gnatcatcher, © Bruce Farnsworth

The Nature Conservancy booklet on Natural Community Conservation Planning, 1991-1998, Courtesy of The Nature Conservancy

Laguna Beach Dudleya, © Wayne Johnson

Least Bell's Vireo, © Moose Peterson

Orange Whiptail Lizard, © Bruce Farnsworth, Place Stock Photography

"train wreck" yet. Proposed by Gov. Pete Wilson and adopted by the California legislature in 1991, NCCP sets a framework for the regional protection and management of wildlife habitat while allowing development to continue in certain areas that biologists consider less critical to the ecosystem.

"Unlike the way we've usually approached conservation—reacting to each crisis that comes up—NCCP allows us to create large-scale, proactive conservation solutions," says Michael O'Connell, the Conservancy's NCCP project director. "It essentially creates an off ramp to survival for species speeding down the road to extinction."

Conservation planning had its beginnings in a 1982 amendment to the federal Endangered Species Act allowing private landowners and developers to disturb or destroy endangered species habitat in exchange for a habitat conservation plan (HCP) that would protect or restore other high-quality habitat. HCPs offer a way for landowners to comply with the law and still continue their business, helping resolve conflict over what some view as critical habitat, others as prime real estate.

"But NCCP is a real breakthrough," explains O'Connell. "The beauty of it is that it focuses on whole natural communities; it can encompass hundreds of species and thousands of landowners at a time, and the process begins before a situation gets out of control." By contrast, most HCPs have been created around a single protected species, one at a time, in reaction to the threat of enforcement of the Endangered Species Act.

In 1993, The Nature Conservancy geared up to test out the novel NCCP approach with funding from the Hewlett, Irvine and Compton foundations. Steve Johnson, director of science for the Conservancy's California program, facilitated meetings among a group of conservation scientists, developers, landowners, conservationists and representatives from local, state and federal governments. Together they hammered out a system of large, interconnected coastal sage scrub reserves designed to protect habitat for the gnatcatcher and other imperiled species.

With the approval of the California Department of Fish and Game and the USFWS, the NCCP plan would free participating landowners from future endangered species permit review for land they wanted to develop outside the reserve's boundaries. "So when landowners voluntarily commit to NCCP, they're really going beyond what the law requires," says O'Connell. "They're not just doing as little as possible to squeak by; they're doing what's right for the ecosystem."

Landowners receive binding assurances from the wildlife agencies that if the NCCP plan ever needs adjusting—if more land must be protected or managed differently, or more funds committed – the public will pick up the tab. This policy has been the most controversial, but it's what brings landowners to the table and keeps them there. It gives them certainty and a streamlined process.

Early on, Johnson and NCCP's other architects identified the linchpin of a reserve system surrounded by developed land: The grand plan had to be based on good science—the latest, best thinking about the requirements for species and ecosystem function. To that end, the state appointed an independent scientific review panel composed of five prominent ecologists and biologists and chaired by Dr. Dennis Murphy of Stanford University. Their vision: keep habitats contiguous, reserves linked through corridors and habitat buffered from encroaching development.

In early 1996, the Orange County Board of Supervisors unanimously approved the conservation plan, three years in the making. Soon after, the wildlife agencies approved the plan, and in July 1996, the 38,000-acre Orange County Nature Reserve officially opened. This permanent reserve was created by combining 21,000 acres of land set aside by The Irvine Company, the county's largest landowner and developer, with 17,000 acres held by other local entities, including county and state parks. Private landowners and public agencies, including the Orange County Transportation Corridor Agencies, are slated to contribute a $10.6 million permanent endowment to manage the reserve system over time. All reserve land, regardless of its current use, must be managed with conservation as the highest priority.

Why did a landowner like The Irvine Company take such a big risk on an untried program and give up so much expensive real estate? "We knew NCCP was a bold experiment, but it's a much more promising alternative to traditional enforcement of the Endangered Species Act," says Monica Florian, senior vice president at The Irvine Company. "It accommodates reasonable economic growth while protecting the richest, most biologically vital habitat in the region."

The Orange County Nature Reserve stretches from the coast at Laguna Beach to the base of Saddleback Mountain, from Costa Mesa down to San Juan Capistrano. (A second NCCP plan in the county, if completed, would protect an additional 40,000 acres in southern reaches of the county.) Among the reserve's wildlife residents are 40 imperiled species, including the tiny arboreal salamander, a lizard called the orange-throated whiptail, a flower known as the Laguna Beach Dudleya and many endangered birds: least Bell's vireo, peregrine falcon, southwestern willow flycatcher and, of course, the California gnatcatcher. The NCCP plan protects not only the habitats these species currently occupy, but most important, other habitats essential to their survival and areas that incorporate the

Willow Flycatcher, © Anthony Mercieca

Peregrine Falcon, © Craig Koppie, U.S. Fish and Wildlife Service

261

Maurice Braun, *San Diego Countryside with River*, Private Collection, Courtesy of The Irvine Museum

natural processes that sustain the whole system. The foresight underlying this reserve design is nearly impossible to achieve using the regulatory hammer of the Endangered Species Act alone.

But NCCP is not without its critics. Some conservationists worry that regional reserves will never fully materialize in some areas because of the huge amount of money needed for land acquisition. They also wonder whether city and regional governments are equipped to manage the reserves for their biological values in this day and age of shrinking tax-supported budgets, overworked bureaucracies and competing civic interests.

"Saying the program is visionary is one thing, making it so is another," says Joel Reynolds, senior attorney with the Natural Resources Defense Council. "The real proof will be whether politics or science will determine the shape and size of the reserves and whether local governments will manage them for the protection of ecosystems and species after the politicians, federal agencies and public interest groups have left the bargaining table."

Proponents of NCCP concede the program has flaws, but, as the Conservancy's Steve Johnson says, "Perfection is the enemy of good in regional conservation planning. All you have to do is fly over Southern California and see what has resulted from trying to preserve land project by project. What you get are tiny islands of habitat surrounded by a sea of red-tile-roofed homes. NCCP can do better than that."

SAN DIEGO COUNTY

East of San Diego, where the tentacles of housing developments have halted their slide eastward toward the desert and asphalt drops down into the hard brown earth, the native scrub still holds sway. Steep, shrubby ravines choked with lemonadeberry bushes and buckwheat are flecked with gnatcatchers and frequented by mountain lions. Here along the Mexican border, the Otay Mesa represents one of the single largest blocks of coastal sage scrub remaining in Southern California.

A recent county-by-county study reported in the journal Science identified San Diego County as a biological "hot spot." Concentrated in California, Hawaii and Florida, such hot spots mark where native species are most diverse and where they're backed into ever-shrinking corners by the march of development. According to Dr. Ted Case, professor of biology at the University of California – San Diego, San Diego County has more threatened species of plants and animals than any other county in the continental United States.

"It's become clear that Endangered Species Act listings simply cannot keep up with the rate of biological loss here," says Michael Beck, a grassroots environmentalist and director of the San Diego chapter of the Endangered Habitats League. "That's why we agreed to the NCCP approach. We needed a way to make preservation possible in a phenomenally complex world of politics, economics, science and ethics."

RIGHT AND BELOW: Santa Margarita Plateau, photos by Joan Irvine Smith

Spade-Footed Toad, © Stephen Francis Photography

Indeed, in San Diego County, making NCCP happen is no mean feat. Some 20,000 landowners hold property in the planning area—an overwhelming number of players, especially when compared to central Orange County's single big private landowner, The Irvine Company. Some 200,000 acres of coastal sage scrub habitat are in question, nearly triple the amount in Orange County, and almost 100 species are imperiled.

"The size, scope and complexity of the San Diego area is simply staggering," says O'Connell. "We're dealing with several cities, thousands of landowners, dozens of species and habitats—yet it's got to be tackled."

Two plans are under way in San Diego County that, when completed, will create the biggest NCCP reserve to date. The first of these is designed to protect nearly 172,000 acres and some 85 imperiled species, including many unique to this corner of the world, such as the San Diego fairy shrimp and the Otay Mesa mint.

In March, the San Diego City Council unanimously approved its share of one of the plans—a 900-square-mile study area in the southwest portion of the country, including the Otay Mesa and parts of San Diego proper.

Much of the land that will comprise the reserve system is already owned by public agencies or will be donated by private landowners. Approximately 27,000 acres, however, will need to be purchased. State and federal authorities and local governments have divided the estimated price tag of between $260 million and $360 million for land acquisition equally among them, though the sources of these funds have yet to be identified.

To help deal with the issue of funding, the Conservancy has partnered with other stakeholders to catalyze public support for funding and has created a new local nonprofit entity, The Naturelands Project, to take the lead. "Response has been encouraging," says Jim Sulentich, the Conservancy's NCCP team member in San Diego. "You get the sense that the community has been wanting something like this for a long time."

San Diego Fairy Shrimp, U.S. Fish and Wildlife Service

Otay Mesa Mint, © Greg Mason

"San Diego is a case study other local communities can look to when developing their own plans," says Ron Rempel, NCCP manager for the California Department of Fish and Game, pointing to other regional conservation debates, such as that in the San Francisco Bay—Delta. "Other states are taking a look, too," Rempel says. "We've talked with Colorado's wildlife agency about how NCCP might help deal with the high plains ecosystem east of Denver. We've also had similar discussions with folks in Austin to see if NCCP can be used to expand the preserves at Balcones Canyonlands." The Balcones Canyonlands Conservation Plan created reserves near Austin, Texas, using the HCP process.

Maurice Braun, *San Diego River Valley*, Private Collection, Courtesy of The Irvine Museum

Alfred Mitchell, *Sunset Glow*, 1924, Courtesy of DeRus' Fine Arts, Laguna Beach

California's home-grown regional planning process may also have a big impact in Washington, D.C. Marc Ebbin, who serves as Interior Secretary Bruce Babbitt's California-based representative for NCCP affairs, believes NCCP will help end the long-standing debate over the need to overhaul the Endangered Species Act. With that serving as a safety net, he says, NCCP can be used far in advance to head off endangered species conflicts before they escalate.

For the Conservancy's part, Steve Johnson observes that the organization has participated in NCCP to make sure the planning reflects conservation values and, at the same time, to learn how to improve the results of conservation planning on the ground. He predicts conservation planning along the lines of NCCP will play an increasingly important role across the country as the Conservancy seeks ways to conserve habitat in areas where real estate prices are high. "For us NCCP has a big multiplier effect when we step out the door," he says. "We can achieve maximum amount of conservation gain for the effort we put in."

HOPES AND PROMISES

Of course, it will be some years before NCCP can truly be credited with saving Southern California's coastal sage scrub and the wildlife that depends on it. But, as I found on a recent visit to the heart of Orange County's reserve near Laguna Beach, things are definitely off to a good start. It was a windy but cloudless March day when I stood on top of an emerald ridge dotted with orange-blossomed fiddlenecks, purple-petaled lupine and blue dicks. Open space stretched around me in all directions. There wasn't a red-tiled roof in sight. I watched a pair of courting harriers perform an aerial dance. A cactus wren called somewhere in the distance. I plucked some coastal sage, rubbed it beneath my nose and breathed deeply of my youth. It smelled of hope and promise.

IN 1999, MY COUSINS Linda and Harvey Smith contacted me about a musical pageant on the early history of California and the Mission San Juan Capistrano, which they were producing with the drama department of California State University at Fullerton. They wished to hold the event at The Oaks/Blenheim/Rancho Mission Viejo Riding Park in August of that year. I thought it was a wonderful idea and told them that I would of course assist them personally and give them financial support through the Joan Irvine Smith & Athalie R. Clarke Foundation. The Irvine Museum produced a pamphlet entitled *California's True Gold: Her priceless and irreplaceable cultural and historical monuments, and her beautiful and fragile environment, so "...very close to the earthly paradise,"* which presented a brief overview of California history from prehistoric times to the present, with emphasis on the Mission period. It also gave a brief overview of the Natural Community Conservation Planning (NCCP) process for reaching a broad consensus about the limits of development on remaining natural lands in a large area.

Ricardo Montalbán and I were named as co-chairs for the event, which opened on August 28 at the east end of the grass field of the riding park and was attended by a wide cross section of Orange County's community leaders. It was a beautiful production, with lovely music and lyrics, splendid historical costumes and many sensational special effects. The pageant continued annually until 2001, when it was presented at the Mission San Juan Capistrano.

As my granddaughter Antoinette Athalie ("Toni") Smith, who is learning to ride at The Oaks, has strabismus and has always worn glasses for nearsightedness, my son Morton Irvine Smith and his wife, Marianne, hosted an event called "Vision in Vogue," benefiting the UCI Department of Ophthalmology headed by Dr. George Baerveldt. Among other things, it featured a fashion show that included both children and adults modeling designer eyeglasses. The

FRONT ROW FROM LEFT: Joan Irvine Smith, Ricardo Montalban, and Linda Irvine Smith. BACK ROW: Anita Ziebe and Harvey Smith at a fundraising event for the Mission Pageant at the Mission San Juan Capistrano, photograph, Courtesy of Mission San Juan Capistrano

first two events were held in 2001 and 2002 at Saks Fifth Avenue in Mission Viejo, and the third in 2003 at Nordstrom's at South Coast Plaza in Costa Mesa. The Joan Irvine Smith & Athalie R. Clarke Foundation has supported Vision in Vogue. Morton is a director of The Irvine Museum, a director of the Crystal Cove Conservancy and also chairs the City of San Juan Capistrano Traffic Commission.

FROM LEFT: Joan Irvine Smith with Morton, Marianne and Toni Smith at the Vision in Vogue fashion show benefiting the UCI Department of Ophthalmology held at Saks Fifth Avenue in Mission Viejo in 2001, photo by Brian Cummings

Elizabeth Penniman, photo by Brian Cummings

Jase Swinden, photo by Brian Cummings

Marianne and Toni Smith, photo by Brian Cummings

Rex Penniman and friend, photo by Brian Cummings

FROM LEFT: Marianne, Toni and Morton Smith with Nathalie Cooper at The Oaks, with Cappy Smith and Alletta Smith Cooper seated in background

Charlotte, Virginia Rose, and Toni Smith grooming the ponies at The Oaks

Alletta Smith Cooper and Cappy Smith at The Oaks

FROM LEFT: Charlotte, Virginia Rose and Toni Smith

Toni Smith riding Bubbles

Charlotte Smith riding Night Light

Jorge Gonzales leading Virginia Rose on Apple

ON OCTOBER 30, 2003, I attended the Climate Change Conference held by the UCI Newkirk Center for Science and Society. The panel participants included, among others: Chancellor Ralph Cicerone, Dr. F. Sherwood Rowland, Newkirk Center Director Dr. Joseph DiMento, and Andrew Revkin of the *New York Times*, who covers subjects ranging from anthrax attacks to changes in the sea ice at the North Pole, to the political clash over global warming.

The aim of the conference was to explain the greenhouse effect and what it would mean for us and for future generations of Californians. The conference reviewed much information and raised many issues that had been set forth in the EPA article of September 1997 entitled "Climate Change and California."

Frank Cuprien, *A Summer Evening*, Private Collection, Courtesy of The Irvine Museum

Maurice Braun, *Along the Merced River*, Private Collection, Courtesy of The Irvine Museum

Edgar Payne, *Rugged Peaks, High Sierra*, The Irvine Museum

The article reads:

The earth's climate is predicted to change because human activities are altering the chemical composition of the atmosphere through the buildup of greenhouse gases—primarily carbon dioxide, methane, nitrous oxide, and chlorofluorocarbons. The heat-trapping property of these greenhouse gases is undisputed. Although there is uncertainty about exactly how and when the earth's climate will respond to enhanced concentrations of greenhouse gases, observations indicate that detectable changes are underway. There most likely will be increases in temperature and changes in precipitation, soil moisture, and sea level, which could have adverse effects on many ecological systems, as well as on human health and the economy...

Since the beginning of the industrial revolution, human activities have been adding measurably to natural background levels of greenhouse gases. The burning of fossil fuels—coal, oil, and natural gas—for energy is the primary source of emissions. Energy burned to run cars and trucks, heat homes and businesses, and power factories is responsible for about 80 percent of global carbon dioxide emissions, about 25 percent of U.S. methane emissions, and about 20 percent of global nitrous oxide emissions. Increased agriculture and deforestation, landfills, and industrial production and mining also contribute a significant share of emissions. In 1994, the United States emitted about one-fifth of total global greenhouse gases.

Since the pre-industrial era, atmospheric concentrations of carbon dioxide have increased nearly 30 percent, methane concentrations have more than doubled, and nitrous oxide concentrations have risen about 15 percent. These increases have enhanced the heat-trapping capability of the earth's atmosphere...

Global mean surface temperatures increased 0.6 to 1.2 degrees F since the late 19th century. The nine warmest years of the 20th century have all occurred in the last fourteen years.

Several pieces of additional evidence consistent with warming, such as a decrease in Northern Hemisphere snow cover, a decrease in Arctic Sea ice, and continued melting of alpine glaciers, have been corroborated. Globally, sea levels have risen 4 to 10 inches over the past century…

Trees and forests are adapted to specific climate conditions, and as climate warms, forests will change. These changes could include changes in species, geographic extent, and health and productivity. If conditions also become drier, the current range and density of forests could be reduced and replaced by grasslands and pasture…These changes could occur during the lifetimes of today's children, particularly if they are accelerated by other stresses such as fire, pests, and diseases. Some of these stresses would themselves be worsened by a warmer and drier climate…

Hotter, drier weather could increase the frequency and intensity of wildfires, threatening both property and forests. Along the Sierras, drier conditions could reduce the range and productivity of conifer and oak forests. Farther north and along the northern coast, drier conditions could reduce growth of the Douglas fir and redwood forests. A significant increase in the extent of grasslands and chaparral throughout the state could result. These changes would affect the character of California forests and the activities that depend on them.

Jack Wilkinson Smith, *Sierra Landscape*, Private Collection, Courtesy of The Irvine Museum

ABOVE: Edgar Payne, *Landscape with Distant Mountains*, Private Collection, Courtesy of The Irvine Museum

Frederick Shafer, *The Russian River*, Courtesy of DeRu's Fine Arts, Laguna Beach

Harry Casey Best, *Redwoods*, The Irvine Museum

Paul Grimm, *Lake Arrowhead*, Private Collection, Courtesy of The Irvine Museum

Paul Lauritz, *Autumn Near Big Bear Lake*, The Irvine Museum

One of the worst droughts recorded in Southern California history has weakened our pine forests to such an extent that they have become vulnerable to infestations by colonies of voracious native black beetles. In October 2003, these dry, dead and dying trees provided substantial fuel to the raging wildfires that burned almost one million acres in our state, causing twenty deaths and more than $2 billion of damage.

An article entitled "Forest Die-Off Linked to Global Warming" which appeared in the *Los Angeles Times* on October 15, 2005 states the following:

Researchers believe the massive die-offs of New Mexico's state tree, the pinyon, during the drought of 2002 and 2003 could be a harbinger of life in a warming world.

High-elevation pinyon forests that had survived previous droughts endured as much as 90% mortality during that drought, Arizona researchers reported in the Proceedings of the National Academy of Sciences. Drought weakened the trees enough for bark beetles to kill them, and warmer temperatures—only 1 to 2 degrees Fahrenheit higher than the long-term average—appear to have contributed, the scientists found.

An article from the Associated Press on August 17, 2004, entitled "Study: Global Warming Could Affect California," indicates:

Global warming could cause dramatically hotter summers and a depleted snow pack in California, leading to a sharp increase in heat-related deaths and jeopardizing the water supply, according to a study released on August 16…

The study, published in the Proceedings of the National Academy of Scientists, focused on California because of its diverse climate, large economy, agricultural interior, and profuse pollution from industries and population centers.

The researchers used computer models they said illustrate the consequences of doing nothing, or adopting "relatively aggressive" policies such as the greater use of renewable energy sources rather than fossil fuels.

California can avoid the worst effects by quickly cutting how much carbon dioxide and other heat-trapping gases are released into the atmosphere, the scientists said.

The nineteen scientists who prepared the report include experts from Stanford University and the University of California, Berkeley, along with consultants and members of the Union of Concerned Scientists.

"If we do not take action now to reduce emissions of greenhouse gases, the consequences for California after about 2050 will become significantly more harmful than if we do take action now," said Michael Hanemann, director of the California Climate Change Center at University of California at Berkeley.

Paul Grimm, *Cloud Study*, Private Collection, Courtesy of The Irvine Museum

Marion K. Wachtel, *Near Mount Whitney*, Private Collection, Courtesy of The Irvine Museum

Edgar Payne, *The Sierra Divide*, 1921, Private Collection,
Courtesy of The Irvine Museum

John Frost, *Near Lone Pine*, 1924, The James Irvine Swinden Family Collection

Elmer Wachtel, *Convict Lake*, The Irvine Museum

Marion K. Wachtel, *Long Lake, Sierra Nevada*, The Irvine Museum

Under the most optimistic computer model, periods of extreme heat would quadruple in Los Angeles by the end of the century, killing two to three times more people than in heat waves today; the Sierra Nevada snow pack would decline by 30 percent to 70 percent; and alpine forests would shrink 50 percent to 75 percent.

The most pessimistic model projects five to seven times as many heat-related deaths in Los Angeles, with six to eight times as many heat waves. Snow pack and high altitude forests would shrink up to 90 percent.

The scientists' temperature projections are higher than previous estimates, particularly in summer. Their predictions of an extreme decline in snow pack, alpine forests and the spread of desert areas all exceed earlier projections…Among other predictions, the report says spring melt-off will come earlier, increasing the risk of flooding and decreasing how much snow-melt could be captured in reservoirs. The state will rely more on increasingly scarce groundwater, even as droughts become more frequent and more severe.

Paul Dougherty, *Rocks and Surf*, Private Collection, Courtesy of The Irvine Museum

An article by Andrew C. Revkin entitled "Global Warming Is Expected to Raise Hurricane Intensity" appeared in the *New York Times* on September 30, 2004, indicating:

Global warming is likely to produce a significant increase in the intensity and rainfall of hurricanes in coming decades, according to the most comprehensive computer analysis done so far.

By the 2080's, seas warmed by rising atmospheric concentrations of heat-trapping greenhouse gases could cause a typical hurricane to intensify about an extra half step on the five-step scale of destructive power, says the study, done on supercomputers at the Commerce Department's Geophysical Fluid Dynamics Laboratory in Princeton, NJ, and rainfall up to 60 miles from the core would be nearly 20 percent more intense.

Other computer modeling efforts have also predicted that hurricanes will grow stronger and wetter as a result of global warming. But this study is particularly significant, independent experts said, because it used half a dozen computer simulations of global climate, devised by separate groups at institutions around the world. The long-term trends it identifies are independent of the normal lulls and surges in hurricane activity that have been on display in recent decades. The study was published online by *The Journal of Climate* and can be found at www.gfdl.noaa.gov/reference/bibliography/2004/tk0401.pdf.

The new study of hurricanes and warming "is by far and away the most comprehensive effort" to assess the question using powerful computer simulations, said Dr. Kerry A. Emanuel, a hurricane expert at the Massachusetts Institute of Technology who has seen the paper but did not work on it. About the link between the warming of tropical oceans and storm intensity, he said, "This clinches the issue." Dr. Emanuel and the study's authors cautioned that

it was too soon to know whether hurricanes would form more or less frequently in a warmer world. Even as seas warm, for example, accelerating high-level winds can shred the towering cloud formations of a tropical storm. But the authors said that even if the number of storms simply stayed the same, the increased intensity would substantially increase their potential for destruction. Experts also said that rising sea levels caused by global warming would lead to more flooding from hurricanes—a point underlined at the United Nations this week by leaders of several small island nations, who pleaded for more attention to the potential for devastation from tidal surges.

The new study used four climate centers' mathematical approximations of the physics by which ocean heat fuels tropical storms. With almost every combination of greenhouse-warmed oceans and atmosphere and formulas for storm dynamics, the results were the same: more powerful storms and more rainfall, said Robert Tuleya, one of the paper's two authors. He is a hurricane expert who recently retired after 31 years at the fluid dynamics laboratory and teaches at Old Dominion University in Norfolk, Va. The other author was Dr. Thomas R. Knutson of the Princeton laboratory.

Altogether, the researchers spawned around 1,300 virtual hurricanes using a more powerful version of the same supercomputer simulations that generates Commerce Department forecasts of the tracks and behavior of real hurricanes. Dr. James B. Elsner, a hurricane expert at Florida State University who was among the first to predict the recent surge in Atlantic storm activity, said the new study was a significant step in examining the impacts of a warmer future. But like Dr. Emanuel, he also emphasized that the extraordinary complexity of the oceans and atmosphere made any scientific progress "baby steps toward a final answer."

Frank Cuprien, *Summer Evening, Laguna*, Private Collection, Courtesy of The Irvine Museum

In 1999, when environmental engineer Dr. Stanley B. Grant of UCI began conducting research on microbial pollution for the National Water Research Institute, I became active in opposing urban runoff. His Coastal Runoff Impact Study, which was prompted by the beach closures in Huntington Beach that year, focused on the sources, dynamics and nature of microbial pollution in a coastal watershed in Orange County, with the goal of examining the impact of urban runoff on the seashore. The "Dynamics of Point and Non-point Source Fecal Pollution from an Urban Watershed in Southern California" project will examine how storms affect fecal indicator bacteria sources, ecology and transport within several sub-drainages of the Santa Ana River watershed.

Dr. Grant studies the sources, fate and transport of pathogens and indicator organisms in drinking water, urban runoff and the coastal ocean. He is a member of the EPA's Science Advisory Board (on the Drinking Water Panel) and the lead on several multi-disciplinary research projects, including one on the influence of tidal wetlands on coastal pollution (joint with researchers from UC Irvine, Scripps Institution of Oceanography and UCLA, funded by the University of California Marine Council); another on the association of pathogens and particles in storm runoff (joint with

Pollution in the Bolsa Chica Wetlands due to urban runoff, Courtesy of Bolsa Chica Land Trust

researchers from UCI and the University of California at Santa Barbara, funded by the U.S. Geological Survey and the National Water Research Institute); and a third on the contribution of marinas to fecal indicator bacteria impairment in tidal embayments (in support of the Newport Bay Fecal Coliform Total Maximum Daily Load, funded by the California State Water Quality Control Board).

A recent EPA report pertaining to polluted runoff indicates:

The most recent National Water Quality Inventory reports that runoff from urban areas is the leading source of impairments to surveyed estuaries and the third-largest source of water quality impairments to surveyed lakes. In addition, population and development trends indicate that by 2010 more than half of the nation will live in coastal towns and cities. Runoff from these rapidly growing urban areas will continue to degrade coastal waters.

To protect surface water and ground water quality, urban development and household activities must be guided by plans that limit runoff and reduce pollutant loadings. Communities can address urban water quality problems on both a local and watershed level and garner the institutional support to help address urban runoff problems.

The porous and varied terrain of natural landscapes like forests, wetlands, and grasslands trap rainwater and snow melt and allow it to slowly filter into the ground. Runoff reaches receiving waters gradually; in contrast, nonporous urban landscapes like roads, bridges, parking lots, and buildings don't let runoff slowly percolate into the ground. Water remains at the surface, accumulates, and runs off in large amounts.

Cities install storm sewer systems that quickly channel this runoff from roads and other impervious surfaces. Runoff gathers speed once it enters the storm sewer system. When it leaves the system and empties into a stream, large volumes of quickly flowing runoff erode stream banks, damage streamside vegetation, and widen stream channels. In turn, this will result in lower water depths during non-storm periods, higher-than-normal water levels during wet weather periods, increased sediment loads, and higher water temperatures. Native fish and other aquatic life cannot survive in urban streams severely impacted by urban runoff.

Maurice Askenazy, *Sunset Boulevard*, The Irvine Museum

Paul Lauritz, *Rocks and Surf*, photograph, Courtesy of Bonhams and Butterfields

Pelicans, Courtesy of Bolsa Chica Land Trust

Urbanization also increases the variety and amount of pollutants transported to receiving waters: sediment from development and new construction; oil, grease, and toxic chemicals from automobiles; nutrients and pesticides from turf management and gardening; viruses and bacteria from failing septic systems; road salts; and heavy metals are examples of pollutants generated in urban areas. Sediments and solids constitute the largest volume of pollutant loads to receiving waters in urban areas.

When runoff enters storm drains, it carries many of these pollutants with it. In older cities, this polluted runoff is often released directly into the water without any treatment. Increased pollutant loads can harm fish and wildlife populations, kill native vegetation, foul drinking water supplies, and make recreational areas unsafe.

Coral Reef, © Eugene Weber, California Academy of Science

William Ritschel, *Boats Returning Home*,
The James Irvine Swinden Family Collection

Donna Schuster, *Los Angeles Harbor*, Private Collection,
Courtesy of The Irvine Museum

A *Los Angeles Times* article entitled "Panel Presses New Ocean Safeguards," published on April 21, 2004, states:

A commission authorized by Congress and appointed by President Bush has issued a gloomy report on America's oceans, urging the government to intervene in hundreds of ways—from curtailing pollution to controlling coastal development—in order to nurse the ailing waters back to health.

The 450-page report from the U.S. Commission on Ocean Policy details what has gone wrong: seafood contaminated with bacteria and chemicals such as mercury and dioxins; urban runoff laden with oil, trash and human waste; farm runoff that causes blooms of algae that suffocate all life and create oceanic "dead zones"; and rising sea temperatures that are killing coral reefs and spreading water-borne viruses.

The report lays blame on a variety of human activities. It singles out commercial fishermen who deplete fish stocks and discard up to a quarter of their catch. It also faults poorly planned coastal development that degrades estuaries and wetlands and puts people in the path of violent storms.

The report will please and provoke many of the groups that share an interest in the oceans, from conservationists and fishermen to the oil industry and the military. It calls for weakening the authority of regional fishery management councils controlled by the fishing industry. It also encourages new techniques of sea-floor mining and calls for relaxing restrictions on the use of industrial sonar, which can disturb whales and dolphins.

"Everyone agrees the oceans are in trouble," said commission Chairman James D. Watkins, a retired Navy admiral, referring to the 16 panel members, who included oil and shipping executives as well as scientists and government officials. "We know if we don't get moving now, in 10 years we may not be able to recover." Watkins said the overwhelming evidence collected at public hearings and site visits made it easy for the commissioners to reach consensus on the urgency of their mission.

The report, the first comprehensive analysis of the oceans in thirty-five years, emphasizes their role in providing food and jobs, as well as their intangible benefits. "We also love the oceans for their beauty and majesty and for their intrinsic power to relax, rejuvenate and inspire," the report says. "Unfortunately, we are starting to love our oceans to death." The report recommends that Bush set up a National Ocean Council, appoint a White House assistant to lead it, and bring order to the chaos of 20 federal agencies that implement 140 federal laws related to America's oceans.

George K. Brandriff, *Cannery Row, Newport Beach*, The Irvine Museum

George K. Brandriff, *Newport Harbor*, Private Collection, Courtesy of The Irvine Museum

Humpback Whales, © James D. Watt/Innerspace Visions, Courtesy of Greenpeace International

Bottlenose Dolphins, © Richard Jackson

Frank Cuprien, *An Evening Symphony* (detail), The James Irvine Swinden Family Collection

Saim Caglayan, *Overlooking Crystal Cove*, 2004, Courtesy of the artist

Frank Cuprien, *Evening Gold*, Private Collection, Courtesy of
The Irvine Museum

ALTHOUGH MY MOTHER AND I had not been shareholders in The Irvine Company since 1983, we still had a very personal interest in how the company's lands and Orange County were developed. To that end, we attended numerous Orange County Board of Supervisors meetings and city council and water board meetings, including those of the Irvine Ranch Water District, which I attend regularly to this day. We also continued to have a very personal interest in what took place at Crystal Cove State Park. On a number of occasions before my mother died, we would drive along Newport Coast Road, overlooking Crystal Cove State Park, and she would say, "Your grandfather and your father wanted this land to be a park, I want it to be a park, and you must see that it remains a park for the people forever."

In 1995, under Governor Pete Wilson's administration, an Assembly bill ended up with a "trailer bill" that said: "notwithstanding any other provision of law, the [State Parks] department is authorized to enter into a concession contract for the development, operation, and maintenance of the Crystal Cove Historic District as a public use facility for a period of up to sixty years, upon those terms and conditions that the department determines to be in the best interest of the State." In other state parks, the term is for ten years, and the concessionaire contracts must be put out to open bid. In the case of Crystal Cove, however, not one public hearing was held on this matter.

What the public was never informed of was that the proposed resort in the Crystal Cove Historic District was to serve as a model for other resorts to be built in state parks throughout California. This plan was similar to one proposed under President Ronald Reagan's administration when Secretary of the Interior James Watt was forced to step down for his support of a program to sell off federal parkland to real estate developers.

In November 1995, State Parks issued a request for proposals on a Crystal Cove Historic District Concessions Project. Three submissions were received. In December, the tenants of the Historic District filed a lawsuit asking to remain on a month-to-month lease until development began. A month later, their request was granted. In April 1996, Crystal Cove Preservation Partners of San Francisco was selected for the concession.

In 1997, State Parks reached a sixty-year contract with Crystal Cove Preservation Partners, which proposed renovating the cottages and creating a luxury resort at the Crystal Cove Historic District. Ten percent of the rooms had to be discounted at half the regular rate. The state stood to make 1 percent of the gross receipts.

On December 27, 2000, I read a letter in the *Los Angeles Times* from Laura Davick, founder of the Alliance to Rescue Crystal Cove and an ardent opponent of urban runoff in Crystal Cove State Park. She opposed Michael Freed's Preservation Partners luxury resort in the park's Historic District. At that time, I called Laura and told her that I wanted to meet with her. She later told me that she thought at first that someone was playing a joke on her, until I asked her to join me for lunch the following day at my farm, The Oaks in San Juan Capistrano.

That afternoon, Laura and I went to the Crystal Cove State Park Historic District to see her home and the other cottages. For me, the experience was like deja vu. The fog blanketed the coast, blocking any view of the development in Newport Beach; the surf was flat and lapped against the sand on the deserted beach; and the small painted wooden cottages reminded me of days gone by and the little green house at Irvine Cove. This was truly "An Island in Time." On January 17, I publicly joined Laura Davick in her efforts to stop the resort.

Liv Saether, *Crystal Cove Solitude*, Private Collection, Courtesy of
The Irvine Museum

Joan Irvine Smith at an event sponsored by the Alliance to Rescue Crystal Cove
held at Crystal Cove State Park, photograph, Courtesy of *Coastline News*

John Cosby, *Hazy Morning, Crystal Cove*, Courtesy of the artist

Back in 1979, when the contract was drafted for the sale of
The Irvine Company's coastal property to the state for Crystal Cove
State Park, I had insisted that the agreement contain a provision
indicating that should the state decide to lease any portion of the
property for development purposes, the company had the right of
first refusal. At my first opportunity, I asked Donald Bren if he had
any interest in developing the Historic District at Crystal Cove State
Park. He indicated to me that he did not, and that he wanted the
park "to remain as beautiful and pristine as it is, in perpetuity." I
knew then that my actions to preserve the cottages and protect the
park's natural resources would not adversely affect my agreement
with him not to impede The Irvine Company's development plans.

On January 18, 2001, I joined the Alliance to Rescue
Crystal Cove, the Natural Resources Defense Council, the Sierra
Club and other organizations and concerned residents at the first
informational meeting on the proposed luxury resort. Almost
immediately, the meeting turned contentious when the audience of
more than 600 people began chanting, "No Resort! No Resort!" On
February 1, 2001, State Parks officials announced that they would
send thirty-day eviction notices to cottage residents beginning
February 15.

The environmentalists' and local residents' strong opposition to the resort plan prompted the Davis administration to nullify the Wilson administration's action and seek money to buy out
Crystal Cove Preservation Partners' contract. On March 22, 2001,
the California Coastal Conservancy voted unanimously to spend up
to $2 million to buy out the sixty-year contract. The buyout propos-
al was crafted by Paul Morabito, a Laguna Beach resident and the
conservancy's first Orange County board member.

Governor Davis praised the breakthrough agreement, saying it was a "triple-win" solution to the ongoing controversy surrounding future plans for the Historic District of Crystal Cove State
Park: "It is responsive to the local community, expands environmental protection, and reimburses the developer for costs incurred up to
now."

In April 2001, I received a call from First Lady Sharon
Davis. She asked if she could meet with me, as she was coming to
Orange County for a board meeting. I invited her to join me for
lunch at my farm, The Oaks. It was during a horse show, and Susan
Samueli and my son Morton also joined us.

I had met Gray and Sharon Davis earlier that year and had
given them a copy of Native Grandeur, a book that The Irvine
Museum had produced with the Nature Conservancy. I had told
them about the museum, the books that we had published and our
in-house and traveling exhibitions.

Edgar Payne, *High Sierra*, Private Collection, Courtesy of The Irvine Museum

After lunch, Sharon asked me if I would consider sending some of the museum's paintings to Sacramento to be displayed in the State Capitol, which I thought was a wonderful idea. She mentioned that after Gray became governor, she had asked Elizabeth Smart, Director of the State Museum Resource Center, and Vito Sgromo, Curator of the California State Capitol Museum, to give her a tour of the Capitol. When she saw the building's bare walls, she felt that there was definitely room for improvement, so asked Carol Finley, Special Assistant to the Governor, to spearhead a program to find paintings, drawings, prints and other artifacts and furnishings that would improve the Capitol's décor. The first project was to search through what State Parks had stored throughout the state, to acquire artworks from the State Fair and the Summer School for the Arts and to borrow paintings from California museums to put on display.

John Gamble, *Goleta Point*, Private Collection, Courtesy of The Irvine Museum

Millard Sheets, *Pomona Ranch House*, Private Collection, Courtesy of The Irvine Museum

Frank Cuprien, *The Afterglow*, Private Collection, Courtesy of The Irvine Museum

California First Lady Sharon Davis, Jean Stern and Joan Irvine Smith at The Irvine Museum

At that time, I told Sharon about Laura Davick's and my project to save and restore the cottages in the Crystal Cove Historic District. I also shared with her our plan to have a painting competition there to raise funds for the restoration. She told me that she was very interested in the restoration and preservation of California's historical and cultural treasures, and that she and my friend Cheryl Lyles—then the assistant to State Parks Director Rusty Areias—were involved in the restoration of the Leland Stanford Mansion in Sacramento. She also said that she was very supportive of the Arts in the Parks program, and that she was most interested in our plan for the plein air painting competition in the Historic District.

Before Sharon left, I gave her two of our Irvine Museum books, *Reflections of California*, which I had written as a memorial to my mother, and *Romance of the Bells*, which is a history of our California missions. During the time that Governor Davis was in office, Sharon gave copies of *Romance of the Bells* to visiting dignitaries. And when The Irvine Museum published its history book, *California, This Golden Land of Promise*, which Jean Stern and I wrote, Gray gave that book to visiting dignitaries as well. It is also sold in the Capitol bookstore.

I had known Cheryl Lyles for about twenty years, as she had a lovely Grand Prix horse named Dutch Chocolate, and we often sat together and talked at the various horse shows that I attended in Southern California. Although I had not seen her in some time, we immediately renewed our friendship and began working on the Conservancy's plan to have the plein air painting competition at the Historic District in Crystal Cove State Park. At that time, we also discussed at length her idea to create a cultural and historical conservancy in California.

Rob Gage and Dutch Chocolate compete in a Grand Prix at The Oaks for Owner Cheryl Lyles, photo by Tish Quirk

Architectural rendition of the proposed Wheeler Library, Courtesy of the Orange County Public Library

THE JOAN IRVINE SMITH & ATHALIE R. CLARKE Foundation is supporting the Irvine Historical Society in its efforts to rebuild the historic main section of the original San Joaquin Ranch House, which was demolished by Irvine Company management in 1961. The remaining portion currently serves as home to the Irvine Historical Museum.

With regard to the restoration of the ranch house in Tustin, which was the Irvine family home and which was torn down by Irvine Company management in 1965 after a minor fire, the Orange County Public Library will use a $1 million grant from the James Irvine Foundation to build its new Katie Wheeler Branch as a replica of the house on the original site. The headquarters building, a number of barns and farm buildings, as well as old tenant houses and other homes, remain on the property, which is slated to become an Orange County historic park.

Irvine Historical Society historian Judy Liebeck writes in *Irvine: A History of Innovation and Growth*:

> At one time, the Irvine Ranch had the finest collection of tenant farm homes in the southwestern United States. Now, only about 20 of those homes still exist. These remaining structures serve as reminders of the ranch's rich agricultural history. The families who lived in them were the labor force of the agricultural era, a period which greatly determined the future growth and development of Orange County. The structures represent more than 50 years of economic and social change, from the days when the Irvine Ranch was one of the most productive farms in the world to today's master-planned city of Irvine.

The Irvine Historical Society became aware that the historical community needed to begin the process to save historic buildings before plans for developments were finalized. At the society's request, The Irvine Company leased the oldest building on the ranch, a wing addition of the original San Joaquin Ranch House, to the city, who in turn leased it to the society for use as a museum to house the society's collection. Immediately after the opening of the museum in 1980, the society shifted its focus to saving East Irvine, the old shipping center for dry crops.

As early as 1981, plans were being discussed to preserve as much of East Irvine as possible. Sand Canyon Avenue, the two-lane road that bisected the town, was slated to become the third busiest street in the city of Irvine. The AT&SF railroad tracks, which bordered the town on the south side, were targeted for a multi-billion dollar Bullet Train project, and were to be lowered four feet. A 35-foot-high railroad overpass was to be built to accommodate the six-lane divided Sand Canyon Avenue. The Santa Ana Freeway to the north was to be widened toward the town, further encroaching on the dozen acres that made up East Irvine. In addition, plans called for the site of the historic warehouses to be the eastern boundary of the company's Irvine Industrial Complex East. The bean and grain warehouses were to be removed and an industrial warehouse built in their stead. A large residential development, known as Village 14, was to be built along the southwest. Jets from El Toro Marine Corps Air Station flew over the area daily, creating a significant noise impact and crash hazard area.

Saving the town was labeled "impossible" by everyone who understood what was involved in historic preservation. Under the leadership of Barbara Wiener, an expert in community affairs, saving the town became a reality.

The old shipping center in Irvine, photograph, Courtesy of historian Judy Gauntt

Wooden windmill on the Irvine Ranch, photograph, Courtesy of historian
Judy Gauntt

Peer Swan, former president of the Irvine Ranch Water District, was responsible for saving the last wooden windmill on the Irvine Ranch, now located at the district's Michelson Reclamation Plant. He also saved three tenant houses when he had them moved to the San Joaquin Wildlife Sanctuary, on the same site.

Because Orange County is located on the Pacific Flyway for migratory birds, ducks and Canada geese were so plentiful during the early part of the twentieth century that a dozen birds could be brought down with a single shot. Some of the gun clubs in Orange County were grand estates with expensive memberships. The Irvine Ranch clubs, however, were rustic and inexpensive: one could shoot by invitation only.

Irvine tenant houses which were moved to the Duck Club at the San Joaquin
Wildlife Sanctuary, photograph, Courtesy of historian Judy Gauntt

The San Joaquin Wildlife Sanctuary, photograph, Courtesy of Irvine Ranch
Water District

The Duck Club at the San Joaquin Wildlife Sanctuary, a 300 acre coastal freshwater
wetlands that has recently been restored under the stewardship of the Irvine Ranch
Water District and The Irvine Company, photo by Trude Hurd, Sea and Sage Audubon

The Irvine Ranch had the best shooting in Orange County, and there was a gun club at almost every reservoir and marsh. There were so many ducks and geese around the San Joaquin Gun Club that when they took wing, they would darken the sky. The gun club was located at today's San Joaquin Wildlife Sanctuary, a 300-acre coastal freshwater wetlands that has recently been restored under the stewardship of the Irvine Ranch Water District and The Irvine Company.

The project provides many of North America's migratory and local birds with a place to rest, nest and feed. Some of the birds seen at this sanctuary include the Canada goose, the red-tailed hawk, the great blue heron, the snowy egret and the ruddy duck. It also serves as a safe haven for a variety of threatened and endangered species, such as the least Bell's vireo, the willow flycatcher and the peregrine falcon. The sanctuary has won first place in a national bird-watching competition for having the highest number of bird species sighted.

Canada Geese at the San Joaquin Wildlife Sanctuary, photograph, Courtesy of
Irvine Ranch Water District

Mary Nichols, former Secretary of the California Resources Agency, said of the sanctuary's restoration: "Thanks to a truly collaborative effort, including the hard work of scientists, engineers, committed individuals and organizations, the San Joaquin Marsh is once again a vital habitat for fish and birds. These restoration activities are a wonderful example of how we really can reclaim California's natural heritage."

In order to create a more appealing wildlife habitat, the restoration involved replacing 70 acres of non-native vegetation with quality habitat, and creating 69 acres of naturalized ponds and nesting islands. Wetlands cannot survive without a reliable water supply. An important component of the restoration project was the development of dependable water sources to supply the sanctuary with water year round. Water is diverted from San Diego Creek into the sanctuary, a process that dramatically improves the water quality of Newport Bay by preventing 15 tons of nitrogen from entering it each year. The project created several sediment-trapping basins in the creek that also provide a variety of other ecological benefits to the Bay, such as protecting Bay vegetation and maintaining mud flats.

With regard to the first 40 planned wetlands being built by the Irvine Ranch Water District in Irvine, part of a $41 million project over the 118 square-mile drainage area that feeds in to San Diego Creek, an article entitled "Workhorse Wetlands Ready to Assist Irvine: A system of human-engineered wetlands is being built across the county to reduce water pollution, help wildlife, by Pat Brennan, which appeared in *The Orange County Register* on Monday, November 28, 2005, indicates the following:

Once they were swamps, good for little but draining and filling. These days they're called wetlands, and with the name change comes new respect. The briny, meandering waterways on the coast, full of birds, reeds and cattails, or their freshwater counterparts farther inland, turned out to be highly valuable.

They are home to spectacular wildlife and act as natural filters for contaminants. The Irvine Ranch Water District is building chains of wetlands across central Orange County. Together they are called the Natural Treatment System, and the first four are now under construction in a relatively new development in Irvine called Quail Hill.

The largest is a 9-acre system of ponds that will destroy nitrates, kill harmful bacteria, snag trash and provide a haven for local birds (and bird watchers). And it will do all these things, its builders say, without breeding too many mosquitoes.

Unlike the county's bigger, better-known wetland restoration at Bolsa Chica, creating new wildlife habitat isn't the goal in this case, but something of a fringe benefit. The more than 40 planned wetlands on 31 sites are really working wetlands, with pollution control at the top of the list of priorities.

The 300 acre San Joaquin Wildlife Sanctuary, photograph, Courtesy of Irvine Ranch Water District

"The primary reason for the constructed wetlands is to treat urban runoff," said Norris Brandt, the district's environmental quality manager. But once they build them, the fringe benefits will come.

The 9-acre wetland, to be completed this spring, is next to an open-space preserve. Egrets and red-winged blackbirds will probably take up residence. Coyotes and bobcats might hunt or drink there. Roadrunners might even stop by to pluck insects or reptiles from the marsh's edge.

The wetland is also next to a staging area for a coastal trail system.

Once construction is finished, Brandt said, "we invite people to walk around the road outside of the wetland." And while they walk, the wetlands will be chugging away, scrubbing runoff water before it reaches the ocean.

The wetland, patterned after the much larger constructed wetland at San Joaquin Marsh, is a series of ponds, linked by channels and separated by removable barriers known as weirs.

Nitrates, fertilizer remnants that can cause excessive blooms of algae, will be broken up in the mud at the bottom of the ponds by "good" bacteria, giving off nitrogen—a harmless gas and the main component of the atmosphere. The reeds in the ponds also absorb some nitrate and will help provide stable, deep-water habitat for the nitrate-munching bacteria.

The water will remain in the ponds for seven to ten days. That's long enough for "bad" bacteria, the kind that washes down storm drains, to be killed by exposure to ultraviolet light from the sun. Trash will be trapped in the wetlands as well and periodically removed by maintenance workers.

And what about those West Nile mosquitoes? Taken care of, Brandt says. In meetings with the Orange County Vector Control District while the wetlands were in the planning stages, the water district picked up advice for keeping mosquito populations down.

An important element is reducing the amount of shallow, stagnant water where mosquitoes breed. Deeper ponds should help. And the wetland—unlike some built by other agencies in the county before West Nile was a problem—includes easy access for Vector Control technicians.

"The main thing is design it and maintain it so you don't have vegetation all the way to the shore—that way we have access, so we can treat it," said Michael Hearst, spokesman for Vector Control.

Last, the ponds will be home to a resident population of hungry mosquito fish.
The bare basins now being dug will soon be full of water, edged with cattails and bulrushes and noisy with birds, a blend of nature and human engineering.

If it's a swamp, then it's a super-swamp, an ecological workhorse and an increasingly common sight in urban Orange County.

For more on the water district's Natural Treatment System, go to www.naturaltreatmentsystems.org or call (949) 453-5500.

Amid business centers, a university and a bustling city, the San Joaquin Wildlife Sanctuary attracts visitors with its surprising sense of stillness in an urban setting. With its sweet smells and the rustling sounds of willow, alder and cottonwood, the sanctuary feels more like a faraway, peaceful paradise than a rejuvenated wetland near one of California's busiest freeways. It is a place for a family to enjoy an afternoon stroll while a tree swallow makes a nest. Visitors can walk along 12 miles of trails, rest on the benches, bird watch or simply relax under a native willow and listen to the sounds of nature.

The sanctuary serves as a living laboratory for students, teachers and the public, with its more than 200 species of birds. In cooperation with the local chapter of the National Audubon Society, the sanctuary offers a variety of wildlife education programs and tours, including an active school field-trip program.

In many ways, this rejuvenated wetlands is still in its infancy. Together the community will watch it grow to become an environmental haven and restful escape in the heart of Irvine. Nearly two-thirds the size of New York City's Central Park, the San Joaquin Wildlife Sanctuary is expected to become one of Southern California's most notable nature respites.

Sadly, nearly 90 percent of California's wetlands suffered another fate and disappeared during the twentieth century. Understanding the value of wetlands to the environment, the Irvine Ranch Water District, The Irvine Company and the voters of Irvine, through the Open Space Initiative, have given new life to one of the state's most important resources. These groups have worked with the city of Irvine to restore and enhance the largest coastal freshwater wetland reserve in Southern California.

The San Joaquin Wildlife Sanctuary encompasses 300 acres, half of which are being restored to a more natural state through the innovation and stewardship of the Irvine Ranch Water District and The Irvine Company. The remaining acres are quality habitat and are not in need of restoration.

In the effort to preserve and revitalize this important wetland, The Irvine Company has pledged $1.5 million over a five-year period. An annual gift of $300,000 will support the efforts of the sanctuary to further restore and preserve the tremendous wildlife and habitat in the San Joaquin Marsh and to expand the sanctuary's outstanding public education programs.

The San Joaquin Wildlife Sanctuary is free to the public and open from dawn to dusk, seven days a week. Educational programs under the direction of Trude Hurd are available at the Sea and Sage Audubon House, which is a restored Irvine Company tenant house. For information go to www.seaandsageaudubon.org/chapteroffice.htm or call (949) 261-7963. The Joan Irvine Smith & Athalie R. Clarke Foundation has long supported the National Audubon Society's work at this sanctuary.

The Audubon House at the San Joaquin Wildlife Sanctuary, photograph, Courtesy of Irvine Ranch Water District

Pacific Coast Highway, looking south to Tyron's Camp, c. 1927, First American Trust and Title Historical Collection

El Morro Beach with Trailers, 2005, photograph, Courtesy of Crystal Cove Alliance

AT CRYSTAL COVE STATE PARK, at least thirty extensive Native American archeological sites have been identified at various elevations. They are of three types: occupation sites, areas where people lived for some time, either returning seasonally or remaining in residence throughout the year; task sites, areas that were used only for performing specific tasks, such as shellfish gathering and processing; and rock shelters, some of which represent certain aspects of occupation sites while others have certain aspects of task sites. Most of these shelters were used as temporary occupation sites at various times of the year. One particular six-acre site in Morro Canyon dates back more than 5,000 years and is considered to be one of the most important archeological sites on the California coast.

In 1979, when the state of California purchased the land for Crystal Cove State Park from The Irvine Company, the intent was to ensure that the natural, cultural, archeological, historical and recreational resources of the area would be preserved, protected and made accessible to all. At that time, the tenants of El Morro Village mobile home park, located in El Morro Canyon within the park, chose a twenty-year lease extension in lieu of receiving relocation expenses. The agreement provided two decades, plus an additional five-year term from 1999 to 2004, to plan for departure. The agreed-upon lease required the tenants to cover all costs associated with moving personal property, including the mobile homes.

In 1982, following the full public comment and approval process, the Crystal Cove State Park General Plan was adopted. The plan identified the public access and restoration improvements for the El Morro area of the park, the last component for readying the park for full public enjoyment. The park, one of the last publicly owned and accessible coastal open space areas in Orange County, is now virtually surrounded by urbanization and private development. The El Morro area in particular is vital to all elements of the park plan, especially for full public access to passive and active recreational activities.

On February 20, 2002, Assemblyman John Campbell, whose district includes Crystal Cove State Park, introduced Assembly Bill 2190. This legislation proposed postponing the El Morro evictions—scheduled for 2004—and increasing the rents there to help pay for the improvements to the Historic District.

The previous year, I had founded the Crystal Cove Conservancy, whose mission is to retain the existing ambience of Crystal Cove State Park in perpetuity and to support the preservation and protection of all park natural and cultural resources. The board of directors included me as president, Laura Davick as vice president and Louise Arnold. Recently, my son Morton Smith, the head of the Traffic Commission in the city of San Juan Capistrano, has taken over Louise Arnold's seat on the board. The Conservancy receives funding from The Joan Irvine Smith & Athalie R. Clarke Foundation.

After founding the Conservancy, I wrote a booklet entitled *Crystal Cove State Park: An Island in Time*, which narrates California's history from the time of its early native inhabitants to the present day, especially as it relates to Crystal Cove State Park. Another pamphlet I designed was on the inhabitants and preservation of tide pools; this was produced by the Crystal Cove Conservancy and is given out to children visiting the park. It is currently also distributed by the Birch Aquarium at the Scripps Institution of Oceanography in La Jolla, the Ocean Institute at Dana Point, the Orange County Board of Education, the city of Newport Beach and a number of other organizations.

The pamphlet designed by Joan Irvine Smith on the inhabitants and preservation of tide pools which is produced by the Crystal Cove Conservancy

FROM LEFT: Bill and Alletta Cooper with Willem, Nathalie and Little Alletta, Morton Smith, Anita Ziebe, Joan Irvine Smith, Jim and Madeline Swinden with Jase, and Russ and Carol Penniman with Elizabeth and Rex and their dog Max at Abalone Beach

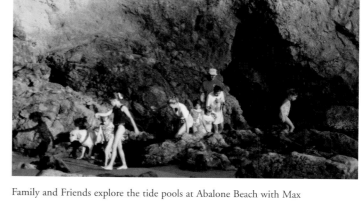

Family and Friends explore the tide pools at Abalone Beach with Max

LEFT: Madeline and Jim Swinden with Jase
ABOVE: Russ Penniman with Elizabeth and Rex

Nathalie Cooper and Elizabeth Penniman

Rex and Carol Penniman

My family and I have spent many summer days at Abalone Beach in Irvine Cove where the little green house once stood. My children have learned and are now teaching my grandchildren the vital necessity of protecting our beaches and oceans and the creatures that inhabit them. It is our wish that the natural and cultural resources of Crystal Cove State Park be preserved and protected and made available to all the people forever.

FROM LEFT: Joan Irvine Smith, Madeline and Jim Swinden with Jase at a seal release

Skippy and Sissy at Abalone Beach

Seals released by Friends of the Sea Lion in Laguna Beach

Virginia Rose and Charlotte Smith at Crystal Cove

Jack Wilkinson Smith, *Tide Pools, Crystal Cove*, Private Collection, Courtesy of The Irvine Museum

Toni Smith and her fourth grade class explore the tide pools at Crystal Cove

Guy Rose, *Indian Tobacco Trees, La Jolla*, Private Collection, Courtesy of The Irvine Museum

California Sea Lions feeding on sea urchins, © Joseph Dougherty

My good friend Dr. Charles F. Kennel, Vice Chancellor of Marine Sciences, Director of the Scripps Institution of Oceanography, and Dean of the Graduate School of Marine Sciences, and Chair of the NASA Advisory Council, has long advised me on environmental matters. Dr. Kennel envisions marine missions, like the early California missions, along the coast to inform visitors on the plight of our endangered marine environment and educate them on what can be done to protect our coastal waters and their inhabitants. These educational facilities could begin with Birch Aquarium at Scripps in La Jolla, include the Ocean Institute and Crystal Cove State Park in Orange County and similar facilities along the California coast.

The Joan Irvine Smith & Athalie R. Clarke Foundation supports research at the Scripps Institution of Oceanography, including its recent Kelp Bed Reforestation project. My son Russell Penniman is a member of the Director's Cabinet at the institution. Appointed by Governor Davis, he serves on the board of the California 22nd District Agricultural Association in San Diego County, which oversees the San Diego County Fairgrounds, including the Del Mar Race Track and Horse Park. He also chairs the Fairground's annual Del Mar Horse Show and was recently appointed president of the California Race Track Authority.

The Ocean Institute at Dana Point, headed by Daniel Gee, uses the ocean as a unique teaching tool to inspire learning, literacy and love of the environment. The institute, which is also supported by the Joan Irvine Smith & Athalie R. Clarke Foundation, provides children from pre-kindergarten age through college age with hands-on opportunities to become research scientists, oceanographers and explorers through programs that complement the school curriculum. These include the Ocean Institute Watershed Education program, the goal of which is to create an increase in concern and knowledge about watershed/water-quality issues in southern California. The Ocean Institute is at the site where a reproduction of the historic brig Pilgrim is docked; guided tours of the Pilgrim and educational cruises are also offered.

On June 9, 2001, with the support of Sharon Davis, Cheryl Lyles and Rusty Areias, the Crystal Cove Conservancy hosted Images of Crystal Cove, an art competition in which the signature members of the Laguna Plein Air Painters Association painted for one month at the Crystal Cove Historic District. The $10,000 in prize money offered by Joan Irvine Smith Fine Arts, Inc. consisted of $5,000 for first place, $3,000 for second and $2,000 for third.

FROM LEFT: Wyland, Joan Irvine Smith and Susan Samueli at the ground breaking for the new facility at the Ocean Institute, photograph, Courtesy of the Ocean Institute, Dana Point

The Ocean Institute research ship Sea Explorer, photograph, Courtesy of The Ocean Institute, Dana Point

Rick Delanty, *Dana Point*, Courtesy of the artist

Signature members of the Laguna Plein Air Painters Association members painting at the Crystal Cove Historic District, photograph, Courtesy of the Alliance to Rescue Crystal Cove

Anita Hampton, *Remembered Community*, Private Collection, Courtesy of The Irvine Museum

Ken Auster, *Good Morning Crystal Cove*, Private Collection, Courtesy of The Irvine Museum

289

The judging took place at the Joan Irvine Smith Fine Arts gallery in Laguna Beach. The judges were Rusty Areias, Roy C. Rose, grand-nephew of California Impressionist artist Guy Rose, and Thomas B. Stiles, who with his wife, Barbara, is a noted collector of historic California plein air art. The show was displayed to the public at my gallery for more than a month. In addition, I donated $44,000, or 40 percent of the proceeds from the sale of the paintings, to the Crystal Cove Conservancy, and I purchased the three prize-winning paintings for use in future Conservancy events. An exhibition of the Crystal Cove Historic District paintings was later presented at the California State Capitol Museum in Sacramento.

California Assembly Leader Marco Firebaugh of Los Angeles was among the attendees at the art judging, as was Cheryl Lyles. During the event, Cheryl had an opportunity to discuss with Assemblyman Firebaugh her idea of creating a cultural and historical conservancy in the state of California. Firebaugh went on to author a bill to create such a conservancy under California State Parks; thereafter, Senator John Burton introduced legislation that created the California Cultural and Historical Endowment, headed by the State Librarian, who at that time was Dr. Kevin Starr. My son James Swinden was appointed by Governor Davis and later by Governor Schwarzenegger to the board of the Endowment.

John Budicin

Anita Hampton

PAINTINGS OF CRYSTAL COVE BY VARIOUS ARTISTS

RIGHT: Scott Jennings
FAR RIGHT: John Budicin
BELOW, LEFT TO RIGHT:
John Budicin, Dan
Goozeé, Anita Hampton

RIGHT: Anita Hampton
FAR RIGHT: Scott Jennings

In the summer of 2001, Laura Davick and I organized an environmental fair to be hosted by the Crystal Cove Conservancy in October at the Crystal Cove Historic District. We brought together a host committee that included myself, the Crystal Cove Conservancy, the Alliance to Rescue Crystal Cove, California State Parks, the California State Parks Foundation, the Crystal Cove Interpretive Association, Quest-Tek, Saddleback College, Ocean Technology Systems, Cox Communications, RoseTel, the Ocean Institute, Orange County Coastkeeper, the Coastal Dolphin Survey Project, the Rocky Intertidal Preservation Program, Orange Coast College, the Orange County Department of Education, The Irvine Museum, the National Water Research Institute, the League for Coastal Protection, the California Coastal Protection Network, Friends of Harbors, Beaches, and Parks, and the Laguna Plein Air Painters Association.

On October 20, 2001, we presented educational programs throughout the day at the Crystal Cove Historic District. Visitors were able to view the Crystal Cove Underwater Park via video and wireless transmission and also converse with the divers. The Crystal Cove Kelp Reforestation Project was demonstrated live and hands on with Eco-Carts. From the mountains to the sea, our local watershed was depicted by a diorama that shows how actual water travels through our cities, picks up pollutants and is carried to the sea. Information revealing the discovery of dolphin birthing circles and dolphin nursery behavior was also exhibited. An interactive display demonstrated the effect of humans on intertidal areas, specifically tide pools. Tours of the tide pools and the historic cottages were conducted, and a pictorial display showed early Native American inhabitants from 1100 AD and how local Orange County history up to the present day has affected the park.

Garibaldi, photo by Ken Kramer, Superintendent of Crystal Cove State Park

Kelp Reforestation at Crystal Cove State Park, photo by Ken Kramer

Bottlenose Dolphins, © Richard Jackson

RIGHT: Bottlenose Dolphin at Sunset, © Richard Jackson

ABOVE: Jackie Nuñes teaching a class of school children about Native American culture, photograph, Courtesy of Mission San Juan Capistrano

LEFT: Mortar and pestle found offshore at Crystal Cove State Park, photo by Ken Kramer

Frank Cuprien, *Iridescent Evening*, Private Collection, Courtesy of The Irvine Museum

On February 26, 2002, Laura Davick and I hosted a fundraiser for Proposition 40, a bond issue that raised $2.6 billion for park projects and environmental initiatives across California. On March 14, 2002, voters approved the measure, which included $225 million earmarked for improvements to existing parks, $267 million for historic and cultural resources and $200 million for the California Coastal Conservancy for various open space projects. Although Assemblyman John Campbell opposed Proposition 40, he indicated that he would withdraw his Bill 2190, which had met with considerable resistance, if the bond issue was approved.

Governor Davis' budget proposal released on May 14, 2002 set aside $9.2 million of Proposition 40 funds for the restoration project in the Crystal Cove State Park Historic District. When Proposition 40 passed, State Parks officials promised that the cottages at Crystal Cove would be high on the list of projects recommended for use with those funds. In addition to the allotted $9.2 million, the revised budget also allocated $96,000 from Proposition 40 for sewers and $800,000 from Proposition 12 for El Morro State Beach, which holds the trailer park slated to be emptied in 2004.

In the spring of 2002, in another effort to protect our marine environment, I joined with Laura Davick of the Alliance to Rescue Crystal Cove and other environmental organizations, including the Ocean Outfall Group headed by Dr. Jan Vandersloot, the Natural Resources Defense Council, Coast Keepers and the Surfrider Foundation, to convince the Orange County Sanitation District to go to full secondary treatment on the 243 million gallons of moderately treated sewage it discharges into the ocean daily. Out of the nation's 16,000 sewage agencies, the Orange County Sanitation District (OCSD) was one of only thirty-six agencies nationwide holding a five-year waiver to the federal Clean Water Act that allowed them to discharge dirtier sewage into the ocean.

ABOVE: John Cosby, *Reflections, Crystal Cove*, Courtesy of the artist
RIGHT: Jack Wilkinson Smith, *Laguna Beach*, Private Collection, Courtesy of The Irvine Museum

An article entitled "Ocean-Bound Sewage to Be Fully Treated, Environment: Orange County Sanitation District, persuaded by clean-beach arguments, agrees to drop its waiver," which appeared in the *Los Angeles Times* on July 18, 2002, indicates that on the previous day:

By one vote, the Orange County Sanitation District opted to abandon a federal waiver that allows it to release into the ocean dirtier sewage than nearly all of the nation's 16,000 other sewer agencies. In doing so, the district agreed to comply with the requirements of the federal Clean Water Act.

"By us developing a policy of full secondary [standard of treatment], there's no need for a waiver," said Brian Brady, a representative of the Irvine Ranch Water District, who made the motion not to seek another waiver. He said the sanitation district will have to negotiate with federal regulators, "but I have full confidence that [sanitation district staff] can do that." County Supervisor Tom Wilson, who opposed seeking another waiver, said that "as long as we're going in the right direction with the right speed, those agencies will applaud us for what we're doing, not penalize us."

An overflow crowd of more than 200 people listened to the speakers' comments during the nearly four-hour meeting. They packed the boardroom, another nearby room and spilled out onto the lawn. When the vote was announced, the spectators cheered, and Christopher J. Evans, executive director of the Surfrider Foundation said, "What happened today is a victory for future generations in Orange County, and marine life and the economy."

The Clean Water Act requires two levels of treatment to kill most bacteria and viruses before sewage is discharged into oceans, rivers and lakes. Since 1977, the U.S. Environmental Protection Agency has been allowed to grant waivers to this requirement in cases where it would not harm the environment or public health.

Williams Lees Judson, *Morning Fog, Laguna Beach*, Private Collection, Courtesy of The Irvine Museum

Edgar Payne, *Seascape, Laguna Beach*, Private Collection, Courtesy of The Irvine Museum

John Comer, *Surfer, Crystal Cove*, Courtesy of the artist

Frank Cuprien, *A Summer Evening*, Private Collection, Courtesy of The Irvine Museum

The Orange County Sanitation District opted for full secondary treatment and has not reapplied for a waiver from the EPA allowing a lesser level of treatment. On September 17, 2004, the Santa Ana Regional Board of the California Regional Water Quality Control Board approved a resolution authorizing the Executive Officer to enter into a consent decree with the EPA and the Orange County Sanitation District that would establish a time schedule for the Orange County Sanitation District to achieve compliance with secondary treatment standards.

According to Robert P. Ghirelli, D.Env., Director of Technical Services at the Orange County Sanitation District, "The consent decree was successfully negotiated among the three parties—the OCSD, EPA and the state—and submitted to the federal district court. The public comment period closed in December 2004, and the decree was filed with the court in its final form in January 2005. The consent decree sets interim ocean discharge standards, deadlines for completion of new secondary treatment facilities at both plants and regular reporting of progress. Semi-annual progress reports will be prepared by the OCSD and submitted to EPA and the state on March 1 and September 1 of each year, through 2012. The OCSD will not receive any monetary penalties under the consent decree unless the district fails to comply with the terms of the agreement."

With the encouragement of the regulatory agencies, OCSD and the National Water Research Institute (NWRI) organized a Blue Ribbon Advisory Panel that will meet semi-annually for the duration of the project to provide advice and guidance regarding the technical issues associated with reaching full secondary treatment. The NWRI Executive Director, Ronald Linsky, selected Panel members who are recognized for their expertise from academia, public utilities and, the private sector to optimize the value of the services the Panel will provide to OSCD.

On September 19, 2002, I joined with Dr. Jan Vandersloot of the Ocean Outfall Group, Jean Watt of Friends of Harbors, Beaches, and Parks, and the Bolsa Chica Land Trust, headed by Flossie Horgan, to host a reception in support of Proposition 50, the Clean Water and Coastal Protection Bond of 2002, which passed in November of that year. The measure's funding categories included: 1) Water Quality–$955 million, 2) CALFED Bay Delta Program–$825 million, 3) Regional Projects–$710 million, and 4) Coastal Protection–$950 million.

One of the most unique and significant archeological sites in coastal Southern California lies within the Bolsa Chica in Huntington Beach. Known as ORA-83, this site contains evidence of an 8,000-year-old village and burial ground, located on a grassland mesa that is now proposed for a residential tract. It is the last remaining Early Holocene coastal village in Orange County and has at least twenty-five known burial sites. The precious nature of this site has become even more profound with the loss of a second nearby site for the construction of housing units.

Artist painting at Bolsa Chica, photograph, Courtesy of Bolsa Chica Land Trust

Lee Mothes, *The Bolsa Chica*, 1998, Courtesy of Bolsa Chica Land Trust

J. Daniel Rogers, Ph.D., Head of the Division of Archeology at the Smithsonian National Museum of Natural History, says of this site: "I am now convinced that every effort should be made to preserve as much of this site as possible. ORA-83 is almost certainly the last remaining major coastal habitation site between Los Angeles and San Diego. Carefully consider what its loss will mean to California and the nation."

More than twenty-three known archeological sites have been identified within one mile of the Bolsa Chica lowland, on the mesas. More than 400 "cogged" stones have been found on the Bolsa Chica Mesa, indicating that it was possibly a manufacturing site for these mysterious artifacts. Various theories about the religious or social use of the cogged stones abound. Only a few cogged stones are found at other sites in the region, but no other site shows indications of cogged-stone manufacture. In prehistoric times, this site was situated near the mouth of the Santa Ana River before the river changed its course in the late 1800s, and it was the beginning of a known natural transportation corridor that stretched into the Mojave Desert. This site had a profound influence on the region and probably was the hub of a ritual interaction sphere.

Shell middens, the debris from eating shellfish, are scattered throughout the Bolsa Chica, testifying to the abundance of seafood that was available to early inhabitants. Radiocarbon dating indicates that the site was occupied from about 8,000 to 2,000 years ago. The shell middens can provide the information needed to trace environmental changes and to study the corresponding changes in natural resource exploitation by the early inhabitants of the Bolsa Chica. Steatite, or soapstone artifacts, have been found with burials, indicating the existence of a trade network with communities on Santa Catalina Island, where the steatite was mined.

Granville Redmond, *Morning on the Pacific*, Private Collection, Courtesy of The Irvine Museum

Prehistoric "Cog Stones," © Stephen Mueller, photograph, Courtesy of Bolsa Chica Land Trust

Coyote, © Clair de Beauvoir, Courtesy of Bolsa Chica Land Trust

Jack Rabbit, © Connie Boardman, Courtesy of Bolsa Chica Land Trust

Great Horned Owl with Owlets, © Clair de Beauvoir, Courtesy of Bolsa Chica Land Trust

In 2003, my friends Jean Watt from Friends of Harbors Beaches and Parks, urban planner Terry Watt from Terrell Watt Planning Consultants in San Francisco, and Flossie Horgan from Bolsa Chica Land Trust initiated the Orange County Green Vision Project. It has been embraced by such community groups as The Nature Conservancy, Trust for Public Land, Hills for Everyone, Laguna Canyon Foundation, Sea and Sage Audubon, Friends of Harbors Beaches and Parks and the Bolsa Chica Land Trust. The purpose of the Green Vision Project is threefold: first, to formulate and articulate an open space vision for Orange County wildlands and wilderness areas; second, through coalition building to support local and state funding measures; and third, to establish broad-based private funding sources in the county for the acquisition and preservation of these areas.

As the second most densely populated county in the state and the fifth most densely populated county in the country, Orange County faces tremendous development pressures. With more than 3,300 people per square mile, Orange County far exceeds Los Angeles County's 2,400 residents per square mile. Well over 60,000 new housing units are currently proposed, approved or under construction in the county. This booming population, and the development that comes with it, are jeopardizing Orange County's unique natural heritage.

The Orange County Green Vision Project has received a start-up grant from the Orange County Community Foundation to explore the various funding mechanisms and the feasibility of such options. It is an excellent example of how to create new policy direction from the ground up. Over the next ten years, remaining wildlands and wilderness areas in the county will either be protected for future generations or lost to urban sprawl. The Green Vision Project will address this issue and work collaboratively to bring about the preservation of open space in Orange County.

Poison Oak, Campo Amantes, Rancho Mission Viejo, © Stephen Francis Photography

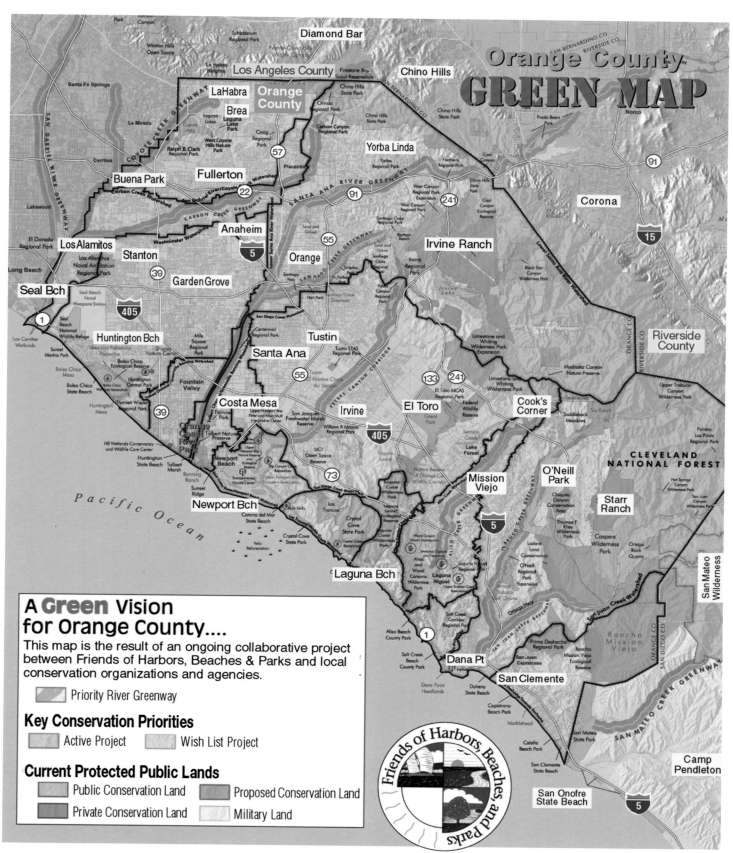

Orange County GREEN MAP

Friends of Harbors, Beaches & Parks (FHBP), in Newport Beach, coordinates Green Vision activities with over 30 county groups. The Green Map, updated regularly, shows the progress made through their combined efforts throughout Orange County.

Orange County Green Map, Courtesy of Friends of Harbors, Beaches and Parks

Scenic Path through Bolsa Chica Wetlands, photo courtesy of Bolsa Chica Land Trust

California Brown Pelicans at Bolsa Chica Wetlands, photo courtesy of Bolsa Chica Land Trust

Tern Rookery at Bolsa Chica Wetlands, © Connie Boardman, photo courtesy of Bolsa Chica Land Trust

An article entitled "No State OK for Project at Bolsa Chica: Coastal panel worries about environmental impact, Builder's parent firm says if there is no development, there may be no land sale to state," which appeared in the *Los Angeles Times* on October 14, 2004, states the following:

A plan to build 379 homes on a mesa above the Bolsa Chica wetlands in Huntington Beach stalled on October 13 when the California Coastal Commission raised concerns about the project's environmental impact. Unable to win approval at the commission meeting in San Diego, Hearthside Homes withdrew its application to the agency and vowed to correct potential violations of the state Coastal Act, which regulates development on the coast.

Hearthside wants to build 379 homes and a park on 105 acres on a mesa overlooking the 1,100-acre Bolsa Chica Ecological Reserve, which is undergoing a $65-million restoration. The housing project represents the last fight over the wetlands after almost three decades of controversy to protect the salt marsh and its mesas from development. In 1980, there were plans to build at least 5,700 homes, several marinas and hundreds of acres of commercial buildings.

Commissioners were concerned about protecting environmentally sensitive habitat for tar plant, the burrowing owl and eucalyptus trees on the land. They also said the project's required buffer zones between homes and the adjacent Bolsa Chica Ecological Reserve must be free of gravel roads, parking spaces, water retention basins and trails.

The Coastal Commission staff recommended against approving the current project because of potential adverse affects on wildlife habitat, water quality and public access to Bolsa Chica. A favorable decision is expected to clear the way for the state to buy 103 acres from Hearthside's parent company, California Coastal Communities Inc., in an adjacent section of the mesa and preserve it as part of the Bolsa Chica restoration. California Coastal Communities has agreed to sell the land for $65 million. The purchase will be funded by Proposition 50, a 2002 initiative providing $3.4 billion for environmental projects.

Pollution due to urban runoff at Bolsa Chica Wetlands, photo courtesy of Bolsa Chica Land Trust

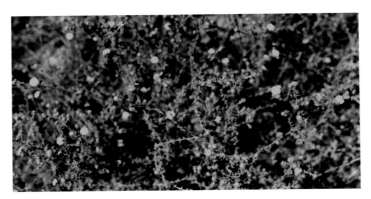

Southern Tar Plant in Bloom at Bolsa Chica Wetlands, photo courtesy of Bolsa Chica Land Trust

An article entitled "State OKs Homes for Mesa at Bolsa Chica Wetlands, Coastal Commission's approval of 349 luxury houses, to be built on 105 acres overlooking the salt marsh reserve, ends a 30-year fight" from the *Los Angeles Times* of April 15, 2005 indicates the following:

Plans to build luxury homes on a mesa overlooking the Bolsa Chica wetlands in Huntington Beach won approval on April 14 from the California Coastal Commission, ending a 30-year battle that saved the salt marsh from development.

Hearthside Homes will build 349 houses and a park on 105 acres overlooking the 1,100-acre Bolsa Chica Ecological Reserve, which is undergoing a $65-million restoration—the largest such undertaking in Southern California. The Coastal Commission voted 11 to 1 in favor of the project, adding more than two dozen conditions the developers must follow.

Though the vote was a landmark moment in the preservation battle, some environmentalists were disappointed by the decision to finally allow development in the Bolsa Chica area. "It's a bitter pill to have the proposed development be approved," said Flossie Horgan, a founding member of the Bolsa Chica Land Trust, which fought to preserve the upland areas of the wetlands. "While we're not excited about it, we are proud that we worked so hard with so many people to do what we've done."

Burrowing Owl on Sign, © Clair de Beauvoir

Peregrine Falcon, © Clair de Beauvoir

California Brown Pelican, Courtesy of Bolsa Chica Land Trust

White-Tailed Kites, © Clair de Beauvoir

Snowy Plover, © Clair de Beauvoir

Osprey, © Clair de Beauvoir

Black Skimmer, © Steven Eric Smith

Allen's Hummingbird, © Clair de Beauvoir

Mallard Female with Ducklings, © Clair de Beauvoir

ABOVE: Great Blue Herons Nesting in Tree, © Clair de Beauvoir
RIGHT: Great Blue Heron, Courtesy of Bolsa Chica Land Trust

American Avocets, Courtesy of Bolsa Chica Land Trust

Douglass Fraser, *Creeping Shadows, Vallejo*, Private Collection, Courtesy of The Irvine Museum

Alson S. Clark, *La Jolla Seascape*, 1924, Private Collection, Courtesy of The Irvine Museum

Paul Grimm, *Approaching Storm*, Private Collection, Courtesy of The Irvine Museum

Richard L. Partington, *Looking Across the Golden Gate*, 1908, Private Collection, Courtesy of The Irvine Museum

ON DECEMBER 10, 2002, I hosted a holiday dinner with the Natural Resources Defense Council (NRDC) in Huntington Beach. The theme of the event was "The Role of Business in Protecting the Environment," and it was announced as "An Evening with Robert F. Kennedy, Jr., the NRDC Senior Attorney." The following are some of the remarks that he made that evening:

* Good environmental policy is good economic policy.
* Economic indicators should be based upon dignified jobs, community well-being and a healthy environment.
* Pollution-based prosperity gives our nation the allusion of prosperity.
* Poor health, denuded landscapes, huge cleanup costs are what our kids will inherit...and won't be able to afford. We are passing the costs of our prosperity onto the backs of our children. By 1970, the Cuyahoga River was on fire, Lake Eerie was dead, and no one could swim in the Potomac or Charles rivers. Following the first Earth Day in 1970, President Nixon created the Environmental Protection Agency. That same year, NRDC was founded

and went on to help write 28 major federal environmental laws.

* While these environmental laws now serve as the model for 150 nations around the world, there are some nations that chose not to make that investment in the environment. For example: The former Soviet Union never passed legislation similar to the National Environmental Policy Act, and as a result, the Aral Sea is now a desert. Because it never created a Clean Water Act, the Sea of Azov is now a biological wasteland. In Turkey, there is no Clean Water Act, and the Black Sea will be dead in 10 years. Thailand has no Clean Air Act. People there are wearing gas masks, and the average child who has reached the age of 6 will have lost 7 IQ points. In Mexico City, smog inversions kill 10,000 people per year.

* An investment in the environment does not diminish our nation's wealth. It is an investment in infrastructure—the same as investing in communications and road construction—to ensure economic vitality from one generation to the next.

Albert DeRome, *Sardine Purse Seiner*, Courtesy of James (Jase) Irvine Swinden, Jr.

Hunting Beach with Oil Derricks, c. 1930, Vintage postcard, Private Collection

* Local and community control are the essence of democracy. But that devolution of power, from the federal to the state and local level, means corporate control. For example: In New York, General Electric left behind a $2 billion cleanup bill, and the Hudson River fish are still contaminated with PCBs. Hudson Valley residents have PCBs in their flesh, and mothers have PCBs in their breast milk.

* Four out of every five toxic waste dumps are in black neighborhoods. The most contaminated zip code in California is in East Los Angeles.

* When you see environmental injury, it is a subsidy. Someone is stealing something that belongs to you. The best thing that could happen to the environment is a free market economy in which people pay their way.

* You show me pollution, and I'll show you a subsidy for someone who has enough political clout to escape the discipline of the free market, someone who is cheating us out of something we own.

* The economy is a wholly owned subsidiary of the environment.

* We must be tireless in our efforts to re-impose the free market economy, to make sure people are not trading higher standards of living for themselves, at the expense of a lower quality of life for the rest of us and future generations.

At the conclusion of his remarks, Kennedy quoted an ancient Indian proverb that says, "Treat the Earth well. We do not inherit it from our ancestors; we borrow it from our children."

The event, which was a tremendous success, introduced the NRDC to Orange County. Two hundred guests attended, including landowners and developers, business executives, public officials, heads of both the university and museum communities, as well as research and environmental organizations.

FROM LEFT: Morton Smith, Joan Irvine Smith, Robert F. Kennedy Jr., Natural Resources Defense Council Senior Attorney, Marianne Smith, and Jim and Madeline Swinden

Robert Kennedy with his mentor Dr. F. Sherwood Rowland, a 1995 UCI Nobel Laureate for his world-renowned atmospheric chemistry research efforts

Ron Linsky, Executive Director of the National Water Research Institute

Robert Kennedy and Joan Irvine Smith

Bob Epstein a Natural Resources Defense Council Trustee and Environmental Entrepreneurs Co-Founder, opened the ceremonies, photographs, Courtesy of NRDC

FROM LEFT: Joan Irvine Smith, Joanne and Dr. Sherwood F. Rowland and Carol Cicerone

A table setting with a California oak tree as the centerpiece

FROM LEFT: Mr. Richard J. O'Neill, Laura Davick, President and Founder of Crystal Cove Alliance, Robert Kennedy and Joan Irvine Smith

FROM LEFT: Joan Irvine Smith, Orange County Sheriff Mike Corona and UCI Chancellor Ralph Cicerone

David and Ruth Seigle

Katrina Lutge and Gloria Brandes

Nancy Golden of NRDC and Dane Chapin

Chris Copps and his wife Saxon Baines

FROM LEFT: San Juan Capistrano Mayor Joe Soto with his wife Carol and daughter Vanessa

FROM LEFT: Laura Saari and her husband Santa Ana Mayor Miguel Pulido, Joel Reynolds, a NRDC Senior Attorney, Robert Kennedy and Susan Salter Reynolds

Jean Stern Executive Director of The Irvine Museum and R.J. Brandes

FROM LEFT: Robert Kennedy and Dan and Althea Brimm

FROM LEFT: Bob Caustin, President and Founder of Defend The Bay, Robert Kennedy and David Beckman, a NRDC Attorney

FROM LEFT: California State Park Superintendent, Mike Tope, Crystal Cove State Park Superintendent, Ken Kramer and Laura Davick

FROM LEFT: Alden Pierce, Carolina Winston and Howard Freidman

FROM LEFT: Bob Hernreich, Cheryl Lyles Joan Irvine Smith and Robert Kennedy

FROM LEFT: Sonny Lowe, Joan Irvine Smith and Cara Blessley Lowe

FROM LEFT: Mark Sanderson of The Nature Conservancy, Sheri Grady and Dan Merkle

303

CRYSTAL COVE STATE PARK CONTAINS some of the last remaining undeveloped coastal property in Southern California, as well as scenic upland canyons and ridges, coastal bench lands and bluffs, excellent swimming beaches and significant offshore marine features, including the Crystal Cove Underwater Park and the Irvine Coast Marine Life Refuge. Besides its important Native American sites, the park contains a variety of natural resources, including such rare and endangered species of plants and animals as the coastal sage scrub and the California gnat catcher. It is also one of the birthing sites of the bottlenose dolphin on the California coast.

In 2003, the California State Park Commission and the California Coastal Commission adopted the Preservation and Public Use Plan (PPUP) that preserves the historic cottages in the Historic District for interpretive public uses. Developed under the leadership of the Alliance to Rescue Crystal Cove and with my support, the plan balances the desires of participating organizations in an adaptive reuse plan that provides for the public's use of the property and addresses pressing historical, cultural and environmental issues.

The plan's four interrelated components are: overnight accommodations, educational and interpretive programs (the Community, Arts, Research, and Education, or CARE, program), State Park operations and other visitor services. It provides for affordable overnight rentals, park lectures, historic tours, painting classes, art exhibitions, tide pool exploration and ocean recreation. Visitors who enjoy rotating exhibits may catch glimpses of marine research center activities, including studies on water quality, marine habitat and dolphin behavior. The impact of these educational and interpretive programs extends beyond the park's boundaries into classrooms and communities through state-of-the-art video conferencing and wireless technologies.

Michael Obermayer, *Scotchman's Cove, Laguna Beach*, Courtesy of Jean and Linda Stern

In September 2003, the Alliance to Rescue Crystal Cove held its first Tropical Gala at the Crystal Cove Historic District, called "Celebrating the Past and Rebuilding for the Future." This event featured an exhibition and sale of plein air paintings of Crystal Cove State Park by signature artists from the Laguna Plein Air Painters Association, the California Art Club and the Southern California Plein Air Painters Association. It was judged by Jean Stern, executive director of The Irvine Museum. More than 180 paintings were produced and offered for sale, raising more than $60,000 for the benefit of the park. At the gala, it was announced that with the rescue of the cottages accomplished, the Alliance to Rescue Crystal Cove was to be renamed the Crystal Cove Alliance (CCA), as it was now the non-profit Cooperating Association benefiting the Crystal Cove State Park Historic District. Through this new contractual relationship with California State Parks, CCA raises vital funds for ongoing restoration and educational programs for the Crystal Cove Historic District.

Bottlenose Dolphin and Baby, photograph, Courtesy of Crystal Cove Alliance

FROM LEFT: Joan Irvine Smith, R.J. Brandes and Laura Davick at the first Tropical Gala hosted by the Alliance to Rescue Crystal Cove held at the Crystal Cove Historic District in September 2003, photograph, Courtesy of Crystal Cove Alliance

Jesse Powell, *Picket Fence, Crystal Cove*, Courtesy of the Crystal Cove Alliance

Mark Kirckhoff, *Keyhole Rock, Laguna*, Courtesy of the Crystal Cove Alliance

According to Crystal Cove State Park Superintendent Ken Kramer, "Phase I of the historic restoration, including 22 of the cove's 46 cottages, began on March 8, 2004, funded by $9.2 million from Proposition 40 funds and $2.8 million from the California Coastal Commission. Phase I of the Historic District is projected to be open to their new owners, the general public, in late 2005. Phase II, restoration of the remaining 24 cottages, will begin as soon as funds are secured."

Since September 2003, the Crystal Cove Alliance has raised $350,000 for the restoration of cottage No. 13, the Marine Research Facility. Of these funds, $250,000 was donated by the Samueli Foundation and $100,000 by UCI. Susan Bryant, Dean of Biological Sciences at UCI, heads the project. Other UCI faculty on the advisory committee include Executive Vice Chancellor Michael Gottfredson, Karol Gottfredson of the Department of Education and Peter Bowler of the Department of Ecology and Evolutionary Biology. The Alliance is currently launching a $9.2 million capital campaign to assist California State Parks with the funding for the remaining 24 cottages in Phase II.

On September 11, 2004, the Crystal Cove Alliance held its second annual Tropical Gala, "Golden Memories and Future Visions," as well as "Coastal Splendor," an invitational art competition and sale at the Historic District. This competition was also judged by Jean Stern. The event was a tremendous success, raising $100,000 for the Alliance's educational programs for environmental preservation, cultural arts and historic preservation.

Gregory Hull, *Nobody Home, Crystal Cove*, Courtesy of Redfern Gallery, Laguna Beach

Jesse Powell, *Tidepools, Crystal Cove*, Courtesy of the Crystal Cove Alliance

With respect to the El Morro Village mobile home park, a letter by Sara Feldman, Southern California Director of the California State Parks Foundation, entitled "Scrap Crystal Cove Sweetheart Deal: After 25 years, let's put public interest ahead of beach trailer-park renters," appeared in the Orange County Register on March 25, 2004, stating:

A seemingly local controversy in Orange County has statewide implications. The exclusive use of public land by private individuals and companies challenges Californians to ensure access to its parks and open spaces. This is nowhere more apparent than at Crystal Cove State Park, which was purchased in 1979 from The Irvine Co. with $32.5 million in tax dollars. At the time, it was the most expensive purchase in the history of the state parks system. The purchase included the El Morro trailer park, a collection of trailers along the beach and up the canyon on land leased from The Irvine Co. on a month-to-month basis. In lieu of a monetary "relocation benefit," the residents lobbied for and were given a 20-year, supposedly final, lease. However, in 1998, residents quietly and successfully lobbied for an additional five years. There was no public review of this extension and the public gained nothing in exchange for it. Even the line of trailers right on the beach was allowed to stay.

El Morro Beach, Courtesy of Susan Jordan, californiacoastline.org

El Morro Canyon, Courtesy of Susan Jordan, californiacoastline.org

This lease expires Dec. 31, 2004. The trailer park residents have hired consultants, public relations firms and high-powered lobbyists in an effort to continue their exclusive use of this public land. They intend to ask the governor for another extension under the guise of revenue generation from their leases.

Californians have waited more than 25 years to use and enjoy a park they paid for with tax dollars. Trailer residents will have enjoyed exclusive use of prime public lands at bargain rates for 25 years and have profited from it. Subletting is commonplace, continuing and highly profitable. According to State Parks officials, only 38 percent of the tenants use the El Morro trailer park as their primary mailing address, meaning that fully 62 percent do not live there full-time. Many sublet their trailers by the week and by the month and make very substantial profits.

With the Park Bond Act money already allocated and approximately $2 million having been spent on the planning process and other improvements, the California State Parks Department plans to replace the asphalt-covered canyon with coastal habitat, picnic tables and 60 campsites that will be open to the public. A restored El Morro Canyon and beach will provide panoramic coastal views, a sandy beach, camping and picnic sites unequaled in the state. Affordable campgrounds are in high demand and currently lacking in this state park. Once it is opened to the public, the mobile-home parcel will be the only place in the park where visitors can access the trails to the coastal hills from the beach. Finally, it will be the only place where disabled people can easily access the beach in the state park.

The Draft Environmental Impact Report (DEIR) for these plans was circulated, then certified Aug. 13, 2002. Trailer park residents filed suit, claiming the DEIR was inadequate. The state Attorney General's office vigorously defended the long-delayed implementation of the park's approved General Plan against this frivolous and self-serving litigation.

A community coalition consisting of a wide range of groups submitted an amicus brief in support of the state. The trailer park owners lost that suit, but they have filed an appeal to further delay public access. Amazingly, they contend the Parks Department, an agency entrusted with caring for the state's natural resources, didn't pay enough attention to the endangered California gnat catcher by restoring the canyon to native habitat.

The broad and deeply committed coalition working to open the park has pledged to make this state land accessible to its rightful users—all Californians—and not just a few trailer park residents. The public has waited too long to experience the pleasures of their land, beach and ocean at Crystal Cove State Park.

Trailers at El Morro Beach, 2005, photograph, Courtesy of the Crystal Cove Alliance

The state budget passed by Governor Schwarzenegger in August 2004 included $10.4 million to convert the El Morro mobile home village into an RV park and campsites as part of the 2,791-acre Crystal Cove State Park. In early October, the El Morro residents lost their appeal to avoid eviction by December 31.

On October 13, the California Coastal Commission approved removal of the trailers to make way for this day-use and overnight campground in the park, but in mid-November, the residents filed two lawsuits to block their eviction. When the residents lost both of these suits, the State Attorney General's office filed "unlawful detainers" in Superior Court on January 20, 2005, opening the way for eviction notices to be served on the tenants who have not agreed to leave.

An article entitled "Bills Would Keep Homes at El Morro, Assemblyman proposes extending mobile-unit leases 30 years. The deal would cost tenants $50 million up front plus higher rents," appeared in the *Los Angeles Times* on February 12, 2005. It indicates that even while the state is trying to evict residents of the El Morro Village mobile home park in Crystal Cove State Park to allow development of a public beachfront park, freshman Assemblyman Chuck DeVore (R-Irvine) introduced two bills on February 11 proposing to extend tenant leases for 30 years. According to Ken Kramer, superintendent of Crystal Cove State Park, "The tenants' leases have expired and the land belongs to the public. As to DeVore's proposed legislation, the state parks legislative staff is reviewing the bills and the department will make a recommendation to the governor as soon as possible."

An article entitled "DeVore funding at issue in heat of battle, Campaign-finance reports list $74,000 from sources with stake in El Morro," which appeared in the *Orange County Register* on February 28, 2005 indicates the following:

Assemblyman Chuck DeVore is taking heat from both environmentalists and taxpayer groups for supporting the not-quite-yet-lost cause of El Morro Village, which the state intends to turn into a public park later this year.

It hasn't helped that DeVore's campaign-finance reports show more than $74,000 in loans and donations from residents and managers of the mobile home park.

Most of that money came from the family of El Morro Village Inc. shareholder Roberto Brutocao, who is DeVore's finance chairman. DeVore spent $515,420 in the election.

"It doesn't make too much sense what he is proposing unless you want to give special favors to someone," said Fern Pirkle, president of Friends of the Newport Coast. "It just reveals who he is really working for. He is not working for the benefit of all the taxpayers."

DeVore's actions have infuriated two groups that are not usually found on the same side: Environmentalists, such as Surfrider Foundation and Friends of the Newport Coast; and conservative taxpayers.

On February 14, the Orange County Taxpayers Association urged county legislators to defeat DeVore's bills, calling El Morro residents "taxpayer-subsidized squatters on some of the finest public beach property in the world."

That idea was echoed on February 27 by former Irvine Co. Vice President Gil Ferguson of Newport Beach. Ferguson recalled El Morro residents coming to him for an extension when he was in the Assembly. "I told them to get lost," Ferguson said.

"This park was bought and paid for by the people of California. The highest and best use of this property is to allow the people of California to enjoy it. They can't enjoy it very well if there are people sitting on it."

On April 25, Assemblyman Chuck DeVore dropped his two bills that proposed a lease extension for tenants of the El Morro mobile home park. On November 4, in a settlement reached in Orange County Superior Court, the residents of El Morro Village agreed to vacate their mobile homes in Crystal Cove State Park by March 1, 2006. By February 28, they had vacated their trailers.

Richard Rice, *El Morro Beach*, Courtesy of the Crystal Cove Alliance

An article from the *Daily Pilot* of May 8, 2005 indicates that Senator John Campbell was working on a proposal to take management of the entire Crystal Cove State Park out of the state's hands and put it under the auspices of a nonprofit group. Such a move would have opened the door for private real estate development of all the park land, which is designated for park and recreation purposes. It further indicates that he intended to oppose the Parks and Recreation Department's acquisition of approximately $2 million to complete the first phase of the renovation of the historic district's 46 cottages.

While visiting Crystal Cove State Park and speaking with Laura Davick, Dan Gee and Dave Rahn other representatives of the Crystal Cove Alliance and me on May 8, Senator Campbell scaled back his proposal to limit a nonprofit's role to the historic cottage district and the El Morro area. However, he still believed the state could not afford to spend the $2 million to complete the first phase of the restoration of the cottages, even though this would include the restoration of the cottage for use by handicapped individuals.

Because of delays due to winter storms and structural damage that was not found in the cottages until renovation started, only 70% of the work scheduled to be done at the historic district by March had been completed. However, it is expected that 22 of the cottages will be completed by September.

On May 27, Senator Campbell held a meeting with representatives from California State Parks and the Crystal Cove Alliance executive board. As the balance of the funding for the Phase I restoration of the Crystal Cove State Park Historic District has been approved, the primary topic discussed was the future management of the historic district and the lack of funding for the Phase II restoration. Senator Campbell indicated that he would not attempt to block the funding for Phase II of the project, but instead would help look for a viable funding solution.

Senator John Campbell subsequently introduced legislation that would have provided State Parks with the ability to negotiate with a non-profit organization for the management of the Crystal Cove Historic District. The bill reached the Senate floor as a consent calendar item, where it was pulled at the request of AFSCME, a labor union that includes state park employees. Their concern was that the bill was a "slippery slope," allowing the privatization of state parks and decreasing the number of jobs or potential jobs for unionized state employees. It was subsequently sent to the Senate Labor Committee, who would not be holding any more hearings in 2005.

On September 24, 2005, the Crystal Cove Alliance held its third annual Tropical Gala, "An Evening with the Artists," as well as "Coastal Splendor," an invitational art competition judged by Jean Stern and sale at Pelican Point in Crystal Cove State Park. The event was another tremendous success, raising $140,000 for the Alliance's educational programs for environmental preservation, cultural arts and historic preservation.

FROM LEFT: California State Park District Superintendent Rich Rozzelle, and wife Sheryal, Laura Davick and Former California State Park District Superintendent Mike Tope, photo graph, Courtesy of Crystal Cove Alliance

FROM LEFT: Jeff Mosher, Executive Director of the National Water Research Institute, Madeline Swinden, Laura Davick and Greg McCollum of The Nature Conservancy, photograph, Courtesy of Crystal Cove Alliance

FROM LEFT: Winning artist John Asaro, Dave Rahn and Jean Stern, photograph, Courtesy of Crystal Cove Alliance

AT LEFT: Congressman John Campbell with his wife Catherine and AT RIGHT: UCI Chancellor Michael Drake with his wife Linda, photograph, Courtesy of Crystal Cove Alliance

FROM LEFT: Laura Davick, Joan Irvine Smith and Former California Assembly Woman Marilyn Brewer, photograph, Courtesy of Crystal Cove Alliance

Anne Earhart viewing the paintings photograph, Courtesy of Crystal Cove Alliance

Guests viewing the paintings, photograph, Courtesy of Crystal Cove Alliance

La Jolla Cove, 2005 Crystal Cove Annual First Prize winner by John Asaro, Courtesy of the Crystal Cove Alliance

October 12, 2005 was the last day for businesses and non-profits to submit bids to the California Department of Parks and Recreation to operate 13 cottages along with a restaurant and the Crystal Cove Shake Shack at the Crystal Cove State Park Historic District. Although the Crystal Cove Alliance was the sole bidder, the group was not guaranteed the contract as parks department officials have yet to determine whether the alliance's plan was in accordance with the department's requirements for the district. The department wanted to select an organization to manage the project by January, when they expected the 22 cottages in the first phase of the restoration to be completed.

The Crystal Cove Alliance is one of 80 Co-operating Associations in the state partnering with the Department of Parks and Recreation. Under its current contract it is working with the department to raise money for educational facilities at the Historic District and has been intimately involved in the preservation of the cottages for the last six years.

On January 16, 2006, Crystal Cove Alliance Founder and President, Laura Davick and her nonprofit group signed a 20-year contract to manage the cottages at the Crystal Cove Historic District. The agreement was subsequently approved by the California Attorney General's office, The Irvine Company, and the state Department of General Services. On April 6 it was executed by State Parks Director Ruth Coleman.

The Alliance's contract includes management responsibility for the cottages, the Crystal Cove Shake Shack and a beachfront cafe, the Beachcomber. The 10 overnight cottages and three dormitory-style cottages have been restored to offer visitors a California beach experience from the 1930s. "We are thrilled that we are now in the final countdown for opening this unique and special place," Ruth Coleman said. "With its rustic charm and historic feel, we anticipate a huge demand by people who are eager to spend a night at a place unlike anything found anywhere on the West Coast."

An article by David Reyes from the *Los Angeles Times* of April 28 indicates that the race for reservations for the 13 restored cottages in the Crystal Cove State Park Historic District began on April 27 at 8 a.m., online and by telephone. By 8:46 a.m., there were 16,000 people competing for an overnight stay from late June through October.

According to state parks spokesman Roy Stearns, "There hasn't been this much interest in a state park facility opening in 10 years." Public interest in the cottages has been high for months, even though only 13 of 46 cottages from the 1920s and 1930s will be ready for overnight stays June 26. The average rental for a family of four will be $165 a night.

The cottages will be managed by the Crystal Cove Alliance, which is also helping with the remaining renovation. The state has spent $8.6 million so far to renovate 22 of its 46 cottages. Revenue from the rentals will be used to help maintain the historic district and its cottages. In addition, the alliance has set a fundraising goal of at least $15 million to complete restoration of all the units.

Phil Dyke, *Upper Newport Bay*, c. 1935, Courtesy of John Moran Auctions

WITH REGARD TO UPPER NEWPORT BAY, Orange County Harbors, Beaches and Parks indicates the following:

The white cliffs of Upper Newport Bay are composed primarily of microscopic diatoms representing the Monterey Formation and were formed 15 million years ago. Further north, past Big Canyon is the "newer", brown Capistrano formation. The Bay has been sculpted by the Santa Ana River and carved during the glacial period of the Pleistocene Epoch. Fossils from mammoths, bison and giant sloths have been discovered in the sedimentary deposits on top of an older marine terrace. Until 1862, the Upper Bay flowed directly into the Pacific Ocean.

The earliest human inhabitants of the Bay lands lived here nearly 9,000 years ago. Indians known as Gabrielino dwelled here over 2,000 years ago and subsided on the fish and plants of the Bay. Within 50 years of the advent of the mission period, they had all but disappeared.

Since that time, cattle and sheep have grazed the hills above the bay, called Bolsa de Gengara (bay with high banks) by the Spanish, and then Bolsa de San Joaquin by the Mexicans. The sternwheel steamer "Vaquero" helped generate the current name...in 1870 it carried a load of lumber into the Bay, hence the designation, "New port." James Irvine and partners acquired the Bay in 1864, for 37 cents an acre. These holdings supported a salt works from the 1930's until 1969 when it was destroyed by floods. Shellmaker Island was home to several companies until the late 1980's. Shell material was dredged and sold as a chicken feed supplement, and dredging spoils were deposited by the Arches, on Shellmaker Island and at Big Canyon, among other locations.

Preservation of Upper Newport Bay began with a fight for survival in the 1960's when the area was designated from development to provide a water-skiing area. Approximately ten years of lawsuits ensued by environmentally concerned citizens, and ended in 1975 with the undeveloped portions of the Upper Newport Bay becoming a 752 acre ecological reserve under the jurisdiction of the State of California Department of Fish and Game. In the mid 1980's the County initiated negotiations to obtain title to bluffs surrounding the reserve. In 1989, the county accepted the 140-acre Upper Newport Bay Nature Preserve.

Wild Mustard, Upper Newport Bay, © Michael Salas

Shore Birds, Upper Newport Bay, © Michael Salas

Sunset, Upper Newport Bay, © Richard Jackson

Channel, Upper Newport Bay, © Michael Salas

The White Cliffs of Upper Newport Bay, © Michael Salas

Wetlands, Upper Newport Bay, © Michael Salas

Burrowing Owl on post, © Clair de Beauvoir   Great Blue Heron, © John Modesso, Jr   White Heron, © Michael Salas   California Gnatcatcher, © Clair de Beauvoir

Mallards, © Michael Salas   Mallard and Ducklings, © Richard Jackson   California Clapper Rail, © Joyce Gross

Brown Pelican, © Joyce Gross   Little Green Heron, © Richard Jackson   California Clapper Rail, © Joyce Gross

White Pelicans, © Richard Jackson   Curlews, © Richard Jackson   Dowitchers, © Richard Jackson

Killdeer, © Richard Jackson   Black-Crowned Night Heron, © Richard Jackson

312

Savannah Sparrow, © Tom Greer
2004

Peregrine Falcon, © Don Getty 2003

Cactus Wren, © Mark Bratton 2005

American Bittern, © Richard Jackson

Ash-Throated Flycatcher,
© Richard Jackson

Foster's Tern, © Steven Eric Smith

Upper Newport Bay Nature Preserve and Ecological Reserve represent approximately 1,000 acres of open space. Upper Newport Bay Nature Preserve surrounds the Ecological Reserve. The park includes the Peter and Mary Muth Interpretive Center. Upper Newport Bay Nature Preserve totals approximately 140 acres. The Nature Preserve is made up of the bluffs surrounding the Bay. Three sensitive species use the bluffs: The California Gnatcatcher, San Diego Cactus Wren, and Burrowing Owl. Two important plant communities are found on the bluffs - grasslands and coastal sage scrub. Upper Newport Ecological Reserve totals 752 acres. This coastal wetland, one of the largest in southern California, is renowned as one of the finest bird watching sites in North America. During winter migration up to 35,000 birds may be using the Bay at one time. It is home to six rare or endangered species: Light Footed Clapper Rail, Brown Pelican, Belding's Savannah Sparrow, Black Rail, Peregrine Falcon and California Least Tern. The Bay is home to one endangered plant species - Saltmarsh Bird's Beak. Considered a "critical estuary" habitat - Upper Newport Bay is one of the most pristine remaining estuaries in Southern California.

Education is just a part of what the Upper Newport Bay Nature Preserve offers the community. Each year almost one million visitors leave the noise and exhaust of city streets behind to bike, fish, walk, kayak, bird watch, or simply relax and observe nature in the serene beauty of the Bay. The Preserve provides an unprecedented enhancement to the community through its accessibility to the public, and the fact that it borders an ecosystem that has become one of the most endangered in the state - the Coastal Wetlands. This environmentally sensitive area contributes to the outstanding quality of life in Orange County.

Geoff Kruger, *Water Channels, Upper Newport Bay*, Courtesy of Jean and Linda Stern, photo courtesy of Peter Blake Gallery

Lifting Fog, Upper Newport Bay, photo by Jean Stern

ABOVE: Muth Center, Upper Newport Bay, photo by Jean Stern
RIGHT: "Marsh Birds Rising," bronze sculpture by Van Sant, Muth Center, photo by Jean Stern

Jeff Horn, *Upper Newport Bay*, 1997, Courtesy of Jean and Linda Stern

Pollution in Upper Newport Bay due to urban runoff, photograph, Courtesy of Friends of Harbors, Beaches and Parks

The Peter and Mary Muth Interpretive Center is a 10,000 square foot educational facility built into one of the bluffs on the north side of Upper Newport Bay. It was officially opened by Orange County Supervisor Tom Wilson on Saturday, October 14, 2000. Guests of honor were Fran and Frank Robinson who 30 years ago galvanized the community to save Upper Newport Bay from development, and Peter and Mary Muth whose very generous donation provided the seed money to turn the dream of an Interpretive Center into a reality. Its Mission Statement is "To promote and support the protection and preservation of California Coastal Wetlands through environmental education." Joanette Willert, Senior Park Ranger, Upper Newport Bay Nature Preserve, indicates the following:

Since the birth of the Center in October of 2000 much has been accomplished by the staff and volunteers of the bay to fulfill this mission. The purpose of an interpretive center is not only to educate but also to spark interest and inspire questions. Environmental interpretation involves the translation of the technical language of the natural sciences into relationships and ideas that are fun and easy to understand. Firsthand experiences, original objects and illustrative media are incorporated into the exhibits and activities at the Center to help reveal meanings, ideas, and relationships about the natural world.

There are many things to accomplish in the years to come as we continue to spark interest and inspire questions from the thousands of people visiting the bay every year. We hope to encourage the inquisitive minds of our visitors and continue to broaden their understanding and appreciation of the bay. With this increased sense of stewardship, the protection and preservation of wetlands doesn't seem like such an unattainable idea after all.

The Newport Bay Naturalists and Friends is an organization dedicated to preserving and educating the public about Upper Newport Bay. It supports the Peter and Mary Muth Interpretive Center and the California Department of Fish and Game in the operation of the Back Bay Science Center at Shellmaker Island. The stated mission of the latter is "to provide a hands-on facility where students and the public can study and enjoy the estuarine ecology of Newport Bay and the marine ecology of the Ocean, and to promote natural resource conservation and stewardship throughout the watershed." The current Back Bay Science Center was opened the fall of 1999. It began classes in marine ecology in the summer of 2000.

Urban runoff is the leading source of impairment to Upper Newport Bay. An area of approximately 154 square miles of urban Orange County drains into the estuary. Storm water runoff from this watershed brings with it trash, and other less-obvious pollutants including bacteria and other pathogens, and sediment. The proximity of the surrounding communities brings other threats such as non-native plant invasions and detrimental recreational use that cross jurisdictional boundaries.

By the time the Marine Corps Air Station at El Toro closed in 1999, it had become one of the nation's premier military bases serving from World War II through the Gulf War. The Great Park Conservancy was established in October 2000 as a community-based organization to support the vision of a Great Park—a wonderful countywide public amenity—at the former marine base now dotted with military buildings, bisected by massive runways and surrounded by a chain-link fence.

The vision of the Orange County Great Park is a magnificent—perhaps America's most magnificent—metropolitan park, consisting of nearly 4,000 acres devoted to vast stretches of open space and nature preserves, sports and recreational facilities, museums and cultural institutions, colleges and universities and a veterans' memorial—a park that will equal the beauty of New York's Central Park.

In December 2003, the city of Irvine created the Orange County Great Park Corporation, which will be responsible for creating policy for the development, operation and maintenance of the Orange County Great Park. The Corporation's Board of Directors is made up of five Irvine City Council Members and four independent directors. The independent directors are Newport Beach businessman and philanthropist James "Walkie" Ray, Santa Ana Mayor Miguel Pulido, Laguna Canyon Foundation Founder and President Michael Pinto, and former Irvine Company executive Richard Sim.

To accomplish the vision of building one of America's finest metropolitan parks, the Conservancy will operate as an all-inclusive, public benefit corporation engaged in activities to support the planning, development, financing and operation of the park. In doing so, it will work hand in hand with the Great Park Corporation to ensure a regional focus for the Great Park. Also, it will support the vision of the Great Park as a wonderful public amenity that will offer something for everyone, regardless of age, economic circumstances, or place of residence.

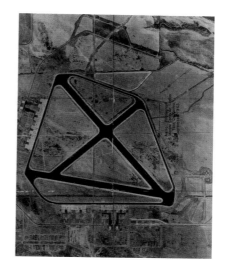

Aerial photograph of MCAS El Toro in September 1943, shortly after the base opened, *Flying Leatherneck Aviation Museum Archives*, photograph, Courtesy of Great Park Conservancy

RIGHT: MCAS El Toro's commissioning ceremony on March 17, 1943, *Flying Leatherneck Aviation Museum Archives*, photograph, Courtesy of Great Park
BELOW: Below: Ariel photograph of El Toro showing boundaries, photograph, Courtesy of Great Park Conservancy

ABOVE: El Toro Marine Corps Air Station, photograph, Courtesy of historian Judy Gauntt

315

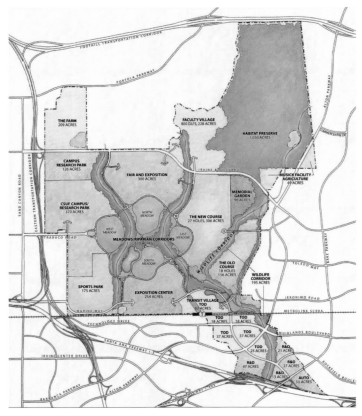

Map of El Toro land showing the Great Park plan, Courtesy of Great Park Conservancy

In March 2004, the city of Irvine annexed the El Toro land; in 2005 the Department of the Navy sold the land to Lennar, a private developer, who in turn donated approximately eighty-five percent back to a public trust for the Great Park. The birth of the Great Park in 2005 is the result of many years of hard work from thousands of residents, elected officials and volunteers who were committed to seeing the land at El Toro continue to retain a proud heritage—a heritage that will maximize the cultural, economic and environmental benefits of reuse of this land for the entire Southern California region.

According to Michael D. Ray, Chair, Great Park Conservancy, "The Great Park is a culmination of a partnership among the Department of the Navy, the city of Irvine and other governmental agencies, and private foundations like the Great Park Conservancy." The Orange County Great Park Advisory Council is composed of 17 mayors and council members from local cities as well as 50 individuals, including my son James Swinden and myself.

Jim and I hope that a world-class design competition will take place for the creation of the Orange County Great Park, and that this design will benefit not only the Orange County community, but also attract both national and international visitors. A significant aspect of this goal would be the establishment of a Great Park Museum Complex that would encompass a variety of museums, such as art, history, human and natural history and science. A "Smithsonian West" museum might be the cornerstone of such a complex and would serve not only Orange County, but California and the Western United States as well.

Another component of the Great Park museum complex should be a world-class Bio-Diversity Center, as suggested by Donald Bren. Such a center would promote environmental awareness through nationally and internationally sponsored symposiums and educational programs geared to the professional as well as the individual. The Bio-Diversity Center would be a model of what might be accomplished locally, nationally and internationally to promote sustainable natural habitats throughout the world.

A major civic enterprise like the Great Park requires far-reaching funding. This funding will come from a variety of sources, including initial park development and assessment fees from private developers; state and federal grants; and donations from Orange County individuals and corporations interested in sponsorship of specific elements of the park. Additionally, the Great Park Conservancy will play an important role in augmenting these financial sources.

Urban park conservancies have become a popular means of support for parks across the country. The Central Park Conservancy in New York has raised more than $270 million for major projects as part of Central Park's restoration and renovation. The Golden Gate National Park Association in San Francisco has raised $40 million for its restoration projects. And, Friends of Hermann Park in Houston has raised $14 million to help underwrite a master plan for their park's restoration.

By providing millions of dollars in private donations, park conservancies have elevated the individual donor to a new height. In Orange County, the participation of many thousands of individual donors is showing that public support for building a great metropolitan park continues to grow.

To choose a Master Designer for the Orange County Great Park, the Great Park Corporation, an entity of the City of Irvine, held an international design competition. This competition drew participation from twenty-five world-wide design firms. Architects and designers from the United States, Europe, and Asia sent their credentials and early concepts for their visions of the Great Park.

Their designs were reviewed by a panel of respected architects, and seven semi-finalist teams were selected. The Great Park Corporation then did research in the Orange County community to find out what residents wanted included at the Great Park. In the Fall of 2005, the Great Park Corporation selected three finalists.

On January 23, 2006, Ken Smith Landscape Architect of New York was chosen to design the Orange County Great Park. Ken Smith's most famous designs to date include New York's East River Waterfront Master Plan, Toronto's Yorkville Park, and San Francisco's Third Street Light Rail Project.

Smith's design, which was a public favorite in the OCGP Corporation's online poll, incorporates several grand features into the Master Plan for the Orange County Great Park. These include a canyon joining the Agua Chinon with a lake and an amphitheatre that faces east across this lake. The design also retains the old runway with fighter planes stationed along its entire length as a linear monument to the military history.

Edgar Payne, *El Toro Eucalyptus Trees*, Private Collection, Courtesy of The Irvine Museum

William Wendt, *A Quiet Brook*, Private Collection, Courtesy of The Irvine Museum

Edgar Payne, *Landscape with Path*, Private Collection, Courtesy of
The Irvine Museum

Mule Deer, U.S. Fish and Wildlife Service

For several decades, a wide range of organizations—
including The Irvine Company, Laguna Canyon Foundation and
The Nature Conservancy—have worked to preserve open space and
habitat areas throughout our region of Southern California.
Together, these groups have made remarkable progress toward safeguarding vast open space areas for future generations.

An important element of the Great Park plan is to link
many of the already-preserved lands into a continuous open space
and wildlife corridor that will stretch from the Cleveland National
Forest, through the Great Park, Laguna Coast Wilderness Park,
Crystal Cove State Park, and finally, all the way to the Pacific Ocean.

Orange County has a stunning natural environment surrounding its cities. Much of this natural beauty is in the form of
open space land that provides a peaceful refuge from the pressures of
modern life. Adding to this open space by incorporating the 1057-
acre Federal habitat preserve and the open space corridor within the
Great Park will enhance this beauty for generations to come.

An article entitled "The Greening of Irvine: Experts say
Great Park should follow example of other energy-efficient projects
in the city" appeared in the *Orange County Register* on December 4,
2004. It indicates:

Orange County's proposed Great Park is destined to
be a green oasis—and if some designers have their way, not
just in trees.

The experts say the city's greatest potential energy
savings at the Great Park could come from "green" buildings, such as the Ford Motor Co. design center just west of
the Santa Ana (I-5) Freeway in Irvine near the Spectrum.
The building's large windows reduce electric-lighting
needs and a fuel cell further reduces electric power that
must be purchased. Recycled water is used in the toilets
and for irrigation.

As the mixed-use park on the old Marine base comes
closer to reality, several experts suggest the development
planned for the park could be among the most energy-efficient in the country. That's because prices have fallen as
technology has improved on fuel cells, water- recycling systems and other energy-saving devices, such as photovoltaic cells, which convert sunlight to electricity.

Just a few years ago, such fittings added cost to a
building; now advances in technology have brought the
cost of green buildings down to that of traditional struc-
tures. "It would be irresponsible to design the Great Park
and not use all the conservation techniques available," says
Malcolm Lewis, president of Constructive Technologies
Group Inc. of Irvine, which helps architects and engineers
design resource-saving buildings.

Lewis hopes his company will be busy on the Great
Park. And his own building provides a glimpse of commercial building's energy-use future. For example, windows
stretch to the ceiling to let in more sunlight, reducing the
need for electric lighting. Some newer buildings are so
energy-efficient that they not only generate enough energy
for their own uses, but they also send surplus electricity to
the utility company.

For example, on sunny days, photovoltaic panels on
the Natural Resources Defense Council building in Santa
Monica generate more electricity than the building can
use. The surplus is sent to the utility company. The building has earned top honors from the U.S. Green Building
Council, which sets standards for green construction.
Great Park buildings can do the same, Lewis and other
experts say.

The Irvine City Council recently has been more
focused on studying the idea of forming its own utility to
serve the Great Park and other new developments than on
the prospects of green buildings. Mayor Larry Agran says
he still wants to continue studying the launch of a city-
owned utility, but he concedes emerging green building
technology raises "a lot of intriguing possibilities." Among
those possibilities are studies that indicate workers are
more efficient in green buildings, says Greg Ander, chief
architect for Southern California Edison, which provides
incentives to encourage green buildings.

The Natural Resources Defense Council building in Santa Monica has earned top honors from the U.S. Green Building Council, which sets standards for green construction. On sunny days, photovoltaic panels on the roof generate more electricity than the building can use. The surplus is scent to the utility company, photograph, Courtesy of NRDC

The Natural Resources Defense Council building in Santa Monica, Courtesy of NRDC

In some respects, green building technology amounts to just getting out of nature's way. At the Patagonia clothing distribution center in Reno, vents let the accumulated hot air out of the building at night, which is replaced by cool night air drawn in at ground level. That reduces the need for electricity to power air-cooling systems.

At its design center in Irvine, Ford uses "daylighting"—the industry term for big windows and skylights that reduce the need for electric lighting. Ford also recycles water and uses a zero-emissions fuel cell, which provides about a third of the electricity needed by the 450 employees at the center. But most striking to visitors is the building's roof. Ford has covered the 100,000-square-foot roof of the design center with plants, which keeps the building cooler in summer and retains heat in winter and extends, Ford expects, the roof's life. The building was finished three years ago; Ford hopes the roof will last 40 years. Moreover, the rooftop garden absorbs carbon dioxide and provides a habitat for birds and insects.

An article entitled "One Bidder Wins It All at El Toro, Home builder Lennar will buy 3,718 acres on O.C.'s closed base for $649.5 million, more than the minimum but less than some expected," appeared in the *Los Angeles Times* on February 17, 2005. It indicates:

The nation's third-largest home builder won an unprecedented federal auction on February 16 to buy the former El Toro Marine Corps Air Station in Irvine, setting the stage for 3,400 new homes in the heart of Orange County and dashing the last hopes for an international airport there.

Bidding $649.5 million for 3,718 acres, Miami-based Lennar Corp. won the property in an online auction that the Defense Department has pledged to use as a model for the sale of future closed military bases. Previously, closed bases were transferred to local governments at little or no cost.

The base's purchase by Lennar "will serve as a model for cooperation between the federal government, local government and the private sector," said Irvine Councilman Larry Agran, the architect of the El Toro redevelopment. The auction, however, does not resolve questions about how much it will cost the Navy to clean up parts of the base that are still off-limits because of contamination. For decades, the military allowed toxic materials such as cleaning solvents to seep into the ground. The Navy has estimated the cost of cleaning El Toro at about $300 million, but some experts have said it may cost much more if more contamination is found during development.

Though Lennar will buy the entire El Toro base, the company will deed about 40% of the land—which includes the most heavily polluted portions—to Irvine for parks, roads, drainage, a 250- acre museum district and other uses.

The rest of the base is slated to become a complex of residential neighborhoods, retail centers, industrial parks, a college campus, a cemetery and a golf course. Lennar will pay the city about $400 million in fees and assessments, including $200 million in assessments to be reimbursed by future buyers.

According to Beth Krom, Mayor of Irvine, "Many years ago, civic leaders in New York, San Francisco, San Diego and other metropolitan areas recognized the value which a great park brings to a growing community. A vast park provides people with an escape from the stress of daily life into a place of beauty and tranquility. The development of great metropolitan parks has been a rarity in modern times due to the rapid pace of development and the scarcity of land and public resources. We in Orange County are very fortunate to have the unique opportunity to create the first great metropolitan park of the 21st century, and I am confident it will be the very best."

Guy Rose, *Low Tide, Honfleur*, c. 1907, Private Collection, Courtesy of The Irvine Museum

FROM LEFT: Katrina Lutge, Joan Irvine Smith, Mikhail Gorbachev, former leader of the Soviet Union and James I. Swinden, photograph Courtesy of UCI

IN 1993, MIKHAIL GORBACHEV, former leader of the Soviet Union and a Nobel Peace Prize laureate, devoted his attention to what he rightly foresaw as the greatest challenge of the 21st century, the environment, through Green Cross International. That same year, Global Green USA was created when Gorbachev invited activist and philanthropist Diane Meyer Simon to join his global environmental movement by founding the American affiliate of Green Cross International.

Today, Green Cross International has 26 affiliate countries with several more in early stages of development. Global Green USA is the only national environmental organization headquartered in Los Angeles, with offices in Washington, D.C. and San Francisco.

Global Green USA establishes collaborative partnerships with local governments, affordable housing organizations, and other public and private entities to facilitate the development, adoption and implementation of sustainable policies, programs and practices. These partnerships inform and direct education, policy development, and advocacy efforts at the local, state and federal levels. Global Green USA also partners with housing developers and public agencies to "green" select affordable housing projects and is currently planning a project in Irvine.

On March 23, 2004, Mikhail Gorbachev visited UCI to accept the inaugural UCI Citizen Peacebuilding Award. My son James I. Swinden, Katrina Lutge and I attended the event. At dinner, I was seated at Chancellor Ralph Cicerone's table with President Gorbachev and his daughter Irina Virganskaya, who works within the Gorbachev Foundation heading up the Raisa Gorbachev Club, which performs charitable activities, mainly for needy children, in Russia.

President Gorbachev's speech was entitled "The Road to a Sustainable Environment and a Safer World." His visit was hosted by the UCI Citizen Peacebuilding Program in the School of Social Sciences, which engages in research, education and action that support grass-roots efforts to prevent violent conflict and promote reconciliation and sustainable peace. Under the direction of Paula Garb, Associate Adjunct Professor of Anthropology, the program's current activities include peace-building efforts in local neighborhoods of Orange County and Los Angeles, as well as communities in Northern Ireland and the former Soviet Union.

Chancellor Cicerone introduced President Mikhail Gorbachev, saying:

> he is recognized as one of the foremost statesmen and leaders for global peace in the 20th century and continues, through different avenues, to have exceptional impact on the world into the current century.

Mikhail Gorbachev was president of the Soviet Union from 1985–1991, instituting sweeping reforms that streamlined and decentralized the governmental system in that country. He oversaw two broad disarmament pacts and the end to Communist rule in Eastern Europe. He also taught us the meaning of the words "perestroika" for government restructuring, and "glasnost" for political openness. He did this by making them more than words, but the very successful agents of social and political change in his country. For these and his many other achievements, he received the 1990 Nobel Peace Prize.

Since leaving political office, President Gorbachev has devoted his efforts to organizations concerned with global issues, including Green Cross International and its U.S. counterpart Global Green. These are groups who assist people affected by the environmental consequences of wars and other violence. And he is also president of the Gorbachev Foundation.

I am very pleased that Mikhail Gorbachev accepted my invitation to come to UC Irvine and to be the first recipient of the UCI Citizen Peacebuilding Award. There is great admiration throughout the world for his realistic approach to achieving peace and disarmament. He is working to spread the message of a secure, sustainable environment for all of us as human beings who must do what we can to safeguard the Earth and its interrelated systems for future generations.

Arthur G. Rider, *On the Beach, Valencia,* c. 1919, Courtesy of Ray and Beverly Redfern

During his speech, Gorbachev stated:

The most predominant characteristic of the world today, particularly since the final decades of the 20th century, is globalization, and the world of the 21st century is facing three main challenges. The first is the challenge of security, including the problem of weapons of mass destruction and their proliferation and the problem of terrorism, which has become a global problem. Second is the challenge of poverty and backwardness, against the background of the fact that the developed world—that is to say 20% of the population of the world today—consumes 80% of the world's resources. Also, the degradation of the environment has now become a third global problem, a global threat. Only one-third of the population of the world lives in decent conditions, conditions worthy of a human being, while all the others survive on $1 to $2 a day.

Today, the human pressure on the environment is at a critical level. To characterize the problem, let me give you a few numbers. At the beginning of the 20th century the population of the world was 1.6 billion people. At the end of the 20th century the world had more than 6 billion people. At the beginning of the 20th century, the annual gross domestic product in the world was $90 billion. At the end of the 20th century this was the amount of GDP produced in one day. That is to say, production grew 365 times. That means tremendous pressure on nature. At the beginning of the 20th century we consumed 300 cubic kilometers of water per year. At the end of the century we consumed 4,000 cubic kilometers of water. So those are the parameters of the problem. That is the kind of pressure that we are exerting on nature and we feel how the environment is being destroyed.

Edgar Payne, *The Matterhorn*, Courtesy of George Stern Fine Arts, Los Angeles and Carmel

Paul Grimm, *Cloud Study*, c. 1925, Private Collection, Courtesy of The Irvine Museum

Frank Cuprien, *Tranquil Evening*, Private Collection, Courtesy of The Irvine Museum

The symptoms of this overload are everywhere—in the process of climate change and global warming, in the deficit of fresh water in many parts of the world, in desertification, and in the pollution of the oceans. This has truly become a global problem. A person who has dedicated his life to problems of security, of nuclear weapons, nuclear non-proliferation, Hans Blix, a person who is probably well known to you, has recently said something that sounded rather paradoxical. Actually, I was surprised to hear this from a person who spends his life on military issues. He said that he was more concerned now, not by the problems of war and peace, but by the problems of the environment, particularly by global warming.

There are also expert opinions of scientists who are close to the U.S. Administration. One of your professors here, Sherwood Rowland, a Nobel Prize winner in chemistry, has given me a scientific report, a report that's not political; a scientific report which I believe is also very important because it contains the science on this issue. Another report that was submitted to the Administration and that has been recently leaked to the media says that the climate processes that are developing now within the next twenty years will lead to major floods and to the humanitarian disasters on a global scale, and inevitably they could result in military conflicts. The authors of that report gave the following scenario. As a result of environmental catastrophes, the reserves of energy, food, and fresh water will shrink so much that the governments of many countries could use weapons of mass destruction in order to protect those resources.

Paul Grimm, *Cloud Study*, Private Collection, Courtesy of The Irvine Museum

Edgar Payne, *Seascape, Laguna Beach*, Private Collection, Courtesy of The Irvine Museum

Bennett Bradbury, *Glacier Bay, Alaska*, Private Collection, Courtesy of The Irvine Museum

WITH RESPECT TO THE DANGERS of global warming, an article by the Associated Press entitled "Scientists Find Arctic Warming Quickly" appeared on November 8, 2004, indicating:

> Scientists say changes in the earth's climate from human influences are occurring particularly intensely in the Arctic region, evidenced by widespread melting of glaciers, thinning sea ice and rising permafrost temperatures.
>
> A study released on November 8 said the annual average amount of sea ice in the Arctic has decreased by about 8 percent in the past 30 years, resulting in the loss of 386,100 square miles of sea ice—an area bigger than Texas and Arizona combined.
>
> "The polar regions are essentially the earth's air conditioner," Michael McCracken, president of the International Association of Meteorology and Atmospheric Sciences, told a news conference that day. "Imagine the earth having a less efficient air conditioner."
>
> Susan Joy Hassol, the report's lead author, said the Arctic probably would warm twice as much as the Earth. A region of extreme light and temperature changes, the Arctic's surfaces of ice, ocean water, vegetation and soil are important in reflecting the sun's heat.
>
> Pointing to the report as a clear signal that global warming is real, Sens. John McCain, R-Ariz., and Joe Lieberman, D-Conn., said on November 8 the "dire consequences" of warming in the Arctic underscore the need for their proposal to require U.S. cuts in emissions of carbon dioxide and other heat-trapping greenhouse gases. President Bush has rejected that approach.

Whale Spouts, © Richard Jackson

Whale Breaching, © Richard Jackson

In the past half-century, average yearly temperatures in Alaska and Siberia rose by about 3.6 degrees to 5.4 degrees Fahrenheit and winters in Alaska and western Canada warmed by an average of 5 degrees to 7 degrees Fahrenheit.

With "some of the most rapid and severe climate change on earth," the Arctic regions' melting contributed to sea levels rising globally by an average of about three inches in the past 20 years, the report said.

"These changes in the Arctic provide an early indication of the environmental and societal significance of global warming," says the Arctic Climate Impact Assessment, a four-year study by 300 scientists in eight Arctic-bordering nations, including the United States.

This most comprehensive study of Arctic warming to date adds yet more impetus to the projections by many of the world's climate scientists that there will be a steady rise in global temperature as the result of greenhouse gases released into the atmosphere from the burning of fossil fuels and other sources.

Paul Grimm, *Cloud Study*, Private Collection, Courtesy of The Irvine Museum

Ringed Seal, © Gerald and Buff Corsi, California Academy of Science

Caribou Crossing Snowy Tundra, © Jo Goldmann, California Academy of Science

Harp Seal in Ice Cave, © Richard Jackson

Polar Bear Female with Two Cubs, © Steve Amstrup, US Fish and Wildlife Service

Polar Bear in Ice Field, © Richard Jackson

It is based on ice core samples and other evidence of climate conditions such as on-the-ground and satellite measurements of surface air temperatures. Nations participating in the study besides the United States are Canada, Denmark, Finland, Iceland, Norway, Russia and Sweden.

"The bottom line is that the Arctic is warming now, much more rapidly than the rest of the globe, and it's impacting people directly," Robert Corell, chairman of the scientists' study panel and a senior fellow with the American Meteorological Society, said on November 7.

The process is only likely to accelerate in the Arctic, a region that provides important resources such as oil, gas and fish, the study finds.

That would wreak havoc on polar bears, ice-dependent seals, caribou and reindeer herds—and local people such as Inuit whose main food source comes from hunting those animals. Some endangered migratory birds are projected to lose more than half their breeding areas.

The study projects that in the next 100 years the yearly average temperatures will increase by 7 to 13 degrees Fahrenheit over land and 13 to 18 degrees over the ocean, mainly because the water absorbs more heat.

Forests would expand into the Arctic tundra, which in turn would expand into the polar ice deserts, because rising temperatures would favor taller, denser vegetation. The areas of Arctic tundra would shrink to their smallest extent since 21,000 years ago, when humans began emerging from the last Ice Age.

Sea levels globally already are expected to rise between another four inches to three feet or more this century. Longer term, sea levels would rise alarmingly if temperatures continue to rise unabated, in the range of 5 degrees to 11 degrees Fahrenheit over the next several centuries.

In that scenario, the study projects "a virtually complete melting of the Greenland Ice Sheet," which would contribute as much as 23 feet to the world's sea level rise.

William Ritschel, *No Man's Land*, a.k.a. *Dat' Devil Sea*, The Irvine Museum

An article by Andrew C. Revkin entitled "Deciding How Much Global Warming Is Too Much" which appeared in *The New York Times* on February 1, 2005 indicates the following:

Under the first treaty addressing global warming, 193 countries, including the United States, pledged to avoid "dangerous" human interference with the climate.

There was one small problem with that treaty, enacted 11 years ago. No one defined dangerous. With no clear goal, smokestack and tailpipe emissions of gases linked to rising temperatures relentlessly climbed.

On Feb. 16, a stricter addendum to that treaty, the Kyoto Protocol, enters into force, requiring participating industrialized countries to cut such emissions.

But its targets and timetable were negotiated with no agreement on what amount of cuts would lead the world toward climatic stability. The arbitrary terms were cited by President Bush when he rejected the Kyoto pact in 2001, leaving the world's biggest source of such gases on the sidelines.

After a decade of cautious circling, some scientists and policy makers are now trying to agree on how much warming is too much.

It has taken this long not just because the "dangerous" question is complicated, but because it holds dangers in and of itself. If scientists offer answers, as some have in recent days, they can be criticized for playing down uncertainties and intruding into the policy arena. If a politician answers, that creates a yardstick for measuring later progress or failure.

It is much easier for everyone simply to call for more research.

But some experts now say that by the time clear evidence is at hand, calamity later in the century will be unavoidable. They say fresh findings show that potentially enormous environmental changes lie ahead.

"I think that the scientific evidence now warrants a new sense of urgency," said Dr. James E. Hansen, a climate scientist and director of NASA's Goddard Institute for Space Studies.

A particular concern is the Arctic. An eight-nation, four-year study concluded in November that accumulating carbon dioxide and other emissions from human activities were contributing to the thawing of tundra and the retreat of sea ice. Recent studies of accelerating flows of ice to the sea in some parts of Antarctica also point to the prospect of a quickening rise in sea levels in a warming world. Other scientists point to the prospect of intensified droughts and floods.

On May 25, Dr. Robert Corell, Senior Research Fellow at Belfer Center for Science & International Affairs, John F. Kennedy School of Government, Harvard University, gave a lecture entitled "Rapid Warming of the Arctic—An early warning for the planet—" at the University of California at Irvine. It was presented by the UCI 2004-2005 Chancellor's Distinguished Fellows Series and hosted by the Schools of Biological Sciences & Physical Sciences.

Dr. Corell chaired and Dr. Pal Prestrud from Norway vice-chaired the Arctic Climate Impact Assessment (ACIA), the four-year study involving eight Arctic countries that confirmed that the Earth's climate is changing more rapidly and persistently than at any time since the beginning of civilization, and that these changes are more severe in the Arctic than elsewhere.

RIGHT: Grizzly Bear Catching a Salmon, © Richard Jackson

Costal Ridges—Irvine Open Space Reserve, © Stephen Francis Photography

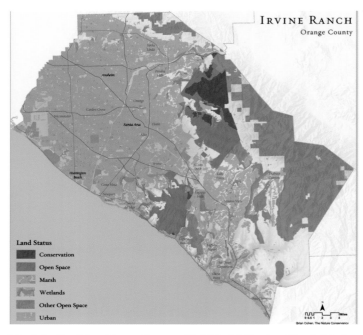

Map Irvine Ranch Land Status, Courtesy of Saddleback Valley Area Historical Society

THE SAME CALIFORNIA ENVIRONMENT that fills us with wonder is an important part of the quality of life that attracts millions of residents to this state, which is now home to more than 36 million people— one out of every eight persons in the United States. Reasonable estimates expect another 18 million citizens to call the state home by the year 2025.

The crush of increasing population and its associated housing, transportation, water, food and other needs, puts an enormous strain on California's natural resources. As 25 percent of all the unique plant species found in the United States and Canada occur in this state, and one-half of them (or 2,140 species) are found nowhere else in the world, local communities, landowners, government, businesses and conservationists are working together through Natural Community Conservation Planning to create reserves that protect wildlife habitat while allowing development to continue in an environmentally responsible manner on remaining natural lands in a large area. The Natural Community Conservation Plan (NCCP), unanimously approved by the Orange County Board of Supervisors in 1996, serves as the model for regional conservation planning in the United States.

The 38,000-acre NCCP reserve stretches from the coast at Laguna Beach to the base of Saddleback Mountain, and from Newport Beach south to Dana Point. This permanent reserve was created by combining more than 21,000 acres of land set aside by Donald Bren and The Irvine Company and managed by The Nature Conservancy, with an additional 17,000 acres held by other entities, including county and state parks.

On November 28, 2001, Bren announced that The Irvine Company was giving 11,000 acres of wildlife habitat in Orange County as an open space gift to the people. He also announced that a 173-acre habitat linkage in Laguna Canyon was to be forever preserved as parkland by a conservation easement to The Nature Conservancy. These two gifts by The Irvine Company have helped to ensure the long-term viability of the NCCP reserve.

The amount of Irvine Ranch land that has been placed by Donald Bren in reserves or that is held by county or state parks is 50,000 acres. This was more than half of the 93,000 acres held by the company in Orange County when I joined the board of directors in 1957. At the conclusion of the announcement ceremony, I told Donald how proud I was of him, and that I could not have done better myself.

A second NCCP plan calls for the protection of an additional 40,000 acres in the southern reaches of the county. Known as the Nature Reserve of Orange County (NROC), this network of undeveloped land is designed to protect large swaths of unique habitats that are home to many rare and threatened species of wildlife. The Nature Conservancy and The Irvine Company conservation easement lands equal an additional 11,500 acres adjacent to but not a part of NROC/NCCP.

William Wendt, *The Three Guardsmen,* 1926, Private Collection, Courtesy of The Irvine Museum

Oak Grove in Limestone Canyon—Irvine Open Space Reserve, © Harold Malde

Donald Bren with Joan Irvine Smith on November 28, 2001 when he announced that The Irvine Company was giving 11,000 acres of wildlife habitat in Orange County as an open space gift to the people. In 1996, Mr. Bren placed more than 21,000 acres of Irvine Company land with The Nature Conservancy. Today this land is the cornerstone of Orange County's Natural Community Conservation Plan program, photograph, Courtesy of The Irvine Company

BELOW LEFT, FROM LEFT: Joan Irvine Smith and Orange County Supervisor Tom Wilson with Donald and Brigitte Bren when The Irvine Company gave a 173-acre habitat linkage in Laguna Canyon to be forever preserved as parkland by a conservation easement to The Nature Conservancy, photograph, Courtesy of The Irvine Company
BELOW RIGHT, FROM LEFT: Paul Morabito of the California Coastal Conservancy, Brigitte Bren, Joan Irvine Smith and Donald Bren, photograph, Courtesy of The Irvine Company

ALL PHOTOS: *Fremont Canyon—Irvine Open Space Reserve,*
© Stephen Francis Photography

ALL PHOTOS: *Fremont Canyon—*
Irvine Open Space Reserve,
© Stephen Francis Photography

Rancho Mission Viejo, photograph, Courtesy of Rancho Mission Viejo

IN 1995, THE O'NEILL AND MOISO FAMILIES opened the 1,000-acre Las Flores community, of which more than 60% was dedicated as open space including key segments of the Chiquita Ridge and Tijeras Canyon. By the end of that year, they had donated to Orange County a total of 977 acres of open space. In addition, Rancho Mission Viejo pledged its support to enroll its remaining land in the Southern Subregion NCCP, a plan for the study and preservation of habitat in exchange for development, ranching and agricultural assurances in less biologically sensitive areas.

In 1996, Tony Moiso and his family began spearheading the 4,000-acre community of Ladera Ranch, which offered a legacy of another 1,600 acres of open space. The following year, the family preserved 1,100 more acres of the Upper Chiquita Canyon.

Today, the O'Neill and Moiso families continue to participate in the NCCP for the preservation of multi-species habitat, while ranching, farming, leasing, planning and developing the Rancho Mission Viejo.

California Gnatcatcher, © Richard Jackson

Alexey Steele, *High Noon at Rancho Mission Viejo*, 2005, Private Collection

Round Up at Chiquita Canyon, Rancho Mission Viejo, 1905, photograph, Courtesy of the San Juan Capistrano Historical Society

Cattle Round Up, Rancho Mission Viejo, © Richard Jackson

An article entitled "Development for 23,000-Acre Rancho Mission Viejo Site OKd" appeared in the *Los Angeles Times* on November 9, 2004, indicating the following:

Clearing the first major hurdle for building homes and businesses on Orange County's largest remaining swath of privately owned open space, the Board of Supervisors on Monday, November 8, unanimously approved development plans for the 23,000-acre Rancho Mission Viejo.

The decision means the land's owner could eventually build as many as 14,000 homes, commercial and community facilities on 380 acres, and 25 acres of golf courses on the south Orange County property.

Under the plan, nearly two-thirds of the land would remain open space. Once the development was complete, the majority of Orange County would either be developed or marked for conservation. The county's last significant piece of undeveloped land and its sheer size have attracted intense public scrutiny since plans were introduced 12 years ago.

More than 300 people attended the standing-room-only meeting in Santa Ana. Many urged supervisors to approve the development, saying it strikes a fair balance between development and conservation. Others asked the board to postpone the decision until state and federal agencies have completed environmental studies.

Baxter's Windmill, Gabino Canyon, Rancho Mission Viejo, © Richard Jackson

Campo Amantes, Rancho Mission Viejo, © Stephen Francis Photography

The California Department of Fish and Game and the U.S. Fish and Wildlife Service are expected to complete those studies next year and have cautioned the county against moving ahead with the zoning changes approved on November 8.

"This is the last big development" in Orange County, said Brittany McKee, a conservation organizer for the Sierra Club. The supervisors "have an obligation to the public to do it right. What's the rush?"

There is no rush, county planning officials said. The land has undergone years of environmental studies, they said, and the zoning changes are compatible with the findings so far. They also pointed out that the developers must clear several other governmental hurdles, giving ample opportunity to adjust construction plans. The county must still review specific community plans and grant building permits, and federal and state agencies must issue environmental permits…

Board approval sets a general footprint for the nearly 7,700 acres of development planned for the ranch in the next two decades. The last holdings of the O'Neill and Moiso families, the land stretches from the southern end of Coto de Caza to Camp Pendleton in San Diego County and from the Cleveland National Forest to San Juan Capistrano. The area is crossed by canyons rich with coastal sage scrub, critical habitat for the California gnatcatcher, an endangered species. There are also acres of agricultural and cattle grazing land, along with cement quarries and silica mines.

Tony Moiso, president of Rancho Mission Viejo, said the land is no longer financially viable as a ranch. "Even though we feel blessed to own 23,000 acres," Moiso told supervisors, "there have been challenges," including financial obligations to maintain the land. "We can't pay bills with envelopes of dirt."

Alexey Steele, *Under Approaching Clouds*, Rancho Mission Viejo, 2005, Private Collection

Alexey Steele, *Last Light*, Rancho Mission Viejo, 2005, Private Collection

Cactus Wren in Prickly Pear Cactus, © Moose Peterson

Alexey Steele, *Embrace of the Hills*,
Rancho Mission Viejo, 2005,
Private Collection

Grey Fox, © Richard Jackson

Pair of Coyotes, © Richard Jackson

Mountain Lion, © Richard Jackson

Bobcat in Sycamores, © Richard Jackson

Alexey Steele, *Real Gold*, Rancho Mission Viejo, 2005, Private Collection

Deer in Tall Grass, © Richard Jackson

Pacific Pond Turtle,
© Richard Jackson

Most of the development will be kept to areas that have been affected by heavy agricultural and other uses, but environmentalists say the plans do not take into consideration the flow of wildlife between the conserved areas.

Some officials in neighboring cities are more concerned about a different kind of traffic flow. "We are terribly congested already," Mission Viejo Vice Mayor Patricia Kelley told supervisors. The development would dump even more traffic onto Mission Viejo's streets, city officials said.

Under a development agreement also approved by the board on November 8, Rancho Mission Viejo would pay about $144 million to improve traffic flow on roads surrounding the project. Officials in Mission Viejo and San Clemente, another city expected to feel the effects of the development, say the funds aren't enough.

Some project opponents said they would sue to reverse the county's approval. "Unfortunately, we are likely to end up in court," McKee said. "This project is not the best deal for Orange County."

Alexey Steele, *Contre-Jour at the Lake*, Rancho Mission Viejo, 2005, Private Collection

Alexey Steele, *Rain is Coming*, Rancho Mission Viejo, 2005, Private Collection

Caspers Park, near Rancho Mission Viejo, © Stephen Francis Photography

Santa Rosa Plateau, © Stephen Francis Photography

Rancho Mission Viejo, © Stephen Francis Photography

ON DECEMBER 8, a coalition of five environmental groups, including the Endangered Habitats League, the Natural Resources Defense Council and the Sierra Club, sued Orange County for approving the Rancho Mission Viejo development plan. Among other things, the suit alleges that the county did not adequately address the project's effect on sensitive habitat.

The following day, the city of Mission Viejo filed its own lawsuit against the plan. That suit alleges that the county did not adequately address the development's impact on traffic.

Regional conservation planning is underway throughout coastal southern California. In 1997, a wide coalition of concerned entities endorsed an NCCP agreement that will safeguard 172,000 acres of rare natural areas in San Diego County. Riverside County has also adopted a similar strategy for its open spaces and rare habitats.

An article entitled "For Those Who Love Preserve, Progress Means Do Nothing" which appeared in the *Los Angeles Times* on November 29, 2004, states:

> If Gen. Gaspar de Portolá and Father Junípero Serra miraculously reappeared in San Juan Capistrano, they wouldn't recognize much of the landscape, except perhaps a parcel several miles east of El Camino Real—the Donna O'Neill Land Conservancy.
>
> Not much has changed there since the 1700s. Mule deer still forage in the rugged hills for moist grass and tender buds. Mountain lions and bobcats roam through the stands of oak and thickets of coastal sage-scrub. Red-tailed hawks soar high above. From the ridgelines are panoramic views of the ocean and Santa Ana Mountains. Never mind the radar dome at the TRW Capistrano Test Site to the south or the isolated patches of nonnative artichoke thistle that the caretakers are trying to eliminate.
>
> "It's an absolute jewel," said Michael Hazzard, an environmental activist in south Orange County who has tangled with developers, including the creators of the preserve. "The Donna O'Neill is one of the finest and last examples of scenic wild lands in Southern California."
>
> The conservancy is 1,200 undeveloped acres set aside by Rancho Mission Viejo, a major south Orange County landholder and developer. Company executives, the county and the city of San Clemente established the preserve as permanent open space almost 14 years ago as a condition for building the nearby Talega housing project.
>
> It was known as the Rancho Mission Viejo Land Conservancy until 2002, when the grounds were renamed to honor Donna O'Neill, the late wife of Richard O'Neill, the aging patriarch of the Moiso, Avery and O'Neill families that own the 23,000-acre ranch. As Hazzard says, the conservancy is a prime example of what much of Southern California looked like before rapid urbanization transformed the natural world.

Trabuco Canyon, O'Neill Park, photograph, Courtesy of Rancho Mission Viejo

Donna and Richard J. O'Neill at the Rancho
Mission Viejo Land Conservancy, renamed the
Donna O'Neil Land Conservancy in 2002, photograph,
Courtesy of Rancho Mission Viejo

Alexey Steele, *The Land of the Hawk*, Rancho Mission Viejo, 2005,
Private Collection

Alexey Steele, *Open Land*, Rancho Mission Viejo, 2005, Private Collection

Oak woodlands, coastal sage-scrub and grasslands
dominate the preserve. Huge sycamores and more than
6,000 coast live oaks fill the canyons and hillsides.
Lemonade berry, toyon, white sage and monkey flower are
among the native plants. The meadows are filled with purple needle grass and perennial wildflowers, such as
California buttercup, lupine, shooting star, checker bloom

Shooting Stars

Field of Lupine

Lupine

California Poppies

Sycamore Tree Hit by Lightning

California Poppies

Wild Hyacinth

Datura

All Photos © Richard Jackson

Lupine

Mariposa Lily

FROM LEFT: Albert R. Valentien, *Buttercup, Lemonade Berry, White Sage, Lupine,* Courtesy of the San Diego Natural History Museum

FROM LEFT: Albert R. Valentien, *Shooting Star, Mariposa Lily, Toyon or Christmas Berry, Purple Needlegrass,* Courtesy of the San Diego Natural History Museum

The Mother Oak, © Stephen Francis Photography

and Mariposa lily. On the edge of the conservancy is an oak tree estimated to be 500 years old. Legend and lore indicate that this is a "mother oak," which provided the seed for most the heritage oaks on the ranch and across South County.

Anthony R. Moiso, president and chief executive of the ranch, thought so much of what was to become conservancy land that his family once considered it a potential homestead. Plans were drawn up for a ranch-style dwelling on 130 acres. Finally considering the parcel too remote, the Moisos and their four daughters abandoned the idea. Moiso said, "Looking back, that land is better served as a permanent gift to the people of Orange County."

Yet whether the conservancy will remain relatively untouched by development is unclear. Thousands of homes are planned for nearby ranchland. On one side is a county landfill, and the Transportation Corridor Agencies, which operate a 51-mile network of tollways in Orange County, want to build a new turnpike, the Foothill South, from Oso Parkway east of Mission Viejo to Interstate 5 in or near San Clemente.

Three of the six proposed routes would go through the Donna O'Neill preserve and the northern part of San Onofre State Beach park. The other options course through San Clemente and require the condemnation of homes to obtain right-of-way. Although they support the Foothill South tollway, Rancho Mission Viejo representatives say they are concerned about the proposed routes through the conservancy, which has been visited by more than 110,000 people, including scientists and schoolchildren.

Clare Climaco, a TCA spokeswoman, said there had been discussions between corridor officials and the O'Neill family about the highway routes. But everything is on hold, she said, until after TCA board members select a route, which could happen the first half of next year.

The Sierra Club and a coalition of environmental groups, such as the Surfrider Foundation, oppose the Foothill South tollway, especially the potentially destructive routes through the conservancy, the California State Park campground at San Mateo Creek and San Onofre. If built, they say, the road would be a disgrace to the memory of Donna O'Neill.

"The conservancy is a wonderful asset to the community," said Brittany McKee, a Sierra Club representative. "Unfortunately, they want to put a toll road through it and develop around it. Because of the Talega development, the conservancy should be saved as intended."

Alexey Steele, *New Day*, Rancho Mission Viejo, 2005, Private Collection

Antonio Parkway near Ortega Highway, photo by Alexey Steele

Kevin Short, *On A Cloudy Day*, Courtesy of the artist

San Mateo Creek, Courtesy of Susan Jordan, www.californiacoastline.org

Kevin Short, *Looking for Strays*, Rancho Mission Viejo,
Courtesy of the artist

345

Rick Delanty, *A Thousand Lights*, San Clemente, Courtesy of the artist

Kevin Short, *Nofi's Hill*, San Juan Capistrano, Courtesy of the artist

Kevin Short, *Last Session at Trestles*, Courtesy of the artist

A commentary entitled "They'd Pave Over Reagan's Park" by Bobby Shriver and Joel Reynolds which appeared in the *Los Angeles Times* on May 10, 2005, indicates the following:

Most Californians see their state parks as places of special natural or historic significance. They protect them by law— forever.

This will change if road builders in Orange County get their way. They have decided that the state park at San Onofre would be better as a toll road. They want to pave it, destroying not only one of the few remaining stretches of Southern California coastal wild land but the fundamental principle of California's state park system: We set aside lands — ancient redwood groves, wildflower-covered desert buttes, Southern California's iconic beaches—to protect them, not to warehouse them for later development.

And there's a bonus. They make money! About 80 million visitors from around the world come to explore California's 278 state parks each year, spending $2.6 billion directly and adding $4 billion in indirect contributions, according to park system estimates.

Gov. Ronald Reagan established San Onofre State Beach in 1971 because he knew its value. It has become one of the five most-visited state parks in California, hosting swimmers, campers, kayakers, birders, fishermen, off-duty Marines, bicyclists and sunbathers. Top surfers compete at its world-renowned Trestles surf breaks. The park contains seven archeological sites, including a Juaneno Indian village. Seven threatened or endangered species live within the park, and it protects significant portions of San Mateo Creek, one of the last relatively unspoiled watersheds in Southern California.

Kevin Short, *Going Surfing*, Courtesy of the artist

Kevin Short, *Lifting Haze, Trestles Beach*, Courtesy of the artist

Kevin Short, *Morning Over Trestles Beach*, Courtesy of the artist

Kevin Short, *Parking Space, San Onofre Beach*, Courtesy of the artist

Kevin Short, *Remembering Your Friends*, Courtesy of the artist

None of this seems to interest the road builders (known as the Transportation Corridor Agencies, or TCA). They want to "connect" undeveloped southeastern Orange County to Interstate 5 in northern San Diego County, bisecting San Onofre State Beach from top to bottom with a huge highway. This massive swath of pavement would force the Parks Department to "relinquish" the majority of the inland wilderness, including the popular San Mateo public campground.

The loss of this coastal haven cannot be compensated. There's no land left. And—here's the kicker—like any major highway in an unspoiled area, the toll road would attract large-scale development to wild lands; generate contaminated runoff, visual blight and noise; and disrupt the natural flow of the creek that maintains the beach and surf breaks. There is no effective mitigation for such damage.

But there is big money to be made by developers. The road builders do not say that. As always, they say the project is needed to address traffic congestion. But identical claims 10 years ago about the neighboring San Joaquin Hills toll road were wrong. That underused toll road disrupted the tranquillity of the Orange County backcountry. It now faces possible default on its bonds and bankruptcy.

Even so, the TCA has refused to seriously consider alternatives to destroying the San Onofre park. Why? Because it is a single-purpose agency. It exists only to build toll roads in Orange County. Among the feasible alternatives it dismissed, or didn't bother to consider, are strategic double-decking on I-5, adding high-occupancy toll lanes on I-5, using congestion fees to alleviate traffic in peak hours, investing in rapid-transit options and combination solutions such as selectively widening I-5 along with expanding certain arterial routes.

This disregard of reasonable, less harmful alternatives is not only illegal but also plain wrong as a matter of public policy and common sense. If a California state park means anything, we must demand that our elected representatives make a stand at San Onofre. Beyond devastating this rare public coastal land, the toll road would set a dangerous, statewide precedent.

As government budgets shrink and the cost of private land rises, public lands, including state parks, will become the path of least resistance—the right of way of choice—for highways or any other infrastructure project that "has to go somewhere." If San Onofre can be taken, so too can other irreplaceable state lands, targeted by shortsighted special interests with too little regard for our natural or cultural heritage.

We agree with Reagan, who said, in establishing the state park at San Onofre, that one of "the greatest legacies we can leave to future generations is the heritage of our land." He went on to say: "But unless we can preserve and protect the unspoiled areas which God has given us, we will have nothing to leave them." His words are as right today as they were 35 years ago. If ever there were a time to act on those words, it is now.

Bobby Shriver is chairman of the California Parks and Recreation Commission and a member of the Santa Monica City Council. Joel Reynolds is a senior attorney with the Natural Resources Defense Council in Los Angeles and director of its urban program

Benjamin Brown, *Wildflowers*, Courtesy of Mr. and Mrs. Thomas B. Stiles II

San Mateo Creek, Courtesy of Susan Jordan, www.californiacoastline.org

William Wendt, *The Trees, They Are My Friends*, Courtesy of the Bowers Museum of Cultural Art, Santa Ana

Intersection of Laguna Canyon Road and Highway 73 Toll Road, photo by Jean Stern

Kevin Short, *Trestles Gold*, Courtesy of the artist

Kevin Short, *Surf Nut*, Courtesy of the artist

An article entitled "Parks Panel Urges State Officials to Block Tollway, Opponents of the road through an O.C. park want governor, attorney general involvement," which appeared in the *Los Angeles Times* on November 19, 2005, states the following:

The fight over a proposed toll road through San Onofre State Beach Park moved north November 18 as the State Park and Recreation Commission urged Gov. Arnold Schwarzenegger to block the controversial 16-mile project.

At a Tahoe City meeting chaired by Commissioner and actor-director Clint Eastwood, the panel unanimously called for Schwarzenegger and Atty. Gen. Bill Lockyer to intervene in the Transportation Corridor Agencies' project to relieve congestion in south Orange County by building an $875-million toll road from Oso Parkway near Mission Viejo to Interstate 5 near San Clemente.

The commission's action followed a contentious Nov. 3 meeting in San Clemente attended by more than 1,000 people who were largely against the most likely route for the proposed Foothill South.

The toll road is opposed by environmental groups and public land advocates because it would slice through 320 acres of the state park's sensitive habitat and within eyesight of the famous Trestles Beach surf break.

"I used to surf down there at San Onofre in the early 1950s," Eastwood said. "I don't find the idea of putting a highway through a state park very appealing."

On December 6, 2005, the Orange County Transportation Corridor Agencies staff members recommended that the controversial Foothill South Toll Road be built through the northern portion of San Onofre State Beach that contains unspoiled wetlands, endangered species, and world-renowned surfing spots. It would also pass through the 1,200-acre Donna O'Neill Land Conservancy. As plans call for a four-lane highway with a right of way that could later be expanded to six lanes, conservancy officials are concerned that the grading required for the tollway would seriously affect wildlife habitat, oaks woodlands, scenic canyons and sensitive watersheds.

The TCA's environmental impact report says that the project would disturb 1,194 acres of open space, including about 385 acres of coastal sage-scrub and about 50 acres of wetlands. Nine areas of habitat for endangered California gnatcatchers and two for endangered arroyo toads would be affected, although other endangered species such as the Least Bell's Vireo and Pacific Pocket Mouse would not.

The public has 30 days to review and comment on the report, as TCA board members are expected to approve the recommended route on January 12, 2006. If all state and federal approvals are obtained, TCA officials hope to start construction of the $875 million Foothill South Tollroad in 2008. The Natural Resources Defense Council is considering a lawsuit to stop the project.

California Gnatcatcher Male at Nest, © Anthony Mercieca

Arroyo Toad, © Richard Jackson

An article entitled "Route for New Tollway Goes Through D.C., Sacramento, Seeking to build a road inside a state park, agency has won highway and environmental exemptions, special legislation in Congress," by Dan Weikel and Janet Wilson which appeared in the *Los Angeles Times* on December 18, indicates the following:

A Southern California toll road agency has relied on high-ranking Bush administration appointees and members of Congress to advance construction of a controversial tollway through a state park.

Over the last six years, the Irvine-based Transportation Corridor Agencies has gained special legislation in Congress, as well as exemptions from the Endangered Species Act and federal highway regulations in its effort to build the Foothill South across San Onofre State Beach Park in north San Diego County.

TCA officials also have tried—but failed—to win congressional exemptions from future or current state laws that might interfere with the project's construction.

The agency's efforts are part of a protracted battle between tollway advocates seeking traffic relief and park supporters who want to protect campsites, wild lands, panoramic views and world-famous surf locales.

So far, the government agency that plans, finances, constructs and operates Orange County's tollways has prevailed, winning a series of federal actions crafted for the Foothill South and successfully lobbying in Sacramento to block proposed protections for state parks.

"They are trying to eviscerate every law standing in their way...for a toll road that should not be built," said James M. Birkelund, an attorney for the Natural Resources Defense Council, a national environmental group opposed to the highway.

But Robert D. Thornton, TCA's general counsel, said the agency's tactics are no different than what its opponents could do. "We aren't doing anything improper," he said. "It is their right to go to Congress, as it is our right to go to Congress."

He said the exemptions and other legislation favoring the tollway are needed to improve mobility in Orange County, where the Foothill South is being called a way to reduce congestion on Interstate 5.

Earlier this month, a $17-million environmental impact study by the TCA recommended that the Foothill South go through the park instead of developed areas of San Clemente where homes and businesses would need to be condemned.

The 16-mile tollway would link Oso Parkway in Rancho Santa Margarita with Interstate 5 south of the city. It would bisect the northern half of the coastal park, which attracted 2.7 million visitors last year.

Last spring, the U.S. Department of the Interior and the U.S. Fish and Wildlife Service cleared a major roadblock for the TCA by eliminating a key protection in the Endangered Species Act.

The protection is known as critical habitat — lands identified as essential to the survival of a species. Critical habitat designations can lead to costly, lengthy project delays to assess and protect the areas.

Seven endangered and threatened species might live in the toll road's proposed path. TCA officials say the road would affect three of the species, while environmentalists say all seven would be harmed.

The first species to be impacted by that decision was the arroyo toad. Overruling their own biologists last April, top Interior officials slashed 97% of critical habitat recommended for the tiny amphibian in eight California counties.

Among the areas cut were free-flowing San Mateo Creek and its banks, part of which could be affected by the toll road. Federal field biologists have repeatedly said that the creek and adjoining shrubby hillsides contained "indispensable" habitat for a "vital" population of the toad.

But citing an amendment to the Endangered Species Act, Assistant Interior Secretary Craig Manson excluded the creek and adjoining lands, saying the cost of protecting an endangered species there outweighed any benefit. The amendment Manson cited was crafted in 1978 by Thornton when he was an attorney for the House of Representatives' subcommittee on fisheries, wildlife conservation and the environment.

Thornton had used the same amendment in 2003 to win TCA and two national homebuilders groups a lawsuit voiding the original, nearly half-million-acre critical habitat designation for the toad. But federal biologists insisted on including San Mateo Creek again in a new critical habitat proposal last January.

Documents obtained under the Freedom of Information Act show that Manson's deputy assistant, Julie A. MacDonald, helped ensure that the TCA won a permanent exemption.

In an interview, MacDonald said that on critical habitat issues, the job of wildlife officials was to "get the developers what they want at the least cost to species." She said alternate management plans, such as one employed by the Marine Corps, were in place to help the toad. The park is on Camp Pendleton, which California leases for a nominal sum from the U.S. Navy.

But biologist Dan Holland, a leading authority on arroyo toads, said the decision by the Interior Department was "clearly not based on science" and could lead to extinction of the species.

Rick Delanty, *San Mateo Creek,* Courtesy of the artist

Last May, Holland hiked the shallows of San Mateo Creek at the edge of Camp Pendleton, searching for the tiny amphibians. "Right around the bend is where they want to put the toll road," he said. "How can they say giant concrete pillars in the middle of one of the last free-flowing creeks in Southern California won't have an impact?"

State park officials who have worked to preserve fragile species at the San Onofre park said they didn't know the cuts had been made until notified by *The Times.* "We want critical habitat," said Roy Stearns, a spokesman for California State Parks. "We're in the business of preserving resources."

Two weeks after the arroyo toad's critical habitat was cut, all critical-habitat designations were permanently eliminated from San Onofre State Beach Park at the request of three Republican congressmen.

Reps. Duncan Hunter of El Cajon, Darrell Issa of Vista and Ken Calvert of Corona said they sought the exemptions to ensure environmental law would not hamper military readiness, and that the park was already covered under an alternate environmental management plan for Camp Pendleton.

Letters obtained by *The Times* show that Navy Secretary Gordon R. England disagreed that the military plan for imperiled species covered the state park. But when the Marine Corps commandant appealed to MacDonald, Manson and others, the blanket exemptions were granted.

It could be a windfall for the TCA, which wants to build the toll road on a federal easement from the Navy through the park. The agency has often used its relationship with Camp Pendleton and defense spending bills as mechanisms to win favorable decisions and legislation.

For instance, Congress placed a rider in the 1999 defense spending bill that gave the Navy the right to grant the TCA an easement on 340 acres within the park. The TCA won another exemption that was slipped into the 2001 defense authorization bill by then-Rep. Ron Packard (R-Carlsbad). No longer would the agency be subject to federal law requiring road builders to exhaust all "feasible and prudent" alternatives before parkland could be used for a highway.

Elizabeth Goldstein, director of the State Parks Foundation, said the TCA sought the exemption because it probably could not comply with the law. She said it also eliminated legal grounds for opponents to challenge the proposed tollway.

Thornton said the TCA went to Congress to eliminate an ambiguous law. He added that the TCA secured the same exemptions for the Foothill-Eastern and San Joaquin Hills toll roads—exemptions that withstood court challenges by the Natural Resources Defense Council.

The TCA also asked Congress in 2002 to nullify any state law that would restrict construction of a toll road through Camp Pendleton, including oversight by the California Coastal Commission, which must approve the highway. A defense bill rider by Calvert was designed to head off attempts by state Sen. Sheila Kuehl (D-Santa Monica) to pass legislation restricting roads in state parks, including the Foothill South.

After being contacted by environmentalists, Sen. Barbara Boxer (D-Calif.) stripped the TCA's exemption from the pending defense bill. Kuehl's measure, which was opposed by TCA as well as other development and business interests, died in committee in Sacramento.

An article entitled "Wilderness in a crossfire, Biologists worry that O.C. toll road would cut through sensitive habitats of endangered species despite precautions by officials" by Pat Brennan which appeared in *The Orange County Register* on January 8, 2006 states that:

SAN ONOFRE STATE BEACH - Explosions from Camp Pendleton echo through the hills to the east. To the west, San Clemente homes shoulder tightly against the county border.

In between is a slice of what once was: rolling, semi-arid foothills covered with scrub brush.

This is the interior of San Onofre State Beach park, one of the state's most popular. Most visitors, especially surfers, spend their time on the beach side, where waves break on a rustic setting.

But it's the rarely visited backcountry, sandwiched between Orange County and Camp Pendleton, that could fuel the biggest debate over wildlife in the path of the proposed Foothill South toll road.

"We're dealing with ever-smaller pieces of high-quality habitat," said state parks ecologist David Pryor on a recent visit to the park's backcountry. "There are more people than critters anymore. That's why we have more and more rare ones."

Last month, Orange County's Transportation Corridor Agencies proposed a wilderness route for the 16-mile Foothill South to complete their regional network of toll roads. The agencies' board will consider approving the route January 12, then the builders must obtain a variety of permits and approval from the state Coastal Commission before construction can begin.

Coastal Sage Scrub, © Moose Peterson

Mustard and Saddleback Mountain, Rancho Mission Viejo, © Richard Jackson

The furor over the agencies' plans to cut a toll road through this remnant slice of wilderness has many flash points: For supporters, future growth that, without the road, could paralyze Interstate 5; for opponents, the possible loss of a big piece of a state park.

But biologists are most concerned about the subdued, yet highly diverse, palette of animals and plants that could be displaced by the road.

A trip early in winter, soon after the plans for the road were announced, doesn't shed much light on what the controversy is about.

Many of the drought-adapted native plants are dormant, looking like clusters of brown and gray weeds.

Even the hilltop home of a highly endangered rodent—the Pacific pocket mouse—shows no activity. The mice are cocooned in their burrows, sleeping away the cold months and saving their energy for their burst of summer activity.

Arroyo toads, another endangered species, are also underground, awaiting the patter of raindrops that will signal the start of their late-winter breeding season.

The big question is whether the corridor agencies' plans to make up the loss by preserving or growing other habitat—and attendant species—will work.

The agencies' latest environmental impact report includes detailed accounts of the species, the land they live on and the possible negative effects of a four-lane tollway through their home turf.

Orange County has been down this road before. Two existing toll roads, the San Joaquin (73) and the Foothill (241), also had their swaths of sensitive habitat and species, as well as formidable opponents seeking to block construction.

But in the end, the agencies overcame the opposition and grew or preserved enough habitat to satisfy federal wildlife officials.

The new toll road's opponents include parks officials like Pryor as well as members of environmental groups and biological consultants those groups have hired.

Arrayed against them is the corridor agencies' army of staff specialists and their own consultants.

Two major wildlife habitats and their species are the big concerns.

One is San Mateo Lagoon, near the mouth of San Mateo Creek, where fish such as endangered tidewater gobies dwell. It's also home to streamside birds such as the threatened southwestern willow flycatcher and least Bell's vireo.

Steelhead trout, another endangered species, don't live in the lagoon, but would pass through it on their way to spawn upstream.

The preferred route for the toll road would not cut through the lagoon, and the roadway would be placed on pillars where it crosses the creek farther upstream to help minimize effects on the streambed.

But some experts say the lagoon species could be affected by sediment and pollutants flowing from toll-road construction.

Toll-road officials say they will install netting, catch basins and other devices to capture sediment and pollution from the roadway.

Yet many of these designs have not been finalized, and activists and some scientists worry that too many measures amount to vague promises. The agencies say many of these measures, called "best management practices," are already in place elsewhere.

"They say they're going to use best management practices," Pryor said. "What if the best isn't good enough?" Worries also linger about polluted water flowing from the roadway after it is finished.

Five years ago, storm-water filters on the 73 toll road were found to be clogged and inadequate, but tollway officials say that maintenance was the responsibility of the state Department of Transportation. They say different technology, relying on settling basins, would be used on the new toll road.

The agency was required to examine all habitat and species within a quarter-mile of the toll road's path, and 10 endangered or threatened species, or their habitat, were found. Two species of fairy shrimp and birds such as the least Bell's vireo, as well as fish in the lagoon, are considered by the agencies to be safe because they are far enough away from the road.

And some biologists who study these species agree that serious harm seems less likely for lagoon species—especially if runoff and sediment are controlled properly.

"We're looking at more of a toad issue than a steelhead issue," said Tim Hovey, associate fisheries biologist with the state Department of Fish and Game.

The other important habitat is upland scrub brush on either side of the creek, farther upstream. And this is likely to be where the real fight between consultants begins.

The upland species include a threatened plant, the thread-leaved brodiaea, the threatened California gnatcatcher, as well as the endangered arroyo toad and highly endangered Pacific pocket mouse.

Toll-road officials say the toad, the brodiaea plant and the gnatcatcher are the only species that will suffer direct effects from the road. Their solution: preserve habitat in Upper Chiquita Canyon on Rancho Mission Viejo, where the brodiaea can be replanted, where gnatcatchers can breed, and where additional habitat can be restored.

Activists say the agencies would use "mitigation credits" it already possesses on Upper Chiquita, which would have been preserved anyway.

California Gnatcatchers, Female and Male, © Clair de Beauvoir

Arroyo Toad,
© Richard Jackson

Pacific Pocket Mouse, photograph, Courtesy of The Natural Resources Defense Council

Small Creek, Rancho Mission Viejo, © Richard Jackson

Chiquita Ridge, Rancho Mission Viejo, © Stephen Francis Photography

Biologists outside the agencies are most concerned about the toad.

This species, they say, is so sensitive it cannot afford to lose any habitat. It breeds in creeks but also forages far and wide in scrub brush. They have been found as much as three-quarters of a mile away from streamside habitat.

And the situation could be even more acute than most people realize, according to herpetologist Dan Holland, a foremost authority on the toad who has, in past years, tramped up and down the toll-road area searching for them.

"The survey results that we had indicate that the average density of arroyo toads, in those areas that would be directly impacted by the toll road, is roughly twice that of anyplace else," Holland said.

The Pacific pocket mouse is another species of great concern to activists and biologists.

Wayne Spencer of the Conservation Biology Institute, who has performed consulting work for the government and conservation groups, says that over many years, the mouse populations might slowly diffuse from one point to another. There are only four known populations left, one on the Dana Point Headlands, one near the toll route, and two on Camp Pendleton.

An article entitled "State Sues to Block Toll Road in Park, Attorney general calls Orange County officials' plan to cut through San Onofre State Beach 'disgraceful.' Two other suits are also filed," by Peter Nicholas and David Reyes which appeared in the *Los Angeles Times* on March 24, 2006 indicates the following:

Atty. Gen. Bill Lockyer filed a lawsuit on March 23 to block a proposed six-lane tollway through San Onofre State Beach, a popular coastal park he described as "a state treasure."

The suit alleges that the Foothill/Eastern Transportation Corridor Agency in Orange County failed to adequately explore more sensible alternatives or assess what environmental harm the 16-mile toll road might cause, in violation of the California Environmental Quality Act.

Lockyer said the plan to push the toll road through the parkland was arrogant and "disgraceful."

"It seems to me that building a six-lane highway through the San Onofre State Beach misses an opportunity to meet transportation needs of this growing region without sacrificing public parklands that should be protected for future generations," Lockyer said.

If built, the thoroughfare will be by far the largest project of its kind that cuts through a state park. Park officials fear it could open the door to other encroachments statewide.

Lockyer's suit was one of three filed March 23, in Superior Court in San Diego seeking to stop the project. The other plaintiffs are a coalition of environmental groups and the Native American Heritage Commission.

Joel Reynolds, senior attorney for the Natural Resources Defense Council—which is part of the environmentalist coalition—described the project as the "poster child for bad transportation policy."

"This project makes no sense, economically, environmentally, spiritually, morally, legally, and it ought to be abandoned," Reynolds said. "So make no mistake, this is a project we intend to stop. We're drawing a line in the sand around San Onofre, because if we can't save this state park, if we can't prevent the TCA from paving over this coastal gem, then it's only a matter of time before a project just like it comes to a state park near you."

The environmental coalition includes the California State Parks Foundation, the Sierra Club, the Surfrider Foundation, Natural Resources Defense Council, and Sea and Sage Audubon Society.

"I hope these concerted actions will wash away the destructive arrogance of this toll road proposal," Lockyer said. "It's disgraceful, and we're going to fight it."

An article by David Reyes from the *Times* of May 6, indicates Democratic Assemblyman Pedro Nava of Santa Barbara, citing environmental concerns, wants to stop the proposed 16-mile toll road through San Onofre State Beach. A former state Coastal Commission member and a member of the Assembly's Budget Committee, he recommended setting aside $450,000 for an independent University of California study to discuss traffic in south Orange County. An Assembly budget subcommittee approved the recommendations at a hearing on March 3. Nava hoped the recommendation would be included in the state budget.

Red-Legged Frog,
© L. Lee Grisner,
US Fish and
Wildlife Service

Steelhead Salmon, Courtesy of US Food and Drug Administration

According to California State Senator Bill Morrow, the San Mateo Creek Steelhead Restoration Project is moving forward. The ultimate goal is restoration to the original habitat. Since 2000 the following project area evaluations have been completed and reports produced on Habitat Assessment, Exotic species removal, and the California Red-legged frog survey. Planning for 2005 is in the scheduling stage. Of the original budgeted funds (from Propositions 12 & 13) about $200,000 has been spent with a remaining balance of approximately $600,000. The goals for 2005 will be to complete the National Environmental Protection Act work in the Cleveland National Forest above Camp Pendleton. Exotic species removal of predator fish and bullfrogs will continue. Stream surveys have begun to see if steelhead entered the stream to spawn during the historic rainy year of 2004. An interpretive sign program to educate the public about the steelhead is in the design stage and volunteer projects involving non-native plant removal and water quality monitoring will continue. Completion of this project is projected for 2007.

Stream, Rancho Mission Viejo, © Richard Jackson

Wildflowers, Rancho Mission Viejo, © Richard Jackson

Rebecca J. Moralez 1993

Whimbrel   American Avocet   Black Skimmer   Estuary

Great Blue Heron

Monkey Flower   Deerweed   Laurel Sumac   California Sagebrush   Chalk Live-forever   Native Grassland   Cactus Wren   Santa Ana Mts. / Saddleback

Diegan Coastal Sage Scrub   Dodder   Red Diamond Rattlesnake   Prickly Pear   California Buckwheat

Sycamore   Coastal Sage Scrub - Chaparral Transition   Ceanothus Chaparral

Canyon Live Oak Ravine Woodland   Matilija Poppy   Mule Fat   Lemonadeberry   Whipple Yucca

Stream Orchid   California Maidenhair   Leopard Lily   Riparian Woodland   White Alder Grove   Coastal Wood Fern   Chain Fern   Bigleaf Maple   Bigcone Spruce / Canyon Live Oak F

California Polypody   Poison Oak   Canyon Tree Frog   Western Toad

Clapper Rail / Great Egret / American Wigeon / Pickleweed / Maritime Coastal Sage Scrub / Mexican Elderberry / Blackberry / California Gnatcatcher / White Sage / Black Sunflower

Raven / Fresh Water Marsh / Tricolored Blackbird / Non-native Grassland / Audubon Cottontail / California Quail / Scrub Jay

Red-tailed Hawk / Chamise Chaparral / Turkey Vulture / Manzanita Chaparral / Santiago Peak / Bigcone Spruce

Yellow-rumped Warbler / Cooper's Hawk / Coast Live Oak Woodlands / Cynipid Wasp Gall / House Wren

Murals by Rebecca Jo Morales, © 1993,
Courtesy of the Donna O'Neill Land Conservancy

359

Karl Yens, *Half Dome, Yosemite*, The Irvine Museum

William Wendt, *Tioga Pass*, Courtesy of George Stern Fine Arts, Los Angeles and Carmel

With regard to California's ancient redwood groves, the website hikewithyourdog.com indicates the following:

> Like Yosemite National Park, its neighbors to the south, Kings Canyon and Sequoia national parks, boasting the largest concentration of giant sequoias in the world, do not allow dogs on the trail. About five miles north of Kings Canyon National Park and the famous General Grant Grove, however, is the Converse Basin Grove where your dog can get up close to a famous giant sequoia, the Boole Tree.

> Converse Basin is a giant sequoia graveyard where once the largest living things on earth grew in majestic abundance. This area was once quite possibly the finest sequoia grove that ever was. Massive trees over 300 feet high were enthusiastically felled by loggers - often for little more than shingles. One 285-foot sequoia known as the General Noble Tree was cut in 1893 to display at the Columbian Exposition in Chicago and the Chicago Stump can be seen today. Among the trees destroyed in the Converse Basin was the oldest known giant sequoia to have been cut down - 3200 annual growth rings were counted. So many trees were taken that the area is known as Stump Meadow.

> If you have spent the day looking at giant sequoias in the landscaped national parks, your encounter with the Boole Tree might come as a bit of a shock. It is related to its brothers in Kings Canyon National Park like the wolf is to your dog. Surrounded by dense forest growth, it is actually possible to not immediately recognize the Boole Tree from the main trail. But once you see your dog up against its massive trunk - its ground perimeter of 113 feet is the greatest of all giant sequoias—there is no mistaking this special tree.

Abandoned Logs, Converse Basin, USDA Forest Service photo

Logging Remains, Carl Alwin Schenck Papers, North Carolina State University

Stumps of Redwood Trees Cut Down in the 1890s, Converse Basin, USDA Forest Service photo

Forty-Three Men Standing on the Base of the Boole Tree, Converse Basin, c. 1890, Private Collection

17½ foot diameter Redwood
Felled at
Union Lumber Company's holdings
Fort Bragg, California
Jan 8, 1933
9-20' saw logs cut from this tree

Fallen Redwood, 17.5 Feet Diameter, c. 1900, Vintage Postcard, Private Collection

The drive to preserve the redwoods on the northern coast of California began in 1917, after the completion of Highway 101, when several prominent conservationists traveled to Humboldt and Del Norte counties to view the magnificent redwood groves there. These conservationists were John C. Merriam, University of California paleontologist and later President of the Carnegie Institute, Madison Grant of the New York Zoological Society and Henry Fairfield Osborn of the American Museum of Natural History. They saw widespread destruction of the forests along the new highway, and were appalled to find that not one tree was owned by any public agency or protected for public enjoyment in any way.

These great conservationists were impressed by the urgent need to preserve redwood groves in public parks for their unique beauty and scientific interest. In an article which appeared in the *National Geographic* magazine, they revealed the coast redwoods to the American public, and made a plea for the preservation of redwood forests. Together, in the spring of 1918, they organized Save-the-Redwoods League. Its objective was to rescue from destruction representative areas of primeval redwood forests, and to cooperate with state and national park services in establishing redwood parks. Through donations and matching state funds, the League bought over 100,000 acres of redwood forest between 1920 and 1960.

Undercutting a Redwood Prior to Felling,
Carl Alwin Schenck Papers,
North Carolina State University

There were thousands of small donations, as well as large. Edward Harkness contributed a half-a-million dollars for the purchase of lands in Prairie Creek, and John D. Rockefeller, over the years, donated a total of around $3 million. Thanks to a generous and timely contribution from my grandfather, James Irvine, the Save the Redwoods League was able to complete its 1943 payment for the Mill Creek Redwoods project. At that time, by action of the California State Parks Commission, the James Irvine Redwood Grove was established within the Prairie Creek Redwoods State Park. It is a primeval forest of 160 acres, northeast of the State Park headquarters. A loop of the picturesque old County Road passes through it, rejoining the Redwood Highway about a quarter-mile from the entrance. An outstanding feature is a Redwood Giant rising above the road, 17 feet 7 inches in diameter, measured breast high.

Mussel Point, Redwood National Park, Courtesy of Susan Jordan, www.californiacoastline.org

FROM LEFT: Diana and Tracy Gaede at the James Irvine Grove in the Prairie Creek Redwoods State Park, photograph, Courtesy of Linda Irvine Gaede Smith

Albert R. Valentien, *California Polypody*, Courtesy of the San Diego Natural History Museum. The lush fern banks on shaded canyons and streamsides seem to vanish with the arrival of dry summer days, as the leaves curl and break off at their bases and the plants await the rains of the next season. The numerous, knotty extremities of the rhizome are the "many feet" referred to by the name Polypodium. —M. Dykens

Giant Redwood in James Irvine Grove, Prairie Creek, California, The Irvine Family Archives

Felling a Giant Redwood, c. 1890s, Vintage Postcard, Private Collection

Felling a 330 Foot Giant, 21 Feet Diameter, Vintage Postcard, Private Collection

Today, the League's mission remains the same. While redwoods have been preserved in our network of national and state parks, in many areas they are still under threat. With regard to the protection of our national forests, an editorial entitled "Forest Non-Planning" appeared in the *Los Angeles Times* on December 27, 2004, stating the following:

In some areas of the West, decisions made in Washington about public lands grate on local officials. They grit their teeth at endless paperwork and bureaucratic delay. Why not trade a few environmental protections for easier commercial use of those lands? The White House has heard those complaints, echoed by the timber and mining industries, and come up with one whopping Christmas present.

The price tag may include loss of endangered species and habitat, irreparable damage to wild land owned by all Americans and the silencing of public comments on logging and mining in remote areas, all in the name of "efficiency."

[In late December 2004], the administration issued new National Forest regulations that push management more into the hands of local and regional forest supervisors, especially when it comes to drawing up new forest plans, which happens every 15 years or so. The administration also aims to speed the development of those plans.

Neither idea is bad by itself. Local managers know their forests best. And it's always been incomprehensible that the U.S. Forest Service takes an average of five years to develop a plan meant to last 15. But instead of strengthening standards to make up for a shorter bureaucratic process, the new rules weaken and in some cases get rid of standards.

Forest planners could bypass the National Environmental Policy Act altogether, eliminating environmental impact studies. Rather than maintaining populations of native animals, foresters must ensure only some unspecified level of species "diversity." They no longer need to keep wildlife from becoming endangered; that's been muddied into a meaningless requirement to protect natural resources.

Loggers Peeling a Fallen Redwood, Carl Alwin Schenck Papers, North Carolina State University

A Group of Men and Horse Teams on a Peeled Giant Redwood, Converse Basin, c. 1890, Archival photo, Private Collection

Oxen Train Dragging Logs, Vintage Postcard, Private Collection

A Lumber Truck on a Log Bridge, c. 1900, Archival photo, Private Collection

Lorenzo P. Latimer, *Old Road in the Redwoods* (detail), Courtesy of Bonhams and Butterfields Auction

Albert R. Valentien, *Five-Finger Fern* (left), Courtesy of San Diego Natural History Museum. This cold-climate Maidenhair fern is abundant on damp forest floors and cliffs in northern California, and ranges north to Alaska and across the Rocky Mountains. In this and other maidenhairs, the spore-bearing tissues are concealed beneath the rolled-under edges of the fan-shaped leaflets.—M. Dykens

Albert R. Valentien, Oscillated Humboldt Lily (right), Courtesy of San Diego Natural History Museum. Openings and meadows in the pine forest and shaded stream edges may be enlivened in late spring by the glowing blooms of this rare lily, arrayed on stalks that are shoulder-high or higher. The name ocellatum refers to the maroon spots on the petals, which have a dark center surrounded by a ring of lighter color.—M. Dykens

In fact, there are no longer actual standards at all. Previous limits on logging transform into "directives" that have less legal power. Instead of meeting specified standards, forest plans must follow "guidelines" that regional forest managers can veer from when they see fit. The public's role is undermined by cutting the comment period to 30 days from the usual 90. Forest plans are complicated, acre-by-acre documents detailed in thousands of pages; the 30-day limit precludes well-researched challenges.

The new rules call for regular "independent audits," but the auditors needn't be very independent. A plan that allows unconscionable logging of old-growth forest could be audited by timber interests, if the regional forester desires.

This isn't more efficient, effective forest planning. It's a loosey-goosey system for avoiding any meaningful planning at all.

An article from the *Times* of December 30 entitled "Bush Official to Probe Sierra Logging Rules: Environmentalists fear the review could lead to revisions that would weaken protections on national forest land in the mountain range" states the following:

A Bush administration official has decided to review a new plan that increases logging levels in the Sierra Nevada, adding another twist to a decade-long fight over the future of national forest land in California's most famous mountain range.

The review by Agriculture Undersecretary Mark E. Rey opens the possibility of further revisions to a plan that has been criticized by the timber industry for not allowing enough logging and by environmentalists for allowing too much.

The plan Rey has chosen to review is itself a revision of a wide-ranging set of protections adopted for the Sierra's 11.5 million acres of national forest land during the Clinton administration.

Those guidelines de-emphasized commercial timber harvesting, set aside 4 million acres of old-growth reserves where only small trees could be cut, and relied heavily on controlled burning to reduce the risk of wildfire.

After Bush took office, his administration moved to weaken the Clinton rules, saying they were too restrictive and didn't do enough to thin dense growth that can fuel forest fires.

Early [in 2004], Regional Forester Jack Blackwell amended the Clinton plan to allow for more logging of larger trees, effectively eliminating the old-growth reserves and loosening habitat protections for rare species such as the California spotted owl and the Pacific fisher.

In the background is a lawsuit filed by the timber industry—and the promise of more lawsuits to come from environmentalists and the California attorney general's office.

The administration has elsewhere cited industry lawsuits in dropping environmental protections.

Earlier [in 2004], for instance, it eased restrictions on logging old growth in the Pacific Northwest and parts of Northern California after settling a timber industry suit challenging the regulations....

Efforts to overhaul management of the Sierra's 11 national forests began in the early 1990s with concern over decline of the California spotted owl and loss of the old-growth habitat it favors. Years of scientific and Forest Service reviews produced the Clinton regulations, which signaled a major shift toward ecosystem and wildlife protection and away from commercial timber production. The Bush administration's move to weaken the Clinton rules was criticized by Democrats as well as by Republican Arnold Schwarzenegger when he was running for governor.

Candidate Schwarzenegger called the Clinton plan "a model of forest ecosystem resource protection" and vowed that "as governor, I will direct all relevant agencies to comply fully with [it] and call on the federal government to abide by the policies."

Northern Spotted Owl, © John and Karen Hollingsworth, US Fish and Wildlife Service

Elk in Velvet, © Robert Karges II, US Fish and Wildlife Service

White-Tailed Deer Doe, © Fred Youngblood, US Fish and Wildlife Service

Mountain Lion Cub at Stream, © Richard Jackson

White-Tailed Deer Buck, © John Stehn, US Fish and Wildlife Service

White-Tailed Deer Fawn, © W. J. Berg, US Fish and Wildlife Service

Black Bear Cub in Pond, © R. I. Bridges, US Fish and Wildlife Service

Mountain Lion Cub, California Department of Fish and Game

Bald Eagle in Flight, © Don Getty, California Academy of Science

Pacific Fisher, The Pacific Biodiversity Institute

Pacific Fisher with Prey, www.kswild.org

Another article from the *Times* of January 28, 2005 entitled "Suit Filed over Sequoia Logging: Environmentalists seek to block Forest Service plans to allow cutting in a national monument" indicates the following:

The Sierra Club and five other conservation groups filed a federal lawsuit on January 27, 2005, asking the courts to overturn a plan that would allow extensive logging in the 5-year-old Giant Sequoia National Monument in the southern Sierra.

The lawsuit is the latest skirmish in a long-running battle over management of nearly three dozen groves of the world's largest trees found on national forest land, beyond the confines of nearby Sequoia and Kings Canyon National Parks.

Logging in the national forest groves in the 1980s provoked a preservation drive that led to creation of the 328,000-acre monument by President Clinton in 2000.

The monument banned logging, mining and off-road vehicle use in and around the towering groves, prompting a lawsuit by timber interests. Their challenge failed, but controversy continued when the U.S. Forest Service issued land-use plans that called for extensive timber cutting in the name of fire prevention and ecosystem restoration.

In the lawsuit filed in U.S. District Court in San Francisco, six conservation groups claim the Forest Service plan violates national environmental laws, permits logging that would harm rare wildlife, and runs counter to both the spirit and the letter of the monument designation.

"The plan will allow significant logging, reduction in forest cover and removal of large trees which are critical to survival of already threatened species such as the Pacific fisher," said Sierra Club legal director Patrick Gallagher, who helped prepare the suit. "The giant sequoia is the largest living thing on earth, and this is the only place they are found, and we ought to give them the utmost protection."

Under the plan, enough trees could be cut in the monument to fill more than 2,000 logging trucks a year. The biggest, oldest sequoias could not be touched, but trees as old as 130 years and as large as 30 inches in diameter—including sequoias—could be felled. The clearing of forest openings as large as a couple of football fields would be permitted. The plan additionally calls for the use of controlled burns to clean out dense brush and small trees that fuel wildfire.

The fight over the monument plan mirrors disputes throughout the West, where conservationists contend that the Bush administration is using the threat of wildfire to pursue logging projects on public land that are more about helping the timber industry than reducing the fire risk. In the Sequoia monument, they say, the Forest Service should rely much more heavily on controlled burning to thin overgrown land—as does Sequoia National Park, which has a long-established program of such burns.

Clear-Cut Forest in Oregon, © Steve Hildebrand, US Fish and Wildlife Service

Redwood Flora by Albert R. Valentien, Courtesy of the San Diego Natural History Museum. TOP, FROM LEFT: *Western Sword Fern, Redwood Lily*; BOTTOM, FROM LEFT: *Coast Redwood, Redwood Sorrel*

California Attorney General Bill Lockyer and a coalition of conservation groups filed back-to-back lawsuits in U.S. District Court in Sacramento on January 31 and February 1, 2005 to block the Bush administration plan to increase logging and scale back wildlife protections in the Sierra Nevada. An article from the *Times* of February 2 entitled "Suits Target Sierra Logging Plan: Activists and the state seek to bar new Forest Service rules that allow cutting of more trees" indicates the following:

> In his lawsuit, Atty. Gen. Bill Lockyer attacked the rollback as an arbitrary move that lacked scientific or legal justification. "The Bush administration just tossed that plan," Lockyer said, calling the Bush revisions "this new pro-timber company plan."
>
> Lockyer, a Democrat, said he has invited Republican Gov. Schwarzenegger to join the lawsuit. "We have informed his office, and hope they will wish to participate."

An article from the *Times* of February 10 entitled "U.S. Scientists Say They Are Told to Alter Findings, More than 200 Fish and Wildlife researchers cite cases where conclusions were reversed to weaken protections and favor business, a survey finds" states the following:

> More than 200 scientists employed by the U.S. Fish and Wildlife Service say they have been directed to alter official findings to lessen protections for plants and animals, a survey released February 9 says. The survey of the agency's scientific staff of 1,400 had a 30% response rate and was conducted jointly by the Union of Concerned Scientists and Public Employees for Environmental Responsibility.
>
> A division of the Department of the Interior, the Fish and Wildlife Service is charged with determining which animals and plants should be placed on the endangered species list and designating areas where such species need to be protected. More than half of the biologists and other researchers who responded to the survey said they knew of cases in which commercial interests, including timber, grazing, development and energy companies, had applied political pressure to reverse scientific conclusions deemed harmful to their business.
>
> Bush administration officials, including Craig Manson, an assistant secretary of the Interior who oversees the Fish and Wildlife Service, have been critical of the 1973 Endangered Species Act, contending that its implementation has imposed hardships on developers and others while failing to restore healthy populations of wildlife. Along with Republican leaders in Congress, the administration is pushing to revamp the act. The president's proposed budget calls for a $3-million reduction in funding of Fish and Wildlife's endangered species programs.
>
> "The pressure to alter scientific reports for political reasons has become pervasive at Fish and Wildlife offices around the country," said Lexi Shultz of the Union of Concerned Scientists. Fish and Wildlife scientists in 90 national offices were asked 42 questions and given space to respond in essay form in the mail-in survey sent in November.
>
> One scientist working in the Pacific region, which includes California, wrote: "I have been through the reversal of two listing decisions due to political pressure. Science was ignored—and worse, manipulated, to build a bogus rationale for reversal of these listing decisions."
>
> Sally Stefferud, a biologist who retired in 2002 after 20 years with the agency, said February 9 she was not surprised by the survey results, saying she had been ordered to change a finding on a biological opinion. "Political pressures influence the outcome of almost all the cases," she said. "As a scientist, I would probably say you really can't trust the science coming out of the agency."

California Attorney General Bill Lockyer filed another federal lawsuit on March 3, 2005, to block the U.S. Forest Service plan to permit commercial logging in the Giant Sequoia National Monument. This suit, which follows the one filed in January by conservation groups, alleges that the Forest Service is violating protections granted by President Clinton in 2000, when he established the 328,000-acre monument in the southern Sierra northeast of Bakersfield. An article entitled "Lockyer Suit Seeks to Save Sequoias" from the *Los Angeles Times* of March 4 indicates the following:

Clinton's declaration barred timber production, saying that trees could be removed in the monument "only if clearly needed for ecological restoration and maintenance or public safety."

The Forest Service's 2003 management plan nonetheless allows enough timber-cutting to fill more than 2,000 logging trucks a year. Ancient sequoias could not be cut, but sequoias and other trees up to 30 inches in diameter and a century old could be logged.

The Forest Service said the logging was not being done for commercial purposes but to restore the monument's 34 groves of giant sequoias, which contain the largest—and some of the oldest—trees in the world. The agency said the groves grew too dense under the government's longtime policy of putting out wildfires that naturally clean out smaller trees and underbrush.

But the U.S. District Court suit contends that the management plan is confusing and fails to justify the timber-cutting.

The suit says that the proposed annual logging levels amount to 42% of the average annual timber yield in the last 10 years for the entire Sequoia National Forest. Yet the monument covers less than a third of the forest.

For some time, I have been corresponding with Governor Schwarzenegger with regard to the plight of our magnificent Sequoia trees in the Giant Sequoia National Monument, created by President Clinton in 2000. At a dinner with the Governor on March 22, 2005, I had the opportunity to speak with him directly on the matter. The next day, he sent me the following letter (*opposite*):

Thomas Hill, *Redwoods*, Courtesy of Dr. and Mrs. Edwin H. Boseker

Albert R. Valentien, *Mountain California Lady's-Slipper* (RIGHT), Courtesy of San Diego Natural History Museum. Mountain Lady's Slipper is a threatened species of orchid found in central and northern California and other western states in moist areas, dry slopes, and mixed coniferous forests. Orchids such as this species can sometimes take as long as 16 years to bloom and have very exacting requirements for reproduction to take place. Specific fungi are necessary for germination to occur. These requirements, coupled with the threats to orchid habitat by logging and development, often result in drastically reduced numbers of new plants.—M. Dykens

Albert R. Valentien, *California Lady's-Slipper* (FAR RIGHT), Courtesy of San Diego Natural History Museum. California Lady's-Slipper, like many other species in the Orchid family, is threatened by logging and over-collecting. Because it has very specific requirements for germination, new plants are also very few and far between. It is found on moist slopes and along streambanks in central and northern California.—M. Dykens

OFFICE OF THE GOVERNOR

March 23, 2005

Joan Irvine Smith
P.O. Box 1453
San Juan Capistrano, CA 92693

Dear Joan,

Thank you for your letters of concern for the protection of our federal forest resources. I also appreciate your patience in awaiting a response. My Administration supports protecting California's unique natural assets like our giant sequoias and fully embraces that the future health of our environment and economy rely upon one another.

As the Sequoia is the world's largest tree, I share your interest in the long-term health of our majestic giant sequoia groves on National Forest System lands in California. To this end, a Presidential Proclamation created the 328,000-acre Giant Sequoia National Monument on April 15, 2000. The Proclamation identified two critical problems facing the giant sequoias and their ecosystems: 1) an unprecedented failure in giant sequoia reproduction, and 2) an unprecedented buildup of woody debris and surface fuels, leading to an increased hazard from severe wildfires that were rarely encountered in pre-Euro-American times.

The recently released Forest Service Final Giant Sequoia National Monument Management Plan provides for the care and management of all natural resources in the National Monument. According to this plan, prescribed fire will be the preferred treatment method and will be considered first to meet ecological restoration and public safety objectives, including the need to manage forest structure or create small openings (gaps) to promote giant sequoia regeneration. Other methods, including tree removal is permitted only if a site-specific project analysis determines and documents that mechanical treatments and/or tree removal are clearly needed for ecological restoration and maintenance or public safety.

I believe that states must play a stronger role with federal land management agencies to achieve coordinated and comprehensive resource stewardship that can be thoughtfully implemented. We will work with the USDA Forest Service to ensure the future protection of our State's National Forests. The State will actively monitor forest management activities at the Giant Sequoia National Monument to ensure that the sequoia groves are being properly protected for future generations.

Sincerely,

Arnold Schwarzenegger

The Grand Canyon of the Yellowstone, Yellowstone National Park photo

An editorial entitled "Destroying the National Parks" which appeared in *The New York Times* on August 29, 2005 indicates the following:

Most of us think of America's national parks as everlasting places, parts of the bedrock of how we know our own country. But they are shaped and protected by an underlying body of legislation, which is distilled into a basic policy document that governs their operation. Over time, that document has slowly evolved, but it has always stayed true to the fundamental principle of leaving the parks unimpaired for future generations. That has meant, in part, sacrificing some of the ways we might use the parks today in order to protect them for tomorrow.

Recently, a secret draft revision of the national park system's basic management policy document has been circulating within the Interior Department. It was prepared, without consultation within the National Park Service, by Paul Hoffman, a deputy assistant secretary at Interior who once ran the Chamber of Commerce in Cody, Wyo., was a Congressional aide to Dick Cheney and has no park service experience.

Within national park circles, this rewrite of park rules has been met with profound dismay, for it essentially undermines the protected status of the national parks. The document makes it perfectly clear that this rewrite was not prompted by a compelling change in the park system's circumstances. It was prompted by a change in political circumstances—the opportunity to craft a vision of the national parks that suits the Bush administration.

Some of Mr. Hoffman's changes are trivial, although even apparently subtle changes in wording—from "protect" to '"conserve,'" for instance—soften the standard used to judge the environmental effects of park policy.

But there is nothing subtle about the main thrust of this rewrite. It is a frontal attack on the idea of "impairment.'" According to the act that established the national parks, preventing impairment of park resources—including the landscape, wildlife and such intangibles as the soundscape of Yellowstone, for instance—is the "fundamental purpose." In Mr. Hoffman's world, it is now merely one of the purposes.

Mr. Hoffman's rewrite would open up nearly every park in the nation to off-road vehicles, snowmobiles and Jet Skis. According to his revision, the use of such vehicles would become one of the parks' purposes. To accommodate such activities, he redefines impairment to mean an irreversible impact. To prove that an activity is impairing the parks, under Mr. Hoffman's rules, you would have to prove that it is doing so irreversibly—a very high standard of proof. This would have a genuinely erosive effect on the standards used to protect the national parks.

The pattern prevails throughout this 194-page document—easing the rules that limit how visitors use the parks and toughening the standard of proof needed to block those uses. Behind this pattern, too, there is a fundamental shift in how the parks are regarded. If the laws establishing the national park system were fundamentally forward-looking—if their mission, first and foremost, was protecting the parks for the future—Mr. Hoffman's revisions place a new, unwelcome and unnecessary emphasis on the present, on what he calls "opportunities for visitors to use and enjoy their parks."

There is no question that we go to national parks to use and enjoy them. But part of the enjoyment of being in a place like Yosemite or the Grand Canyon is knowing that no matter how much it changes in the natural processes of time, it will continue to exist substantially unchanged.

There are other issues too. Mr. Hoffman would explicitly allow the sale of religious merchandise, and he removes from the policy document any reference to evolution or evolutionary processes. He does everything possible to strip away a scientific basis for park management. His rules would essentially require park superintendents to subordinate the management of their parks to local and state agendas. He also envisions a much wider range of commercial activity within the parks.

In short, this is not a policy for protecting the parks. It is a policy for destroying them. The Interior Department has already begun to distance itself from this rewrite, which it kept hidden from park service employees. But what Mr. Hoffman has given us is a road map of what could happen to the parks if Mr. Bush's political appointees are allowed to have their way.

Old Faithful in Winter, Yellowstone National Park photo

It is clear by now that Mr. Bush has no real intention of living up to his campaign promise to fully finance the national parks. This document offers a vivid picture of the divide between the National Park Service, whose career employees remain committed to the fundamental purpose of leaving the parks unimpaired, and an Interior Department whose political appointees seem willing to alter them beyond recognition, partly in the service of commercial objectives.

Suddenly, many things—like the administration's efforts to force snowmobiles back into Yellowstone— seem very easy to explain.

Kevin Short, *Long Division*, Crystal Cove, Courtesy of Crystal Cove Alliance

WITH REGARD TO URBAN RUNOFF, an article entitled "Not all plan to go with stopping the runoff flow, High cost has some cities, agencies seeking exemption from state order to keep contaminants out of ocean," appeared in the *Orange County Register* on February 21, 2005. It indicates the following:

> The letters came as a shock to cities, parks, developers and public-works agencies up and down the state, including five in Orange County: Stop contaminated water from trickling into sensitive ocean habitat, or face the consequences.
>
> The protests soon followed. The ultimatum by state water regulators in October could cost hundreds of millions of dollars to put into effect statewide, the agencies say, and many already feel cash-strapped from years of lean budgets.
>
> The California Department of Transportation alone could face as much as $300 million in costs, the agency estimates. Coastal roads and highways, including Pacific Coast Highway, are prime sources of contaminated runoff because rainwater picks up metal, brake dust, oil and other pollutants and washes them off roads and into the sea.
>
> Stopping the runoff requires either eliminating its source or paying for potentially expensive installation of filters, catch basins and other devices that trap contaminated water.
>
> "What we are going to try to do is identify the solutions that are least environmentally damaging," said Dominic Gregorio of the state Water Board's division of water quality. He is keeping track of the responses to the agency's letters.

Run-off at Treasure Cove, near Crystal Cove, photograph, Courtesy of Crystal Cove Alliance

Run-off pipe, Crystal Cove, photograph, Courtesy of Crystal Cove Alliance

Junn Roca, *Crystal Cove*, Private Collection, Courtesy of The Irvine Museum

Even those agencies seeking an exemption from the mandate—more than 20 so far—could end up spending millions on environmental studies and monitoring, they say, to track contaminated water. Exemptions can be given to agencies that are able to show, among other things, that the discharge won't cause harm to ocean water.

The regulatory push began five years ago in Orange County, when the Santa Ana Regional Water Quality Control Board ordered Caltrans to stop contaminated runoff from flowing into Crystal Cove, one of three "areas of special biological significance" on the Orange County coast.

The order was prompted in part by a lawsuit by Orange County Coastkeeper. The activist group said the state Ocean Plan prohibits discharging wastewater into these biologically significant sections of coastline. After initial protests, Caltrans eventually capitulated and agreed to install runoff-control devices known as bioswales. These beds of soil and plants are now being installed along Pacific Coast Highway in Newport Beach, and they should prevent further contamination when they are completed Feb. 28. Soon after the Crystal Cove matter was resolved, the state Water Resources Control Board—the parent agency for the regional boards—realized that what applies in Orange County ought to apply everywhere on the coast. Each of the state's 34 areas of special biological significance, they said, must be protected.

"We're delighted with the job the state's doing," said Coastkeeper executive director Garry Brown. "It's all positive, forward movement."

Joseph Kleitsch, *Tidepools, Laguna Beach*, Courtesy of Bonhams and Butterfields Auction

Rick Delanty, *After the Rain, San Clemente*, Courtesy of the artist

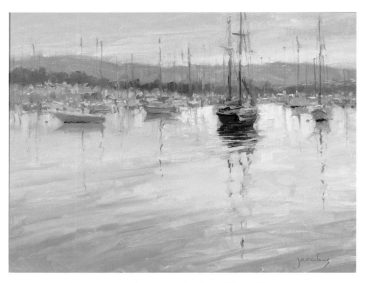

Jacobus Baas, *Newport Boats*, Courtesy of the Crystal Cove Alliance

Michael Situ, *Laguna Beach*, Private Collection, Courtesy of The Irvine Museum

Ken Auster, *Before Nightfall, Laguna*, Courtesy of the artist

John Cosby, *Heisler Park, Laguna*, Courtesy of the artist

Ken Auster, *Wine and Roses, Laguna*, Courtesy of the artist

But stopping runoff is difficult. Contaminated water from lawns, roads and businesses trickles steadily into sensitive ocean habitat in countless locations in California.

Newport Beach has a powerful waterfall that is gradually eating a large gouge in a coastal bluff. The waterfall, which runs year-round, even during dry weather, is almost entirely composed of excess urban runoff. It would not exist naturally.

Runoff funneled to the coast from miles of creeks and storm channels can contain animal feces and pesticides and fertilizers from homeowners' lawns, along with other forms of pollution.

Environmental officials at Orange County agencies who received the letters had varying reactions.

Newport Beach officials decided simply to take care of the problem, rather than go through the laborious—and potentially costly—exemption process.

In Laguna Beach, the situation is not so clear-cut. Large amounts of storm water flowing through the city's Heisler Park during the rainy season would be too hard to control, said Assistant City Manager John Pietig, so he will seek an exemption. But the city also is making $1.6 million worth of water-quality improvements in the area and has modified its plans in order to incorporate many of the state's requirements, he said.

The state asked a Westminster research group to survey all the places—pipes, storm drains, leaky stairs or back yards, for example—from which runoff flows into areas of special biological significance.

Orange County three biologically significant areas. Crystal Cove, listed as the Irvine Coast Marine Life Reserve, Heisler Park Ecological Reserve and Newport Beach Marine Life Reserve have runoff points that total only in the teens. Others are far higher. The area of the coast with the most sites of runoff discharge into the ocean is Mugu Lagoon, the state water board's Gregorio said, with nearly 500 of them.

San Diego also was among the places with the most discharge sites, with 184.

Even remote parts of the California coast—including the Farallon Islands, a wildlife refuge about 30 miles off San Francisco—were not spared the water board's mandate.

Agencies that don't comply with the mandate or seek an exemption could find themselves in hot water. Cease-and-desist orders - much like the one that prompted action by Caltrans at Crystal Cove five years ago—are already being considered by regional water-quality officials against Monterey, Pacific Grove, Carmel and the Pebble Beach Co.

Alfred R. Mitchell, *La Jolla Shores*, (detail) The Irvine Museum

George Gardner Symons, *Rocky Coast*, The Irvine Museum

Arthur Hill Gilbert, *Land of Grey Dunes*, Monterey, The Irvine Museum

Another article entitled "Buzz swirls over using bioswales to spare sea" appeared in the *Register* on February 21. It indicates:

Soil and plants are being pressed into service to help stem the flow of polluted water into Orange County's marine environment.

Biofiltration swales—dirt depressions filled with native grasses—are being installed along Pacific Coast Highway to filter highway runoff flowing into Crystal Cove.

The devices are the first such system in Orange County, part of a growing state trend to use plants to filter runoff. A similar project is planned on realigned sections of Laguna Canyon Road, now under construction.

"We're looking to preserve what we have out there," said Sylvia Vega, Caltrans chief of environmental planning in Orange County, adding that an increase in houses and cars has contributed to the runoff.

Essentially, the swales act like a natural filter. During or after rainstorms, dirt, oils and metals from vehicles traveling along PCH mix with water. The runoff flows off the highway and into a network of ditches, called biofiltration swales or bioswales.

Those ditches, filled with low-growing grass, such as pinpoint clover, California poppy and salt meadow barley, remove about 65 percent to 70 percent of harmful pollutants before the water flows into two adjacent creeks, and then into the ocean away from Crystal Cove.

The $2.1 million roadwork on Pacific Coast Highway, expected to wrap up Feb. 28, comes in response to a November 2000 order by local water regulators requiring the California Department of Transportation to stop roadway contaminants, such as dirt, oil and brake dust, from flowing into the area's beaches and sandy coves.

Laura Davick in Crystal Cove Run-off pipe, photograph, Courtesy of the Crystal Cove Alliance

Work on the filtration devices began last September. Environmentalists said the filters are a victory for the community and future generations.

Laura Davick, founder of the Crystal Cove Alliance, said she is pleased. "We are behind this 100 percent. I'm happy. I know the dolphins and sea creatures are happy, too."

Davick has been involved with issues related to the area since 1999. She crawled through pipes in 2000 to document illegal runoff from a housing development.

"For me, it's really about trying to provide that same experience I've had at Crystal Cove to other people," she said.

Each year about 1 million people visit Crystal Cove's 3.2 miles of beaches, with seven rocky coves, 400 acres of coastal bluff and 2,400 acres of undeveloped wooded areas. Visitors see sharks, rays, seals, sea lions and dolphins.

Dan Goozeé, *Beach Bluffs*, Courtesy of the artist

John Cosby, *Summer Day, Crystal Cove*, Courtesy of the artist

Jesse Powell, *Tidepools, Crystal Cove*, Courtesy of the Crystal Cove Alliance

Millard Sheets, *Sunset, Gualala Coast*, Private Collection

The park, also a home to tide pools and rare birds, is one of 34 state-designated "areas of special biological significance." The bioswale technology is meant to protect the area.

"It sets the bar very high for where everybody needs to head," said Ken Kramer, Crystal Cove park superintendent. "This puts us on the leading edge of environmental protection."

Pam Gorniak, a Caltrans spokeswoman, said the state decided to install the swales—instead of putting filters in existing drains—because they didn't involve mechanical parts, are easy to maintain and don't tend to cause flooding.

"It was a scientifically proven filtration system," she said.

Regulators didn't specify the capture devices needed, just that Caltrans had to stop runoff. There are swale projects in Los Angeles and San Diego.

Millard Sheets, *Los Angeles River*, 1928, Courtesy of Bonhams and Butterfields Auction

The Crystal Cove Development, photograph, Courtesy of The Irvine Company

Sat Tamaribuchi on Pelican Hill, photograph, Courtesy of The Irvine Company

A further article entitled "Newport Coast limits urban runoff" also appeared in the *Register* on February 21. It states:

Activists were initially critical of the Irvine Co.'s Newport Coast development and sued the developer, fearing the new homes would increase the flow of urban runoff into the ocean.

The Irvine Co. redesigned its project, and now state regulators consider it a model for runoff control.

Storm drains are fitted with filters that screen out oil and heavy metals.

Wetlands dotting the development cut the velocity of runoff water that might otherwise erode slopes and flow into the ocean. Wetland plants absorb pollutants deposited in mud.

"First-flush" rainfall—the first -¾ inch of rain after a dry season—usually carries a large burden of contaminants that have built up in storm channels for months. The development includes basins designed to catch these flows and hold them for up to 40 hours, cutting the amount of sediment flowing into the ocean and capturing pollutants.

An article entitled "The Runoff Stops Here" which appeared in the Summer 2004 issue of *Orange County Coastkeeper* magazine indicates the following:

The site of the new 115-acre Pelican Hill resort is so close to the special marine habitat of Crystal Cove State Park that The Irvine Company is going to unprecedented lengths to create an elaborate water quality system based on conservation and recycling.

In charge of that effort is Sat Tamaribuchi, the developer's vice president of environmental affairs, who says in this case it is "worth the extra push."

Frank Cuprien, *Seascape with Pine Trees*, Private Collection, Courtesy of The Irvine Museum

Sat Tamaribuchi is on a mission—a seemingly impossible mission, even with all the resources of The Irvine Company behind him. One of Orange County's most influential master plan developers and its environmental officer seek to defy a fundamental law of nature: Water flows downhill.

The rolling hills of the exclusive Pelican Hill Golf Club stretch before Tamaribuchi with stunning views of the Pacific Ocean in the distance. This will be the site of a new resort taking shape in Newport Coast, a low-profile and environmentally sensitive enclave that The Irvine Company has been planning for years.

If nature had its way, the runoff would flow down the rugged washes to Crystal Cove State Park with its fragile tide pools, sensitive marine life and struggling kelp forests.

But The Irvine Company has a different plan in mind, one that will stop new runoff from getting anywhere close to the coast. Beneath the surface of the Pelican Hill Golf Club, the master plan developer envisions a sophisticated water quality system to promote conservation and recycling—a labyrinth of filters, enormous cisterns and catch basins that will trap and treat all runoff at the new resort. "Our goal is to mimic and even improve upon nature," said Tamaribuchi. The captured runoff will be treated and used to help irrigate the two championship golf courses that have been operated for more than a dozen years.

"The smart use of technology to control urban runoff is important to the protection of our natural resources in Orange County, but is especially critical with coastal projects such as Pelican Hill because pollutants picked up by runoff can have an immediate and harmful effect on the ocean," Tamaribuchi said.

Construction of the Pelican Hill water quality system is expected to begin in the fall of 2004. But already the plan has received the blessing of many environmental experts and activists, who say it's the most advanced water quality management program they've seen on the California coast. It has the endorsement of Orange County Coastkeeper, whose officers were consulted early in the planning process.

"The goal of this project is quite extraordinary and will become a model of water quality for California and possibly the entire nation," said Garry Brown, founder and executive director of Orange County Coastkeeper. "This commitment far exceeds what is required by law. We appreciate the fact The Irvine Company wants so much to do the right thing they are spending significant extra dollars to protect the special biological area that lies in the ocean in front of their property."

On March 16, 2005, the United States Senate voted to open part of the Arctic National Wildlife Refuge to oil and gas drilling, marking a turning point in one of the nation's most contentious environmental issues. An article entitled "Refuge Has Long Been a Major Environmental Battleground, The nation's oil and gas needs help Bush gain support for drilling. But foes say the limited supply isn't worth the lasting damage," from the *Los Angeles Times* of March 17, states:

No environmental battle in the last 25 years has aroused more passion than the seesaw struggle over the future of a strip of coastal tundra at the northern tip of Alaska.

The Senate's vote on March 16 to allow oil and gas drilling there did not seal the fate of the Arctic National Wildlife Refuge. Legislative hurdles remain. But for the first time in more than 20 years of debate, the president and Congress have signaled that they agree the nation's energy needs justify tapping into the nation's largest wildlife preserve, a place many Americans believe should be untouchable.

Moreover, both proponents and critics of drilling in the preserve see the March 16 vote as the opening wedge in a broader campaign, reflected in pending legislation to open other areas currently off limits to energy exploration, including areas off California's coast.

Oil industry executives have tied exploring the preserve to a larger agenda of opening areas that are closed to exploration. In a speech in Washington in June, Exxon Chief Executive Lee R. Raymond said: "We will need to muster the political will, based on a realistic energy outlook, to allow further development of the energy resources to be found in the United States. This includes those that may be [in] offshore California and Florida, in the Rocky Mountains and in northern Alaska."

Language in the pending energy bill would give the Interior secretary the authority to override California's bipartisan opposition to exploratory drilling off the coast, where, according to some industry estimates, there are at least 1 billion barrels of untapped oil.

"Dog Beach" at Huntington Beach, photograph, Courtesy of historian Judy Gauntt

Loggerhead Turtle hatchlings going to the ocean, US Fish and Wildlife Service

Elk Herd in the Rocky Mountains, © Chuck Bargeron, US Fish and Wildlife Service

Snow Geese Migration, Alaska, , US Fish and Wildlife Service

"If this refuge is not special enough to be saved, then there is no place in the United States that is safe from oil rigs, including the coastlines that for now are protected from offshore drilling," said House Democratic Leader Nancy Pelosi of San Francisco.

The 19-million-acre refuge, which lies between the Beaufort Sea and the 9,000-foot peaks of the Brooks Range, was created in 1960 to protect wildlife. In 1980, Congress and President Carter earmarked the 1.5-million-acre coastal slice of the preserve as a potential site for energy development.

Although drilling in the Alaskan preserve would affect, at most, 8% of the total area, opponents argue that the targeted zone that borders the Beaufort Sea is the biological heart—a marshy tableland that supports millions of migratory birds, polar bears, marine mammals and musk oxen. It is also the summer range for the 150,000-strong Porcupine caribou herd that travels hundreds of miles each year to bear its offspring on the coastal plain.

Caribou Feeding in Alaskan Tundra, © Dean Biggins, US Fish and Wildlife Service

Caribou Herd in Alaska, © Aaron Collins, Togiak National Wildlife Refuge

Grizzly Bears, © Chris Servheen, US Fish and Wildlife Service

Canada Geese and Chicks, US Fish and Wildlife Service photo

Tundra Swan on Nest, US Fish and Wildlife Service photo

Bald Eagle Landing in Nest, © Dave Menke, US Fish and Wildlife Service

Walrus, US Fish and Wildlife Service photo

Polar Bear, © Connie Barclay, US Fish and Wildlife Service

Polar Bear with Two Cubs, © Richard Jackson

Musk Ox Bull, US Fish and Wildlife Service photo

Ringed Seal, Canadian Arctic Profiles photo

Only one exploratory well has been drilled in the refuge, and that was nearly two decades ago. Environmentalists contend that the Arctic contains a six-month supply of oil at most, and will never supply more than 2% of the national demand.

The oil industry, in contrast, has long regarded the preserve as potentially one of the most significant petroleum fields in the nation. But drilling in the Arctic refuge, however successful it proves to be, won't offer a quick fix to the nation's oil needs. Interior Secretary Gale A. Norton has said it will be 10 years before oil from the refuge flows into America's refineries.

An article from the *Los Angeles Times* of May 20 entitled "House Rebuffs Push to Soften Offshore Drilling Ban, Environ-mentalists and industry officials alike see tougher battles ahead over moratorium" indicates the following:

A bipartisan coalition of coastal-state lawmakers beat back an effort in the House on May 19 to weaken the decades-old ban on new oil and gas drilling offshore, but it is bracing for a potentially tougher battle ahead.

The vote was 262 to 157 to defeat an effort to exempt new natural gas drilling from the federal moratorium, which covers most coastal waters except for large parts of the Gulf of Mexico.

Opposition to easing the restrictions came from coastal-state delegations, including those from California, New York, Massachusetts and Florida.

While environmentalists celebrated their victory, they said they were worried about other efforts in Congress to break through the federal moratorium on new offshore drilling.

Bipartisan efforts are underway in the Senate, for example, to offer billions of dollars to entice financially hurting states to opt out of the moratorium.

The bill's sponsors hope to include the measure in a sweeping overhaul of national energy policy now being drafted in the Senate.

The push to ease the restrictions is being driven by a combination of economic and political factors: Lawmakers are under pressure to do something about high energy prices, and energy industry groups and their congressional allies have been emboldened by the Senate vote earlier this year, after years of debate, to open part of Alaska's Arctic National Wildlife Refuge to energy exploration.

Richard A. Charter, a longtime drilling foe who is co-chairman of the National Outer Continental Shelf Coalition, an environmental advocacy group, called the House vote "only the beginning" of efforts in Congress to open coastal areas to drilling.

"This is a good time not to take your favorite beach for granted, because it could disappear while you're there," he said.

The issue has created unusual political alliances, bringing together environmentalists with pro-business Republicans worried about the impact of drilling on beach tourism.

During the May 19 debate, Rep. Randy "Duke" Cunningham (R-San Diego) called drilling a threat to California beaches. "We invite you to come spend your money in California," he said, "but you're not going to come if we start poking holes in the bottom of the Pacific."

Santa Barbara, Courtesy of Susan Jordan, www.californiacoastline.org

California Brown Pelicans, © Dr. Antonio J. Kerreira, California Academy of Science

Oil-Smeared Pelican, © J. de la Torre Ponce, International Bird Rescue Center

Coronado Beach, Courtesy of Susan Jordan, www.californiacoastline.org

An article from the *Times* of June 22 entitled "Senate OKs Offshore Energy Survey, Lawmakers from coastal states fear that the move may lead to overturning the ban on new drilling" states:

Jittery about political fallout from high gasoline prices, the Senate advanced a measure on June 21 that would allow a survey of offshore oil and gas resources, overriding the objections of coastal-state lawmakers.

The critics warned that the survey could prove the first step toward overturning the decades-old moratorium on new drilling in most U.S. coastal waters.

The Senate is likely to reject an effort on June 22 to establish a mandatory program to reduce greenhouse gases blamed for global warming. On June 21, the Senate backed a voluntary plan.

Both issues were intensely debated as the Senate worked toward passage of a sweeping energy bill that President Bush has sought since 2001.

Opponents of the survey of offshore oil and gas resources sought to strip it from the bill; their motion was defeated, 52 to 44.

It is uncertain whether it will survive negotiations with the House, which did not include a similar provision in the energy bill it approved in April. But Rep. Joe Barton (R-Texas), chairman of the House Energy Committee, who will play a key role in writing a final energy bill, said he supported the inventory.

Democratic and Republican lawmakers representing coastal states warned that the inventory could lead to undoing the moratorium on drilling and hurt tourism that is crucial to their states' economies.

"We've been told not to worry, that all they're talking about is an inventory," said Sen. Elizabeth Dole (R-N.C.). "Why would we inventory an area we don't plan to later drill?"

She was among 12 Republicans who voted against the inventory, along with 31 Democrats—including California Sens. Barbara Boxer and Dianne Feinstein—and one independent. Supporting the inventory were 42 Republicans and 10 Democrats.

The moratorium, first put in place in 1982 and extended by presidential directive until 2012, applies to most coastal waters except for a large part of the Gulf of Mexico.

All photos Courtesy of Susan Jordan, www.californiacoastline.org

Long's Cove, Mendocino

Tennessee Point

Point Sur, Big Sur

Cypress Point, Carmel

McWay Canyon

San Simeon Point

Loon Point, Summerland

Camp Pendleton

Sen. Bill Nelson (D-Fla.) called the inventory "the proverbial camel's nose under the tent."

Boxer brought to the Senate floor pictures of pristine coastline in California. "To me, it's almost a moral issue that we protect the beauty that we've been given," she said.

The proposal for a mandatory cap on industrial emissions of greenhouse gases was proposed by Sens. John McCain (R-Ariz.) and Joe Lieberman (D-Conn.). It faced opposition from the coal and oil industries, and a similar proposal failed two years ago.

"The generation to come will rightfully look back and ask why…we left them a global environment in danger," Lieberman said.

In a plea for support for the McCain-Lieberman proposal, Feinstein summarized scientific predictions that temperatures and sea levels would rise over the next century as a result of global warming, focusing on the potential effect in California.

Feinstein said experts had predicted that the state could lose enough mountain snowfall, a crucial source of water in the West, to sustain 16 million people—about as many as now live in the greater Los Angeles region.

If left unchecked, global warming represents "Armageddon to California, Armageddon to the fifth-largest economy on Earth," Feinstein said.

The Senate approved an amendment by Sens. Chuck Hagel (R-Neb.) and Mark Pryor (D-Ark.) that would promote voluntary reductions in greenhouse gases and subsidize energy technologies low in carbon emissions. The vote was 66 to 29, with Feinstein supporting the provision and Boxer opposing it.

Environmental groups called it a toothless proposal that essentially continued the status quo under the Bush administration, which rejected the Kyoto Protocol to reduce greenhouse gases and had continued to oppose mandatory limits on emissions. The U.S. is the only major developed nation other than Australia not to sign the international pact, which would have required U.S. greenhouse gases to be reduced to 7% below 1990 levels by 2012.

All photos Courtesy of Susan Jordan, www.californiacoastline.org

Paul Grimm,
Purple Hues, Private
Collection, Courtesy of
The Irvine Museum

An article from the *Times* of June 23 regarding the proposal by Sens. Joe Lieberman and John McCain to establish a mandatory cap on industrial emissions of greenhouse gases blamed for global warming indicates the measure was rejected by the Senate 38 to 60. It further indicates:

Sen. Barbara Boxer (D-Calif.) had voted for that proposal but withdrew her support this time because of a new provision that could have provided subsidies for nuclear power plants. Her California Democratic colleague, Sen. Dianne Feinstein, supported the McCain-Lieberman proposal.

Republicans criticized a mandatory limit as an unfair burden on the U.S. economy, and noted that many other large emitters of greenhouse gases—including China—had not committed to reducing them. Democrats focused on recent scientific calls for action on global warming and argued that the U.S., the world's largest emitter of greenhouse gases, had a duty to respond.

Lieberman argued that despite the Senate's apparent lack of interest in his proposal, momentum was clearly building among businesses, states and U.S. mayors to deal with global warming in a serious way.

"The science is changing to be clearer and clearer," he said. "What's not changing is the failure of all my colleagues to recognize that science."

The Senate did pass a bipartisan resolution supporting, in principle, a mandatory limit on greenhouse gas emissions. Supporters of stronger action on global warming argued that the "sense of the Senate" resolution, approved on a voice vote, signaled that lawmakers' views on the issue were shifting.

"The Senate is clearly moving beyond a discussion of whether America will begin to deal with the issue, and instead is beginning to focus on what to do about it," said Fred Krupp, president of Environmental Defense.

On June 28 the Senate approved by a bipartisan 85-12 vote a new national energy policy that would provide more than $18 billion in tax breaks to spur more efficient use of resources, greater development of nuclear energy and increased reliance on renewable fuels such as ethanol.

With regard to global warming, an article entitled "Court Backs EPA Decision on Greenhouse Emissions, The ruling is a setback for environmental groups and states seeking to regulate carbon dioxide under the Clean Air Act," which appeared in the *Los Angeles Times* on July 16, 2005 states:

The Environmental Protection Agency was justified in refusing to regulate carbon dioxide, the primary greenhouse gas linked to global warming, as a pollutant under the Clean Air Act, a federal court ruled July 15, in a major legal victory for the Bush administration.

A coalition of 12 states, including California, and numerous environmental groups had argued that the EPA was legally bound to regulate carbon dioxide under the Clean Air Act because global warming was a demonstrable threat to public health and safety.

But in a 2-1 decision, a three-judge panel of the U.S. Circuit Court of Appeals for the District of Columbia concluded that agency officials acted within their authority two years ago when they rejected a petition demanding that they begin regulating carbon exhaust from new cars and trucks.

The decision ensures that the federal government will not force businesses to make reductions in greenhouse gases while President Bush is in office unless it is compelled to do so by Congress. A spokeswoman for California Atty. Gen. Bill Lockyer said the states that brought the suit were considering an appeal to the U.S. Supreme Court.

Bush promised to regulate carbon dioxide emissions from power plants during his first campaign for president, but reversed his position after he took office. He now contends that mandatory measures to cut greenhouse gases would cripple the U.S. economy.

Under Bush, the United States rejected the Kyoto Protocol, an international pact to reduce greenhouse gases. The administration instead has chosen to pursue only voluntary reductions programs to address scientists' concerns that global warming will lead to dangerous increases in temperature and rises in sea level. The United States, the world's largest emitter of carbon dioxide, and Australia, the world's largest coal exporter, are the only two major developed nations to reject the Kyoto Protocol. It requires participating countries to reduce greenhouse gases to about 5% below 1990 levels by 2012.

Though many coastal states and conservation groups joined the legal challenge, several Midwestern states and industry groups entered the case in support of the administration's position, showcasing significant national differences on the proper response to global warming.

The ruling was applauded by attorneys general from Texas and Michigan, who were among the 11 states that filed arguments in favor of the administration's stance, as well as the automobile industry, which also intervened in the case.

However, California officials and other supporters of regulation noted that the court did not offer an opinion on whether the agency had the authority to curtail greenhouse gases if it wanted to, a central issue in the dispute.

Moreover, California officials pointed out that the federal decision did not prevent states from adopting their own measures to combat global warming—a step many states around the country had begun to take.

"This administration is a lost cause," said Sierra Club lawyer David Bookbinder, who helped argue the case on behalf of environmental groups. "But as long as we can preserve California's authority, that's all we care about right now."

California has passed a groundbreaking law that requires auto makers to reduce greenhouse gas emissions from cars and trucks about 30% by 2016. It is being challenged in federal court by most domestic and foreign car companies.

"Today's decision reinforces the critical importance of states retaining their statutory authority under the Clean Air Act to adopt more stringent vehicle emissions standards, including for greenhouse gases, especially where the federal government is unable or unwilling to act," said Bill Becker, executive director of the Assn. of Local Air Pollution Control Officials in Washington.

John Gamble, *Morning Mists, Wild Lilac*, Private Collection, Courtesy of The Irvine Museum

An article entitled "Energy Policy Overhaul Wins Senate Approval, President Bush says he will sign the long-sought bill, which he called 'critically important.' The measure had strong bipartisan support," which appeared in the *Los Angeles Times* on July 30, 2005 indicates the following:

Congress completed work July 29 on President Bush's cherished goal of the first overhaul of national energy policy in more than a decade.

That same day, the Senate approved the bill, 74 to 26; the previous day, the House passed it, 275 to 156.
The 1,745-page measure seeks to increase and diversify domestically produced fuel sources. It provides $11.5 billion in tax breaks to promote conservation and spur production of oil, gas, coal and nuclear energy.

It extends daylight saving time beginning in 2007 and requires greater use of mostly corn-based ethanol in the nation's gasoline supply. In addition, it includes provisions aimed at strengthening electricity grids.

While the bill would do little to provide immediate relief from high gasoline prices, its supporters said it could help keep prices down over the long term.

Even with the measure's passage, energy policy is likely to remain a hot topic on Capitol Hill.

When Congress returns from its August recess, it is expected to take up another long-sought Bush initiative: opening a portion of Alaska's Arctic National Wildlife Refuge to energy exploration.

And a provision of the energy bill that would allow for an offshore survey of oil and gas resources is expected to be followed up with legislation that would allow states to opt out of the long-standing moratorium on new drilling in most U.S. coastal waters.

The energy bill drew the support of 25 Senate Democrats, many from farm states enthusiastic about the provision requiring refiners to nearly double, to 7.5 billion gallons, ethanol that must be added to gasoline.

All but six of the chamber's Republicans supported the bill.

Nineteen Democrats voted against it, including California Sens. Dianne Feinstein and Barbara Boxer.

"What's far worse than what's in the bill is what's not in the bill," said Sen. Charles E. Schumer of New York, another Democrat who opposed the measure. "The effort to conserve is negligible."

Boxer and Feinstein expressed similar complaints.

The energy bill includes a number of recommendations made by a task force established by Bush in 2001 and headed by Vice President Dick Cheney.

The task force's private meetings with energy industry lobbyists later became the subject of a legal fight that reached the Supreme Court, which set aside a judge's order that would have required Cheney to turn over documents showing those he met with.

Energy legislation passed the House in 2003, but fell two votes short of overcoming a filibuster in the Senate, largely because of a dispute over whether producers of a gasoline additive, Methyl Tertiary Butyl Ether (MTBE), blamed for contaminating water supplies should be shielded from suits seeking cleanup money.

That legal protection was dropped from the latest bill, clearing the way for its passage.

Edouard Vysekal, *Late Afternoon Mood*, 1915, Courtesy of Jean and Linda Stern

Thomas Hill, *Deer in a Forest*, Courtesy of Bonhams and Butterfields Auction

In July 2005, Ralph J. Cicerone, chancellor of the University of California, Irvine since 1998, took office as the new president of the prestigious National Academy of Sciences. He was succeeded by Dr. Michael Drake, fifth chancellor of the University of California, Irvine.

Prior to becoming chancellor, Dr. Drake, an eminent physician, served as University of California vice president for Health Affairs, a post he had held since March 2000. In that capacity, he oversaw education and research activities at the University of California's fifteen health sciences schools located on seven campuses, in fields that include medicine, dentistry, nursing, pharmacy, public health, optometry, and veterinary medicine. The university is the largest single producer of trained physicians in the United States. Additionally, as director of the Office of Health Affairs, Dr. Drake oversaw the University of California Special Research Programs, such as the Tobacco-Related Disease Research Program, the Breast Cancer Research and HIV/AIDS Research Programs, the California/Mexico Health Initiative and the newly developed California Health Benefits Review Program.

Dr. Drake is a member of several national scientific and scholarly societies. In 1998, he was elected to the National Academy of Sciences' Institute of Medicine. He is the current president of the Alpha Omega Alpha Honor Medical Society and serves as a trustee of the Association of Academic Health Centers. Additionally, he has received a number of awards for teaching, public service, mentoring, and research, including the School of Medicine's Clinical Teaching Award, the Chancellor's Award for Public Service and the Martin Luther King Jr. Award.

On August 18, my family and I hosted a reception for Chancellor and Mrs. Drake at The Irvine Museum. This was in keeping with the unique association the Irvine family has maintained with UCI over the past fifty years, from my very first appeal to have the university on the Irvine Ranch and the ensuing gift of 1,000 acres of land, through to the present day, a family tradition of unqualified support for excellence in academics that will continue with my sons and their families.

Former UCI Chancellor Ralph Cicerone is now President of the prestigious National Academy of Sciences, photograph, Courtesy of UCI

UCI Chancellor Dr. Michael V. Drake is a member of the National Academy of Sciences' Institute of Medicine, photograph, Courtesy of UCI

FROM LEFT TO RIGHT: Francisco J. Ayala, Ph.D. and Mrs. Hana Ayala; Henry Samueli, Ph.D. and Joan Irvine Smith; F. Sherwood Rowland and Joanne Rowland; Michael V. Drake, M.D. and Mrs. Brenda Drake; Hazem Hikmat Chehabi, M.D. and Salma A. Chehabi; Mr. Donald Bren and Mrs. Brigette Bren at the UCI Medal Dinner 2005, photo by Laurel Hungerford

Jesse Powell, *Bommer Canyon*, Courtesy of the artist

William Wendt, *Shady Canyon*, Private Collection, Courtesy of The Irvine Museum

Donald Bren and U.S. Interior Secretary Gale A. Norton walking through the Irvine Ranch Land Reserve on May 26, 2005. Secretary Norton praised his plans for the reserve, saying "The Irvine Ranch illustrates what cooperative conservation is all about. A conservation-minded corporate citizen is working hand-in-hand with federal and state agencies, the Nature Conservancy, local communities, private citizens and other partners to thoughtfully and purposefully create an environment where both people and wildlife can thrive." Photograph, Courtesy of The Irvine Company

I AM VERY PROUD OF DONALD BREN, not only has he kept the Irvine Ranch intact, but also has done an excellent job in developing the property under the master plan that I convinced The Irvine Company board of directors to establish in April 1960. Furthermore, on May 26, 2005 standing amid giant sycamores in Irvine Regional Park, he pledged $20 million to expand the public's access to 50,000 acres of Irvine ranch land he has set aside as open space. This gift brings to $50 million the amount donated by the Donald Bren Foundation to make sure the land is protected and remains in its rugged state.

Speaking before 200 invited guests, including U.S. Interior Secretary Gale A. Norton, Donald also announced the creation of the Irvine Ranch Land Reserve Trust, a nonprofit that guarantees that the acreage will be permanently preserved. It is his vision "that the reserve will set a new standard for conservation stewardship and recreation that will be understood and appreciated, not just in Orange County, but throughout the United States." He further stated that he believed "we can create a world-renowned park…a place where the people from Orange County can enjoy nature close to their homes."

Secretary Norton praised Donald's plans for the reserve, saying "The Irvine Ranch illustrates what cooperative conservation is all about. A conservation-minded corporate citizen is working hand-in-hand with federal and state agencies, the Nature Conservancy, local communities, private citizens and other partners to thoughtfully and purposefully create an environment where both people and wildlife can thrive."

On August 16, 2005 the Orange County Board of Supervisors approved the settlement of a lawsuit brought by environmentalists seeking to block the Rancho Mission Viejo development of 14,000 homes over the next two decades. Although the number of homes stays the same as in an earlier plan, the project acreage was cut 25%, with 17,000 of the 23,000-acre ranch left protected.

The agreement reduces development in key wildlife habitat areas and increases open space for wildlife. It was signed by the county, Rancho Mission Viejo and environmental groups, including the Endangered Habitats League, the Natural Resources Defense Council, the Sierra Club, Laguna Greenbelt Inc. and the Sea and Sage chapter of the Audubon Society.

The protected 17,000 acres includes 12,000 acres in the San Mateo watershed, which provides drinking water to Camp Pendleton. It also includes acres of coastal sage-scrub that is home to a threatened bird species, the California gnatcatcher, and habitat for the endangered arroyo toad.

An article entitled "U.S. House Votes to Revamp Endangered Species Act, Hundreds of critical habitats would be redesignated. Backers see better protection for landowners and species. An alternative plan dies," by Johanna Neuman and Janet Wilson which appeared in the *Los Angeles Times* on September 30, 2005 indicates the following:

The House of Representatives, in a major overhaul of the Endangered Species Act, voted on September 29 to rescind existing protections on more than 150 million acres and to pay property owners whose land use is restricted because of an endangered species.

An alternative proposal, which would have offered incentives to landowners to help protect species on their property, failed to pass by 10 votes. Both eliminated the "critical habitat" provisions of the Endangered Species Act, with Democrats conceding that the litigation the law spawned had hurt its appeal.

The bill now goes to the Senate, where it may not be considered until next year. Sen. Lincoln Chafee (R-R.I.), a key subcommittee chairman, has said he would not favor eliminating the provisions requiring species protection in their critical habitats.

Southern Right Whale Diving, © Joseph Dougherty, Courtesy of Ecology.org

"If you gut the habitat, you're really gutting the act," he said.

The overhaul was a victory for Rep. Richard W. Pombo (R-Tracy), who has been fighting the Endangered Species Act, first enacted in 1973, since he was elected in 1992.

Pombo said the bill would cancel existing critical habitat protection for hundreds of plants and animals on both public and private land and would require new habitat designations by new teams of "stakeholders," including biologists, landowners, public officials and environmentalists. The U.S. secretary of Interior would have the final say. Up to now, critical habitat determinations have been based on government findings, often in response to lawsuits brought by environmental groups.

Bighorn Ram, © Dean Boggins, US Fish and Wildlife Service

He argued that the new approach would provide better protection for species as well as landowners.

Critics disagreed, saying the bill would threaten the survival of such creatures as the northern spotted owl and right whales, peninsular bighorn sheep, Steller sea lion and desert tortoise.

"Habitat destruction is the main cause of extinction," said Kieran Suckling, head of the Center for Biological Diversity. "This bill sends conservation back to the Stone Age."

"We can do better than the current law, but it's hard to do worse than the legislation being proposed," said House Minority Leader Nancy Pelosi (D-San Francisco),

California Desert Tortoise, © Michael W. Tuma

who noted that the yew tree was a source for the breast-cancer drug Taxol. She also invoked the Bible's book of Psalms to remind members that God created the creatures "and in wisdom we should preserve and protect them."

Critics of the Republican overhaul said it would gut the protection that was already in trouble because of budgetary restraints. "This is a gun to the head, an attack on America's great heritage," said Rep. Sam Farr (D-Carmel), who praised the economic benefits to his district of tourists coming to view "watchable wildlife."

Philip E. Clapp, president of the National Environmental Trust, called the legislation a "sweeping attack" on a major environmental law. "With plummeting poll numbers, an indicted leader, two hurricanes, a war and an exploding budget deficit, House members have now added outright repeal of a major environmental law to their list of political liabilities," he said.

An editorial entitled "An Endangered Law" which appeared in *The New York Times* on October 9, 2005 indicates the following:

Although timber companies, developers and other interests have complained bitterly about the Endangered Species Act ever since Richard Nixon signed it in 1973, the public has broadly supported the law's protections for threatened plants and animals, as well as for the habitat these species need to survive. Attempts to weaken the law have always failed. But the House of Representatives' recent approval of a bill written by Richard Pombo of California has given critics fresh hope that their campaign may yet succeed.

Mr. Pombo advertises his measure as a long-overdue balancing of the interests of private property owners and

those of nature. It is in fact a dreadfully one-sided bill, cynical and fiscally irresponsible in the bargain.

Of the bill's multiple flaws perhaps the most glaring is its fundamental premise, namely that there is something wrong with the law because only a handful of the nearly 1,300 species listed as endangered or threatened have recovered to the point where they can be taken off the list. A species already on the brink of extinction can hardly be expected to rebuild healthy populations overnight, or even in several decades.

A better measure of the act's success is that only a handful of listed species have actually become extinct. An even better measure, one suggesting slow but steady progress, is the government's own finding that two-thirds of the species whose conditions are known are stable and improving.

But the House swallowed Mr. Pombo's dubious line of thinking, and that made it easy to sign on to a host of damaging provisions. One would give political appointees authority to make important scientific judgments now reserved for wildlife biologists. Another would weaken the current system of designating critical habitat by making it voluntary, not mandatory.

Among the worst provisions—one that Mr. Pombo personally regards as the most important— is a requirement that government reimburse property owners who lose money by forgoing commercial use of land required to protect the species. This would, in a stroke, destroy years of painstaking effort by past administrations to reconcile the claims of private landowners with the public's larger interest in protecting endangered animals.

The Clinton administration's answer was to negotiate "habitat conservation plans": individual deals under which landowners would agree to leave some property untouched in return for the right to develop the rest. Mr. Pombo's solution, by contrast, would ask nothing of the developer and everything of the taxpayer, who in effect would be required to pay people for obeying the law. The net result could be an open-ended entitlement program that could bankrupt federal conservation efforts already starved for money.

So far there is no companion bill in the Senate, although various right-wing enthusiasts—among them James Inhofe of Oklahoma and Michael Crapo of Idaho—are making noises about writing one. The Senate should resist. Even its most ardent proponents agree that the Endangered Species Act would benefit from careful revision—to simplify its cumbersome procedures, to make it less vulnerable to litigation and to provide positive incentives to landowners to preserve habitat. But the Pombo approach is wholly misguided.

Bennett Bradbury, *Driving to East*, Private Collection, Courtesy of The Irvine Museum

ON SUNDAY AUGUST 27, 2005, Hurricane Katrina hit the coasts of Louisiana, Mississippi, and Alabama on the Gulf of Mexico causing one of the worst natural disasters in the history of this country. Although the strongest winds struck elsewhere, a day later breached levees flooded the city of New Orleans. A commentary entitled "They Saw It Coming" by Mark Fischetti which appeared in *The New York Times* on September 2, 2005 states:

The deaths caused by Hurricane Katrina are heart-rending. The suffering of survivors is wrenching. Property destruction is shocking. But perhaps the most agonizing part is that much of what happened in New Orleans this week might have been avoided.

Watching the TV images of the storm approaching the Mississippi Delta on Sunday, I was sick to my stomach. Not only because I knew the hell it could unleash (I wrote an article for Scientific American in 2001 that described the very situation that was unfolding) but because I knew that a large-scale engineering plan called Coast 2050—developed in 1998 by scientists, Army engineers, metro-politan planners and Louisiana officials - might have helped save the city, but had gone unrealized.

The debate over New Orleans's vulnerability to hurri-canes has raged for a century. By the late 1990's, scientists at Louisiana State University and the University of New Orleans had perfected computer models showing exactly how a sea surge would overwhelm the levee system, and had recommended a set of solutions. The Army Corps of Engineers, which built the levees, had proposed different projects.

Yet some scientists reflexively disregarded practical considerations pointed out by the Army engineers; more often, the engineers scoffed at scientific studies indicating that the basic facts of geology and hydrology meant that significant design changes were needed. Meanwhile, local politicians lobbied Congress for financing for myriad spe-cial interest groups, from oil companies to oyster farmers. Congress did not hear a unified voice, making it easier to turn a deaf ear.

Fed up with the splintered efforts, Len Bahr, then the head of the Louisiana Governor's Office of Coastal Activities, somehow dragged all the parties to one table in 1998 and got them to agree on a coordinated solution: Coast 2050. Completing every recommended project over a decade or more would have cost an estimated $14 billion, so Louisiana turned to the federal government. While this may seem an astronomical sum, it isn't in terms of large public works; in 2000 Congress began a $7 billion engineering program to refresh the dying Florida Everglades. But Congress had other priorities, Louisiana politicians had other priorities, and the magic moment of consensus was lost.

Thus, in true American fashion, we ignored an inevitable problem until disaster focused our attention. Fortunately, as we rebuild New Orleans, we can protect it—by engineering solutions that work with nature, not against it.

The conceit that we can control the natural world is what made New Orleans vulnerable. For more than a century the Army Corps, with Congress's blessing, leveed the Mississippi River to prevent its annual floods, so that farms and industries could expand along its banks. Those same floods, however, had dumped huge amounts of sediment and freshwater across the Mississippi Delta, rebuilding each year what gulf tides and storms had worn away and holding back infusions of saltwater that kill marsh vegetation. These vast delta wetlands created a lush, hardy buffer that could absorb sea surges and weaken high winds.

The flooding at the river's mouth also sent great volumes of sediment west and east into the Gulf of Mexico, to a string of barrier islands that cut down surges and waves, compensating for regular ocean erosion. Stopping the Mississippi's floods starved the wetlands and the islands; both are rapidly disintegrating, leaving the city naked against the sea.

What can we do to restore these natural protections? Although the parties that devised Coast 2050, and other independent scientists and engineers who have floated rival plans, may disagree on details, they do concur on several major initiatives that would shield New Orleans, reconstitute the delta and, as a side benefit, improve ports and shipping lanes for the oil and natural gas industries in the Gulf of Mexico.

Cut several channels in the levees on the Mississippi River's southern bank (the side that doesn't abut the city) and secure them with powerful floodgates that could be opened at certain times of the year to allow sediment and freshwater to flow down into the delta, re-establishing it.

Build a new navigation channel from the Gulf into the Mississippi, about 40 miles south of New Orleans, so ships don't have to enter the river at its three southernmost tips 30 miles further away. For decades the corps has dredged shipping channels along those final miles to keep them navigable, creating underwater chutes that propel river sediment out into the deep ocean. The dredging

could then be stopped, the river mouth would fill in naturally, and sediment would again spill to the barrier islands, lengthening and widening them. Some planners also propose a modern port at the new access point that would replace those along the river that are too shallow to handle the huge new ships now being built worldwide.

Erect huge seagates across the pair of narrow straits that connect the eastern edge of Lake Pontchartrain, which lies north of the city, to the gulf. Now, any hurricane that blows in from the south will push a wall of water through these straits into the huge lake, which in turn will threaten to overflow into the city. That is what has filled the bowl that is New Orleans this week. But seagates at the straits can stop the wall of water from flowing in. The Netherlands has built similar gates to hold back the turbulent North Sea and they work splendidly.

Finally, and most obviously, raise, extend and strengthen the city's existing but aging levees, canal walls and pumping systems that worked so poorly in recent days.

It's hard to say how much of this work could have been completed by today had Coast 2050 become a reality. Certainly, the delta wetlands and barrier islands would not have rebounded substantially yet. But undoubtedly progress would have been made that would have spared someone's life, someone's home, some jazz club or gumbo joint, some city district, some part of the region's unique culture that the entire country revels in. And we would have been well on our way to a long-term solution. For there is one thing we know for sure: hurricanes will howl through the Mississippi Delta again.

Mark Fischetti is a contributing editor to Scientific American *magazine.*

Jessie Arms Botke, *Pelicans and Gulls*, Private Collection, Courtesy of The Irvine Museum

An editorial entitled "Redemption in the Bayou" which appeared in *The New York Times* on September 5, 2005 indicates the following:

People keep making bets against nature, and in the end nature usually wins. This is as true in the rainforests of Central America, where clear-cutting has led to disastrous floods, as it is in the steep California canyons, where people have no business building houses.

It is no less true of the Mississippi Delta and its biggest city, New Orleans, whose heart-rending tragedy is partly traceable to years of federal efforts to manage the Mississippi River in ways that it did not intend to be managed, keeping it from going where it wanted to go and thus weakening the natural defenses that might have spared the city the worst.

Amends can be made. Before Congress is a $14 billion plan to restore the vanishing wetlands and barrier islands off the Louisiana coast that in times past would have served as a buffer against the storm. The House has approved a modest $1.9 billion down payment on this plan, but it needs a push from President Bush and the Senate majority leader, Bill Frist, to ensure Senate approval. The plan would involve some delicate re-engineering of the natural system and is not without risk. Still, it could provide a measure of redemption for years of environmental carelessness for which Congress itself is largely responsible.

The problem, in a nutshell, is this: the Louisiana coast, its protective fringe of barrier islands and coastal marshlands, is disappearing. Over the last 75 years, 1.9 million acres have vanished. Every year, another 25 square miles, an area roughly the size of Manhattan, sinks quietly beneath the waves. In some places, the coastline has receded 15 miles from where it was in the 1920's.

The soil in the delta compacts and sinks naturally. Historically, however, the Mississippi replenished the loss with sediment gathered from its many tributaries and then deposited like clockwork in the delta with the spring floods. Or so it did until 1927, when Congress ordered the Army Corps of Engineers to find ways to control the floods so as to make the river safe for farming, homes and commerce.

As it would later do in the Everglades (with equally disastrous results for the Florida ecosystem), the corps then proceeded to construct a network of dams, levees and canals throughout the river basin. The upstream dams reduced the river's sediment load well below historical levels; the sediment that remained, while considerable, was then routed away from the Louisiana coast by a system of levees and navigation channels. The effect of all these engineering changes was to hurry the river along and, at its mouth, propel its contents deep into the Gulf of Mexico, as if shot from a cannon, bypassing the coastal marshes and barrier islands that most needed its nourishment.

Add to all this the demands of a growing population, plus thousands of miles of pipes and canals dug through the marsh for a booming oil and gas industry, and the result was inevitable: a shrunken, degraded and essentially defenseless landscape.

More is at stake, of course, than the landscape. These may be the hardest-working wetlands in America. They support one of the country's largest fisheries; almost every fish caught in the Gulf of Mexico spends part of its life in the Louisiana marsh. They are the wintering ground or refueling stop for most of the migratory waterfowl that travel the Mississippi flyway. And as everyone who has bought gasoline in the last few days knows by now, they are vital to the production, refining and transportation of much of the nation's oil. Indeed, the oil and gas industry has as much incentive as anyone to protect the marshes from further erosion. Most of its equipment cannot survive in open water.

The conditions are thus ripe for a major effort to restore the Louisiana coast. The program before Congress was hatched by the state's politicians and in its universities and drafted by the Army Corps of Engineers. It is supported by both industry and advocacy groups like the National Audubon Society and Environmental Defense, which helped with its design. It would start small, with three or four carefully calibrated pilot programs to divert water flow to the marshes, then go from there.

What it has always required is the enthusiastic support of Washington's political leaders. It is hard to believe that the events of the last week haven't caught their attention.

Jessie Arms Botke, *Mural from the East Wall of the Oaks Hotel, Ojai,* (detail) The Irvine Museum

Jessie Arms Botke, *Egrets*, Private Collection, Courtesy of
The Irvine Museum

Jessie Arms Botke, *Flamingos*, The Irvine Museum

Amédée Joullin, *Marsh at Sunset*, The Irvine Museum

An article entitled "Lawmakers Say Katrina Is Wake-Up Call to Repair State's Levee System" which appeared in the *Los Angeles Times* on September 7, 2005 indicates the following:

Saying New Orleans' catastrophic levee breaks were "a wake-up call for Californians," Sen. Dianne Feinstein and Rep. Richard Pombo urged the Army Corps of Engineers Tuesday to turn its attention to the deteriorating condition of the state's vast levee system.

"For years, we have known about the severe flood risks we face, but like Louisiana have been unable to find the funding to do the necessary repairs," they wrote Lt. Gen. Carl A. Strock.

Feinstein, a Democrat, and Pombo, a Republican from Tracy, cited predictions by UC Davis geologist Jeffrey Mount.

In a recently published paper, Mount predicted a 2-in-3 chance that a major earthquake or storm would cause widespread levee failures in the Sacramento-San Joaquin Delta in the next 50 years.

"A major breach in these levees could imperil hundreds of thousands of people and endanger most of the state's water supply," Feinstein said in a statement. "As we have seen in New Orleans, it would be a dramatic mistake to further delay the repairs that are necessary to protect communities from the ravages of floodwaters."

Last year's federal legislation reauthorizing CalFed, a state-federal delta improvement program, included $90 million for delta levee repairs.

But the funds have yet to be appropriated.

And that sum represents just a fraction of what would likely be needed.

"The $90 million is a very small beginning of what we're going to be able to do to reduce the damage and risks in the delta," said Brandon Muncy, chief of the water resources branch in the corps' Sacramento district.

The Feinstein-Pombo letter raises the possibility of a joint federal and state study to explore long-term levee repairs.

"Clearly, over the long term, much more needs to be done. At this point, we don't even have a good handle on the different options, and what they might cost," wrote Feinstein and Pombo, who is chairman of the House Resources Committee.

Muncy said a pending water appropriations bill in Congress includes $900,000 that could help fund a comprehensive review of levee risks and repairs.

The state has started such a study, which the corps would be willing to join, Muncy said.

The delta, roughly the size of Orange County, is a maze of canals, wetlands and drained farmlands that lie below sea level.

It is a major source of drinking water for more than 20 million Californians.

It is crisscrossed by more than 1,000 miles of earthen levees, most built by farmers on top of deep layers of decomposing peat.

A major breach in the system not only would cause extensive flooding but also would send salt water rushing toward the massive pumps that divert irrigation and drinking water to the Central Valley and Southern California, officials said.

"In addition to the human tragedies, a massive flood could devastate our agricultural economy the same way Katrina decimated one of America's largest and most important sources of energy," Pombo said.

On February 24, 2006, Governor Arnold Schwarzenegger announced a state of emergency to deal with the state's crumbling system of levees in Northern California. He pointed to the Hurricane Katrina disaster as a reason for concern in our state. The Associated Press reported "Two Central Valley levees broke on April 4, forcing evacuations from residential neighborhoods and inundating farmland amid soaking rains." On April 10, the governor declared his second state of emergency as a result of winter rainstorms that threatened to overburden California's system of reservoirs, levees, aqueducts and rivers.

Kevin Courter, *Wetlands Embers*, (Sacramento Delta), Courtesy of the artist

Kim Fancher Lordier, *Swollen Fields, Butte County*, Courtesy of the artist

An article entitled "Severe Hurricanes Increasing, Study Finds" by Juliet Eilperin which appeared in *The Washington Post* on September 16, 2005 states:

A new study concludes that rising sea temperatures have been accompanied by a significant global increase in the most destructive hurricanes, adding fuel to an international debate over whether global warming contributed to the devastation wrought by Hurricane Katrina.

The study, published today in the journal *Science*, is the second in six weeks to draw this conclusion, but other climatologists dispute the findings and argue that a recent spate of severe storms reflects nothing more than normal weather variability.

Katrina's destructiveness has given a sharp new edge to the ongoing debate over whether the United States should do more to curb greenhouse gas emissions linked to global warming. Domestic and European critics have pointed to Katrina as a reason to take action, while skeptics say climate activists are capitalizing on a national disaster to further their own agenda.

According to data gathered by researchers at the School of Earth and Atmospheric Sciences at Georgia Tech and the National Center for Atmospheric Research, the number of major Category 4 and 5 hurricanes worldwide has nearly doubled over the past 35 years, even though the total number of hurricanes, including weaker ones, has dropped since the 1990s. Katrina was a Category 4 storm when it made landfall.

Using satellite data, the four researchers found that the average number of Category 4 and 5 hurricanes—those with winds of 131 mph or higher—rose from 10 a year in the 1970s to 18 a year since 1990. Average tropical sea surface temperatures have increased as much as 1 degree Fahrenheit during the same period, after remaining stable between 1900 and the mid-1960s.

Georgia Tech atmospheric scientist Judith A. Curry—co-author of the study with colleagues Peter J. Webster and Hai-Ru Chang, and NCAR's Greg J. Holland—said in an interview that their survey, coupled with computer models and scientists' understanding of how hurricanes work, has given the researchers a better sense of how rising sea temperatures are linked to more-intense storms.

"There is increasing confidence, as the result of our study, that there's some level of greenhouse warming in what we're seeing," Curry said. "Is it the whole story? We don't know."

Higher ocean temperatures result in more water vapor in the air, which, combined with certain wind patterns, helps power stronger hurricanes, Webster said. Small increases in sea temperature, he added, can "exponentially provide more and more fuel for the hurricanes."

William Ritschel, *The Glorious Pacific*, a.k.a. *Our Dream Coast of Monterey*, Private Collection, Courtesy of The Irvine Museum

Satellite Photo of Hurricane Katrina Hitting New Orleans, NASA photo

Other studies and computer models also have pointed to an increase in storm intensity: Massachusetts Institute of Technology atmospheric scientist Kerry A. Emanuel wrote last month in the journal *Nature* that the duration and maximum wind speeds of storms in the North Atlantic and North Pacific have increased about 50 percent since the mid-1970s. The storms' growing violence stemmed in part from higher ocean temperatures, he concluded.

Some researchers, however, question the connection with more severe hurricanes and cyclones. Gerry Bell, the lead seasonal hurricane forecaster at the National Oceanic and Atmospheric Administration, said the rise in strong hurricanes reflects a natural weather pattern spanning several decades. Hurricanes in the Atlantic Ocean were more powerful in the 1950s and '60s, weakened in the 1970s, '80s and early '90s, and have strengthened again since 1995.

"It's not linked to global warming or anything like that," Bell said. "This is normal climate variability. It's just that this trend lasts for decades."

Florida State University meteorology and oceanography professor James O'Brien, who writes for the online free-market journal Tech Central Station, said his survey of government data on Atlantic storms between 1850 and 2005 shows that "there's no indication of an increase in intensity."

But both Emanuel and Gavin Schmidt, a climatologist at NASA's Goddard Institute for Space Studies, said today's Science paper is important because it examines worldwide hurricane patterns.

"If you look at it on the global basis, it makes that signal of global warming easier to see," Schmidt said. "You have to be extremely conservative—with a small 'c'—to think [rising sea temperatures and stronger hurricanes] are not related."

And some hurricane experts who previously have questioned the influence of global warming now say the evidence is mounting that it has contributed to recent intense tropical storms.

Florida International University researcher Hugh Willoughby, who headed NOAA's hurricane research division between 1995 and 2003, said the recent two hurricane studies are "very persuasive" and helped move him "toward the climate corner" of the debate.

"It's really hard to find any holes in this, and I'm the kind of person who's inclined to look for holes," he said of the new study in Science. The arguments against the connection between climate change and more intense storms, he added, are "looking weaker and weaker as time goes by."

Katrina reanimated a transatlantic argument over global warming policy as critics of the Bush administration have seized on it to promote mandatory limits on greenhouse gas emissions.

"The American president shuts his eyes to the economic and human damage that the failure to protect the climate inflicts on his country and the world through natural catastrophes like Katrina," Germany's environmental minister, Jurgen Trittin, wrote in an opinion piece printed Aug. 30 in the *Frankfurter Rundschau* newspaper.

Arguing that the science of global warming remains uncertain, President Bush in 2001 disavowed the Kyoto treaty that sets mandatory targets for reducing greenhouse gas emissions, and he has pursued policies calling for more research and voluntary efforts to limit emissions.

William Ritschel, *Moonbeams*, Private Collection, Courtesy of The Irvine Museum

Adelie Penguins Diving Off Iceberg, © Richard Jackson

During an interview on *Meet the Press* on September 18, 2005, Tim Russert asked President Bill Clinton if the he thought "global warming, influences, effects, creates hurricanes or the severity of them?" In response Mr. Clinton stated that "Whenever there's a marked change in the weather, it has ramifications across a whole wide range of activities." Although he did not think anyone could tell you that Katrina was caused by global warming, he said the following:

What we do know, what the evidence shows, is that there is an increase in the number and severity of bad weather events all across the globe. We know that.

Keep in mind, in the last decade, 12 blocks of ice the size of the state of Rhode Island have broken off the South Pole. We now have some significant evidence that the North Pole and, even worse, the ice cap on Greenland, the massive island of Greenland, are thinning. This is going to lift the water levels. It's going to complicate the rebuilding of New Orleans. If we don't reverse it within 50 years, we'll lose 50 feet of Manhattan Island. That—one of these little countries I'm working with, the Maldives, the water will just roll over it; we'll never recover it.

So I think that we just need to face the fact that the climate is changing. and this is one of the consequences.

Bennett Bradbury, *West by Southwest*, Private Collection, Courtesy of The Irvine Museum

An article entitled "Report Says Global Warming Could Spark Conflict" by Reuters which appeared in *The New York Times* on September 22, 2005 indicates:

Rising world temperatures could cause a significant increase in disease across Asia and Pacific Island nations, leading to conflict and leaving hundreds of millions of people displaced, a new report said on September 22.

Global warming by the year 2100 could also lead to more droughts, floods and typhoons, and increase the incidence of malaria, dengue fever and cholera, the report into the health impact of rising temperatures found.

Compiled by the Australian Medical Association (AMA) and the Australian Conservation Foundation, the country's leading medical and environment groups, the study predicts average temperatures will rise by between 1 degree Celsius (1.8 Fahrenheit) and 6 degrees by 2100.

"We're not just talking about a longer summer or a shorter ski season," AMA president Mukesh Haikerwal told reporters.

"Climate change will damage our health. People will get sick as a direct result. People will die in larger numbers as our earth, our world, our home, heats up."

Internationally, higher world temperatures would increase the incidence of violent storms and droughts, and could lead to crop failures which could cause political and social upheaval.

"As stresses increase there is likely to be a shift toward authoritarian governments," the report said.

"At the worst case, large scale state failure and major conflict may generate hundreds of millions of displaced people in the Asia-Pacific region, a widespread collapse of law, and numerous abuses of human rights."

The report said crop yields were likely to increase in parts of Northern Asia, but would decrease in countries in Southern Asia, where the incidence of floods, droughts, forest fires and tropical cyclones would all increase.

The report, titled Climate Change Health Impacts in Australia; Effects of Dramatic CO2 Emission Reductions, calls on governments to cut carbon dioxide emissions to limit the impact of global warming.

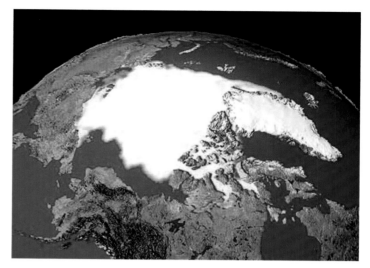

Satellite View of Arctic Ice Cap, March, 1979

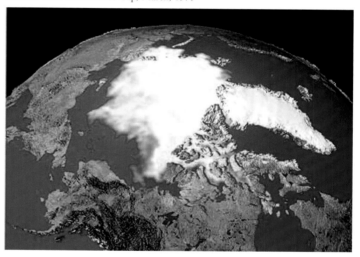

Satellite View of Arctic Ice Cap, March, 2003, showing ice loss

Both photos: Courtesy of National Oceanic and Atmospheric Administration

Jack Wilkinson Smith, *Dog Head's Point, La Jolla*, Private Collection, Courtesy of The Irvine Museum

Emil J. Kosa Jr., *Silver Luster*, Private Collection, Courtesy of The Irvine Museum

Bennett Bradbury, *Moon in Pisces*, Private Collection, Courtesy of The Irvine Museum

In less than a month from the time Hurricane Katrina devastated New Orleans, Hurricane Rita ripped across the Florida Keys and slammed into the Texas and Louisiana coasts on the Gulf of Mexico. A commentary entitled "Managing the next disaster" by Roger A. Pielke Jr. and Daniel Sarewitz which appeared in the *Los Angeles Times* on September 23, 2005 states the following:

Like a bad horror movie in which the villain keeps coming back, Hurricane Rita, the 18th storm of the season, is spinning toward an inevitable rendezvous with the Gulf Coast. We've already seen more death and destruction than the last 35 hurricane seasons combined. And many people, including some European and U.S. politicians, are hoping that the carnage—represented most poignantly by the destruction in New Orleans—will help bring this country to its senses on dealing with global warming.

But understanding what this hurricane season is really telling us about why we're so vulnerable to climate-related catastrophes means facing up to an unavoidable fact: Efforts to slow global warming will have no discernible effect on hurricanes for the foreseeable future. Reducing greenhouse gas emissions and adequately preparing for future disasters are essentially separate problems.

Reducing emissions is a crucial environmental, economic and geopolitical goal. But if we are concerned about hurricanes, then we need to manage what is within our control on the ground, not what is proving to be beyond our control in the atmosphere.

The truth is, the number and scale of disasters worldwide has been rising rapidly in recent decades because of changes in society, not global warming. In the case of hurricanes, the continuing development and urbanization of coastal regions around the world accounts for all of the increases in economic and human losses that we have experienced.

Even if tomorrow we could somehow magically put an end to global warming, the frequency and magnitude of climate-related disasters would continue to rise unabated into the indefinite future as more people inhabit vulnerable locations around the world. Our research suggests that for every $1 of future hurricane damage that scientists expect in 2050 related to climate change, we should expect an additional $22 to $60 in damage resulting from putting more people and property in harm's way.

None of this means that we should not pursue reducing greenhouse gas emissions, or that mitigating climate change is a bad idea. But we simply cannot expect to control the climate's behavior through energy policies aimed at lowering greenhouse gas emissions.

The current international policy framework for reducing greenhouse gas emissions—the Kyoto Protocol—is far too modest to have any meaningful effect on the behavior of the climate system. And even the modest agreements reached under Kyoto are failing.

For example, the European Environment Agency reported in 2004 that 11 of the 15 European Union signatories to Kyoto "are heading toward overshooting their emission targets, some by a substantial margin." And the other four are meeting their targets only because of non-repeatable circumstances, such as Britain's long-term move away from coal-based energy generation. To make matters much worse, most of the growth in emissions in coming decades will occur in rapidly industrializing nations such as China and India, which are exempt from Kyoto targets.

To make matters still worse, because of the way that greenhouse gases behave in the atmosphere, even emissions reductions far more rapid and radical than those mandated under Kyoto would have little or no effect on the behavior of the climate for decades. As James Hurrell, a scientist at the U.S. National Center for Atmospheric Research, testified before the U.S. Senate in July, "It should be recognized that [emissions reductions actions] taken now mainly have benefits 50 years and beyond now."

The implications are clear: More storms like Katrina are inevitable. And the effects of future Katrinas and Ritas will be determined not by our efforts to manage changes in the climate but by the decisions we make now about where and how to build and rebuild in vulnerable locations.

Do we have the will to pay the upfront economic and political costs of strict building-code enforcement and prudent land-use restrictions? Will we have the imagination to build resilience into the local economy, rewarding companies that find ways to preserve jobs after a disaster and contribute to a faster recovery? Do we have the decency to counter the market forces that cause poor people to live in the most vulnerable areas?

As we learn the lessons of this terrible hurricane season, the answers we give to these kinds of questions will create the conditions that determine the effects of future hurricanes. We are, that is, about to begin the process of managing the next disaster. What kind of disaster do we want it to be?

ROGER A. PIELKE JR. is director of the Center for Science and Technology Policy Research at the University of Colorado, Boulder. DANIEL SAREWITZ is director of the Consortium for Science, Policy and Outcomes at Arizona State University.

An article entitled "In a Melting Trend, Less Arctic Ice to Go Around" by Andrew C. Revkin which appeared in *The New York Times* on September 29, 2005 indicates the following:

The floating cap of sea ice on the Arctic Ocean shrank this summer to what is probably its smallest size in at least a century of record keeping, continuing a trend toward less summer ice, a team of climate experts reported yesterday.

That shift is hard to explain without attributing it in part to human-caused global warming, the team's members and other experts on the region said.

The change also appears to be headed toward becoming self-sustaining: the increased open water absorbs solar energy that would otherwise be reflected back into space by bright white ice, said Ted A. Scambos, a scientist at the National Snow and Ice Data Center in Boulder, Colo., which compiled the data along with the National Aeronautics and Space Administration.

"Feedbacks in the system are starting to take hold," Dr. Scambos said.

The data was released on the center's Web site, www.nsidc.org.

The findings are consistent with recent computer simulations showing that a buildup of smokestack and tailpipe emissions of greenhouse gases could lead to a profoundly transformed Arctic later this century, when much of the once ice-locked ocean would routinely become open water in summers.

Expanding areas of open water in the summer could be a boon to whales and cod stocks, and the ice retreat could create summertime shipping shortcuts between the Atlantic and the Pacific.

But a host of troubles lie ahead as well. One of the most important consequences of Arctic warming will be increased flows of meltwater and icebergs from glaciers and ice sheets, and thus an accelerated rise in sea levels, threatening coastal areas. The loss of sea ice could also hurt both polar bears and Eskimo seal hunters.

The Arctic ice cap always grows in the winter and shrinks in the summer. The average minimum area from 1979, when precise satellite mapping began, until 2000 was 2.69 million square miles, similar in size to the contiguous area of the United States. The new summer low, measured on Sept. 19, was 20 percent below that.
Before 1979, scientists estimated the size of the ice cap based on reports from ships and airplanes.

The difference between the average ice area and the area that persisted this summer was about 500,000 square miles, an area about twice the size of Texas, the scientists said.

This summer was the fourth in a row with the ice cap areas sharply below the long-term average, said Mark C. Serreze, a senior scientist at the snow and ice center and a professor at the University of Colorado, Boulder.

Dr. Scambos said the consecutive reductions in the ice cap "make it pretty certain a long-term decline is under way."

A natural cycle in the polar atmosphere called the Arctic oscillation, which contributed to the reduction in Arctic ice in the past, did not appear to be a factor in the past several years, Dr. Serreze said.

He said the role of accumulating greenhouse gas emissions had become increasingly apparent with rising air and sea temperatures. Still, many scientists say it is not yet possible to determine what portion of Arctic change is being caused by rising levels of carbon dioxide and other emissions from human sources and how much is just climate's usual wiggles.

Dr. Serreze and other scientists said that more variability could lie ahead and that the area of sea ice could actually increase some years. But the scientists have found few hints that other factors, like more Arctic cloudiness in a warming world, will reverse the trend.

"With all that dark open water, you start to see an increase in Arctic Ocean heat storage," Dr. Serreze said. "Come autumn and winter that makes it a lot harder to grow ice, and the next spring you're left with less and thinner ice. And it's easier to lose even more the next year."

The result, he said, is that the Arctic is "becoming a profoundly different place than we grew up thinking about."

Other experts on Arctic ice and climate disagreed on details. For example, Ignatius G. Rigor at the University of Washington said the change was probably linked to a mix of factors, including influences of the atmospheric cycle.

But he agreed with Dr. Serreze that the influence from greenhouse gases had to be involved.

"The global warming idea has to be a good part of the story," Dr. Rigor said. "I think we have a different climate state in the Arctic now. All of these feedbacks are starting to kick in and really snuffing the ice out by the end of summer."

Bennett Bradbury, *Glacier Bay*, Private Collection, Courtesy of The Irvine Museum

Killer Whale Pod in Prince William Sound, Alaska, Hosking photo, US Fish and Wildlife Service

An article entitled "Plan for Coastal Drilling Emerges, Pointing to Katrina's hit to fuel supplies, some in Congress seek to diversify by loosening a ban covering areas such as offshore California," which appeared in the *Los Angeles Times* on October 3, 2005 states the following:

Citing hurricane damage to the oil and gas industry in the Gulf of Mexico, key lawmakers are trying to relax a decades-old federal ban on new drilling off California and the Atlantic Seaboard and to encourage energy prospecting in the Rocky Mountains.

Congressional proposals also aim to waive some air pollution rules to encourage expansion of oil refineries and to authorize oil drilling beneath Alaska's Arctic National Wildlife Refuge.

"Mother Nature proved just how vulnerable America is to supply disruption," said House Resources Committee Chairman Richard W. Pombo (R-Tracy). "We must do more to increase and to diversify domestic supplies."

The legislation, likely to be voted on soon in the House, comes as oil- and natural-gas-dependent manufacturers have urged Congress to reopen the "85% of all federally controlled coastal waters [that] are currently off-limits to energy production."

"The nation is paying the price for concentrating so much of its energy infrastructure in a small geographic area," wrote the American Gas Assn. and more than 100 other petrochemical companies and manufacturers. "As we go about the business of recovering from Hurricane Katrina…Congress has an opportunity to reduce the nation's vulnerability to sudden energy shocks by expanding our sources and supplies of energy—especially in our coastal waters."

Yet opponents in Congress point to the 191,000 barrels of oil that have gushed into the gulf from ruptured pipelines and hurricane-battered oil facilities as a reminder of the difficult-to-contain disasters that can accompany offshore production. Spills brought about by Hurricane Katrina amount to about 80% of the oil that despoiled Alaskan waters when the Exxon Valdez tanker ran aground in 1989.

Some lawmakers, including Sen. Mel Martinez (R-Fla.), worry that hasty federal policy changes could expose fragile coastal environments, fisheries and beach-dependent tourism to disaster risks. "It keeps getting more threatening all the time," Martinez said.

Others are incensed at what they consider raw opportunism to exploit high gas prices and hurricane damage.

"This just looks like the oil and gas industry are shamelessly using the tragedy of Katrina and Rita to try and push their special-interest agenda through Congress," said Rep. Lois Capps, a Santa Barbara Democrat who represents a district that experienced a devastating oil platform blowout in 1969. "We need to address our energy needs, but we don't need to jeopardize our environment and economy to do it, and we shouldn't use a national tragedy as cover for bad policy."

States control oil and gas drilling within three miles of their coastlines. Federal waters begin where states' end and extend 200 miles off the coast. The federal Minerals Management Service regulates drilling there.

For more than two decades, bipartisan lawmaker coalitions have resisted challenges to Congress' ban on new offshore oil and gas leasing on the West and East Coasts and much of Florida.

Congress first passed the moratorium in 1981 to cover waters off Northern California and Massachusetts in response to then-Interior Secretary James G. Watt's plan to open the entire outer continental shelf to new oil and gas development. The ban was expanded in 1985 to include most of the rest of U.S. coastal waters and has been renewed every year since.

Last week, the House Resources Committee approved Pombo's legislation to let states "opt out" of the moratorium in exchange for a larger federal share of the royalties. Supporters say that would be especially helpful to Louisiana, which already allows offshore drilling and needs billions of dollars for post-hurricane reconstruction.

The California Ocean Protection Council, speaking on behalf of Gov. Arnold Schwarzenegger, requested in a letter to Pombo that "future congressional legislation exclude any language that threatens this moratorium that has been protecting our shores more than two decades."

Florida Gov. Jeb Bush seems to favor much of Pombo's bill, especially a portion that would allow Florida to adopt a permanent no-drilling buffer zone within 125 miles of the state's coastline.

Florida's members of Congress, many of them Republican, have been a critical component of the bipartisan annual renewal of the congressional moratorium on new offshore drilling, joining a number of Democratic lawmakers from California and New England.

Drilling foes worry that lawmakers who favor energy development have devised a divide-and-conquer strategy to unravel the moratorium coalition.

William Wendt, *The Silent Summer Sea*, 1915, Private Collection, Courtesy of The Irvine Museum

Guy Rose, *Point Lobos*, The James Irvine Swinden Family Collection

Guy Rose, *Carmel Shore*,
Private Collection, Courtesy of
The Irvine Museum

Alson S. Clark, *Yacht Race, San Diego*,
Private Collection, Courtesy of
The Irvine Museum

Eunice MacLellan, *Pelicans*, Private Collection, Courtesy of The Irvine Museum

Barse Miller, *Bird Rock, Laguna*, Private Collection, Courtesy of The Irvine Museum

"If, all of a sudden, the Florida delegation drops out of the equation, it makes the rest of the country much more vulnerable," said Lisa Speer, senior policy analyst for the Natural Resources Defense Council. "The coastal states that don't want to see [outer continental shelf] development really need to hang together, or they're going to hang separately."

The House Resources Committee's top Democrat, Nick J. Rahall II of West Virginia, agreed that Pombo's bill endangered the moratorium. "States that opt not to drill but are adjacent to those that choose to drill will be vulnerable to the consequences of their neighbors' actions," he said.

Pombo's 168-page bill has scores of proposals to encourage energy development—and remove obstacles—both on- and offshore.

It would allow new exemptions from environmental rules, shorten public comment periods and limit lawsuits over leasing decisions made by the Bureau of Land Management.

The bill proposes to kick-start the dormant shale oil industry by greatly discounting the royalty rate that companies would pay in the first 15 years of production. Shale oil is found in deposits in western Colorado.

It would allow a waiver of the National Historic Preservation Act on private lands, so that oil and gas development could proceed without assessing potential effects on Native American burial or archeological sites.

House Energy and Commerce Committee Chairman Joe Barton (R-Texas) has advanced his own package of incentives to build new refineries, including certain waivers to the Clean Air Act.

A surprise amendment to Pombo's legislation, by Rep. John E. Peterson (R-Pa.), would lift the offshore moratorium nationwide for companies seeking to drill for natural gas.

The industry scored a victory this year with a requirement in the energy bill signed by President Bush for an inventory of offshore oil and natural gas resources.

The array of new energy proposals in the House may face strong resistance in the Senate, according to energy industry lobbyists.

On October 19, the Senate Energy and Natural Resources Committee voted to include a measure authorizing opening a portion of Alaska's Arctic National Wildlife Refuge to oil and gas drilling in a budget bill. Supporters of the drilling initiative hoped that by attaching it to another bill they would avoid the filibusters that have blocked energy exploration in the refuge. However, the measure which has been strongly opposed by environmentalists in a decades old dispute still could be stalled by an unrelated issue: a fight over federal spending cuts to pay for rebuilding the gulf coast.

An article entitled "House Drops Bid to Open Refuge, Coasts to Drilling, GOP concessions to moderates may ease passage of a budget bill. But a mining measure could mean the sale of Western public lands," which appeared in the *Los Angeles Times* on November 10, 2005 indicates:

In a rare victory for environmentalists in the House of Representatives, Republican leaders November 9, night abandoned a measure to open the Arctic National Wildlife Refuge to oil and gas drilling.

They also jettisoned a provision to relax a long-standing ban on new energy exploration off the Atlantic and Pacific coasts. However, they apparently left in the budget package a mining law provision that would permit the sale of public lands in the West for private development.

A rewrite of the Mining Law of 1872, it has drawn less attention than the Arctic drilling provision but could have a farther-reaching effect on public lands. Drafted by the House Resources Committee, the measure would allow the sale of potentially millions of federal acres, including national park and forest holdings.

Such a law could mean "the biggest privatization of federal land in the last 100 years," said John Leshy, who was the Interior Department's top lawyer in the 1990s and is now a professor at UC Hastings College of the Law. "Nothing like this has ever surfaced before."

The proposal would lift an 11-year-old congressional moratorium on mining patents, letting mining companies buy federal land with valuable mineral deposits for nominal fees. It would also make it easier to purchase federal land for nonmining uses, dropping the requirement that the acreage contain a valuable mineral discovery. And it would let the public stake new claims next to existing mining claims and buy that adjacent land for economic development unrelated to mining.

The concessions to moderate Republicans on drilling in the Arctic National Wildlife Refuge grew out of the party leadership's effort to salvage the broad spending-cut bill to which the oil-drilling and mining measures were attached.

A spokesman for House Resources Committee Chairman Richard W. Pombo (R-Tracy) said Pombo was inclined to oppose the bill "if it does nothing to increase domestic energy supplies and lower prices."

Wednesday's developments do not kill the prospect of drilling in the Arctic National Wildlife Refuge. The Senate included drilling in its spending-cut bill, passed last week, and the provision could survive an eventual House-Senate compromise.

'We win for now," Sierra Club lobbyist Melinda Pierce said. "It's going to come back, no doubt. For them,

Jessie Arms Botke, *Wild Geese in a Birchwood*, Private Collection, Courtesy of The Irvine Museum

they win once and it's all over. For us, we win, and we just live to fight another day."

In a letter to GOP leadership this week, about two dozen moderate House Republicans said they would not vote for a bill that contained the provision on Arctic drilling, which would threaten a "national treasure." The spending-cut bill is "far too important to jeopardize" by including it, they wrote.

A spokesman for REP America, a group of Republican activists who support environmental conservation, praised the legislators who opposed the provision.

"We are particularly pleased that many of them have already warned leadership against trying to put Arctic drilling back into the legislation in conference with the Senate," said David Jenkins, government affairs director of REP America.

Although the mining proposal from the House Resources Committee excludes national parks and wilderness areas, a caveat recognizes "valid existing rights"—which critics say means that pockets of national park land could be sold. There are 903 mining claims, averaging 20 acres each, in the park system nationwide that predate the parks' establishment. Most of those claims are in California, including 432 in the Mojave National Preserve and 286 in Death Valley National Park.

Paul Grimm, *The Desert in All It's Glory*, Private Collection, Courtesy of The Irvine Museum

Helen Forbes, *Furnace Creek Wash*, The Irvine Museum

The House Resources Committee's top Democrat, Rep. Nick J. Rahall II of West Virginia, asked the House Rules Committee to drop Pombo's language from the budget measure, saying it would "turn what is supposed to be a mining law into a general real estate sales program for Western public lands."

Sen. Dianne Feinstein (D-Calif.) cited the possibility of land sales in a letter November 9, that called for Pombo to withdraw the proposal. "I am deeply concerned that you propose to sell off significant parts of America's treasured public lands, including areas in national parks, wilderness areas and national forests, as part of the House budget reconciliation bill," Feinstein wrote.

Paul Grimm, *Celestial Architecture*, 1932, The Russell and Carol Penniman Collection

The $50 billion budget bill squeaked by the House of Representatives late on November 17. Although the oil drilling provisions off the nation's coasts and in the Artic National Wildlife Refuge had been stripped from the measure, the provision allowing the government to sell off millions of acres of public land remained until December 13 when Congressman Jim Gibbons (R-NV) announced that he was officially dropping the controversial mining legislation that he and House Resources Committee Chairman Richard Pombo inserted into the budget reconcilliation bill. On December 18, the second day of a rare weekend session, House and Senate leaders approved spending cuts to domestic social programs and agreed to attach a proposal by Senator Ted Stevens (R-Alaska) allowing drilling in the Arctic National Wildlife Refuge to a bill funding the U.S. military. The following morning the Senate met and passed the military spending bill, which included the drilling measure. On December 21, after a contentious debate, the Senate stripped the measure to open the Arctic National Wildlife Refuge to oil drilling from the defense spending bill before passing it.

Albert R. Valentien, *Howell's Lewisia*. Named after Captain Meriwether Lewis of the Lewis and Clark Expedition, this species of *Lewisia* is a fascinating plant found clinging by a very stout taproot to rocky outcrops, wedged into crevices, and in cracks on canyon walls. The flowers with their pink and white candy-striping are charming and showy against the backdrop of a basal rosette of dark green leaves. This beautiful plant is a threatened species in northern California.
–M. Dykens, Courtesy of the San Diego Natural History Museum

John Hilton, *Dawn of the Primrose*, Private Collection, Courtesy of The Irvine Museum

Edgar Payne, *The Surf at Laguna*, Private Collection, Courtesy of The Irvine Museum

An article entitled "Saving the Environment, One Quarterly Earnings Report at a Time" by Claudia H. Deutsch which appeared in *The New York Times* on November 22, 2005 states the following:

A few years ago, scientists at Cargill Inc. learned how to make rigid, transparent plastics from corn sugars. There was just one problem: they cost a lot more than the oil-based plastics they would replace.

But that was before the price of oil shot up and companies came under pressure from consumers and investors to find economically sound ways to adopt "green" packaging and other environmentally friendly products and processes. This year, Wal-Mart, Wild Oats Market and many other retailers, as well as food suppliers like Del Monte and Newman's Own Organics, all embraced corn-based packaging for fresh produce.

Sales at NatureWorks, the Cargill subsidiary that makes the plastic, grew 200 percent in the first half of this year over the period last year. "The early adopters were more influenced by environmental concerns than costs," said Kathleen M. Bader, chairwoman of NatureWorks. "But now we're competitive with petrochemicals, too."

Cargill is one of several companies profiting from the concerns -- of shareholders, communities and consumers -- about global warming, leaking landfills and other potential environmental hazards. Huge companies like General Electric and Chevron now have separate businesses to market what they are calling environment-friendly products.

And new companies and university projects appear each day. Cornell University's College of Engineering, for one, expects to have a commercial process for using bacteria to recoup energy from wastewater treatment within three years.

"There are a lot of creative types looking for the next big thing," said Bob Sheppard, deputy director for corporate programs at Clean Air-Cool Planet, a nonprofit environmental education organization. "Well, these days, environment is it."

It is impossible to quantify the size of the environmental industry. Many of the newer companies are privately held. And many "green" products—more efficient power generators, say, or biodegradable plastics—are parts of other industries.

But investors are clearly funneling ever more money into green technologies. Last year, the California Public Employees Retirement System, or Calpers, said it would invest $200 million in what it called the "burgeoning environmental technology sector." This year, 27 members of the Investor Network on Climate Risk promised to invest $1 billion in companies with green products.

Paul Grimm, *Cloud Study*, Private Collection, Courtesy of The Irvine Museum

"The environmental industry is about to take off, as more investors realize that they can reap returns from cleaner technologies," said Dan Bakal, director of electric power programs at Ceres, a coalition of investors and environmental organizations that runs the investor network. Entrepreneurs say the change is palpable. Northern Biodiesel, a small company in Ontario, N.Y., recently got financing for a plant to turn cooking oils and agricultural waste into diesel fuel. "Banks used to dismiss me as a tree-hugger when I tried to borrow for an environmentally advantaged product," said Bob Bechtold, the company's vice president.

In one sense, the current environmental boon is a replay of the 1970's, when regulations spawned a profitable industry to sell electrostatic precipitators, air scrubbers and other air cleaning devices. New federal rules limiting diesel emissions are spurring sales now, too.

But this time, other powerful motivators are at play. The United States did not sign the Kyoto treaty regulating greenhouse gases, but companies feel pressure to reduce gas emissions to do business comfortably in countries that did sign. Moreover, "people know that regulations will come here, too," said Judi Greenwald, director of innovative solutions at the Pew Center on Global Climate Change, a nonprofit research group.

Even without rules to force their hands, companies are responding to societal pressures to act in an environmentally aware manner. "Investors believe it is simply not acceptable to be environmentally irresponsible," said Abby Joseph Cohen, chief United States investment strategist at Goldman Sachs, which just announced its own comprehensive environmental policy.

William Wendt, *New Corn*, 1920, Private Collection, Courtesy of The Irvine Museum

William Wendt, *When Fields Lie Fallow*, 1931, Private Collection, Courtesy of The Irvine Museum

Another article by Ms. Deutsch entitled "Goldman to Encourage Solutions to Environmental Issues" which appeared in the *Times* on November 22 further states:

As of today, the Goldman Sachs Group is officially green.

The big investment banking firm has announced a policy that details how its 24,000 employees—be they bankers, analysts or purchasing agents—should promote activities that protect forests and guard against climate change.

Goldman, which counts paper companies, refiners and car companies among its clients, stopped short of saying it would reject clients with questionable environmental practices. Instead, it said it would "encourage" clients in "environmentally sensitive" areas to use "appropriate safeguards."

It committed itself to investing $1 billion in projects that generate energy from sources other than oil and gas. And it strongly endorsed stringent federal regulation. Goldman said it would establish a Center for Environmental Markets to study how the free-market system can solve environmental problems. Henry M. Paulson Jr., Goldman's chairman, said the center—which will cost $5 million to set up and will be operating within six months—would help shape public policy.

"We don't have a lot more time to deal with climate change," said Mr. Paulson, an outspoken environmentalist who is also chairman of the Nature Conservancy. "We need the right balance between regulation and market-based approaches."

Goldman is not the first financial services firm to adopt an environmental policy. In response to a 2003 campaign led by the Rainforest Action Network, more than 30 commercial banks signed the Equator Principles, which call for them to assess environmental risk before financing a project.

This year, J. P. Morgan Chase set out strict environmental dos and don'ts for each part of its business. And Merrill Lynch now includes environmental issues in the due-diligence checklist its bankers use before underwriting stock issues.

But environmental advocates say that the Goldman policy keeps going where others leave off.

"They are spending intellectual capital and energy on finding market-based solutions to environmental problems," said Michelle Chan-Fishel, program manager for green investments at Friends of the Earth.

Jonathan Lash, president of the World Resources Institute, was more blunt. "Goldman has given us things to measure them by," he said.

The Goldman policy is certainly the most explicit. J. P. Morgan calls for public policy that "establishes certainty for investors and allows significant investments in greenhouse gas emissions." Goldman endorses a "strong policy framework that creates long-term value for greenhouse gas emissions reductions and consistently supports and incentivizes the development of new technologies that lead to a less carbon-intensive economy."

Goldman, which already owns wind farms and power plants and recently contributed land for a protected forest in Chile, has also set such quantifiable goals as reducing greenhouse gases from its office buildings by 7 percent by 2012 and developing uniform green building standards for all its properties.

It has pledged to increase its activities in carbon trading, which grants companies the right to emit set quantities of carbon dioxide and sell the rights if they emit less than allowed. It has also committed its equity research department to do extensive environmental studies.

"Goldman is expressly acknowledging the financial risks of investing in a company with weak environmental performance," said Michael J. Brune, executive director for Rainforest Action Network.

Goldman said it would insist that its own buildings be constructed of certified wood—wood that was not illegally logged—and would "prefer" to finance forestry projects that have been similarly certified. Similarly, it said, it would "prefer" to finance projects in which the local communities were consulted.

"It is not our job to dictate to clients what they must do," Mr. Paulson said. "We won't finance projects that damage the environment, but we won't refuse to underwrite your security or handle your merger because you are not as environmentally strong as we would like."

Environmentalists wince at some of the omissions, but concede that no bank has pledged to shun clients on environmental grounds.

"We can't expect unilateral disarmament," said Eileen Claussen, president of the Pew Center on Global Climate Change. "If Goldman works to get stricter federal policies, and if it disseminates its research to clients and policy makers, the issue may be rendered moot anyway."

An article entitled "Preserving The Great Bear Rainforest" from a Nature Conservancy marketing piece produced in July, 2005 indicates the following:

On the mainland coast of British Columbia, opposite the northern end of Vancouver Island, north to the Alaskan border, the Great Bear Rainforest stretches for more than 250 miles. Like the rainforests of the nearby

Kermode or Spirit Bear in its habitat, ©Ron Thiele

island archipelago of the Haida Gwaii, the Great Bear Rainforest has been peopled by First Nations for more than 10,000 years. It is a land of history and legend, mist and waterfalls—an ancient rainforest laced with rivers and cut with fjords.

Today, it is a threatened wilderness of giant cedars and Sitka spruce, a haven for salmon, wolves and ghostly white bears. At 21 million acres, the Great Bear Rainforest is part of the largest coastal temperate rainforest left on Earth.

Born of a complex interaction between oceans, mountains, forests and rain, coastal temperate rainforests have always been rare and are considered more threatened than tropical rainforests. Scientists estimate that nearly 60 percent of our planet's original coastal temperate rainforests have been destroyed by logging and development. The Great Bear Rainforest represents fully one-quarter of what remains.

Decisions are being made right now that will determine the future of the Great Bear Rainforest. Following the conclusion of negotiations with First Nations, historic land use agreements in British Columbia could ultimately provide full protection for as much as 30 percent of the Great Bear Rainforest's 21 million acres and establish a process to develop ecosystem-based management practices for the entire rainforest.

These unprecedented consensus agreements between the Great Bear Rainforest's main constituencies—local, regional and provincial governments, industry, communities, workers, small businesses and environmental organizations— offer a rare opportunity to create a new global model of lasting conservation in the region.

The Great Bear Rainforest is valuable both economically and as an irreplaceable ecosystem. The development

Kermode or Spirit Bear, ©Ron Thiele

of dedicated public and private funding sources that support conservation as well as community stability of First Nations is key to ensuring the successful implementation of the consensus agreements.

An ecosystem of global importance, the Great Bear Rainforest is also a vital natural and economic resource for British Columbia. To be successful, conservation here must be more than a wilderness agreement. To be successful in this complicated political, economic and environmental landscape, conservation in the Great Bear Rainforest must not only protect the ecosystem, but also respect indigenous cultures, and strengthen the economies of local communities that depend upon the rainforest for their way of life.

Paul Grimm, *Cloud Study with Oak Trees*, Private Collection, Courtesy of The Irvine Museum

An article entitled "State Looks to Lead Pollution Fight, Breaking with the Bush administration, officials from California propose new fees on greenhouse gas emitters and call for use of alternative fuels," which appeared in the *Los Angeles Times* on December 6, 2005, states the following:

MONTREAL—As diplomats from 189 nations meet here this week to discuss the world's response to global warming, California is unveiling a new set of initiatives to control greenhouse gases that would put it in the forefront of a burgeoning campaign by state and local officials to begin regulating the root causes of climate change.

California's action plan—which includes proposals to cap greenhouse gases and force industries to report emissions of carbon dioxide—sharply contradicts the official position of the Bush administration, which has dispatched a delegation to Montreal to reiterate its message that the United States opposes all mandatory limits on heat-trapping gases because, the administration says, such limits would hamstring the economy.

"We can't control what the national government is doing, but we can control what California is doing," said Alan Lloyd, the state's environmental protection secretary, who is leading a California delegation in Montreal. "We are big enough to effect change, and we are still looked upon as a leader on these issues due to our decades of work on air pollution."

Indeed, the United Nations' Montreal conference on climate change — the largest gathering of its kind since most of the world's nations adopted the Kyoto Protocol to reduce greenhouse gases in 1997 — is attracting state and local officials eager to share the message that some parts of the U.S. have begun to address global warming.

Among the state officials scheduled to attend the Montreal talks are Vermont Gov. James H. Douglas, Connecticut's top environmental official, Gina McCarthy, and Los Angeles Deputy Mayor Nancy Sutley. New Mexico Gov. Bill Richardson, who has pledged to reduce his state's emissions, plans to address the conference by videophone.

Seattle Mayor Greg Nickels, who has organized a grass-roots campaign to tackle global warming that has enlisted the mayors of more than 180 cities, including Los Angeles, plans to meet today with a coalition of international mayors.

He said the goal of his campaign is not just to place pressure on the federal government but to show U.S. politicians that global warming can be good politics. Opinion polls in many states, including California, have shown strong public support for action against global warming, Nickels said.

"Our ultimate goal is to make it impossible for the federal government to continue ignoring this issue," Nickels said. "We want to show that it can be done without devastating impacts on our local economies ... and we want to show other politicians that this is safe."

Earlier this year, Gov. Arnold Schwarzenegger pledged to slash California's greenhouse gas emissions by 80% by 2050. Schwarzenegger has yet to endorse the ideas that state officials have outlined to reach his target, however, making it uncertain whether the proposals set to be officially released December 8, will translate into real policies.

At the same time that Schwarzenegger was promising to lead the world's fight against global warming at a U.N. event in San Francisco earlier this year, his top energy advisor was working on an equally ambitious proposal to build an electricity highway that would move coal-fired power from Wyoming to California.

Coal-burning power plants are the leading emitters of carbon dioxide, which is the most abundant greenhouse gas.

California already receives more than a fifth of its electricity from out-of-state coal-fired power plants in the West. The state's demand for coal power has grown in the last decade despite a state law requiring investment in renewable energy, environmental groups said in a report released last week.

In response to criticism that the Schwarzenegger administration appeared to be contradicting itself, state officials have acknowledged that better coordination—and stricter electricity-buying policies—will be needed to achieve the governor's goals.

The California Public Utilities Commission and Energy Commission have adopted policies that make it more difficult for in-state utilities to purchase new coal power, citing coal's contribution to global warming. The policies have led to legal threats from officials and power plant operators in other Western states, who contend that California is violating constitutional provisions on interstate commerce.

Environmentalists said it remained to be seen whether California's ambitious proposals — which include a new fee on major greenhouse gas emitters to fund state global warming programs, and a renewed push to produce cleaner-burning ethanol as an alternative to gasoline — would survive what is expected to be a fierce lobbying push by oil refiners and other affected industries.

A highly publicized plan by eight Northeastern states to set a ceiling on greenhouse gas emissions from power plants was recently thrown into turmoil when Massachusetts Gov. Mitt Romney raised concerns about electricity costs and asked that the proposal be delayed. The seven other states, which include New York and New Jersey, may move ahead without Massachusetts.

Nonetheless, environmentalists said they were encouraged by what they see as a sincere effort by Schwarzenegger administration officials to examine potential solutions. "This is where Arnold starts to think about his legacy," said V. John White, a veteran Sacramento air quality lobbyist. "There may be some people around him that will try to change his mind, and we know Exxon and the coal companies will try, but there are enough businesses supporting this that it will happen."

Representatives of Calpine, a private power company that generates most of its electricity from natural gas, are in Montreal as part of the state's delegation.

Silicon Valley venture capitalist John Doerr, who has provided seed capital for several of the state's biggest technology companies, has also expressed support for the state proposal to enact a "cap and trade" system that would not only place a ceiling on emissions, but also allow businesses that cut more than their share of the gases to profit by selling "pollution credits" to businesses that do not cut emissions enough.

California's proposals are part of a groundswell of global warming initiatives by state and city leaders nationwide, who are promising to boost clean energy sources and cut greenhouse gases in response to what they see as a failure to act by officials in Washington.

Although the Bush administration contends that setting a ceiling on greenhouse gases would damage the economy, some states disagree, arguing that taking early action to reduce dependence on fossil fuels and conserve energy will save money.

To hammer home the point, California and the Brazilian state of Sao Paulo released a study this week showing that their clean-energy programs over the last two decades, which had the unintended effect of reducing greenhouse gases, have helped to improve their economies. "In the absence of any congressional leadership and action by the Bush administration, we have decided to set climate change goals on our own," said New Mexico Gov. Richardson in an interview with *The Times* last week.

Their stands sharply differ from the position of President Bush, who rejected the Kyoto Protocol, the current international treaty to combat climate change. Bush's delegation is telling other nations that the U.S., the world's largest emitter of greenhouse gases, does not want to negotiate a new global warming treaty.

The Kyoto Protocol requires developed nations to reduce greenhouse gases by roughly 5% below 1990 levels. The United States and Australia are the only large developed nations that have not ratified the treaty. It expires in 2012, and most of the world's nations this week are discussing whether to set a deadline of 2008, 2009 or 2010 for agreement on the treaty's successor.

An article entitled "U.S. Stands Alone at U.N. Climate Conference, Bush administration opposes mandatory limits on emissions. Other nations agree to negotiate a new treaty," which appeared in the *Los Angeles Times* on December 10 indicates the following:

MONTREAL — With the conspicuous exception of the United States, most countries were poised December 9, to agree to negotiate a new treaty to combat global warming before the obligations of the current pact, the 1997 Kyoto Protocol, expire in 2012.

The U.S., which opposes mandatory limits on greenhouse gas emissions, found itself isolated during the United Nations Climate Change Conference here. At one point early that day, the top U.S. negotiator, Harlan L. Watson, walked out of talks on reopening dialogue under a separate 1992 U.N. treaty, which he regarded as an attempt to renew discussions on limiting emissions.

Late that night, Watson indicated that he would agree to an amended version of the dialogue proposal.

The aim of the conference was to lay the groundwork for a future global warming treaty. Delegates believed they would accomplish that before week's end despite U.S. efforts to block even nonbinding discussions of future climate change actions under existing U.N. agreements.

However, as the largest international conference on global warming since Kyoto drew to a close, the gulf between what nations are willing to do and what scientists say is needed to avoid environmental disaster remained as wide as ever.

In addition to the United States, several of the world's top greenhouse gas emitters, including China and India, continued to oppose capping their emissions, even as they agreed to continue allowing discussions to move forward, raising questions about how the U.N. process would achieve progress.

"There is an atmosphere of goodwill and understanding of the seriousness of the problem," said Margaret Beckett, the British environment secretary, describing this week's talks. "Nevertheless, that will not be enough to address climate change with the seriousness with which it needs to be addressed."

The Kyoto Protocol, which requires wealthy countries to reduce emissions of heat-trapping gases that scientists have linked to rising temperatures, was the first effort to craft an international response to global warming. But it has been troubled since it was signed in 1997, and has failed to curtail the rise in greenhouse gas emissions from the burning of fossil fuels such as coal and oil.

The U.N.'s International Energy Agency estimates that greenhouse gas levels two years ago were 25% above 1990 levels. The Kyoto pact, which was finally ratified by enough nations to take effect this year, aims to reduce emissions from wealthy countries to roughly 5% below 1990 levels.

Representatives of some of the more than 150 nations at the Montreal talks said they hoped to deliver the message that they remain committed to reducing emissions through international accords—even if the U.S., the world's largest emitter of greenhouse gases, refuses to take part.

A decision to continue pursuing firm limits on greenhouse gas emissions, expected before the two-week conference ends early this morning, would represent a political setback for President Bush, who rejected the Kyoto pact, saying it would harm the U.S. economy, and who dispatched a delegation to Montreal that adamantly refused to discuss new caps.

Often pointed criticism of the U.S. stance, including a comment by Canadian Prime Minister Paul Martin that the U.S. should remember "there is such a thing as a global conscience," intensified Friday with a hastily arranged speech by former President Clinton.

"I think it's crazy for us to play games with our children's future," Clinton said in a folksy speech before delegates that prompted a spirited ovation.

Alluding to Bush's rationale for the Iraq war as a bulwark against terrorism, Clinton said, "There is nowhere in the world where it is more important to apply the principle of precaution than in fighting climate change." Arguments that capping greenhouse gases would harm the economy, were "flat wrong," he said.

Despite the promises of delegates to continue working on negotiations to address global warming, it was clear that persuading many of the world's major economies to commit to steeper greenhouse gas reductions would be difficult.

Mandatory limits are opposed by China, which is on a pace to surpass the U.S. as the top greenhouse gas emitter within the next quarter of a century.

Brazil and India, among the top 10 emitters, also rejected putting caps on their releases of heat-trapping gases, continuing to argue that wealthy nations should act first because they caused global warming by burning fossil fuels for 150 years.

More than 150 nations, including the U.S., pledged to avoid "dangerous" human interference with the world's climate systems at the 1992 Earth Summit in Rio de Janeiro.

Although the countries that signed the 1992 treaty did not define what dangerous climate impacts meant, many scientists have estimated that greenhouse gases would have to be radically cut over the next 50 years to prevent temperatures from rising several more degrees, which could melt polar icecaps and raise sea levels around the world.

Concentrations of carbon dioxide in the air reached 380 parts per million this year, which experts believe is the highest level in 650,000 years. Two centuries ago, they were 280 ppm. Some scientists have argued that levels need to be capped at 450 ppm to avoid the most damaging consequences of global warming, but no one thinks that will happen under current U.N. plans.

"You can't go on with agreements to limit emissions based on what the politics of the moment will bear," said Michael Oppenheimer, a scientist at Princeton University who was co-author of a paper in the journal Science that examined the greenhouse gas reductions needed to avoid dangerous climate impacts. "At some point, you have to inject scientific reality."

Nonetheless, environmentalists December 9, applauded the nations for moving forward on new global warming negotiations without the U.S., arguing that it proved the majority of the world is serious about the problem.

Activists were particularly optimistic about a proposal by Papua New Guinea and Costa Rica, approved that day by the U.N., that would allow developing nations to receive financial compensation from richer countries for agreeing to preserve their rain forests. The U.S. initially opposed the proposal before agreeing to support it.

Deforestation accounted for as much as a fifth of the greenhouse gas emissions during the last decade, according to estimates by a worldwide panel of scientists. Environmentalists believe that by preserving forests over the next two decades, nations can slow global warming while waiting for better technologies to reduce emissions from fossil fuels—and also give developing nations a financial reason to get more involved in talks.

"The Bush administration appears to be throwing a hissy fit, but it's not having the intended effect," said Alden Meyer, a lobbyist for the Union of Concerned Scientists. "It is only serving to stiffen the resolve of the rest of the world to move forward."

Paul Grimm, *Cloud Study*, Private Collection, Courtesy of The Irvine Museum

Paul Grimm, *Cloud Study*, Private Collection, Courtesy of The Irvine Museum

Paul Grimm, *Cloud Study*, Private Collection, Courtesy of The Irvine Museum

An article entitled "Nations Agree to New Talks on Greenhouse Gas Limits" from the *Los Angeles Times* of December 11, 2005 states:

MONTREAL — Despite the Bush administration's resistance, nearly every industrialized nation agreed December 10, to talks aimed at producing a new set of binding limits on greenhouse gas emissions that would take effect in 2012.

The Bush administration, which rejects the emissions cutbacks required by the current Kyoto Protocol, accepted a second, weaker conference decision, agreeing to join an exploratory global dialogue on steps to combat climate change. However, that agreement ruled out "negotiations leading to new commitments."

The divergent tracks did little to close the gap between Washington and Kyoto supporters, which include Europe and Japan. But environmentalists welcomed the plan.

"The Kyoto Protocol is alive and kicking," said Jennifer Morgan of the World Wide Fund for Nature.

An article entitled "Gas Emissions Reached High in U.S. in '04" by Andrew C. Revkin which appeared in *The New York Times* on December 21 indicates the following:

American emissions of greenhouse gases linked to global warming reached an all-time high in 2004, rising 2 percent from the year before, the Energy Department said, nearly double the average annual rate measured since 1990.

The department's Energy Information Administration, in a report issued December 19, also raised earlier government estimates of emissions for 2003, pushing that year past 2000 into second place.

No estimates were available for United States emissions in 2005, although energy experts say increased economic growth this year is likely to make it another record-setter.

The increases in 2003 and 2004 followed a brief dip in emissions in 2001 and 2002. Government officials said that decline reflected a slowdown in the economy, the departure of some manufacturing industries overseas, and emissions cuts in other industries.

Less than two weeks ago, Bush administration officials at climate-treaty talks in Montreal repeatedly cited the short-lived drop in emissions after 2000 as evidence that President Bush's climate policy, using voluntary measures to slow growth in the gas releases, was working.

In its report, the energy agency said that while overall emissions were growing, the rate of growth continued to slow relative to economic growth, and so remained on the track set by Mr. Bush.

Yesterday, Lord Rees, the president of the Royal Society, an independent British scientific academy similar to the National Academies in the United States, said the new American data showed that all industrialized countries needed to intensify efforts to cut emissions. He noted that Britain's emissions had also risen in the last two years.

Lord Rees said that the two countries and the other members of the Group of 8 biggest industrialized nations clearly had to do more to live up to a statement they issued at a summit meeting in Scotland in July, in which they resolved to act with "urgency" to reduce greenhouse gas emissions.

"We should not underestimate the challenge of achieving economic growth whilst reducing emissions, and the United States is not the only country that is struggling to do this," Lord Rees said in a statement. "But it seems unlikely that the present U.S. strategy of only setting emissions targets relative to economic growth, reducing so-called greenhouse gas intensity, will be enough."

Carbon dioxide, the main greenhouse gas generated by humans, remains an unavoidable byproduct of burning the fossil fuels that underpin modern life. Other powerful greenhouse gases include methane, which leaks from landfills and gas pipelines, and nitrous oxide, released mainly from fertilizer use in large-scale farms.

The gases are measured collectively in tons of carbon dioxide by converting the heat-trapping capacity of each gas into the amount of carbon dioxide that would have the same warming effect.

By this measure, total American emissions of the six major greenhouse gases in 2004 added up to the equivalent of 7.1 billion metric tons of carbon dioxide, up 2 percent from 6.98 billion metric tons in 2003. Emissions in 2000 were 6.97 billion tons, the agency said.

The energy agency's greenhouse gas report is online at HYPERLINK "http://eia.doe.gov/environment.html".

Paul Grimm, *Cloud Study, Passing Storm*, Private Collection, Courtesy of The Irvine Museum

Franz Bischoff, *Alpen Glow, High Sierra*, The Irvine Museum

H. H. Betts, *Half Dome, Yosemite*, Private Collection, Courtesy of The Irvine Museum

An article entitled "Yosemite Fauna on the Up and Up, Scientists studying the park's wildlife wonder if global warming is the primary factor spurring a migration of species to higher elevations," which appeared in the *Times* on December 5 indicates:

Scientists studying Yosemite National Park's bountiful wildlife have found that several animal species have moved to higher altitudes, an uphill migration possibly spawned by the grinding effects of global warming on one of the nation's most protected wildernesses.

The team of scientists from UC Berkeley's Museum of Vertebrate Zoology made the discovery while retracing the pioneering research of biologist Joseph Grinnell, who about 90 years ago cataloged the park's menagerie of mammals, birds and reptiles.

Over the last three summers, the Berkeley researchers revisited many of the spots Grinnell plotted in his landmark study. What they found was an environment that has seen a remarkable shift in many of its wild inhabitants.

Several species of small rodents that once lived in Yosemite's lower elevations have now moved higher up the Sierra's gnarled granite frontier, in some cases shifting their range by as much as 3,000 feet.

Yosemite Valley, meanwhile, has seen a 50% turnover in the types of birds it harbors, and several species have spread to far higher elevations than ever seen in Grinnell's day.

Part of the shift, the scientists said, could be explained by natural variations that species see over time, or by alterations in flora and the forest canopy caused by a century's worth of aggressive wildfire suppression. The California pocket mouse, for instance, may have expanded its range nearly 3,000 feet higher because the chaparral it inhabits has spread farther up the park's western slope.

But in high-elevation spots where fire is not a factor, several small mammal species have fled farther uphill, prompting researchers to suspect that larger forces are at work.

"I didn't go into this expecting any shifts, to be quite honest," said James Patton, the museum's curator and an emeritus professor of integrative biology. "But the changes are clear-cut. The data record is very strong. While the interpretation as to what these changes mean remains open to discussion, they are consistent with expectations of global warming."

Several other studies have documented similar environmental changes in the Sierra, among them disappearing glaciers and alterations in the growth pattern of trees in some types of soil.

Over the last century alone, Patton said, the average annual temperature in Yosemite has risen by 9 degrees Fahrenheit.

While most scientists now accept that global warming has been afoot for more than a century, the exact cause of that trend remains a topic of intense debate in academic and political circles.

Many researchers have implicated man-made greenhouse gases as a principal cause, but doubters contend the rise may be a natural climate shift after centuries of cooler weather.

The findings in Yosemite are "consistent with a lot of work with biological species that are adjusting to an increase in temperature," said William O'Keefe, chief executive at the Marshall Institute, a Washington, D.C.-based think tank.

"But you have to say: So what?" said O'Keefe. "Over the centuries there have been periods when it's been colder, others when it's warmer. And species adjust. The fact is science can't distinguish between natural variability and the human contribution."

Patton and his colleagues have skirted that larger debate while conducting their painstaking review of Grinnell's original work.

Over the course of nearly four decades, Grinnell visited more than 700 locations around California to establish a bedrock database detailing the state's fauna.

Along with a team of young scientists, Grinnell compiled 2,000 photographs and 13,000 pages of field notes. In all, they examined more than 20,000 specimens.

Grinnell, founding director of the Museum of Vertebrate Zoology, visited Yosemite over several years in the mid-1910s. The volume his team compiled, "Animal Life in Yosemite," remains "the seminal description" of the park's fauna, said Leslie Chow, a U.S. Geological Survey wildlife biologist assisting with the new study.

Grinnell's scientific descendants returned to Yosemite in the summer of 2003 and almost immediately saw that fundamental change had taken place.

The rare Inyo shrew, once found no higher than 8,000 feet, now ranges as high as 10,000 feet, the scientists discovered. The western harvest mouse had moved more than 1,000 feet uphill into Yosemite Valley.

Patton said "the big surprise" was the piñon mouse, a ball of fur with Dumbo-size ears that frequents the juniper belt in the eastern Sierra. Known to elevations of 8,000 feet in Grinnell's day, it now ranges above 10,000 feet at Mt. Lyell and is common at 9,000 feet in Tuolumne Meadows.

While several species expanded their range uphill, a few others have retreated to higher ground. The Belding's ground squirrel has disappeared from the lower reaches of its territory of a century ago.

So has the alpine chipmunk, which once ranged as low as 7,900 feet but now can't be found below 10,000 feet.

Among the most provocative discoveries, Patton said, was the upward retrenchment of the pika, a tiny relative of the rabbit. The pika has little tolerance for higher summer temperatures and is seen by some researchers as a sort of canary in the coal mine for global warming. Once found as low as 7,800 feet by Grinnell, the pika now isn't found

Pika on a Rock, © Don Getty

Karl Yens, *Yosemite Valley*, (detail) Private Collection, Courtesy of The Irvine Museum

Maurice Braun, *Yosemite Falls from the Valley*, The Irvine Museum

below 9,500 feet in Yosemite.

Chow said genetic drift and natural range extensions could also explain the upward movement of some of the species, but that global warming may well be the primary factor.

"This is another piece of evidence, in addition to melting ice packs, retreating glaciers and elevations in mean low temperatures," he said.

Still unclear is whether predatory animals are moving uphill. The researchers are reviewing records on the park's carnivores to determine if they too are shifting ranges.

Carol Boggs, director of Stanford University's Center for Conservation Biology, called the Yosemite findings "another signpost that global change is having impacts on the flora and fauna, not just changing temperature."

Boggs noted that other studies have documented biological changes attributed to warming climate—animals and insects showing up at higher latitudes around the globe, plants flowering earlier.

But the Berkeley effort "is particularly strong" because it builds off Grinnell's meticulous historical snapshot, she said. "His notebooks are absolutely a biological treasure. The fact that people can go back and find the same place really strengthens the inferences we can make."

Patton said the findings leave him concerned for the future of some of Yosemite's creatures.

"For species like the alpine chipmunk, there's no more 'up' left," the biologist said. Few Sierra peaks reach above 14,000 feet. "That's it; there's no more room to move higher. If that habitat disappears, the animal could be gone. And it's never going to be back."

An article from the *Los Angeles Times* of December 31 entitled "Tiny Mammal Facing Climate Change, and an Uphill Battle" indicates the following:

Human activity and climate change may be pushing the tiny American pika toward extinction in the mountains of western North America, according to a study published December 29, in the Journal of Biogeography.

The small rabbit-like mammals live in rock-strewn slopes but are gradually being pushed to higher elevations and are running out of places to live.

"Human influences have combined with factors such as climate change operating over longer time scales to produce the diminished distribution of pikas in the Great Basin today," said the study's author, University of Washington archeologist Donald K. Grayson.

Seven of 25 historically described populations of pikas in the Great Basin—the area between the Sierra Nevada and Rocky Mountains—appear to have become extinct by the end of the 20th century, he said. Among the intrusions that appear to imperil the pikas are roads close to their habitat and pressure from grazing livestock.

Grayson examined 57 archeological sites dating as far back as 40,000 years, as well as unpublished studies by other researchers, finding that the tiny mammals have been pushed higher over the years.

"The Great Basin pika is totally isolated on separated mountain ranges and there is no way one of these populations can get to another," he said. "They don't have much up-slope habitat left."

Pikas, which are very sensitive to high temperatures, are considered to be one of the best early warning systems for detecting global warming in the western United States, the study said.

Pika, © Dr. Lloyd Glenn Ingles, California Academy of Science

Adelie Penguins on an Iceberg, © Richard Jackson

An article entitled "Scorched Earth" by Robert L. Park, published in *The New York Times*, on January 15, 2006, states:

NASA has quietly terminated the Deep Space Climate Observatory, citing "competing priorities." The news media took little notice. Few Americans, after all, had even heard of the program. But the entire world may come to mourn its passing.

Earth is growing warmer. Even the most strident global-warming deniers have taken to saying that a little warming is a good thing. If the trend continues, however, it will have catastrophic consequences for life on this planet. Correctly identifying the cause could be the most important problem facing humanity.

Most scientists link global warming to unrestrained burning of fossil fuels, which shrouds Earth in a blanket of carbon dioxide, trapping the Sun's energy. Others, backed by industries that spew pollutants into the atmosphere, insist that greenhouse emissions are not the problem. They prefer to attribute warming to natural variations in solar output. Scientists are skeptical, but they don't deny the

possibility. The issue cries out to be resolved.

Even in a world wracked by wars, battles are not fought over scientific disagreements. In science, nature is the sole arbiter. Disputes are resolved only by better experiments.

The better experiment when it comes to global warming was to be the climate observatory, situated in space at the neutral-gravity point between the Sun and Earth. Called Lagrange 1, or L1, this point is about one million miles from Earth. At L1, with a view of the full disk of the Sun in one direction, and a full sunlit Earth in the opposite, the observatory could continuously monitor Earth's energy balance. It was given a poetic name, Triana, after Rodrigo de Triana, the sailor aboard Christopher Columbus's ship who first sighted the New World.

Development began in November 1998 and it was ready for launching three years later. The cost was only about $100 million. For comparison, that is only one-thousandth the cost of the International Space Station, which serves no useful purpose.

Before Triana could be launched, however, there was a presidential election. Many of the industries favored by the new Bush White House were not anxious to have the cause of global warming pinned down. The launching was put on hold.

The disdain of the Bush White House for Triana goes much deeper than just a desire to avoid the truth about global warming. Triana began life in early 1998 as a brain-child of Al Gore, who was then the vice president. Mr. Gore, the story goes, woke up one morning wondering if it would be possible to beam a continuous image of the full Earth back from space to inspire people with the need to care for our planet. The 1972 portrait of the full Earth, taken from the Moon, had inspired millions with the fragile beauty of our blue planet. Why not beam the image live into classrooms, allowing students to view weather systems marching around the globe?

Scientists had dreamed of such an observatory for years. They hoped Mr. Gore's influence would make it happen. Mr. Gore's support would end up destroying it. Those who hated him, hated Triana. His dream of inspiring environmentalists and schoolchildren served only to trivialize the project. It was ridiculed as "Gore's screen saver."

Triana is terminated, but global warming is not. Someday, there will have to be an observatory at L1. Perhaps the most important lesson from our exploration of the solar system is that the most terrible place on Earth is a Garden of Eden compared to the best place anywhere else. We must find out how to keep it that way.

On February 16, 2005, I attended a fascinating presentation by Vice President Al Gore entitled "The Climate Crisis: What You Don't Know, But Should," which was held at the Beverly Hilton Hotel in Beverly Hills. Pertaining to that presentation an article entitled "Sundance Spotlight on Al Gore" from The Associated Press on January 26, 2006 indicates the following:

Park City Utah – Former Vice President Al Gore is not all that comfortable being a star of the Sundance Film Festival. He's far more concerned that the celebrity watchers hear what he has to say.

The former vice president came to town for the premiere of "An Inconvenient Truth," a documentary chronicling what has become his crusade since losing the 2000 presidential election: Educating the masses that global warming is about to toast our ecology and our way of life.

Gore has been saying it for decades, since a college class in the 1960s convinced him that greenhouse gases from oil, coal and other carbon emissions were trapping the sun's heat in the atmosphere, resulting in a glacial meltdown that could flood much of the planet.

Americans have been hearing it for decades, wavering between belief and skepticism that it all may just be a natural part of Earth's cyclical warming and cooling phases.

And politicians and corporations have been ignoring the issue for decades, to the point that unless drastic measures to reduce greenhouse gases are taken within the next 10 years, the world will reach a point of no return, Gore said.

He sees the situation as "a true planetary emergency."

"If you accept the truth of that, then nothing else really matters that much," Gore said in an interview with The Associated Press. "We have to organize quickly to come up with a coherent and really strong response, and that's what I'm devoting myself to."

"An Inconvenient Truth" takes its title from the notion that consumers, politicians and corporations hooked on energy-inefficient vehicles and emission-heavy power sources may not want to hear the facts, Gore said.

The film centers on the elaborate slideshow presentations Gore conducts around the world for live audiences on the perils of global warming. He presents alarming images of ice-cap meltdowns and graphs linking the rise and fall of atmospheric carbon-dioxide to rising and falling temperatures.

If the pace of pollution continues, Gore's projections for carbon-dioxide levels are off the charts within a few decades.

Among the worst-case consequences: A new ice age in Europe, and massive flooding of regions in India, China and elsewhere that could make refugees of tens of millions of people.

Gore makes his case using copious scientific data and a surprising amount of humor for a politician who found it necessary during campaigns to poke fun at his own stiff image.

"I benefit from low expectations," Gore joked.

"An Inconvenient Truth" also lays out events in Gore's personal life and how they influenced his global-warming mission: A car accident that nearly killed his young son, his sister's death from lung cancer after 30 years as a smoker, his family's legacy as former tobacco farmers, the photo finish of the 2000 election.

Calling himself a "recovering politician," Gore reiterated to a Sundance audience at the film's premiere that he would not run for office again.

"What really attracted us to this presentation is the tone Al strikes," said "An Inconvenient Truth" director Davis Guggenheim. "It's not righteous. It doesn't have a political agenda. It lands right in the middle, and Al just lays out what is this inconvenient truth. And I think that's why the audience is willing to receive it."

Gore said U.S. government and business leaders must follow the lead of other nations that have enacted stricter mileage standards for cars. Utility companies worldwide must adopt cleaner methods of burning fossil fuels and focus on renewable energy sources such as solar and wind power, he said.

The filmmakers brought "An Inconvenient Truth" to Sundance hoping to land a distributor that will put the documentary in theaters.

"I'm thrilled to have a chance to get this message to a broader audience, because doing it retail a few hundred people at a time is pretty exhausting," Gore said. "I'm committed to it and I'm continuing to do it, but if we can get it before a much larger audience more quickly, that serves the larger purpose."

Polar Bear Devouring its Prey, © Dave Olson, US Fish and Wildlife Service

William Ritschel, *Purple Tide*, Private Collection, Courtesy of The Irvine Museum

An article entitled "Glaciers Flow to Sea at a Faster Pace, Study Says" by Andrew C. Revkin which appeared in *The New York Times* on February 17, 2006 states:

The amount of ice flowing into the sea from large glaciers in southern Greenland has almost doubled in the last 10 years, possibly requiring scientists to increase estimates of how much the world's oceans could rise under the influence of global warming, according to a study being published today in the journal *Science*.

The study said there was evidence that the rise in flows would soon spread to glaciers farther north in Greenland, which is covered with an ancient ice sheet nearly two miles thick in places, and which holds enough water to raise global sea levels 20 feet or more should it all flow into the ocean.

The study compared various satellite measurements of the creeping ice in 1996, 2000 and 2005, and was done by researchers at NASA's Jet Propulsion Laboratory in Pasadena, Calif., and the University of Kansas.

Glaciers are creeping rivers of ice that accelerate or slow and grow thicker or shrink depending on the interplay of a variety of conditions including rates of snowfall and temperature and whether water lubricates the interface between ice and the rock below.

Sometimes the rate of movement in a particular glacier can change abruptly, but the speedup in Greenland has been detected simultaneously in many glaciers, said Eric J. Rignot, the study's author, who has extensively studied glacier flows at both ends of the earth.

"When you have this widespread behavior of the glaciers, where they all speed up, it's clearly a climate signal," he said in an interview. "The fact that this has been going on now over 10 years in southern Greenland suggests this is not a short-lived phenomenon."

Richard B. Alley, an expert on Greenland's ice at Pennsylvania State University who did not participate in the study, agreed that the speedup of glaciers in various places supported the idea that this was an important new trend and not some fluke.

"There's no way that the Jakobshavn Glacier on the west side can call up the Helheim on the other side of the ice sheet and say, 'Let's get going,'" he said.

A separate commentary published in *Science* by Julian A. Dowdeswell of the Scott Polar Research Institute in Britain noted that the rising flows could be a result of both the rapid deterioration of the miles of floating "tongues" of ice where the glaciers enter the sea and an increase in water melting on the ice surface and percolating down through crevasses, where it can reduce friction with the underlying rock.

An article entitled "Loss of Antarctic Ice Increases" by Mr. Revkin which appeared in the *Times* on March 3 indicates:

Two new satellite surveys show that warming air and water are causing Antarctica to lose ice faster than it can be replenished by interior snowfall, and thus are contributing to rising global sea levels.

The studies differed significantly in estimates of how much water was being added to the oceans this way, but their authors both said that the work added credence to recent conclusions that global warming caused by humans was likely to lead to higher sea levels than previous studies had predicted.

The earlier projections presumed that snowfall over Antarctica, as well as Greenland, would increase as warming added moisture to the air, compensating for the losses of ice from crumbling or melting along coasts.

Several independent experts agreed with the new conclusions, saying they meshed both with more localized studies of trends in Antarctica and with evidence from warm spells before the last ice age.

"Snowfall will matter less and less," said Robert Bindschadler, an expert on polar ice at the National Aeronautics and Space Administration who was not involved in either study. "We know that warmer climates eventually lead to less ice."

Most of the ice is being lost in western Antarctica, where warming air and seawater have recently broken up huge floating shelves of ice, resembling the brim of a hat. That, in turn, has allowed ice in the interior to flow more readily to the coast.

One of the new surveys, led by H. Jay Zwally, a NASA scientist, used satellites and aircraft to measure changes in the height of ice sheets in Antarctica and Greenland over the decade ended in 2002. It found a loss of volume in Antarctica and a small overall gain in Greenland, where inland snows have outpaced ice flowing into the sea, at least temporarily. It was just published in The Journal of Glaciology.

The other study, by scientists at the University of Colorado, looked at changes from 2002 to 2005 using NASA satellites that detect subtle changes in Earth's gravitational field that can be used to estimate the weight of water in an ice sheet.

"The changes we are seeing are probably a good indicator of the changing climatic conditions there," said Isabella Velicogna, the lead author of the gravity-sensing study, which was published online yesterday by the journal *Science*.

An article entitled "Climate Data Hint at Irreversible Rise in Seas" by Andrew C. Revkin which appeared in *The New York Times* on March 24, 2006 states:

Within the next 100 years, the growing human influence on Earth's climate could lead to a long and irreversible rise in sea levels by eroding the planet's vast polar ice sheets, according to new observations and analysis by several teams of scientists.

One team, using computer models of climate and ice, found that by about 2100, average temperatures could be four degrees higher than today and that over the coming centuries, the oceans could rise 13 to 20 feet—conditions last seen 129,000 years ago, between the last two ice ages.

The findings, being reported today in the journal *Science*, are consistent with other recent studies of melting and erosion at the poles. Many experts say there are still uncertainties about timing, extent and causes.

But Jonathan T. Overpeck of the University of Arizona, a lead author of one of the studies, said the new findings made a strong case for the danger of failing to curb emissions of carbon dioxide and other gases that trap heat in a greenhouselike effect.

"If we don't like the idea of flooding out New Orleans, major portions of South Florida, and many other valued parts of the coastal U.S.," Dr. Overpeck said, "we will have to commit soon to a major effort to stop most emissions of carbon to the atmosphere."

According to the computer simulations, the global nature of the warming from greenhouse gases, which diffuse around the atmosphere, could amplify the melting around Antarctica beyond that of the last warm period, which was driven mainly by extra sunlight reaching the Northern Hemisphere.

The researchers also said that stains from dark soot drifting from power plants and vehicles could hasten melting in the Arctic by increasing the amount of solar energy absorbed by ice.

The rise in sea levels, driven by loss of ice from Greenland and West Antarctica, would occur over many centuries and be largely irreversible, but could be delayed by curbing emissions of the greenhouse gases, said Dr. Overpeck and his fellow lead author, Bette L. Otto-Bliesner of the National Center for Atmospheric Research in Boulder, Colo.

In a second article in *Science*, researchers say they have detected a rising frequency of earthquakelike rumblings in the bedrock beneath Greenland's two-mile-thick ice cap in late summer since 1993. They say there is no obvious explanation other than abrupt movements of the overlying ice caused by surface melting.

The jostling of that giant ice-cloaked island is five times more frequent in summer than in winter, and has greatly intensified since 2002, the researchers found. The data mesh with recent satellite readings showing that the ice can lurch toward the sea during the melting season.

The analysis was led by Goran Ekstrom of Harvard and Meredith Nettles of the Lamont-Doherty Earth Observatory in Palisades, N.Y., part of Columbia University.

H. Jay Zwally, a NASA scientist studying the polar ice sheets with satellites, said the seismic signals from ice movement were consistent with his discovery in 2002 that summer melting on the surface of Greenland's ice sheets could almost immediately spur them to shift measurably. The meltwater apparently trickles through fissures and lubricates the interface between ice and underlying rock.

"Models are important, but measurements tell the real story," Dr. Zwally said. "During the last 10 years, we have seen only about 10 percent of the greenhouse warming expected during the next 100 years, but already the polar ice sheets are responding in ways we didn't even know about only a few years ago."

In both Antarctica and Greenland, it appears that warming waters are also at work, melting the protruding tongues of ice where glaciers flow into the sea or intruding beneath ice sheets, like those in western Antarctica, that lie mostly below sea level. Both processes can cause the ice to flow more readily, scientists say.

Many experts on climate and the poles, citing evidence from past natural warm periods, agreed with the general notion that a world much warmer than today's, regardless of the cause of warming, will have higher sea levels.

But significant disagreements remain over whether recent changes in sea level and ice conditions cited in the new studies could be attributed to rising concentrations of the greenhouse gases and temperatures linked by most experts to human activities.

Sea levels have been rising for thousands of years as an aftereffect of the warming and polar melting that followed the last ice age, which ended about 10,000 years ago. Discriminating between that residual effect and any new influence from human actions remains impossible for the moment, many experts say.

Satellites and tide gauges show that seas rose about eight inches over the last century and the pace has picked up markedly since the 1990's.

Dr. Overpeck, the co-author of the paper on rising sea levels, acknowledged the uncertainties about the causes. But he said that in a world in which humans, rich and poor, increasingly clustered on coasts, the risks were great enough to justify prompt action.

Frank Cuprien, *Seascape,* Courtesy of the Russ and Joan Allen Collection

An article entitled "Study Says U.S. Companies Lag on Global Warming" by Claudia H. Deutsch which appeared in *The New York Times* on March 22, indicates:

European and Asian companies are paying more attention to global warming than their American counterparts. And chemical companies are more focused on the issue than oil companies.

Those are two conclusions from "Corporate Governance and Climate Change: Making the Connection," a report that Ceres, a coalition of investors and environmentalists, expects will influence investment decisions.

The report, released yesterday, scored 100 global corporations—74 of them based in the United States—on their strategies for curbing greenhouse gases. It covered 10 industries—oil and gas, chemicals, metals, electric power, automotive, forest products, coal, food, industrial equipment and airlines—whose activities were most likely to emit greenhouse gases. It evaluated companies on their board oversight, management performance, public disclosure, greenhouse gas emissions, accounting and strategic planning.

The report gave the chemical industry the highest overall marks, with a score of 51.9 out of a possible 100; DuPont, with 85 points, was the highest-ranking American company in any of the industries. Airlines, in contrast, ranked lowest, with a score of 16.6; UAL, the parent of United Airlines, received just 3 points.

The study gave General Electric, American Electric Power and Cinergy among the highest scores in their industries. But over all, it concluded, American companies '"are playing catch-up" with international competitors like BP, Toyota, Alcan, Unilever and Rio Tinto.

"Dozens of U.S. businesses are ignoring the issue with 'business as usual' responses that are putting their companies, and their shareholders, at risk," said Mindy S. Lubber, president of Ceres and director of the Investor Network on Climate Risk, a group whose members control a total of $3 trillion in investment capital. "When Cinergy and American Electric Power are tackling this issue, and Sempra and Dominion Resources are not, that should be a red flag to investors."

Art Larson, a Sempra Energy spokesman, took exception to Sempra's score of 24. He said that Sempra, based in San Diego, had been "aggressive in promoting energy efficiency and procuring renewable energy sources," and that "in the area of environmental responsibility, Ceres seems to give more weight to words over action." Hunter Applewhite, a spokesman for Dominion, a big electric utility in Richmond, Va., that scored 27, said the company had no comment on its ranking.

Members of the Investor Network said they would take the report's conclusions seriously. "We need to continue to press poor-performing companies to clean up their act," said California's state treasurer, Phil Angelides, who is on the board of two pension funds that collectively manage more than $300 billion in assets.

Connecticut's state treasurer, Denise L. Nappier, who administers a $22 billion investment fund, lauded the report as an "unprecedented window into how companies most affected by climate risk are responding at the board level, through C.E.O. leadership and strategic planning."

The report does show progress since 2003, when a much smaller Ceres study concluded that most American companies were ignoring the threat of climate change. Since then, Ceres notes, Chevron Texaco has invested $100 million in developing cleaner fuels, Ford Motor introduced the first American hybrid car, American Electric Power has committed itself to "clean coal" technologies and G.E. has introduced its Ecomagination program stressing "green" products. And many companies including Dow Chemical, Anadarko Petroleum and Cinergy have board committees that oversee the curbing of greenhouse gases.

"More U.S. companies realize that climate change is an enormous business issue that they need to manage immediately," Ms. Lubber said.

Still, the top-scoring company, with 90 points, was BP, a British company that has said it will invest $8 billion in solar, wind and other clean-energy technologies in the next decade. "BP understands that all companies must work to reduce their carbon footprint, starting with fossil fuels," Ms. Lubber said.

Paul Grimm, *Approaching Storm* (detail), Private Collection, Courtesy of The Irvine Museum

An article entitled "Gov. Backs Greenhouse Gas Strategy, Aides say he plans to endorse the far-ranging program to curb global warming today, despite opposition from GOP and business leaders" by Janet Wilson and Marc Lifsher, which appeared in the *Los Angeles Times* on April 11, 2006 states:

Gov. Arnold Schwarzenegger will announce today his support for a strategy to combat global warming that has drawn criticism from Republicans and business leaders, aides said April 10.

The market-based approach would include controversial "cap-and-trade" requirements mandating greenhouse gas producers who exceed certain tonnages of harmful emissions to buy credits from other companies that have lowered emissions.

Schwarzenegger is expected to make the announcement, endorsing major components of his climate action team's plan, at a summit he has convened in San Francisco this afternoon bringing together economists, investors, business executives, environmentalists and lawmakers.

Legislative approval could be needed to enact key elements of the 1,300-page plan, including the cap-and-trade system and a registry for businesses to report the amounts of greenhouse gases they emit.

Terry Tamminen, special advisor to the governor on environment and energy issues, said that under the market-based program, power plants, for instance, would be able to buy emissions credits not just from other power plants but also from other industries, including timber companies that set aside forests to trap carbon dioxide, a key greenhouse gas. Tamminen said such broad access to the credit market would help to drive prices down.

Limited versions of such market-based programs are operating in Chicago and Europe, he said, adding that California's would go much further. Schwarzenegger has said he wants to reduce greenhouse gases by 80% by 2050, putting the state ahead of the rest of the world.

Tamminen said one-third of those reductions could come from a market-based cap-and-trade program. The plan calls for two years of study to design the program.

Cap-and-trade programs are opposed by the Bush administration as well as by many of Schwarzenegger's business backers, including major oil companies and the California Chamber of Commerce.

Allan Zaremberg, president of the chamber, said his members would "be concerned about any cap program that encourages arbitrary reductions in emissions and encourages companies to migrate operations to other parts of the world where there are no carbon dioxide controls."

Tamminen said industries had expressed similar concerns 35 years ago when the Clean Air Act was put into place but had not left the state or hurt the economy through compliance.

Another high-ranking administration source said that Schwarzenegger was well aware of the business concerns and wanted careful study and design but that it would happen.

"He's endorsing the concept and saying we need to have this, but there's an acknowledgment this has to be done carefully," the source said.

Philosophical differences among Schwarzenegger's staffers, legal challenges by automakers and hostile actions by the Bush administration could also stymie pieces of the plan.

One-third of the greenhouse gas reductions outlined in the climate action team's report would come from a tailpipe control law already in place, sponsored by Assemblywoman Fran Pavley (D-Agoura Hills). Automakers are challenging that law in court, arguing that California does not have the legal right to regulate carbon dioxide, a major greenhouse gas.

"This is a tough case," said lawyer Jim Marston of Environmental Defense, a national environmental group that has intervened on the automakers' lawsuit. He said the U.S. Environmental Protection Agency also needs to sign a waiver approving the Pavley law and said California might have to wait for a new president for that to happen.

But he said California has quietly inserted a police powers clause into laws giving them the right to regulate greenhouse gases to protect public health.

Adding another potential roadblock, the National Highway Traffic Safety Administration recently said in a new fuel economy rule that no state has the right to regulate carbon dioxide.

"The real question is while we're sitting here congratulating ourselves, are the feds getting ready to cut our throats?" said V. John White, an environmental lobbyist.

The Center for Biological Diversity, an environmental group, sued the highway agency on April 6, seeking to have the fuel economy rule thrown out.

Schwarzenegger said in a news conference last week, "I have to say that the federal government has so far fallen short with showing leadership when it comes to the environment. I think that I, as governor, don't want to wait for the federal government or for any other states, as far as that goes [to act on global warming].... California has always been innovative and has always been bold about those kind of things, and I think that this is a very bold move, this report."

The plan outlines four dozen initiatives, many of which do not need federal approval.

For example, it seeks to persuade farmers to plant grass and rice for use in manufacturing "bio-fuel" to replace oil and gas, would require utilities to buy "clean" power and would call for carbon dioxide to be trapped in vast forests or buried in caverns.

Supporters say progress has already been made, often at Schwarzenegger's behest.

The state Board of Forestry is identifying lands and working with an existing voluntary emissions registry already in place. The Public Utilities Commission adopted key pieces of the governor's solar power initiative after it failed in the Legislature; those actions are part of the new package.

A dozen more bills that would implement other measures in the plan were introduced this week.

But many business leaders are nervous. Representatives of most oil companies, concrete makers, rubber producers and automakers argue that global warming is an international problem that shouldn't be tackled by a single state.

Jack Coffey, Chevron's government affairs manager, said most oil companies — except for BP, the Royal/Dutch Shell Group and others based in Europe — oppose mandatory reporting or caps on greenhouse emissions.

"The problem is there is pressure put on California industries to reduce, and no one else is doing it, not our neighbors over in Nevada or Oregon or Arizona," said Frank Sheets, a spokesman for Texas Industries Inc., a cement manufacturer with plants in Riverside and near Victorville. "We'd rather see a national system…"

Plan backers note California wants to work with neighboring states, and that 10 other states are moving to adopt tough tailpipe emissions laws.

Schwarzenegger said last week he would bring the report to the next Western governors conference.

There are also growing divisions over global warming within industry groups

"Business is not monolithic in its opposition," said Tamminen.

Many venture capitalists and some utilities are eager to see the new technology initiatives move forward.

A letter signed by BP, the London-based oil giant; Pacific Gas and Electric; a Silicon Valley business association; and three environmental groups commended the governor for the climate action plan's call for "a rigorous and comprehensive system for reporting greenhouse gas emissions" and its recommendations "to provide credit to businesses that take early action to reduce emissions."

In a statement distributed at an environmental conference in San Francisco on April 6, Governor Schwarzenegger said "We cannot reduce emissions unless we have market- based solutions, like trading mechanisms, in addition to regulatory solutions." He also released a letter he sent to President Bush reiterating the state's request for a waiver from the federal government to allow the auto rules to remain in effect.

TODAY, CONSERVING THE ENVIRONMENT and preserving the imperiled diversity of life on our planet are two of the most important issues facing humankind. The need to balance economic growth with environmental preservation has become our most pressing obligation. To achieve a balance between nature and humankind, the environmental community must recognize the necessity of a strong and productive economy that will support environmental projects, and the development community must serve its own enlightened self-interest by pursuing a positive environmental approach. Only by doing our part to preserve California's vanishing natural landscape can we be sure that our grandchildren will experience these wild places firsthand, and not merely through paintings and photographs.

By the middle of the twenty-first century, human activity will dominate natural systems on earth. Environmental issues will be at center stage. What we do in the next fifty years will be critical to our planet's destiny. What we do in the next ten years will determine what is possible in the next fifty. What we do now will decide what kind of world future generations will face.

If we are ever to achieve peace on earth, we must not only protect California's environment, but join together with other nations to protect the world's natural resources as well. Instead of treating the planet as if it were a business in liquidation, we should be addressing the role we can play in the critical search for a sustainable environment. Each generation in its turn is the steward of the land, the water and the air. Our time is now.

William Wendt, *Rincon, from the Montecito Hills*, c. 1903,
Private Collection, Courtesy of The Irvine Museum

The Irvine Museum in Perspective

JEAN STERN

The Irvine Museum opened its doors on January 15, 1993. Nine months earlier, on April 15, 1992, I started my first day as Executive Director and sole employee of The Irvine Museum, not long after Joan Irvine Smith and her mother, Athalie R. Clarke, had signed the documents to create the museum.

At that time, there was no such place as "The Irvine Museum," and so for several months, I went to work every day at The Oaks, Joan Irvine Smith's ranch and private equestrian training center in San Juan Capistrano. The Oaks is well known for training world-class horses for jumping and hunting, and the daily agendum that Mrs. Smith supervises there is precise and exhausting.

Mrs. Smith and I had daily meetings at The Oaks, often with her son James Irvine Swinden attending. As the Vice President of the museum, Jim was essential to the planning and eventual realization of The Irvine Museum. Each day, in the course of our continual series of meetings, I accompanied Mrs. Smith while she managed the various aspects of equestrian training. Whenever we could, we returned to our in-depth discussions of how we would set up and run the museum. The topics we discussed varied from how to properly catalogue and store the works of art, to how to produce our first traveling exhibition, including setting up the various museum venues and publishing our first book for the show.

Even before we opened our doors, we received our first important gift on June 6, 1992. A superb mural, painted in oil paint and gold leaf by Jessie Arms Botke, assisted by her husband Cornelis Botke, was offered as a gift to the Irvine Museum. The large mural, measuring six and one-half feet by twenty-six feet, had been commissioned for the east wall of the ballroom of the Oaks Hotel, in Ojai, California.

Painted between 1954-56, the mural had been the pride of the Oaks Hotel for over forty years. By the 1990s, the venerable hotel had become a health spa and the old ballroom that held the mural became the Coral Spa, or the aerobics exercise room. With a general renovation of the hotel underway, the wall that displayed the mural was scheduled to be demolished in order to greatly expand the exercise area.

After meeting with the owners of the spa, we gratefully accepted the significant gift. It came with the sole proviso that the museum had to bear all costs of removal and conservation. In other words, if we managed to take it off the wall, it was ours.

We arranged to have Scott Haskins, an expert mural conservator, examine it and find a way to remove it. Fortunately, the mural had been painted on canvas that had been glued to the wall. Had the mural been painted directly on the wall, it would not have been feasible to remove it. The mural was in fact painted on two large pieces of canvas, one piece was six and one-half feet high by 12 feet long, while the other was six and one-half feet high by fourteen feet long. Over the years, one small piece of the mural along the top edge had been cut out to allow for an exit sign. Also, one or two other peripheral strips had been cut off near the doorway.

The mural came off the wall very quickly and the two sections were sent to be cleaned and remounted onto two very substantial sets of stretcher bars that were made specifically for our newly acquired Botke mural. We awaited delivery of the restored mural with great anticipation as there was nothing else like it in any museum or private collections.

Guy Rose, *Laguna Eucalyptus,*
The Irvine Museum

The delivery of the Botke mural to the Irvine Museum caused great excitement among the tenants of our building. The sight of the two large sections, painted in vivid colors and gold leaf, drew a large crowd to the lobby. However, in those early years, the museum was located in a large suite on the twelfth floor, and after much brainstorming and careful measuring, the building engineer declared that neither section would fit in any of the six elevators that serve the building.

Once the disappointment had passed, Mrs. Smith arranged to have both mural sections shown on a long-term loan basis at UCI's Joan Irvine Smith Hall, where the dean and administrators of the UCI Medical School have their offices. The awe inspiring mural instantly dominates the field of vision as one enters the building. As of this writing, they are still displayed at Joan Irvine Smith Hall and may be viewed by the public.

Jessie Arms Botke, assisted by Cornelis Botke, *Mural for the East Wall of the Ballroom, Oaks Hotel, Ojai*, c. 1954–56, The Irvine Museum, Gift of the Oaks Hotel, Ojai

Over the years, the Irvine Museum has received numerous gifts of art works, some which we consider important examples of the style, such as the Botke mural, and some very interesting minor works, such as watercolors and drawings, which serve to fill out our holdings of a particular artist. Here are a few of the important paintings that were accessioned as gifts.

In October 1993, Jack and Suzie Kennefick gave The Irvine Museum a painting entitled *Girl with Calabash of Fruit* painted by Millard Sheets in 1968. Although quite late for our collection's focus, we were delighted to have a fine example of Sheets' late work.

Millard Sheets, *Girl with Calabash of Fruit*, The Irvine Museum, Gift of Jack and Suzie Kennefick

Guy Rose, *Lifting Fog, Laguna*, The Irvine Museum, Gift of James and Linda Ries

Armin C. Hansen, *The Farmhouse, Monterey*, The Irvine Museum, Gift of
James and Linda Ries

In November of 1993, the Irvine Museum received a very
generous gift from James and Linda Ries of two important paintings,
Lifting Fog, Laguna by Guy Rose, and *The Farmhouse, Monterey* by
Armin C. Hansen.

In 1994, we were delighted to accept from Rory White the
gift of a magnificent painting entitled *On Fishermen's Wharf,
Monterey*, by Frank Gavencky. Although not of the era of the
California Impressionist style, Gavencky represents the modernist
period that came with the Great Depression and ended with the
advent of Abstract Expressionism in the late 1950s.

Frank Gavencky, *On Fishermen's Wharf, Monterey*, The Irvine Museum,
Gift of Rory White

447

Granville Redmond, *Bringing Home the Flock*, 1903, The Irvine Museum, Gift of Ray Redfern

Hamilton Wolf, *Halos*, The Irvine Museum, Gift of George and Irene Stern

In 1995, Ray Redfern, of the Redfern Gallery in Laguna Beach, donated a magnificent large early painting by Granville Redmond. Painted in Southern California in 1903, *Bringing Home the Flock* shows a shepherd taking his sheep home at the end of the day. While the sky is painted in brilliant end-of-the-day colors, the landscape is rendered in moody, dark tones, characteristic of the French Barbizon influence.

Later that year, George and Irene Stern, of George Stern Fine Arts in Los Angeles and Carmel, donated *Halos* a rare major painting by Hamilton Wolf. This large Regionalist style painting is a significant example of Industrial Modernism in California.

In 1996, we received a gift of a large, superb painting entitled *In Laguna Canyon*, dated 1928, painted by Laguna Beach resident artist William Griffith. The painting came as a gift from Mrs. Josephine N. Milnor, at the suggestion of Ray Redfern. It shows Laguna Canyon Road near Big Bend, as an unpaved path along a gravel-strewn stream bed.

In December, 1996, our good friend Robert McChesney Bethea gave the museum an imposing oil painting by Arthur G. Rider, his step-father. *Morning in Taxco* is a large, light-filled view of a plaza near the cathedral. In addition, the gift came with the companion pencil study for the painting.

In 2004, noted collectors Thomas and Barbara Stiles gave us a large figural painting by Charles Reiffel entitled *Nymphs by the Sea*. Reiffel made a lasting contribution to the art communities of San Diego and Silvermine, Connecticut.

Arthur G. Rider, *Morning in Taxco*, The Irvine Museum, Gift of Robert McChesney Bethea

Charles Reiffel, *Nymphs by the Sea*, The Irvine Museum, Gift of Mr. and Mrs. Thomas B. Stiles II

William Griffith, *In Laguna Canyon*, 1928, The Irvine Museum, Gift of Josephine N. Milnor

Granville Redmond, *Southern California Landscape with Flowers*, The Irvine Museum

Selections from The Irvine Museum, 1992

Invitation to Grand Opening of The Irvine Museum, 1993

The Irvine Museum's inaugural exhibition was *Selections from The Irvine Museum*, which curiously opened not in Irvine but in Scottsdale in 1992, a few weeks prior to our own museum's grand opening. The exhibition tour was originally scheduled to open at The Irvine Museum, continue to the Fleischer Museum in Scottsdale, Arizona, and then move on to the Oakland Museum of California. However, as we approached the opening date, it became evident that we could not meet the schedule because our museum, which was under construction in a temporary location, would not be ready in time. We discussed the issue with Mort and Donna Fleischer in Scottsdale and revised the show so that it would be shown first at the Fleischer Museum, then continue to Oakland, and end its tour in Irvine. James Irvine Swinden and I attended the black-tie opening at the Fleischer Museum, as we have done for every single venue of each traveling exhibition to date. Russell Penniman, Jim's brother and a museum board member, also attended the opening in Scottsdale.

We published our first Irvine Museum book, *Selections from The Irvine Museum*, as a companion volume to the exhibition, with an introduction by Joan Irvine Smith and essays by Harvey Jones, Senior Curator of the Oakland Museum; Janet Blake Dominik, at that time Curator of Art at The Irvine Museum, and myself. The book proved extremely popular, and within two years, we ordered a second printing.

At that time, just after the publication of our first book, Mrs. Smith and the board of directors of the museum instituted a policy that any public, non-profit institution that requested the museum's books for its library would receive a complete set in hardbound editions, free of charge. The only requirement was to have the request presented on the institution's letterhead. This policy, administered by James Swinden, has been in effect since 1993. One single gift of Irvine Museum books to the California State Library System in 2004 comprised 1,000 sets. To date, it is estimated that more than 2,000 sets of books have been given to libraries in public schools, private schools and colleges, as well as local, county and state public libraries.

On the evening of January 14, 1993, The Irvine Museum celebrated its grand opening with a gala reception; the following morning, on January 15, we opened our doors to the public for the very first time. Our initial location was in Suite 1250, on the twelfth floor of Tower 17, a beautiful building located at 18881 Von Karman Avenue in Irvine. Most people who visited us expressed their astonishment that a museum was located in an office building, but their bewilderment quickly changed to enchantment after a tour of the exhibition.

The entire staff of The Irvine Museum on the occasion of its opening and during those first few months of operation consisted of just two full-time employees, Janet Blake Dominik as Curator and myself as Executive Director, with Allison Beaumont as part-time Assistant Curator and Gwen Brewton as receptionist. Gwen was "on loan" from Joan Irvine Smith Fine Arts, Inc., which had not yet opened its doors. From the beginning, our museum administration was managed by James Swinden in his offices in Newport Center. Additionally, we had the as-needed services of Pam Ludwig, the then director of Joan Irvine Smith Fine Arts, who managed our art inventory and storage needs.

Orange County Congressman Christopher Cox presenting a Congressional Proclamation for The Irvine Museum to Joan Irvine Smith at the Grand Opening

Jean Stern and Joan Irvine Smith in front of Frank Cuprien's *Evening's Iridescence*, at the Grand Opening, photo by Lori Brysten

Tower 17, Irvine, site of The Irvine Museum

In 1992, even before we had opened the museum, we mounted exhibitions to accompany The Oaks Classic and The Oaks Fall Classic, two Grand Prix horse jumping events held at The Oaks, Mrs. Smith's equestrian training facility in San Juan Capistrano. These art shows were held for two days, twice a year, until 1998, when the art exhibitions were discontinued. The exhibitions were displayed in a large tent that was air conditioned for the benefit of the paintings. Accompanying the art shows were displays by a selection of art dealers that specialized in California paintings.

Janet Blake Dominik, Allison Beaumont Hahn and Jean Stern in the Irvine Museum tent at The Oaks Classic, 1992

Paintings in the Irvine Museum tent, at The Oaks Classic, 1992

Jean Stern in front of Irvine Museum tent at The Oaks Classic in 1992

The Thoroughbred Spread Barbecue in The Oak Grove at The Oaks Classic, 1994

Ray Redfern in the Redfern Gallery booth

Art Dealers' booths

Karges Fine Arts booth

De McCall and Debby Flores in the DeRu's Fine Arts booth

North Point Gallery booth

George Stern Fine Arts booth

Reflections of California: The Athalie Richardson Irvine Clarke Memorial Exhibition, 1994

Romance of the Bells: The California Missions in Art, 1994

When Athalie Richardson Irvine Clarke, Joan Irvine Smith's mother and the co-founder of The Irvine Museum, died at ninety years of age on May 22, 1993, the museum started planning *Reflections of California: The Athalie Richardson Irvine Clarke Memorial Exhibition*, its second traveling exhibition. Because Mrs. Clarke had been a longtime friend of President and Mrs. Richard Nixon, and because she had been appointed by President Nixon to the Committee for the Preservation of the White House, her memorial exhibition opened at the Richard Nixon Library & Birthplace in Yorba Linda, California. As Mrs. Clarke had also been re-appointed to that committee by President Ford and President Carter, the show traveled on to the Jimmy Carter Library in Atlanta and to the Palm Springs Desert Museum before coming home to Irvine.

In recognition of his friendship with Mrs. Clarke, President Nixon had readily agreed to officiate at the opening of her memorial show in Yorba Linda, but he fell ill and died just a few days prior to opening night. As part of the period of national mourning, President Nixon's body lay in state at the Nixon Library at the same time that *Reflections of California* was displayed there. The many thousands of people who came to pay their respects to the late president also viewed our exhibition. This remarkable timing of events afforded us the unlikely satisfaction that, as a very young museum, we had a show that claimed more than 100,000 visitors.

Reflections of California was accompanied by a fully illustrated book featuring a superb essay by Joan Irvine Smith that is distinguished both as an eloquent tribute to her mother and as a synopsis of the history of Orange County. To accompany her text, I wrote an essay discussing the paintings that comprise the show. *Reflections of California* was produced by our incomparable graphic designer Lilli Colton, who has designed most of our books since.

Also in 1994, the museum organized a sweeping exhibition and book on the historic Franciscan missions of California. *Romance of the Bells: The California Missions in Art* was a compilation of paintings, watercolors and etchings of the twenty-one California missions, painted in the period between 1880 and 1940. The book, which has an introduction by Joan Irvine Smith and essays by Gerald J. Miller, Pamela Hallan-Gibson, Norman Neuerburg and myself, has received popular acclaim as a readable survey of California's historic missions and their representations in art.

Romance of the Bells: The California Missions in Art opened at the Mission San Juan Capistrano with a dramatic and magnificent evening gala in the historic mission courtyard. Many of the paintings, which were painted there more than a century ago, were displayed in the two-hundred-year-old arcade, using a hanging method that did not impact the ancient adobe walls, and were illuminated by a lighting system installed specifically for the event. It was a unique and mystical experience to stroll the softly lit grounds of the time-honored mission and see the historic paintings in the same setting.

Romance of the Bells was displayed in several museums and academic institutions throughout California, including the Mission San Luis Rey, the University of San Diego Art Gallery, the Santa Barbara Historical Society Museum, the Bakersfield Museum of Art,

Lillli Colton, Joan Irvine Smith and Jean Stern at work on *Reflections of California*, 1993

the Monterey Museum of Art, the Santa Cruz Museum and the Redding Museum.

In 1995, three small museums in California approached The Irvine Museum with the idea of organizing a show and publishing a catalogue that featured landscapes from each museum's immediate region. This wonderful idea became *Palette of Light*, which was organized and displayed at the Santa Cruz Museum, the Redding Museum, the Bakersfield Museum of Art and The Irvine Museum. I wrote a text to accompany the fully illustrated catalogue of the exhibition.

One of the very first projects initiated by the museum while we were still holding all of our meetings at The Oaks was the *Guy Rose* exhibition and monograph. This idea, first pursued in 1992, brought us together with several of the leading figures in the young field of California Impressionism, including Ray Redfern of the Redfern Gallery, Roy Rose of the Rose Family Archives and Harvey Jones of the Oakland Museum of California. Guy Rose (1867–1925) was the most important of our Impressionist painters, and after numerous failed attempts by others to document his life and works, we felt certain that we would succeed.

In 1995, after three years of preparation, The Irvine Museum and the Oakland Museum of California jointly produced *Guy Rose: American Impressionist*, a retrospective exhibition accompanied by a definitive book on the artist. Dr. Will South, a scholar on American art, was commissioned to write a comprehensive biography of Guy Rose, and noted American art history professor William H. Gerdts wrote an introduction. Mrs. Smith wrote an introduction, and I wrote an essay that examined Rose's unique and important role in the California art community.

As part of the Guy Rose project, The Irvine Museum and the Oakland Museum of California sponsored a video documentary on the life of the artist. The captivating twenty-six-minute film, produced by Robert Boudreaux, aired on many local PBS television stations.

Guy Rose: American Impressionist opened to a tremendous attendance at the Oakland Museum and continued with great popularity at The Irvine Museum, the Montclair Art Museum in New Jersey and the Greenville Museum in South Carolina. For many years, *Guy Rose* claimed the highest attendance of any of our exhibitions.

Palette of Light: California Paintings from The Irvine Museum, 1995

Guy Rose: American Impressionist, 1995

In 1996, The Irvine Museum became one of the few museums in the United States to be invited to participate in the Olympic Games Cultural Olympiad Arts Festival. Working with the University of Georgia Art Museum in Athens, Georgia, one of the venues for the Games, we produced *California Impressionists*, the most important show of California paintings up to that time. Drawn from our collection as well as from several notable private collections, this superb exhibition was documented in an accompanying book with introductions by Joan Irvine Smith and James Swinden and essays by Dr. Susan Landauer, Donald D. Keyes, curator of the Georgia Museum of Art, and myself.

California Impressionists opened at the University of Georgia Art Museum in Athens in conjunction with the opening ceremonies of the Olympic Games in Atlanta. The show continued to the Cummer Museum in Jacksonville, Florida; the Gibbes Museum in Charleston, South Carolina; the University of Utah Museum in Provo, Utah; the Crocker Art Museum in Sacramento and The Irvine Museum.

Also in 1996, a PBS video project called *Impressions of California*, with lead funding by the Joan Irvine Smith & Athalie R. Clarke Foundation, came to fruition. A few months before, Paul Bockhorst, an award-winning filmmaker and producer at KOCE-TV in Huntington Beach, had completed a PBS documentary entitled *Visions of California*, which examined the art and artists of California during the Great Depression. Soon after the station aired Visions of California, he approached the museum for assistance in producing the second installment of a planned three-part series, to be called *Impressions of California*. This was to be a "prequel" to Visions in that it would examine an earlier period of art in California, between the 1870s and the 1920s. Since some of the key artists featured in Visions were aging but still available for interviews, he realized that time was of the essence and acted quickly to tape the second segment first.

To accompany *Impressions of California*, the Irvine Museum and KOCE jointly produced an exhibition of paintings and an illustrated book to complement the video. The book boasts essays by a who's who of California art historians, including Harvey Jones of the Oakland Museum of California, Bolton Colburn and Janet Blake of the Laguna Art Museum, Martin Petersen of the San Diego Museum of Art, noted art writer Ruth Westphal, Nancy Dustin Wall Moure, Susan M. Anderson and myself. The program is still shown on various PBS stations.

In 1998, a long-term project between the Art Gallery at California State University, Dominguez Hills and The Irvine Museum came to fruition with the opening of *Painted Light: California Impressionist Paintings from the Gardena High School–Los Angeles Unified School District Collection*. This superb exhibition, organized by Kathy Zimmerer and curated by myself, featured the well-respected Gardena High School art collection, amassed by the student body over a period of thirty-five years.

California Impressionists, official event of the 1996 Atlanta Olympic Games Cultural Olympiad

Impressions of California, joint project of The Irvine Museum and KOCE-TV (PBS) Huntington Beach, 1996

Starting in 1917, Gardena High initiated a policy of having the graduating class purchase a work of art for the school collection. This tradition continued into the 1950s, with two, or sometimes three, paintings added each year.

As an art historian in the field of California painting, I had heard of this collection and had seen it on several occasions starting in the late 1970s. The collection was superb, but its handling, storage and conservation were alarming. Gardena High School did all it could to protect the paintings, but after years of mishandling, damage and destructive "restoration" by well-meaning art teachers, several of the pieces had become irretrievably damaged and others were very near that point.

At the suggestion of Kathy Zimmerer, I attended a meeting at Gardena High School to see if something could be done to preserve the collection. Also in attendance were various representatives of the faculty, school district and alumni. Most importantly, Kathy had invited DeWitt Clinton McCall, an art dealer and conservation expert that I've known and respected since 1978, when I was director of Petersen Galleries in Beverly Hills and first asked him to clean one of my paintings. Since that first job, De cleaned and repaired more than a thousand works of art that came through Petersen Galleries.

The meeting at Gardena High School led to an agreement on initiating this difficult and costly project—that is, to prepare the paintings for display, to document and publish a book on the collection, and to tour the collection in a traveling exhibition. Not long afterward, Kathy called me and De McCall to announce that she had secured funding from the W. M. Keck Foundation, which allowed us to start the project.

Painted Light was a tremendous success. The exhibition was shown at California State University, Dominguez Hills, The Irvine Museum and the Autry Museum of Western Heritage. The story of how this remarkable collection was saved became an episode in Huell Howser's *California's Gold* program, which airs on PBS stations.

Gardena's method of building an art collection through gifts of art by each graduating class was at one time widespread in Southern California, but only a few other schools continued it past a few years and accumulated great works of art. Following the success of the Gardena High School collection exhibition, the Irvine Museum has since been approached by two other schools wishing to repair, document and publish their incomparable long-term collections. Severe budget limitation, however, has hampered any progress on these proposals.

Our first traveling exhibition to reach the Northeastern United States, *All Things Bright & Beautiful*, was organized in 1998, with noted American art authority William H. Gerdts serving as Guest Curator. The show consisted of a selection of fifty-eight paintings drawn from our collections as well as from those of several private lenders, representing the best exhibition of California Impressionists to date.

Kathy Zimmerer, Huell Howser and Jean Stern at *Painted Light: The Gardena High School-Los Angeles Unified School District Collection*, in The Irvine Museum, 1998

All Things Bright & Beautiful was shown at the National Academy Museum in New York, the Terra Museum of American Art in Chicago, the Dixon Gallery and Gardens in Memphis, the Oakland Museum of California as well as The Irvine Museum. This was the first time that an exhibition of California Impressionist paintings was displayed in New York or Chicago.

As is usual with The Irvine Museum, we published a full-color book to accompany the show, with an congratulatory letter by Governor Pete Wilson, introductions by Joan Irvine Smith and James Swinden, and scholarly essays by Professor Gerdts, myself, Harvey Jones of the Oakland Museum of California, and David Dearinger, curator of the National Academy Museum. In addition, I presented a slide-illustrated lecture at the Terra Museum in Chicago, and Professor Gerdts and I each presented lectures on Impressionist paintings at the National Academy.

All Things Bright & Beautiful: California Impressionist Paintings from The Irvine Museum, 1998

A significant gift to The Irvine Museum was presented by the Geoffrey Beaumont family in December 1998. The gift consisted of a large collection of watercolors, drawings and other artwork by the celebrated painter of U.S. Navy scenes Arthur E. Beaumont (1890–1978).

Beaumont was born in England as Arthur Eadwine Crabbe. In 1908, he went to Canada to work on a horse ranch in Saskatchewan. After a year of cowboy life, he moved to Oakland, California, and in 1910, enrolled at the San Francisco School of Art. After one year of art studies, he returned to ranch work as a cowboy in the San Joaquin Valley.

He moved to Los Angeles in 1915, and began, for reasons that are unclear, to use the name Arthur Beaumont Crabbe, and not long thereafter, simply "Arthur Beaumont." He supported his art studies by taking construction jobs, and on one of those, at the Los Angeles Bible Institute, he met Dorothy Dean, his future bride. By 1917, he had opened his own commercial art studio and devoted himself to art on a full-time basis. In 1919, he married Dorothy, and the couple moved in with her parents in Los Angeles.

In 1921, Beaumont enrolled at the Chouinard School of Art and took classes with the modernist Stanton MacDonald-Wright (1890–1973), all the while continuing his career as a commercial artist. He accepted a scholarship from the Chouinard Art

Arthur E. Beaumont, *Planes Roar into Action from US Aircraft Carriers Wasp and Enterprise*, 1941, The Irvine Museum, Gift of the Geoffrey Beaumont Family, © 1941 National Geographic Society

Arthur E. Beaumont, *Heavy and Light Cruisers Range Far to Scout or Fight, USS Astoria and USS Phoenix*, 1941, The Irvine Museum, Gift of the Geoffrey Beaumont Family, © 1941 National Geographic Society

Institute in Los Angeles in 1925, and later went to Europe to further his art education. He returned to Los Angeles in 1927, and took a teaching position at Chouinard.

The great turning point in Beaumont's career came in 1932, when he painted the first of three formal portraits of Admiral William D. Leahy. Knowing of Beaumont's love of ships and of his earnestness, Leahy arranged a commission for Beaumont as Lieutenant in the U.S. Naval Reserve, a position he held for two years. Thereafter, from 1932 to 1977, Beaumont was the Official Artist of the U.S. Navy, and he devoted his life and career to documenting the Navy.

In 1935, he was commissioned to paint backdrops for the movie Mutiny on the Bounty and was selected as one of America's 50 best watercolor artists. That same year, he was elected president of the Long Beach Art Association, a post he held several years. Beaumont's renown was growing every year. In 1939, he was chosen Chairman of the Art Jury for the Golden Gate International Exposition in San Francisco.

In 1941, the National Geographic Society selected Beaumont to paint "Ships That Guard Our Ocean Ramparts," a series of paintings of battleships, destroyers and other naval vessels. The article was especially timely as it appeared in the September issue, barely three months before the attack on Pearl Harbor. The tremendous popularity of these paintings prompted the National Geographic Society to commission Beaumont to paint a similar series on the U.S. Army. These were published in 1942. In 1943, Beaumont served on the citizens committee that raised $40 million to build the cruiser USS Los Angeles. His paintings and posters of the proposed ship were used in the fundraising drive and accounted for more than $1.5 million of the money raised.

Throughout World War II, Beaumont's paintings of the ships and crews that fought in the various battles were instrumental in shaping the public's view of the gallantry and determination of the U.S. Navy. After the war, he continued as Official Artist of the U.S. Navy by recording the testing of the atomic bomb on Bikini Atoll. His series of more than 180 watercolors described the effects of two tests of the atomic bomb. These were exhibited at the National Gallery of Art in Washington, D.C., and sent on a nation-wide tour.

In 1957, Beaumont was the Official Artist of the U.S. Navy Arctic Expedition. He painted the North Polar Ice Cap and was one of only a few people to complete the fabled "Northwest Passage" from the Pacific to the Atlantic aboard the USS El Dorado.

Correspondingly, in 1960, he painted at the South Pole as the Official Artist for Operation Deep Freeze. Aboard the USS Glacier, he produced 350 sketches and 25 paintings of the Bellinghausen Sea. Later that year, he returned to Antarctica and produced 25 sketches and 3 paintings of the U.S. South Pole Station and the geographic pole. Moving about in the perilous landscape, Beaumont fell through a snow bridge into a crevasse and narrowly escaped death before being rescued by a New Zealand navy captain.

In 1967, he and Dorothy moved to Leisure World, a senior citizen retirement community in Laguna Hills, California. Far from being retired, he continued to paint aboard a number of Navy ships and exhibited his works throughout the country. In 1964, Beaumont was bestowed the highest civilian award offered by the U.S. Navy, the Meritorious Public Service Citation for his service as "a distinguished marine artist." Arthur Beaumont died in his home on January 23, 1978.

The generous gift of the Geoffrey Beaumont family includes several important paintings from the 1941 National Geographic Society's "Ships That Guard Our Ocean Ramparts" series.

In 1998, Mrs. Smith, The Irvine Museum's President and Founder, proposed an ambitious exhibition that would bring together a large number of environmental, art, cultural, governmental and private organizations that share an enlightened view toward environmental conservation. This momentous show, titled *A Silent Testament: Nature and Humankind in the Balance*, was held at the Bowers Museum of Cultural Art from mid-March through mid-April 1998. It offered insight into the state of biodiversity on a planet-wide scale and suggested approaches for present and future methods of finding workable solutions. Due to the short lead time for *A Silent Testament*, we could only publish a small illustrated pamphlet, which nevertheless gained wide distribution, especially in schools, and required a second printing.

The list of supporting entities for *A Silent Testament* is indeed impressive. It included the Friends of the Nature Reserve of Orange County, the Nature Conservancy, The Irvine Company, the County of Orange, the Bowers Museum of Cultural Art, the American Oceans Campaign, the University of California at Irvine, the National Water Research Institute, the National Audubon Society, the Hubbs-Sea World Research Institute, the Metropolitan Water District of Southern California, the Orange County Water District, the Rancho Mission Viejo Company, the Rancho Mission Viejo Land Conservancy (now known as the Donna O'Neill Land Conservancy) and the Scripps Institute of Oceanography, among many others.

The success of *A Silent Testament* led to a joint project between the Nature Conservancy of California and The Irvine Museum in 2000, entitled *Native Grandeur: Preserving California's Vanishing Landscapes*. This exhibition, co-produced with Mark Sanderson of the Nature Conservancy, featured a stunning group of paintings illustrating the seven ecological regions of California: the South Coast, the Desert, the Central Coast, the North Coast, the Sierra Nevada Mountains, the Great Central Valley and the Shasta-Cascades.

These beautiful paintings of California were selected from The Irvine Museum, the Oakland Museum of California, the Crocker Art Museum, the Hearst Art Gallery, the Kern County Museum and several private collections. The companion book featured 87 color plates, an informative text by David Wicinas, and essays by Harvard Professor E. O. Wilson, Joan Irvine Smith, California State Librarian Dr. Kevin Starr, myself and many others.

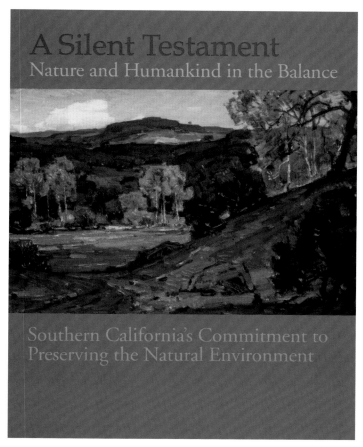

A Silent Testament: Nature and Humankind in the Balance, 1999

Native Grandeur: Preserving California's Vanishing Landscapes, joint project of The Nature Conservancy and The Irvine Museum, 2000

Native Grandeur was shown at the Oakland Museum of California, the Napa Valley Museum, the Santa Barbara Museum of Natural History, the Los Angeles Museum of Natural History and the San Diego Natural History Museum.

California's True Gold, 1999

Another small but very influential pamphlet that grew into an important project was published in 1999, and was entitled *California's True Gold*: Her priceless and irreplaceable cultural and historical monuments and her beautiful and fragile environment so very close to the "earthly paradise." *California's True Gold* was a brief overview of California history, with special emphasis on Orange County and the Mission San Juan Capistrano. It was produced to accompany the mission's first Pageant of Capistrano. It also gave a brief overview of the Natural Community Conservation Planning (NCCP) process for reaching a broad consensus about the limits of development on remaining natural lands in a large area.

The historical discussion in *California's True Gold* spawned a great demand for additional information from schools and numerous interested individuals. We soon learned that in California public schools, California history is taught in the fourth grade only, and not again until college, and then only as an elective. Sensing a need

for an accurate, readable and well-illustrated account of the history of California, we opted to produce an exhibition and book to examine this subject.

Also in 1999, The Irvine Museum accepted another major gift in the form of the estate of Frank H. Myers, given to us by the Patricia Clark Myers Trust. Patricia Clark Myers, the artist's daughter-in-law, had been a close friend of mine for more than twenty years. She was a gentle and caring person and dedicated herself to the legacy of Frank H. Myers. We collaborated on many projects, and I visualize her each time I look at a painting by Myers. Pat and I were introduced by Martin E. Petersen, Curator Emeritus of the San

Frank H. Myers, *The Charleston*, 1926, The Irvine Museum, Gift of the Estate of Patricia Clark Myers and the Brian Myers Trust

Frank H. Myers, *Seagulls' Domain*, The Irvine Museum, Gift of the Estate of Patricia Clark Myers and the Brian Myers Trust

Diego Museum. At the time, I was working under Marty as Guest Curator for The Cross and the Sword, the official U.S. Bicentennial Celebration Exhibition at the San Diego Museum in 1976.

Frank Harmon Myers (1899–1956) was born in Cleves, Ohio, and enrolled at the Cincinnati Art Academy in 1917. He took lessons with Frank Duveneck (1848–1919) and John E. Weis (1892–1962). He earned his tuition by designing greeting cards for two Cincinnati printers. Myers continued his studies by taking summer classes, in 1919 and 1920, at the Pennsylvania Academy of the Fine Arts. In 1921, he visited France, accompanied by Weis. Together they painted in Brittany and briefly visited Giverny. Back in Cincinnati in 1922, Myers began a 23-year teaching career at the Art Academy. In 1923, he returned to Europe and studied at the School of Fine Arts in Fontainebleau.

In 1925, Myers married Ella Price, a young schoolteacher. They spent their honeymoon in Europe, staying in Paris and taking trips throughout Spain. The following year, they made an extended trip west to Colorado and California. On the return trip, they spent several weeks in Santa Fe and Taos, New Mexico, where Myers met Joseph Henry Sharp (1859–1953).

Myers's work included portraits as well as landscapes and urban scenes around Cincinnati, painted in an Impressionistic realism. His early works show Weis's influence, with a strong sense of realism handled in a bold and expressive brushstroke. At other times, Myers produced brightly colored works, showing his keen interest in French Impressionism. Gradually, he developed a strong sense of abstract design, and in the late 1920s, produced a number of remarkably advanced paintings, such as *The Charleston*, in an analytical style that bordered on abstraction.

At the height of the Great Depression, in 1932, Myers took a teaching sabbatical and painted in New Mexico. The series of paintings from this trip, though commercially unsuccessful at the time, represent some of the artist's finest work and can be seen in several museums.

In the late 1930s, Myers' interest increasingly turned toward painting the ocean. At the same time, his health began to falter, and, for no apparent reason, he experienced bouts of severe depression. In 1940, he took a one-year leave of absence and moved to Monterey, California. Thereafter, his work was almost exclusively seascapes, with a few portrait commissions.

Myers was a well-respected leader of the Carmel-Monterey art community, serving as president of the Carmel Art Association in 1953. His painting companions included Armin C. Hansen (1886–1957) and Donald Teague (1897–1991); together, they defined the Monterey art scene for many years. After several years of recurring health problems, Frank Myers died of a heart attack on March 7, 1956.

Myers works are in the National Museum of American Art in Washington, D.C., the Museum of New Mexico, the University of Cincinnati, and of course, The Irvine Museum.

In 2001, we opened *California, This Golden Land of Promise*, an exhibition featuring paintings that documented the historical development of our state and of Orange County. Every day, from the time we opened the exhibition until it closed, we received constantly growing crowds of visitors. To accommodate the large number of visitors, we extended the show from our usual four months to five months. *California, This Golden Land of Promise* was also shown at the Napa Valley Museum, the Bakersfield Museum of Art and the Crocker Art Museum in Sacramento.

The accompanying book, *California, This Golden Land of Promise*, which Joan Irvine Smith and I wrote, includes a detailed timeline by James Swinden and an introduction by Dr. James I. Doti, president of Chapman University. Directed at a general audience, the book is illustrated with historical paintings of California as well as archival photographs, maps, and quotes from original letters, diaries and source books.

To be certain that our text was indeed accurate, Jim Doti selected a committee of history scholars to review the narrative. This committee was made up of Professors Leland L. Estes, Lynne M.

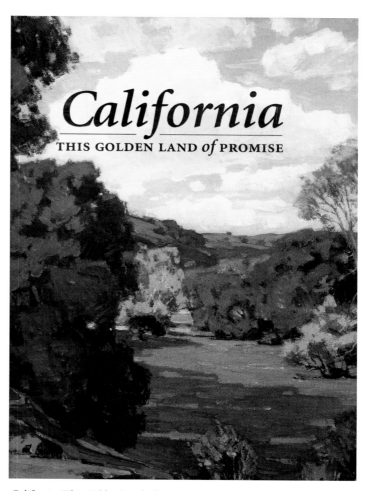

California, This Golden Land of Promise, 2001

James Irvine Swinden, Jean Stern, and Joan Irvine Smith, at a book signing for *California, This Golden Land of Promise*, 2001

Pierson Doti, Robert A. Slayton and James C. Miller, all of Chapman University, as well as Phil Brigandi, an Orange County historian and scholar.

Published jointly by Chapman University Press and The Irvine Museum, *California, This Golden Land of Promise* contains 368 pages with 405 color plates, 88 black-and-white images, a time-line, bibliography and index. It is a historical narrative of California from prehistoric times through the Spanish exploration, colonization, the Mission Period, the Rancho Period, the American Conquest and the Gold Rush. It ends with a chapter on James Irvine I, founder of the Irvine Ranch.

The immediate and truly lasting success of *California, This Golden Land of Promise* has been very gratifying. The book has gained a large readership, not only in public and school libraries, to which the museum distributes for free, but also among students, amateur historians and general readers. In the book's first year of publication, Mrs. Smith, Jim and I appeared at several book signings for various organizations, including the libraries at Chapman University and UCI, the Newport Beach Country Club, the Pacific Club, the California Club in Los Angeles and the Mission San Juan Capistrano, among others.

Also in 2001, our association with author and researcher Nancy Hall came to fruition with the publication of *The Life and Art of Paul de Longpré*, a beautiful and thoroughly researched book on the French-American flower painter. In addition to the main text by Nancy Hall, the book has introductions by Joan Irvine Smith and James Swinden, and an essay I wrote to place the artist within the budding southern California art community of the first decade of the twentieth century.

Paul de Longpré (1855–1911) was born near Lyon, France, and came to the United States as a mature artist who specialized in painting flowers. In 1899, he moved to the newly established city of Hollywood and, until his death in 1911, was internationally known for his beautiful watercolors of flowers. He built a large, Moorish-style mansion on a three-acre lot at the corner of Prospect Avenue (now called Hollywood Boulevard) and Cahuenga Avenue. De Longpré also built a large public garden on his property that was reputed to have more than 2,000 rosebushes representing a multitude of varieties. His home and garden became

The Life and Art of Paul de Longpré, 2001

Paul de Longpré, *Fresh from the Garden*, Courtesy of DeRu's Fine Arts, Laguna Beach

Moving the museum from the Twelfth Floor to the Ground Floor,
March 2002

Hollywood's first spectacular tourist attraction, long before the
arrival of the movie industry. A retrospective exhibition on the work
of de Longpré is scheduled for the near future.

In March 2002, The Irvine Museum moved from its
twelfth-floor suite to the ground-floor suite of Tower 17. Our original
twelfth-floor suite was restricted in space, so we had to make our
offices part of the public exhibition space. Our new site, suite 100,
availed us of not only more display space, but also the opportunity
to design our floor space to best fit our needs for proper viewing
areas as well as private offices.

After seven years of planning and organizing exhibitions
that traveled throughout California and to other parts of the country,
we decided that we were ready to send a show to Europe. In 1999,
Jim Swinden took the lead in producing *Masters of Light*, an exhibition
of the best examples of California Impressionism, gathered from our
collections and from those of fourteen private lenders. As we knew
that we were going to be judged by a discerning and cultivated audience, we resolved that we would send only the very finest art.

From the outset, this exhibition required extraordinary
effort, as there were countless adjustments that came with packing,
crating, documenting and shipping an exhibition across international borders. To cite just two examples, all of the crates had to be
constructed from pre-approved European wood, not from American
lumber, which could harbor insects or organisms that might prove
destructive to European trees; the crates also had to be watertight so
that they would float in case the cargo plane went down in the ocean.

There was one unique philosophical problem that had to
be resolved with the Paris venue. We were told that we could not
label this show as an exhibition of "Impressionist" paintings, as
according to the French art public, only paintings painted in France
in the 1860s and 1870s could properly be termed "Impressionist."

Franz A. Bischoff, *Still-Life of Roses*, The James Irvine Swinden
Family Collection

James Irvine Swinden in front of the Mona Bismarck Foundation,
Paris, 2002

465

Jean Stern and James Irvine Swinden in the Mona Bismarck Foundation, Paris, for Grand Opening of *Masters of Light*, September 22, 2002

Jean Stern in the Old Market Square, Krakow, for *Masters of Light*, February 2, 2003

Jean Stern, Jase Swinden and James Irvine Swinden in front of the Sorolla Museum, Madrid, in conjunction with *Masters of Light*, August 2003

To that end, we agreed to call the exhibition a show of "plein air" paintings, from the French phrase *en plein-air*, signifying that they were painted outdoors.

In order to see the show successfully through its European venues, Jim Swinden dealt with every one of these challenges and eventually mastered this specialized skill, thanks in great part to the assistance of Ms. Mo Shannon, who acted as our special registrar. After three years of planning and attention to hundreds of details, we were ready to send the exhibition to Paris, Krakow and Madrid and then home to Irvine.

As we do for all of our traveling exhibitions, Jim Swinden and I went to Paris for the opening, as well as for interviews and press conferences. The Mona Bismarck Foundation is a well-established venue that hosts a variety of American exhibitions. Mona Bismarck was an American woman from Kentucky who, after four marriages, married the grandson of Otto von Bismarck and became the Countess Bismarck. At her death, she left her palatial home on the Seine, on Avenue de New York just across from the Eiffel Tower, to her foundation to foster Franco-American goodwill through cultural exchanges. Over the years, these American exhibitions have been well attended and have gained widespread respect and support from French museum-goers.

On his arrival at the museum, Jim was greeted by Monica Dunham, curator of the Mona Bismarck, who told him that the show was going to be a big hit. Jim asked Monica how she could be so certain, given that most of the paintings were still leaning against the wall, waiting to be hung. She related that the French professional art installers who were busy hanging the paintings had recently installed the Matisse to Picasso show at the nearby Grand Palais, and they had stated that they liked our paintings much more than the ones they had recently installed.

A few days later, in my native French language, I talked to a group of ladies who were viewing the exhibition. They said they were docents at the Musée d'Orsay, and that at their next meeting, they would suggest a docent group visit to the Mona Bismarck. They told me they had never seen such vivid and brilliant paintings at the Musée d'Orsay.

On press day, Jim and I were pleasantly startled to see more than one hundred journals, magazines and periodicals represented at the press conference. To accommodate the large number of journalists, Jim held a series of one-on-one interviews, and I led three separate press tours. Being a native French speaker, I made an instant hit when, after being introduced as the director of an American museum, I addressed the press conference in fluent French.

On September 25, 2002, *Masters of Light* opened to a large audience at the Mona Bismarck Foundation, hosted by U.S. Ambassador Howard H. Leach and his wife. From the start of the exhibition run, the Mona Bismarck attracted large numbers of sophisticated French visitors who were willing to stand in line on the Avenue de New York to await the opportunity to see our plein air paintings. In fact, the French public was very gracious and showed no preconceived bias against American Impressionist paintings.

In February 2003, *Masters of Light* opened at the International Cultural Centre in Krakow, Poland, in the middle of the Polish winter. We were greeted at the Krakow airport by Professor Jacek Purchla, the director of the center. Huddled in extra-warm clothing, Jim and I attended the opening reception and press interviews. In television interviews, as neither Jim nor I could speak Polish, we donned earphones to listen to the translation prior to giving our response in English, which would then be translated back into Polish.

In Krakow, Jim and I had the occasion to walk around the Market Square where the International Cultural Centre is located, and stroll through the beautiful old part of central Krakow. Recalling the fuss over the use of the term "Impressionist" at the Paris venue, we were both surprised and delighted when we counted at least three huge banners that stretched across various large intersections, boldly announcing the "Impressionist Exhibition" from The Irvine Museum.

Through the kindness of Professor Purchla and his staff, Jim and I were greeted like visiting diplomats. We were amazed at the long lines of patient visitors that snaked out the door and into the snow on a daily basis. To meet the unexpected and extraordinary demand, the Centre had to open one extra day per week and two extra hours per day. The final tally of visitors came to 33,000, far exceeding the Centre's previous record of about 8,000 for a three-month exhibition.

As part of the arrangements between The Irvine Museum and the International Cultural Centre, it was mutually agreed to hold an environmental and cultural symposium in Krakow as part of the show. In late April, in the Polish springtime when it was not nearly so cold, Jim and I attended the conference with our invited guest and colleague, David Beckman of the Natural Resources Defense Council, who presented a paper there.

The third European venue was the Centro Cultural del Conde Duque, a beautiful municipal museum set in an old palace in Madrid. The venue was arranged by our friend and fellow Orange County residents U.S. Ambassador George Argyros. On June 18, 2003, Jim and I represented The Irvine Museum at the opening reception, which was hosted by Mr. and Mrs. Argyros. In addition, we were accompanied by Jim's wife, Madeline Swinden, and their son Jase. *Masters of Light* continued through the summer and drew large crowds of Spanish and foreign visitors.

The most ambitious and successful of our exhibitions up to that date, is of course documented in a book. *Masters of Light* features a congratulatory letter by Governor Gray Davis, scholarly essays by Dr. William H. Gerdts and myself, and introductions by

Masters of Light, Plein-Air Paintings in California 1890-1930, 2002

Joan Irvine Smith and James Swinden. All fifty-eight paintings that comprised the show are illustrated in full-page color, as are the more than forty other images that illustrate the essays.

In 2003, we published a book entitled *Plant Portraits: The Life and Art of Albert R. Valentien*, a joint project with the San Diego Natural History Museum. A special exhibition of eighty of Valentien's watercolor studies of California flora was displayed at the San Diego Natural History Museum and will continue as a traveling exhibition over the next three to four years.

Albert R. Valentien (1862–1925) is widely known as the first chief decorator at Rookwood Pottery in Cincinnati. After a twenty-year career, he and his wife, Anna, came to San Diego in 1903, and in 1907, accepted a commission from philanthropist Ellen Browning Scripps to paint a series of California flower paintings. The Scripps project occupied ten years of their lives, with Anna collecting examples and Albert dutifully painting them. In the end, Albert Valentien painted nearly 1,100 works, which were donated by the Scripps estate to the San Diego Natural History Museum in 1933. And there they remained, locked in a vault for almost seventy years, nearly totally out of view.

Having lived in San Diego for many years, and having worked at the San Diego Art Museum, I knew of this treasure and had seen, from time to time, a few of these works by Albert Valentien on limited display. In 2001, Mrs. Smith, Jim Swinden and I were given a special opportunity to view all of these remarkable

Joseph Kleitsch, *The Old Post Office, Laguna*, Courtesy of the Laguna Art Museum

Plant Portraits: The California Legacy of A. R. Valentien, joint project of The Irvine Museum and the San Diego Natural History Museum, 2003

Joseph Kleitsch, *Red and Green*, The Irvine Museum

paintings. The visual and emotional impact was resounding, and Mrs. Smith quickly offered to have The Irvine Museum publish a book and assist in the task of producing a traveling exhibition.

In addition to the Valentien book, The Irvine Museum is close to completing a five-year project on the art and life of Joseph Kleitsch (1882–1931), one of the most important Impressionist painters of southern California. As part of the project, we will be publishing a fastidiously researched text by Dr. Patricia Trenton, a well-known art historian in the field of American painting. A major retrospective exhibition of Kleitsch's paintings, with Dr. Trenton as Guest Curator, will be organized and sent on tour.

Another important exhibition and book project that is also on our schedule is an examination of the life and art of Arthur E. Beaumont. The elegant and informative text was written by Geoffrey C. Beaumont, son of the artist and a noted authority on his father's work.

Just this year, the museum has commissioned Phil Kovinick, an eminent author and researcher on American art, to write the text for the forthcoming book and exhibition on John Frost (1890–1937). Frost, often called the "lost Impressionist" of California, was the son of Arthur B. Frost, an American painter and illustrator. John Frost was a promising painter who was struck down by tuberculosis at age 46. While small in number, Frost's extant paintings are of superb style and quality. His work is often compared to that of Guy Rose, who was both his friend and his mentor.

In 1995, when we published *Guy Rose, American Impressionist*, we had planned to follow up this volume with a companion book to be called the *Guy Rose Catalogue Raisonné*. This monumental book, containing a list and accompanying photographs of every known work by Guy Rose, is being compiled and

Guy Rose, *The Green Parasol*, Courtesy of John and Patricia Dilks

Guy Rose, *Low Tide, Honfleur*, Private Collection, Courtesy of The Irvine Museum

Guy Rose, *Carmel Seascape*, Private Collection, Courtesy of The Irvine Museum

Elanor Colburn, *Bathing Baby*, 1930,
The Irvine Museum

edited by Roy C. Rose of the Rose Family Collection and Archives. *The Guy Rose Catalogue Raisonné* will be published by The Irvine Museum sometime in the next five to ten years.

Moreover, we are contemplating initiating two more monographs dealing with the life and art of Sam Hyde Harris (1889–1977) and Frank H. Myers (1899-1956). We have had many suggestions as to which California Impressionists should be documented, and we will continue our research and publication programs with the intent of fully documenting the prominent artists of this style.

As our museum's programs and activities expanded, and our role as the principal proponents of historical California paintings brought us additional distinction in Orange County, we accepted, in 2004, the opportunity to establish a working association with the Historical Collections Council (HCC) of Orange County. Over lunch one day at Bistango's Restaurant, James Irvine Swinden and I met with members of the HCC Steering Committee, including Brandon Buza, Andrea Waite, Walter Lachman, Allan Lay, Kirk Edgar, Bob Ehrlich, Bob Hall and Ruth Westphal, and agreed to establish a close working relationship.

On May 21, 1985, a group of dedicated art collectors and dealers, interested in supporting the budding public interest in California Impressionism, met at Petersen Galleries, on Rodeo Drive in Beverly Hills. Since I was director of Petersen Galleries, I served as unofficial chairperson, and after a brief discussion, we signed a roster indicating our desire to organize. Thus the HCC was formed, originally to support the historical paintings collection at the Laguna Beach Museum of art. The sign-up roster of the founding members (in "pass around" order) lists Mary Hamilton (Fieldstone Collection), James Ries (collector), Tobey Moss (dealer), Jim Zidell (collector), Nancy Moure (art historian), Bob Bethea (of the Arthur G. Rider estate), Jay Ingerle (of the Rudolf Ingerle estate), Ken and Kay Roberts (dealers), Terry Callahan, Herb Hilchey, Don C. Jack (collector), Bill Kurschat (collector), Leo Michelson (collector), Julie Noyes (collector), Ray Redfern (dealer), Ed Korb (dealer), Russel Ludwick (collector), Donald W. Grant (collector), George Stern (dealer), Bob and Barbara Ehrlich (collectors), Robert and Nadine Hall (collectors), Bob McDonald (of the Laguna Beach Museum of Art), Robert Simpson (collector), Martin and Brigitte Medak (collectors), Lucinda and Gates Burrows (of the Benjamin C. Brown estate), Ty Brenner (collector), Janet Blake (art historian), and Julia and Frank Tan (collectors). Ruth Westphal (author) and De McCall (dealer) were also founding members.

Together, The Irvine Museum and the HCC will work to

Evelyn Payne Hatcher, Edgar and Elsie Payne's daughter, with Christine DeWitt, Judy Thompson and Merika Gopaul, at DeRu's Gallery, Laguna Beach, 2002

Docent Field Trip to Mayén-Olson Frames, co-owner Victor Mayén is at far right, 2000

Docent Field Trip to De McCall's art conservation lab, 2001, De McCall is at center

enhance the educational and exhibition programs of our museum, as well as lend moral and financial support to any Orange County institution that is interested in our artistic heritage.

In addition to all of the exhibitions and books discussed earlier, we maintain a rigorous exhibition and educational program at the museum. Due to the space limitations of our small museum, we only have one show at a time, which we change every four months; for now, there is no "permanent collection" gallery. Thus, three times a year, all of the paintings are taken down and returned to their respective owners, and a new show is brought in, installed, labeled and properly lit.

At the same time, the educational program is adapted and modified three times a year to meet the demands of each new exhibition. A new curriculum is written, and our docents receive training in preparation for tours and field trips. Finally, for each exhibition, press releases and announcement cards are mailed, and plans and arrangements are readied for the press reception and the invitation-only opening reception.

All of these remarkable accomplishments in such a relatively brief period of time could not have been achieved without a profes-

Our esteemed and dearly missed friend, the late Andy Schuessler of Crate 88, installing an exhibition at The Irvine Museum

Curator of Education Christine DeWitt leading a school tour of The Gardena High School/LAUSD Collection, at the old Twelfth Floor location of The Irvine Museum, 1999

472

Merika Adams Gopaul, *Heading for Dog Beach*,
Collection of Jean and Linda Stern

sional and dependable staff. My staff at The Irvine Museum consists
of five exceptional people, none of which were trained as museum
professionals.

Merika Adams Gopaul, who I had known in San Diego
since the early 1970s, is an accomplished artist in her own right.
When I first met her, I was a guest curator at the San Diego Museum
and she was working as executive assistant to Dan Jacobs, owner of
Orr's Gallery, San Diego's oldest and most prestigious art gallery. We
kept in touch for several years, and in 1994, she contacted me to ask
if I knew of any art-related job openings, as Orr's Gallery was clos-
ing. As it happened, we were looking for an Assistant Director at the
museum, so I immediately invited her to apply. She was interviewed
by Jim Swinden, was hired and has been with the museum ever since.

Christine DeWitt is our Curator of Education. Our first
was Janet Murphy, a retired teacher and art collector who had come
to us as one of the first volunteers at the museum. In 1999, Janet's
husband, Jim, retired from his profession, and soon afterward Janet
resigned her position. After a long search for a replacement, Merika
and I interviewed Christine, who holds a master's degree in education and is a retired teacher. We could clearly see that Christine,
who was born in Paris and speaks fluent French, was just the person
we needed. With the agreement of Jim Swinden, who, in addition
to his other museum administration duties, initiated and oversees
the education and outreach program, Christine was hired. In the
ensuing years, she has become an essential part of our dynamic
educational program.

Assistant Director, Merika Adams Gopaul

That same year, the post of receptionist became vacant, so
we secured the services of a temp firm to assist us in finding a new
employee. After we spent several weeks trying out various people,
the agency sent us Judy Thompson. After Judy's first week on the
job, Christine, Merika and I agreed to inform the agency that we
wanted her for a few more weeks. With Jim Swinden's approval,
Judy was hired as a receptionist, and within a few months, demon-

Coordinator of Visitor Services, Judy Thompson

473

Irvine Museum Staff, 2001, Merika Gopaul, Don Bridges, Jean Stern, Judy Thompson, and Christine DeWitt

James Irvine Swinden (CENTER, SEATED) Hosting the Annual Docent Appreciation Dinner, at Bistango Restaurant, Irvine, 2004

The Irvine Museum. In 2004, we hired Charlett Helm-Pfeiffer as receptionist to replace Judy Thompson, who went to part-time public relations duty.

My fifteen years of association with The Irvine Museum have been remarkable, unique in every way, and thoroughly exciting at all times. I take great satisfaction and pride in knowing that I am a part of this noble endeavor. Mrs. Smith, the board of directors and the staff of the museum have established a lasting legacy by documenting the uniquely beautiful and uplifting art of the California Impressionist period. Singularly, and contrary to other contemporary art styles, California Impressionism is a style that enables us to redeem ourselves by reaffirming nature, the ultimate source of our being and the universal bond of humanity. In doing so, we can only enrich our art and dignify ourselves.

strated that she was capable of greater assignments and responsibilities. Eventually, we created the position of Coordinator of Visitor Services to describe her many contributions to the museum.

When Christine was hired as Curator of Education in 1999, we hired Don Bridges as a part-time employee to assist in the bookstore. Merika, in addition to her duties as Assistant Director and Registrar, was also the Bookstore Manager. In time, owing to our vigorous publication program, the bookstore became progressively more time consuming and complicated to manage, and Don's presence there helped free up Merika for her other responsibilities. In 2001, Don, who had quickly become part of our little museum family, was hired full-time and became the Bookstore Manager at

Jean Stern, at The Oaks Art Exhibition, May 1992

Granville Redmond, *Nocturne*, Private Collection, Courtesy of The Irvine Museum

The Irvine Museum